ŚŪRAṂGAMASAMĀDHISŪTRA

The Concentration of
Heroic Progress

ŚŪRAṂGAMASAMĀDHISŪTRA

The Concentration of Heroic Progress

An early Mahāyāna Buddhist Scripture
translated and annotated by
Étienne Lamotte

English translation by Sara Boin-Webb

UNIVERSITY OF HAWAI‘I PRESS
HONOLULU

in association with
The Buddhist Society (TBSLL)

Printed in the United States of America

14 13 12 11 10 09 6 5 4 3 2 1

First published in English 1998 by Curzon Press
15 The Quadrant, Richmond, Surrey TW9 1BP
in association with
The Buddhist Society London Limited
58 Eccleston Square, London SW1V 1PM

A record of the Cataloging-in-Publication data can be found at
the Library of Congress Web site: http://catalog.loc.gov/

ISBN 978-0-8248-3353-4

University of Hawai‘i Press books are printed on acid-free paper
and meet the guidelines for permanence and durability of the
Council on Library Resources

Printed by Versa Press, Inc.

TABLE OF CONTENTS

ŚŪRAṂGAMASAMĀDHISŪTRA

INTRODUCTION
from the Technical Editor

The *Śūraṃgamasamādhisūtra* (Śgs) is an early Mahāyāna Buddhist scripture. It is ancient, composed anonymously, close to the beginning of the first millenium. It was one of the very first Mahāyāna scriptures to be transmitted to China, where we know its first translation was published in 186 C.E. Because of its popularity the Śgs was translated a further nine times, and the last of these, made by the great translator Kumārajīva at the very beginning of the fifth century C.E., survives to form a part of the modern Chinese Buddhist canon. The other major translation of the Śgs was made into Tibetan at the beginning of the ninth century.

The *Śūraṃgamasamādhisūtra* (The Concentration of Heroic Progress), the first full English translation of Kumārajīva's text, is a welcome addition to the growing library of English language versions of Buddhist scriptures. Lamotte's French version was published in 1965, and now with the publication of Sara Boin-Webb's translation of that the English speaking world has direct access both to an important scriptural text and also to a classic work of Buddhist Studies. Direct comparison can now be made with *The Teaching of Vimalakīrti*, the English version of Lamotte's treatment of the *Vimalakīrtinirdeśa*, to which the present work was conceived as the companion volume.

The title of the text describes in brief its subject. The *Śūraṃgamasamādhisūtra* is the scripture that contains teachings concerning the samādhi that bestows an 'heroic progress', śūraṃgama, on the path to Enlightenment. Samādhi is traditionally understood to denote the altered mental states attainable through meditation techniques, in particular the mental state in which discursive thought is allayed and the mind is calm, concentrated and capable of sustained awareness of a single object, hence 'concentration'. As an integral part of this technology of altered consciousness, samādhi is also understood to bestow power upon the practitioner – not just the power of spiritual insight, but also of magical feat and transformation – and it is this theme which most incited the imagination of Mahāyāna Buddhists to produce an array of 'Mahāyāna samādhis', each accredited with special magical powers of spiritual advancement. As Lamotte explains in his Introduction, he understands the Śgs to be concerned with just such a specific meditative state that is or gives 'heroic progress'.

The Śgs is one of a small group of Mahāyāna sūtras that teach specific, named 'samādhis'. Only one other text from this group is published in English translation – the *Pratyutpannasūtra* (see Bibliography). Others in this genre are the *Samādhirājasūtra*, the *Praśāntaviniścayaprātihāryasamādhisūtra*, and the *Kuan ch'a chu fa hsing ching* (T.649).

The Śgs is not just an object for study and comparison, but was surely composed to be enjoyed, seeking to entertain as it edifies. Nor must we forget that for the community of Buddhist practitioners, to which this text truly belongs, "The sūtras only ask to be believed, remembered, repeated, expounded and put into practice" (p.41).

For this English translation the index has been expanded, the bibliography revised and supplemented, and minor typographic errors of the French edition corrected.

Andrew Skilton, Cardiff

PREFACE

to the original French edition

The Śūraṃgamasamādhisūtra is neither more nor less interesting than the other texts of the Great Vehicle, but it was one of the first Mahāyāna sūtras to be translated into Chinese and, in the periods of the Han, Wei, Wu, Chin, Liang and Ch'in, it enjoyed considerable success. In less than four centuries it was translated some ten times and certain of these translations were subjected to a combined edition; the Sūtra was commented upon several times and it inspired the first Buddhist philosophical school to be established in China: the *Hsin-wu-i*, 'Theory of the non-existence of the mind'.

Yet another reason dictated the choice of this text. Three years ago I published a translation of the Vimalakīrtinirdeśa. In fact, according to well-established custom, those who are interested in the latter work also translate the Śūraṃgamasamādhisūtra. This was the case for Chih Ch'ien, Dharmarakṣa, Shu-lan and Kumārajīva. It has been my wish here to conform to such a justified tradition: the two works are closely related through their ideas and complement each other.

Continuing the interest that he has always taken in my work, Professor Paul Demiéville, Member of the Institut de France, has checked my translation with the talent and care which characterise him. It is a pleasure once again to express my profound gratitude to him.

While publishing, in a new presentation, this thirteenth volume of the Mélanges chinois et bouddhiques, may I be allowed to evoke the memory of their illustrious founder, M. Louis de La Vallée Poussin. May the present work not fall too short of the hopes he set on his successors.

Louvain, 1 May 1965

FOREWORD

to the English edition

by Étienne Lamotte

Curzon Press in association with The Buddhist Society, London,* is now publishing the English version of one of my works, *La Concentration de la marche héroïque* (Śūraṃgamasamādhisūtra) *traduit et annoté*, Mélanges chinois et bouddhiques, Vol.XIII, Bruxelles 1965. Already in 1976, the Pali Text Society had acquired the translation of another of my works: *L'Enseignement de Vimalakīrti* (Vimalakīrtinirdeśa) *traduit et annoté*, Bibliothèque du Muséon, Vol.LI, Louvain 1962, and published it under the title of *The Teaching of Vimalakīrti*.

It is not merely by chance that, among so many other Mahāyāna sūtras, the Vimalakīrtinirdeśa (abbreviated to Vkn) and Śūraṃgamasamādhi (Śgs) should appear together. Both Sanskrit texts, which appeared about the second century of our era but are now lost, figured among the first Mahāyāna sūtras to be rendered into Chinese; they were, over the centuries, the object of many translations into Chinese, the languages of Central Asia and Tibetan. As if through tacit agreement, the Yüeh-chih, Indian and Serindian masters, such as Chih Ch'ien, Chu Fa-hu (Dharmarakṣa) and Kumārajīva, who translated the Vkn into Chinese also produced a version of the Śgs in the same language. We have remained faithful to such a long-standing tradition.

The Introductions that we devoted to both these Sūtras allow us to perceive the close links which unite the Vkn and the Śgs. Along with the Prajñāpāramitā sūtras, they set out the Madhyamaka, the 'Philosophy of the Middle Way', which professes the twofold emptiness of beings and things: they draw up the idealised portrait of the bodhisattva combining Prajñā with Upāyakauśalya. The former is the right vision of the true nature of things which is none other than the absence of any nature; the latter ripens beings by making them aware of the perfect equation between Saṃsāra and Nirvāṇa. This engagement in awareness results in the elimination of false views, the cutting off of idle words and practices (*sarvavādacaryoccheda*) and the calming of the mind. From this point of view, the *Teaching of Vimalakīrti* and the *Concentration of Heroic Progress* are in perfect agreement.

However, if they have ideas in common, these are expressed in different ways. Vimalakīrti, the protagonist of the Vkn, is a lay bodhisattva, a master of paradox who, in order to convince his hearers, does

* *See acknowledgements, p.xviii*

not hesitate to scandalise them. His argument is striking, his style lively and picturesque. In the Śgs, Dṛḍhamati, also a great bodhisattva, is presented as a respectful and meek disciple. He, too, makes use of the traditional language, rich in stock-phrases, of the early canonical sūtras. He is a meditator (*dhyāyin*) who seeks less to win over people than to glean from the Buddha new light on the best of Concentrations. It is not without reason that Japanese scholars classify the Śgs as one of the 'Meditation Sūtras', while they link the Vkn with 'Laymen Buddhism'[1].

In order to understand the Vkn, it is not enough to meditate on the text; account should also be taken of the success achieved by Vimalakīrti, in China from the fourth century under the Eastern Chin, in Japan from the seventh century under the sponsorship of Prince Shōtoku. Even in our own time, in the Far East he incarnates the type of wise and skilful Upāsaka, examining Dharmatā in depth and displaying, not only in our world but also in more distant universes, the full range of Upāya capable of winning over beings. Most of the Buddhist sects and schools have adopted him. Thinkers and philosophers study his message; painters and sculptors devote the best of their talent to depicting him; his Sūtra, translated and retranslated over the centuries and commented upon at length, is the object of public recitation during religious ceremonies and is even introduced into theatrical productions[2].

To return to the Śūraṃgamasamādhi, it should be noted that its title is a cause of difficulty.

According to Professor J.C. Wright[3], "the term Śūraṃgama can scarcely properly denote 'marche héroïque' (*śūrair gamyata iti*), and the alternative resolution proposed, *śūra iva gacchatīti* (to be construed, however, as a Buddha-designation), seems inevitable. In view of the subject-matter of the text, the term is to be accounted a BHSk. reflex of *śū́ramgrāma* 'with pantheon', applied in RV 9.90.3 to *sarvavīra* jétṛ (cf. *mahāvīrá* tuvibādhá, 1.32.6, and *Mahāvīrá* Jina) and indicating that 'Concentration on Śūraṃgama' is fundamentally somewhat older than

[1] H. Nakamura, 'A Survey of Mahāyāna Buddhism with Bibliographical Notes', Journal of Intercultural Studies III, 1976, pp.84, 135-6; repr. in his Indian Buddhism, Delhi 1987, pp.173 and 224-5.

[2] On this subject, see P. Demiéville, 'Vimalakīrti en Chine', in *L'Enseignement de Vimalakīrti*, French translation (only), pp.438-55 (reprinted in *Choix d'Études bouddhiques*, Leiden 1973, pp.347-64); C. Guth, 'Early Perceptions of Vimalakīrti', in *Indianisme et Bouddhisme* (Mélanges Lamotte), *Publications de l'Institut Orientalistes de Louvain* 23, Louvain-la-Neuve 1980, pp.131-42.

[3] *Bulletin of the School of Oriental and African Studies* XXX.2, 1967, pp.417-18.

the 'vieilles conceptions bouddhiques' against which the Sūtra is felt to be in revolt."

Professor R.E. Emmerick[4] does not accept this argument: "We do not know whether the term *śūraṃgama-* has any pre-Buddhist history. J.C. Wright's dogmatic assertion in BSOAS xxx, 2, 1967, 417-8, that 'the term is to be accounted a BHSk. reflex of śū́ragrāma' is entirely arbitrary and without a shred of evidence to support it. Śū́ragrāma, a Rigvedic hapax legomenon, is an epithet of Soma, rendered by K. Geldner 'mit tapferem Clane' and by Renou (ix-40) 'rassemblant les héros'."

Professor J. May[5] proposes a more attractive explanation. For him, [tr.] "the compound *śūraṃ-gama*, in fact is hardly clear and warrants further grammatical investigation. The end syllable in the accusative of the preceding member is hard to explain. BHSD has no mention of it. It is possible that it is one of those terms in which °*gama-* is an appendage and does not represent the root GAM- but the extending of a suffix °ga- wrongly connected with that root. Cf. Renou, *Grammaire sanscrite*, Paris 1961, p.263, referring to Wackernagel II I 201 (201.39-202.16, to be precise). The term already seems to have posed a problem to the Chinese interpreters, who hardly attempted to translate it but merely transcribed it... Perhaps *śūraṃ-gama* means nothing more basically than 'heroic'."

In my opinion, it is not certain that *śūraṃgama* is an Aluk Samāsa with the first member in the accusative. The *ṃ* could be euphonious (*śūra-ṃ-gama*). In fact, alongside the adjectives *śūra-māna* and *śūra-mānin,* there is also to be found, as a euphony, *śūra-ṃ-manya*.

Personally, I would be tempted to split the title into *śūraṃgamaḥ samādhiḥ*, and I would see in *śūraṃgama* (abbreviation of *śūragamana*?) a Vyadhikaraṇa Bahuvrīhi, or attributive compound whose members are not in apposition to each other, i.e., are in different cases when dissolved. A Vyadhikaraṇa Bahuvrīhi is not allowed in any case except in the genitive and locative. Here, it would be a matter of a genitive expressing a term of comparison. Its analysis would therefore be as follows: *śūrasya iva gamanaṃ yasya sa sūraṃgamaḥ samādhiḥ* 'the samādhi whose progress is like that of the hero is *śūraṃgamaḥ samādhiḥ*'. A compound of the same kind often proposed by grammarians is *candrakāntiḥ* analysed into *candrasya iva kāntir yasya sa candrakāntiḥ*. For the author of the Śgs, the hero in question is the

[4] The *Khotanese Śūraṅgamasamādhisūtra*, London Oriental Series 23, Oxford 1970, p.xv, note 13.

[5] *T'oung Pao* LIII, 1-3, 1967, p.223.

cakravartin king, the universal monarch, always accompanied by his seven jewels. Hence this comparison appearing in § 25: 'Just as a noble cakravartin king, while travelling, is followed by his seven jewels, so the Śūraṃgamasamādhi is always followed by all the auxiliary dharmas of enlightenment (*bodhipākṣika dharma*) [and these are associated with it]'.

In 1951, Sir Harold W. Bailey published a long Khotanese fragment of the Śgs, which appeared in his *Khotanese Buddhist Texts*, London, pp.1-7. Since then, our documentation has been considerably enriched. In 1970, Professor R.E. Emmerick produced an excellent critical edition of all the fragments of the Śgs identified at the time: *The Khotanese Śūraṅgamasamādhisūtra*, London Oriental Series, vol. XXIII, Oxford 1970. There appear in the latter three groups of fragments respectively corresponding to §§ 3 and 4, 125 to 134, 134 to 152 of my translation of the Śgs. Group 1 comes from Dandān Öilik, groups 2 and 3, taken from one and the same manuscript, were discovered in Khadalik. Emmerick's work contains three main sections: 1. the Khotanese text of the fragments, accompanied by an English translation; 2. an elaborately detailed linguistic commentary; 3. the Tibetan text from the Kanjur (Otani Cat., No.800) corresponding to the Khotanese fragments; this is a critical edition based on the collation of blockprints from Derge, Lhasa, Narthang and Peking. The Tibetan index and Khotanese glossary which accompany this work make it an extremely valuable working tool.

The portions of the Khotanese Śgs are in the most ancient type of Old Khotanese. They date at the earliest from the seventh century C.E., but are in reality copied from much older manuscripts. The first Khotanese recension of the Śgs is most probably earlier than the Chinese version of the same text compiled by Kumārajīva about 400 C.E.

Emmerick remarks in his Introduction (p.xiii): "We must remember that the aim of the Khotanese translators was not to produce a word for word rendering such as a philologist might desire. They were seeking to make the texts intelligible and did not hesitate to expand or condense." In other words, the Khotanese version is not as scrupulously faithful as are the Tibetan translations, but is more comparable to the Chinese versions which, in order to make themselves better understood, often sacrificed the letter for the spirit. There is one point, however, over which the Khotanese translators did not compromise: this concerns the proper names which they reproduced without change in their original Indian form. Indologists can but be pleased with this, since when one has only the Chinese and Tibetan sources at one's disposal, it is not easy to reconstruct a proper name in Sanskrit, and the equivalents proposed by philologists are always subject to caution.

Another difficulty which should be taken into account is that one and the same sūtra in its Indian form changed greatly in the course of time and was the object of Iranian, Chinese, Tibetan, etc., translations which have notable divergences between them. The reason for this is that they are based on different recensions. To attempt to reconstruct the Urtext of a sūtra by submitting the material at our disposal to a process of textual criticism is an enterprise which is bound to fail. Each recension requires its own study[6].

It would therefore be impossible to restore the original list of bodhisattvas mentioned in § 3 of the Śgs: the Chinese translation counts twenty-six of them, and the Tibetan translation thirty-one. Their names do not agree exactly and are not quoted in the same order. The Khotanese list, incomplete and full of lacunae, only supplies fourteen names[7].

Nevertheless, the Khotanese fragments are not unusable for all that. They enabled Emmerick to correct my translation in two places: the Bodhisattva Meruśikharadhara mentioned in § 50 is called Meruśikharakūṭarāja or, in abbreviated form, Merukūṭarāja; the devaputra Vimalacandragarbha who appears in §§ 136 to 138 had the name of Śaśivimalagarbha; in future ages he will be the Buddha Ekaratnacchatra and his Kṣetra will be called Sarvaratnapratyupta (and not Sarvaratnaracitā).

The Mahāyāna manuscripts from Central Asia published until now have for the most part been rediscovered in the oases bordering on the Silk Road of the Tarim Basin[8]. One of them is the Śgs. It was authoritative among the Mahāyānist Saṃghas of Khotan, while the Śrāvakas continued to resort to the early canonical texts of the Tripiṭaka. A Tibetan document from Tun-huang, 'The Religious Annals of the Li Country'[9] makes the following remarks with regard to the

[6] This is particularly the case for the various recensions of the Lotus; cf. H. Bechert, 'Remarks on the Textual History of the Saddharmapuṇḍarīka', *Studies in Indo-Asian Art and Culture* 2, New Delhi 1972, pp.21-7; 'Über die "Marburger Fragmente" des Saddharma-puṇḍarīka', *Nachrichten der Akademie der Wissenschaften in Göttingen*, 1972, pp.1-81.

[7] They are Prāmodyasvaranirghoṣita, Sarvadevastuti, Dhāraṇīśvararāja, Pratibhānālaṃkāravyūharāja, Mañjuśrī, Maitreya, Sumeruśikharakūṭarāja, Sāgaraguṇaratnavyūhamati, Mahāvyūhamati, Mahāvīrya, Mahāratnaketu, Prabhāketu, Prabhāśrī, ——, ——, ——, Dṛḍhamati, ——.

[8] See L. Sander, 'Buddhist Literature in Central Asia', in *Encyclopaedia of Buddhism* IV, 1, 1979, p.70.

[9] Cf. M. Lalou, *Inventaire des Manuscrits Tibétains de Touen-houang* II, Paris 1950, p.25, No.960. Translated by F.W. Thomas, *Tibetan Literary Texts and Documents concerning Chinese Turkestan* I, Oriental Translation Fund, Vol.XXXII, London 1935, p.311.

Saṃghas of Khotan [tr. Thomas]: "As to the views of the Saṃghas of the two divisions: Of the monks and nuns, two divisions, those of the Mahā-yāna adopt the principles of the *Avikalpa* and the *Śūraṃgama-samādhi*; the śrāvakas adopt the principles of the Four Truths; taking the Saṃghas of both divisions and the laity, as regards the measure of many and few of those who adopt the Mahā-yāna principles and those who adopt the principles of the Śrāvakas, the Mahā-yānists being as the hairs of a horse's body, the Hīnayānists as the hairs of a horse's ear, the measure of many and few is about that."

Thus, the Mahāyānists of Khotan attached very special importance to the Śūraṃgamasamādhi. An even more interesting fact is that Khotan and the neighbouring kingdom of Khargalik had at their disposal a considerable reserve of Mahāyāna sūtras in their long recensions, and the Chinese Fa-ling was able to consult this in 392 C.E.[10]

The English version of the *Śūraṃgamasamādhisūtra* (The Concentration of Heroic Progress) is the work of Sara Boin-Webb. Once again, she has discharged this heavy duty with an eagerness and talent to which I am happy to pay homage. May she accept my profound gratitude.

[10] On this reserve of manuscripts often consulted by the Chinese, see below, Intr, p.103, n.22, and É. Lamotte, 'Mañjuśrī', *T'oung Pao* XLVIII, 1-3, 1960, pp.62-70.

NOTE

from the English Translator

The original French version of this work appeared under the title *La Concentration de la marche héroïque* (Śūraṃgamasamādhisūtra) *traduit et annoté* as Volume XIII in the collection Mélanges chinois et bouddhiques, published by the Institut Belge des Hautes Études Chinoises, Brussels, 1965. Grateful acknowledgement is made to them for granting permission to translate and publish this English version.

For the benefit of readers familiar with the original French version of this book, I should make it clear that all translations herein from the Mahāprajñāpāramitāsūtra (Upadeśa, Ta-chih tu lun, T 1509) are based directly on Prof. Lamotte's version in his five-volume translation of this work, *Le Traité de la grande vertu de sagesse*, and therefore not necessarily the same as he gave in the original of the present volume. All references to his Vimalakīrtinirdeśa translation and *History of Indian Buddhism* are to the relevant English version.

In the pages that follow, any words in square brackets preceded by an obelisk [†] are my additions. Although I was able to consult Prof. Lamotte to a much lesser degree than with the Vimalakīrti translation, some amendments have been made with his agreement.

I wish to express my profound gratitude to the late Dr Arnold Kunst, as well as Prof. T.H. Barrett, for their help in clarifying certain points, Mr John Acquier and Dr Andrew Skilton for their meticulous checking of the proofs and Mr Peter Ma for kindly providing the Chinese characters throughout.

Sara Boin-Webb

ACKNOWLEDGEMENTS

The Pali Text Society first commissioned this translation of the *Śūraṃgamasamādhisūtra* (The Concentration of Heroic Progress) for its series 'The Sacred Books of the Buddhists'. In acknowledging the Pali Text Society's initiating role we would particularly like to thank the late I.B. Horner and the late Arnold Kunst of the School of Oriental and African Studies; also K.R. Norman and N. Franklin.

In the event, the Pali Text Society was unable to publish the work and it lay dormant for several years. It was eventually taken up by the Buddhist Society with the intention of fulfilling Lamotte's wish to make the *Vimalakīrtinirdeśa* and *Śūraṃgamasamādhisūtra* available in translation side by side.

We would like to thank Eric Cheetham for bringing this translation to our attention and Alethea Creighton for her invaluable contribution to the work of the Publishing Committee. We are grateful to the Venerable Myokyo-ni for her encouragement.

We would also like to thank John Swain for his help in getting the typesetting underway, Richard Gombrich for his recommendation on the editing of the text, Andrew Skilton for the great care given to the text, Lulu Sturdy for proofreading and Desmond Biddulph for his guidance and support. Finally, we would like to thank Nina Kidron for her untiring and dedicated work in developing the project for the Society and bringing it to fruition in this volume.

The Buddhist Society, London

ABBREVIATIONS AND BIBLIOGRAPHY

Unless otherwise stated, Pāli texts/translations cited are Pali Text Society publications

*Entries marked with an asterisk refer to the additional bibliography appended

Abhidharmadīpa, ed. P.S. Jaini (Tibetan Sanskrit Works Series IV), Patna 1959

*Abhidharmasamuccaya, ed. V.V. Gokhale, *Journal of the Bombay Branch of the R.A.S.* XXIII, 1947, pp.13-38; rec. P. Pradhan (Visvabharati Studies 12), Santiniketan 1950

Abhisamayālaṃkara, ed. T. Stcherbatsky and E. Obermiller (Bibl. Buddh. 23), Leningrad 1929; tr. E. Conze, *Abhisamayālaṃkara*, Rome 1954

*Akanuma, *Noms propres* = *Dictionnaire des noms propres du bouddhisme indien*, by C. Akanuma, Nagoya 1931

Āloka = Abhisamayālaṃkārāloka, ed. U. Wogihara, Tokyo 1932-35

*Arthaviniścaya, ed. and tr. A. Ferrari, Rome 1944

Aṣṭādaśasāhasrikā [Prajñāpāramitā] ed. and tr. E. Conze, 2 vols, Rome 1962, repr. 1974

Aṣṭasāhasrikā [Prajñāpāramitā], ed. U. Wogihara in Āloka (see above)

Avadānaśataka, ed. J.S. Speyer (Bibl. Buddh. 3) St. Petersburg 1902-09

Bailey, Sir Harold W. ed., *Khotanese Buddhist Texts*, London 1951, repr. Cambridge 1981

Bailey, Sir Harold W., *Khotanese Texts* IV, Cambridge 1961, repr. 1979

Balasooriya, S. et al, ed., *Buddhist Studies in Honour of Walpola Rahula*, London 1980

Bareau, A., *Recherches sur la biographie du Buddha dans les Sūtrapiṭaka et les Vinayapiṭaka anciens*, 3 vols, Paris 1963

Bareau, A., *Les Sectes bouddhiques du Petit Véhicule*, Saigon 1955

Beal, S., *Catena of Buddhist Scriptures from the Chinese*, London 1871, repr. Taipei 1970

Bodh. bhūmi = Bodhisattvabhūmi, ed. U. Wogihara, Tokyo 1930

Bodhicaryāvatārapañjikā, ed. L. de La Vallée Poussin (Bibl. Indica), Calcutta 1901-14

Bodhisattvaprātimokṣasūtra, ed. N. Dutt, IHQ VIII, 1931

bs(s) = bodhisattva(s)

*Buddhacarita, ed. E.H. Johnston (Panjab Univ. Pub. 31), Lahore 1936, repr. Delhi 1984

Chêng = Chêng-yüan hsin-ting shih-chiao mu-lu (T 2157)
Chu = Ch'u san-tsang chi chi (T 2145)
Chung A = Li-tai san-pao chi (T 2034)
Chung B = Chung-ching mu-lu (T 2147)
Chung C = Chung-ching mu-lu (T 2148)
Conze, E., *The Large Sūtra on Perfect Wisdom*, London 1961, repr. Berkeley 1975
Conze, E., *The Prajñāpāramitā Literature*, The Hague 1960, repr. Tokyo 1978
*Daśabhūmika Sūtra, ed. J. Rahder, Louvain 1926
*Daśasāhasrikā [Prajñāpāramitā], rec. S. Konow, Oslo 1941
Demiéville, P., *Le Concile de Lhasa*, Paris 1952, repr. 1987
*Dharmasaṃgraha, ed. M. Müller and H. Wenzel, Oxford 1885, repr. New Delhi 1984
Divyāvadāna, ed. E.B. Cowell and R.A. Neil, Cambridge 1886, repr. Amsterdam 1970
Dutt, N., *Aspects of Mahāyāna Buddhism*, London 1930; rev. ed., *Mahāyāna Buddhism*, Varanasi 1978
Dvādaśamukha Śāstra, rec. N.A. Sastri, *Visva-Bharati Annals* VI, 1954, pp.165-231
Edgerton, *Dictionary* (BHSD) = F. Edgerton, *Buddhist Hybrid Sanskrit Dictionary*, New Haven 1953, repr. Delhi 1993
Edgerton, F., *Buddhist Hybrid Sanskrit Grammar*, New Haven 1953, repr. Delhi 1993
Edkins, J., *Chinese Buddhism*, London 1893, repr. San Francisco 1976
Emmerick, R.E., *A Guide to the Literature of Khotan*, Tokyo 1979, repr. 1992
Emmerick, R.E., ed. and tr., *The Khotanese Śūraṅgamasamādhisūtra* (London Oriental Series 23), Oxford 1970
Foucher, A., *Art gréco-bouddhique du Gandhāra*, 2 vols, Paris 1906-22; 3rd vol. ('additions et corrections'), Hanoi 1951
*Foucher, A., *La Vie du Bouddha*, Paris 1949, repr. 1987
Foucher, A., *Les Vies antérieures du Bouddha*, Paris 1955
Frauwallner, E., *Die Philosophie der Buddhismus*, Berlin 1956, repr. 1994
*Gaṇḍavyūha Sūtra, ed. D.T. Suzuki and H. Idzumi, Kyoto 1934-36
Hōbōgirin = Dictionnaire encyclopédique d'après les sources chinoises et japonaises (ed. in chief, P. Demiéville) Paris-Tokyo 1929 (on-going)
Hoernle, R., *Manuscript Remains of Buddhist Literature found in*

Eastern Turkestan I, Oxford 1916; repr. Amsterdam 1970, New Delhi 1988
Hsü-k'ai = Ta T'ang chêng-yüan hsü k'ai-yüan shih chiao lu (T 2156)
Inde Classique = L. Renou, J. Filliozat et al, ed., *L'Inde Classique*, 2 vols, Paris 1947-53, repr. 1985
*Jñānaprasthānaśāstra, rec. Shanti Bhikshu Sastri, Santiniketan 1955
K'ai = K'ai-yüan shih-chiao mu-lu (T 2154)
Kao — Kao-sêng chuan (T 2059)
*Karuṇāpuṇḍarīka, ed. S.C. Das and S.C. Sastri, Calcutta 1898
*Kāśyapaparivarta, ed. A. v. Staël-Holstein, Shanghai 1926, repr. Tokyo 1977
*Kośa = Abhidharmakośa, tr. L. de La Vallée Poussin, 6 vols, Paris 1923-31, repr. Brussels 1971
Kośavyākhyā = Spūṭārthā Abhidharmakośavyākhyā, ed. U. Wogihara, Tokyo 1932-36
La Vallée Poussin, L. de, *Catalogue of the Tibetan Manuscripts from Tun-huang in the India Office Library*, Oxford 1962
La Vallée Poussin, L. de, *Morale bouddhique*, Paris 1927
*Lalitavistara, ed. S. Lefmann, 2 vols, Halle 1902-8, repr. Tokyo 1977
Lalou, M., *Inventaire des Manuscrits Tibétains de Touen-houang conservés à la Bibliothèque Nationale*, 3 vols, Paris 1939-61
Lalou, M., *Les Religions du Tibet*, Paris 1957
Lamotte, *History* = É. Lamotte, *History of Indian Buddhism, from the Origins to the Śaka Era*, English version by Sara Webb-Boin [correctly, Boin-Webb] (Publ. Inst. Or. Louvain 36), Louvain-la-Neuve 1988
*Laṅkāvatāra, ed. B. Nanjio, Kyoto 1923
Legge, J., *A Record of Buddhistic Kingdoms*, Oxford 1886, repr. San Francisco 1975
Li = Li-tai san-pao chi (T 2034)
Lin Li-Kouang, *L'Aide Mémoire de la Vraie Loi* (Saddharmasmṛty-upasthānasūtra), Paris 1949
*Madh. vṛtti = Mūlamadhyamakakārikās of Nāgārjuna with the Prasannapadā Comm. by Candrakīrti, ed. L. de La Vallée Poussin (Bibl. Buddh. 4), St Petersburg 1913; also see under May, J., *Candrakīrti*
*Madhyāntavibhāga, ed. S. Yamaguchi, 2 vols, Nagoya 1934
Mahākarmavibhaṅga (and Mahākarmavibhaṅgopadeśa), ed. and tr. S. Levi, Paris 1932
*Mahāparinirvāṇa, Sanskrit = Mahāparinirvāṇasūtra, ed.

E. Waldschmidt, Berlin 1950-51
Mahāsaṃnipāta [Ratnaketudhāraṇī], ed. N. Dutt (*Gilgit Manuscripts* IV), Calcutta 1959, repr. Delhi 1984
*Mahāvastu, ed. É. Senart, 3 vols, Paris 1882-97, repr. Tokyo 1977
*Mahāvyut. = Mahāvyutpatti. ed. R. Sakaki, 2 vols, Kyoto 1916-25, repr. Tokyo 1962
Mahāyānasūtrālaṃkāra, see Sūtrālaṃkāra
*Maitreyavyākaraṇa, ed. N. Dutt (*Gilgit Manuscripts* IV), Calcutta 1959, repr. Delhi 1984
Malalasekera, *Proper Names* = *Dictionary of Pāli Proper Names*, by G.P. Malalasekera, 2 vols, London 1937-38; repr. (PTS) London 1975
Mallman, M.-T. de, *Étude iconographique sur Mañjuśrī*, Paris 1964
Marshall, Sir John, and A. Foucher, *The Monuments of Sāñchī*, 3 vols, Calcutta 1940
May, J., *Candrakīrti* = *Candrakīrti Prasannapadā Mūlamadhyamaka-vṛtti, douze chapitres traduits du sanscrit*, by J. May, Paris 1959
Mochizuki, Encyclopaedia = *Bukkyō Daijiten* 2nd ed., 10 vols, Tokyo 1957-63
Mūlasarv. Vin. = Vinayapiṭaka of the Mūlasarvāstivādins (*Gilgit Manuscripts* III), 4 parts, Srinagar 1942-50, repr. Delhi 1984
Mus, P., *Barabuḍur*, 2 vols, Hanoi 1935, repr. New York 1978
Nāgārjuna, *Traité* = *Le Traité de la Grande Vertu de Sagesse de Nāgārjuna*, tr. É. Lamotte, 5 vols, Louvain and Louvain-la-Neuve 1944-80 (English tr. by Sara Boin-Webb in the press)
Nei = Ta T'ang nei tien lu (T 2149)
Obermiller, E., *Analysis of the Abhisamayālaṃkāra*, 2 fascs., London 1933-43
Obermiller, E., 'The Doctrine of the Prajñā-pāramitā', *Acta Orientalia* XI, 1932, repr. as *Prajñāpāramitā in Tibetan Buddhism*, Talent (Oregon) 1984 and Delhi 1988
dPaḥ-bar-ḥgro-baḥi tiṅ-ṅe-ḥdzin = Tibetan version of the Śgs, Tib. Trip, vol.32, No.800
Pañcaviṃśati = Pañcaviṃśatisāhasrikā [Prajñāpāramitā], ed. N. Dutt (Calcutta Oriental Series 28), London 1934
Pañjikā, see Bodhicaryāvatārapañjikā
Petech, L., *Northern India according to the Shui-ching-chu*, Rome 1950
Petech, L., *A Study of the Chronicles of Ladakh*, Calcutta 1939
Renou, L., *Canon bouddhique pāli*, Paris 1949
Renou, L., *Grammaire sanscrite*, 2 vols, Paris 1961

Rhys Davids, *Dictionary* = *Pali-English Dictionary*, ed. T.W. Rhys Davids and W. Stede, Chipstead 1925; repr. London 1972

Rockhill, W.W., *Life of the Buddha*, London 1884, repr. San Francisco 1976, Petaling Jaya 1984

*Saddharmapuṇḍ. = Saddharmapuṇḍarīka, ed. H. Kern and B. Nanjio (Bibl. Buddh. 10) St Petersburg 1908-12; tr. E. Burnouf, *Le Lotus de la Bonne Loi*, Paris 1852, repr. 1989

*Śālistamba Sūtra, ed. N.A. Sastri, Adyar Library, 1950

*Samādhirāja Sūtra, ed. N. Dutt (*Gilgit Manuscripts* II), 3 parts, Srinagar 1941-54, repr. Delhi 1984

*Saṃgraha = Mahāyānasaṃgraha – *La Somme du Grand Véhicule d'Asaṅga* II, tr. É. Lamotte, Louvain 1938-9, repr. (Pub. Inst. Or. Louvain 8) Louvain-la-Neuve 1973

Sarvāstivādin Vin = *Der Vinayavibhaṅga zum Bhikṣuprātimokṣa der Sarvāstivādins*, ed. V. Rosen (Sanskrittexte a.d. Turfanfunden I), Berlin 1959

Śatasāhasrikā [Prajñāpāramitā], ed. P. Ghosa (Bibl. Indica), Calcutta 1914

Śgs = Śūraṃgamasamādhisūtra

Shou-lêng-yen san-mei = Chinese version of the Śgs by Kumārajīva (T 642)

*Siddhi = Vijñaptimātratāsiddhi, tr. L. de La Vallée Poussin, 2 vols, Paris 1928

*Śikṣāsamuccaya, ed. C. Bendall (Bibl. Buddh. 1) St Petersburg 1902

Stein, R.A., *La civilisation tibétaine*, Paris 1962, repr. 1981

*Sukhāvatīvyūha, ed. U. Wogihara, Tokyo 1931 [reproduces, with corrections and new pagination, the edition by M. Müller, Oxford 1883, repr. Amsterdam 1972]

Śuraṅgama Samādhi Sūtra, Excerpts from, tr. Thubten Kalsang Rimpoche and Bhikkhu Pāsādika, Dharamsala 1975

Śūraṅgama Sūtra, The, tr. Charles Luk (Lu K'uan Yu), London 1966, repr. New Delhi 1988

*Sūtrālaṃkāra = Mahāyānasūtrālaṃkāra, ed. S. Lévi, 2 vols, Paris 1907-11, repr. Kyoto 1983

*Suvarṇabhāsa [Uttamasūtra], ed. J. Nobel, Leipzig 1937

T = Taishō Issaikyō, ed. J. Takakusu and K. Watanabe, 55 vols, Tokyo 1924-29

*Tajima, R., *Étude sur le Mahāvairocanasūtra*, Paris 1936, repr. 1992

Thomas, F.W., *Tibetan Literary Texts and Documents concerning Chinese Turkestan*, 4 vols, London 1935-63

Tib. Trip. = Tibetan Tripiṭaka, ed. D.T. Suzuki, 150 vols, Kyoto 1957
Traité – see Nāgārjuna, *Traité*
T'u = Ku chin i ching t'u chi (T 2151)
Tucci, G., *Minor Buddhist Texts* II, Rome 1958, repr. Delhi 1986
Tucci, G., *The Tombs of the Tibetan Kings*, Rome 1950
Upadeśa = Mahāprajñāpāramitopadeśa (Ta chih tu lun, T 1509) see Nāgārjuna, *Traité*
*Vajracchedikā [Prajñāpāramitā], ed. and tr. E. Conze, Rome 1957, rev. ed. 1974
*Vism = Visuddhimagga, ed. H.C. Warren and Dh. Kosambi, Cambridge, Mass., 1950, repr. Delhi 1989
*Vkn = Vimalakīrtinirdeśa. *The Teaching of Vimalakīrti*, tr. É. Lamotte, English version by Sara Boin, London 1976, repr. 1994
Watters, T., *On Yuan Chwang's Travels*, 2 vols, London 1904-05, repr. San Francisco 1975
Wayman, A., *Analysis of the Śrāvakabhūmi*, Berkeley 1961
Woodward, *Concordance* = *Pāli Tipiṭakaṃ Concordance*, ed. F.L. Woodward and E.M. Hare, Pali Text Society, 1952 ff.
Wu = Wu (or Ta) Chou k'an ting chung-ching mu-lu (T 2153)
Yoshimura, S. ed., *The Denkar-ma, an oldest catalogue of the Tibetan Buddhist Canon*, Kyoto 1950
Zürcher, E., *The Buddhist Conquest of China*, 2 vols, Leiden 1959, repr. 1972

ADDITIONAL BIBLIOGRAPHY OF RELATED WORKS

Abhidharmāmṛta, ed. Shanti Bhikshu Sastri, *Visva-Bharati Annals* V, Santiniketan 1953
Abhidharmasamuccaya — tr. W. Rahula, *Le Compendium de la Super-Doctrine (Philosophie)*, PEFEO LXXVIII, Paris 1971, repr. 1980
Abhiniṣkramaṇasūtra — tr. from Chinese by S. Beal, *The Romantic Legend of Śākya Buddha*, London 1875, repr. Delhi 1985
Akanuma — tr. *A Dictionary of Buddhist Proper Names*, Delhi 1994
Arthaviniścaya — see also N.H. Samtani, ed. and ann., Patna 1971; tr. Dharma Publishing, Berkeley, in the press
Avataṃsakasūtra — tr. T. Cleary, *The Flower Ornament Scripture*, 3 vols, Boston 1984-87
Birnbaum, R., *The Healing Buddha*, London 1979, revised ed. Boston 1989
Buddhacarita — tr. E.B. Cowell, 'The Buddha-*k*arita of Aśvaghosha', in *Buddhist Mahāyāna Texts*, Oxford 1894, repr. New York 1969,

Delhi 1985; — tr. E.H. Johnston, *The Buddhacarita or Acts of the Buddha*, Lahore 1936, repr. Delhi 1984

Buddhavaṃsa — tr. B.C. Law, *The Lineage of the Buddhas*, PTS, 1938; — tr. M. Talin, *The Genealogy of the Buddha-s*, Bombay 1969; — tr. I.B. Horner, *Chronicle of Buddhas*, PTS, 1975

Daśabhūmika — tr. M. Honda, 'Annotated translation of the Daśabhūmika-sūtra', in *Studies in South, East, and Central Asia*, ed. D. Sinor, New Delhi 1968, pp.115-276

Daśasāhasrikā [P.P.] — tr. E. Conze in *Selected Sayings from the Perfection of Wisdom*, The Buddhist Society, London 1968, repr. Boulder 1978

Dharmasaṃgraha — tr. Tashi Zangmo and Dechen Chime, Varanasi 1994

Drumakiṃnararājaparipṛcchā, ed. P.M. Harrison, *Druma-Kiṃnara-Rāja-Paripṛcchā-Sūtra (Tibetan Text)*, Tokyo 1992

Emmerick, R.E., *Tibetan Texts concerning Khotan*, London 1967

Gaṇḍavyūhasūtra — tr. T. Cleary in *The Flower Ornament Scripture* 3, Boston 1987

Foucher, A., (abbrev. Engl. tr.) *The Life of the Buddha*, Middletown, Conn., 1963

Gandhāran art — see J. Marshall, *The Buddhist Art of Gandhāra*, Cambridge 1960; — M. Hallade, *The Gandharan Style*, London 1968; *Gandharan Art of North India*, New York 1968; — F. Tissot, *Gandhāra*, Paris 1985; English summary, *The Art of Gandhāra*, 1986; — W. Zwalf, *A Catalogue of the Gandhāra Sculpture in the British Museum*, London 1996

Harrison, P.M., 'The Earliest Chinese Translations of Mahāyāna Buddhist Sūtras: Some Notes on the Work of Lokakṣema', *Buddhist Studies Review* 10, 2, London 1993, pp.135-77

Jñānaprasthāna — see L.N. Hurvitz, 'Path to Salvation in the Jñana-Prasthāna', in *Studies in Indo-Asian Art and Culture* 5, ed. L. Chandra and P. Ratnam, New Delhi, 1977 p.77-102

Karuṇāpuṇḍarīka — see also I. Yamada (ed. & summary), 2 vols, London 1968, repr. New Delhi 1989

Kāśyapaparivarta — tr. Bhikkhu Pāsādika as 'The Dharma-Discourse of the Great Collection of Jewels', 9 parts, *Linh So'n Publication d'Études Bouddhologiques* 1-9, Paris 1977-79; — 'The Sūtra of Assembled Treasures' in Garma C.C. Chang, ed., *A Treasury of Mahāyāna Sūtras*, Penn. State, University Park 1983, repr. Delhi 1991, pp.387-414

Kathāvatthu — tr. S.Z. Aung and C.A.F. Rhys Davids, *Points of Controversy*, PTS, 1915; repr. 1979

Kośa — Engl. tr. [of de La Vallée Poussin's work], L.M. Pruden, *Abhidharmakośabhāṣyam*, 4 vols, Berkeley 1988-90

Lalitavistara — tr. G. Bays, *The Life of the Buddha*, 2 vols, Berkeley 1983

Laṅkāvatāra — tr. D.T. Suzuki, *The Laṅkāvatāra Sūtra*, London 1932; repr. Boulder 1978, Taipei 1991

Madh. vṛtti: Madh. kārikās — tr. K.K. Inada, *Nāgārjuna: Mūlamadhyamakakārikā*, Tokyo 1970, repr. Delhi 1993; Prasannapadā — tr. M. Sprung, *Lucid Exposition of the Middle Way*, London 1979; — tr. J. Garfield, *Fundamental Wisdom of the Middle Way: Nāgārjuna's Mūlamadhyamakakārikā*, London 1996

Madhyāntavibhāga — tr. Th. Stcherbatsky (Bibl. Buddh. 30), Leningrad 1936; repr. Calcutta 1971

Madhyāntavibhāgabhāṣya — tr. S. Anacker, in *Seven Works of Vasubandhu*, Delhi 1984

Mahāparinirvāṇasūtra — tr. from Chinese by K. Yamamoto, 3 vols, Ubeshi 1973-75

Mahāratnakūṭasūtra — see Garma C.C. Chang, ed., *Selections from the Mahāratnakūṭa Sūtra*, Penn. State, University Park 1983; repr. Delhi 1991

Mahāvairocanasūtra, tr. C. Yamamoto, New Delhi 1990

Mahāvaṃsa — tr. W. Geiger and M.H. Bode, PTS, 1915, repr. 1950; — tr. A.W.P. Guruge, Calcutta 1990

Mahāvastu — tr. J.J. Jones, 3 vols, (PTS), London 1949-56; repr. 1976-87

Mahāvyut — ed. Y. Ishihama and Y. Fukuda, *A New Critical Edition of the Mahāvyutpatti*, Tokyo 1989

Paul, D.M., ed., *Women in Buddhism*, Berkeley 1979

Maitreyavyākaraṇa — ed. & tr. S. Lévi in *Études d'Orientalisme* II, Paris 1932; partial tr. E. Conze ('The Prophecy concerning Maitreya') in *Buddhist Scriptures*, Harmondsworth 1959, repr. 1986, pp.238-42

Nettippakaraṇa — tr. Ñāṇamoli, *The Guide*, PTS, 1962, repr. 1977

Paṭisambhidāmagga — tr. Ñāṇamoli, *The Path of Discrimination*, PTS, 1982

Pratyutpanna-Buddha-Saṃmukhāvasthita-Samādhi-Sūtra — ed. P. Harrison, Tokyo 1978; — tr. P. Harrison, *The Samādhi of Direct Encounter with the Buddhas of the Present*, Tokyo 1990; — id.,

'*Buddhānusmṛti* in the *Pratyutpanna-buddha-sammukhāvasthita-samādhi-sūtra*', *Journal of Indian Philosophy* 6, 1978, p.35-57

Puggalapaññatti — tr. B.C. Law, *A Designation of Human Types*, PTS, 1922, repr. 1979

Saddharmapuṇḍarīka — tr. H. Kern, *The Lotus of the True Law*, Oxford 1884, repr. New York 1963, Delhi 1965; — tr. W.E. Soothill, *The Lotus of the Wonderful Law*, Oxford 1930, London 1987; — tr. B. Kato et al, *The Threefold Lotus Sutra*, Tokyo 1975, repr. 1987; — tr. L. Hurvitz, *Scripture of the Lotus Blossom of the Fine Dharma*, New York 1976, repr. 1982; — tr. T. Kubo and A. Yuyama, *The Lotus Sūtra: The White Lotus of the Marvellous Law*, Tokyo and Berkeley 1991; — tr. B. Watson, *The Lotus Sūtra*, New York 1993; — M. Fuss, *Buddhavacana and Dei Verbum — A Phenomonological and Theological Comparison of Scriptural Inspiration in the Saddharmapuṇḍarīka Sūtra and in the Christian Tradition*', Leiden 1990

Śālistamba — tr. S. Frye, 'The Sublime Sūtra of the Great Vehicle Entitled «The Rice Plants»', in *Dreloma*, Drepung Loseling Magazine, Mundgod, Karnataka, Jan. 1985; — tr. J.M. Cooper, 'The Śālistamba Sūtra', in *Buddhist Studies Review* 8, London 1991; — tr. N. Ross Reat, *The Śālistamba Sūtra*, Delhi 1993

Samādhirāja Sūtra — tr. K. Régamey, *Three Chapters* [VIII, XIX, XXII] *from the Samādhirājasūtra*, Warsaw 1938; repr. as *Philosophy in the Samādhirājasūtra*, Delhi 1990; — tr. A.A.G. Bennett, 'Excerpts from the Samādhirāja Sūtra' [Ch.IX], *The Maha Bodhi* 77, Calcutta 1958, pp.295-8; — L.O. Gómez and J.A. Silk (ed.), *Studies in the Literature of the Great Vehicle* (Univ. Michigan), Ann Arbor 1989, Part I. The Sūtra of the *King of Samādhis*: Chapters I-IV; — tr. C. Cuppers, *The IXth Chapter of the Samādhirājasūtra*, Stuttgart 1990; — Thrangpu Rinpoche, *King of Samādhi*, Hong Kong 1994

Saṃgraha — P. Griffiths et al., *The Realm of Awakening: A Translation and Study of the Tenth Chapter of Asanga's* Mahāyānasaṅgraha, New York and Oxford 1989; — tr. from the Chinese by John P. Keenan, *The Summary of the Great Vehicle*, Berkeley 1992

Sasaki, G.H., 'Khanti, Kānti and Kśānti', *Indogaku Bukkyōgaku Kenkyū* 13, 1965, pp.37-42

Satyasiddhiśāstra of Harivarman, ed. and tr. N. Aiyaswami Sastri, 2 vols, Baroda 1975-78

Schuster, N.J. 'Changing the Female Body: Wise Women and the Bodhisattva Career in some Mahāratnakūṭa Sūtras', *Journal of the*

International Association of Buddhist Studies 4, 1981, pp.24-69

Siddhi (or Viṃśatikā) — ed. and tr. M. Tiwari, Varanasi 1967; — ed. and tr. K.N. Chatterjee, *Vasubandhu's Vijñapti-Mātratā-Siddhi*, Varanasi 1980; tr. S. Ganguly, Delhi 1992; tr. from Chinese, *Ch'eng Wei-shih lun: The Doctrine of Mere Consciousness*, Hong Kong 1973

Śikṣāsamuccaya — tr. C. Bendall and W.H.D. Rouse, *A Compendium of Buddhist Doctrine*, London 1922; repr. Delhi 1990

Ṣukhāvatīvyūha (Larger) — tr. F. Max Müller in *Buddhist Mahāyāna Texts*, ed. E.B. Cowell, Oxford 1894; repr. New York 1969, Delhi 1985; — tr. L. Gomez, *The Land of Bliss: The Paradise of the Buddha of Measureless Light*, Honolulu and Kyoto 1996

Sūtrālaṃkāra — tr. S.V. Limaye, *Mahāyānasūtrālaṃkāra*, Delhi 1992

Suvarṇaprabhāsottamasūtra — tr. R.E. Emmerick, *The Sūtra of Golden Light* (PTS), London 1970, rev. ed. 1990

Tsukamoto, Z., *History of Early Chinese Buddhism: From Its Introduction to the Death of Hui-Yuan*, tr. L. Hurvitz, 2 vols, Hawaii 1986

Upāsakaśīlasūtra — tr. Bhikṣuṇī Shih Heng-ching, *The Sūtra of the Upāsaka Precepts*, Berkeley 1994; see R.H. Robinson, 'The Ethic of the Householder Bodhisattva', *Bharati* 9, Banaras Hindu Univ., 1965-66

Vajracchedikā [P.P.] — tr. A.F. Price, *The Jewel of Transcendental Wisdom* (*The Diamond Sūtra*), The Buddhist Society, London 1947, repr. 1955 as *The Diamond Sūtra*; — tr. Bh. Heng Ch'ih, with comm. by Ven. Hsuan Hua, *Vajra Prajna Paramita Sutra*, San Francisco 1974; there are numerous other English translations: see P. Pfandt, ed., *Mahāyāna Texts translated into Western Languages*, Cologne 1986

Vism — tr. Pe Maung Tin, *The Path of Purity*, 3 vols, PTS, 1922-31, 1 vol, PTS, 1975; — tr. Ñāṇamoli, *The Path of Purification*, Colombo 1956; repr. Kandy 1972; 2 vols, Berkeley 1976

Vkn — tr. Lu K'uan Yü (Charles Luk), *The Vimalakīrti Nirdeśa Sūtra* (*Wei Mo Chieh So Shuo Ching*), Shambhala, Berkeley, London 1973; — tr. R.A.F. Thurman, *The Holy Teaching of Vimalakīrti*, University Park and London 1976, repr. 1981; — tr. B. Watson, *Vimalakīrti Sūtra*, New York 1997; — E. Hamlin, 'Magical Upāya in the Vimalakīrtinirdeśa-sūtra', *Journal of the International Association of Buddhist Studies* 11, 1988, pp.89-121

Yang, H-C., *A Record of Buddhist Monasteries in Lo-Yang*, Princeton 1984

Note: Works in the Bibliotheca Buddhica series have been reprinted Osnabrück 1970, Tokyo 1977-79, Delhi 1992

INTRODUCTION

CHAPTER ONE

THE ŚŪRAṂGAMASAMĀDHISŪTRA

I. THE TEXT

Śūraṃgamasamādhisūtra (abbreviation Śgs) means 'Text of the Concentration of Heroic Progress' in Sanskrit. *Samādhi* means concentration, a state of mind fixed on one point (*cittaikāgratā*). The concentration concerned here is the *Śūraṃgama*, Heroic Progress. It is not so much a question of a special concentration as of an aspect of concentration as conceived by the Buddhism of the Great Vehicle. It is called Heroic Progress because whoever possesses it goes everywhere in the manner of a hero (*śūra*) without meeting any resistance, or because it is frequented (*gata*) by those heroes the Buddhas and bodhisattvas.

The work is undoubtedly of Indian origin, but we possess only a few fragments of the Sanskrit original: two quotations in Śāntideva's Śikṣāsamuccaya[1] and one folio of a manuscript discovered in Eastern Turkestan[2]. The complete work is known at present through two translations: a Chinese translation made by Kumārajīva, probably between 402 and 409 C.E.[3] and a Tibetan translation dating from the beginning of the ninth century C.E. ascribed to the collaboration of the Indian pandit Śākyaprabha and the Tibetan exegete Ratnarakṣita[4].

Prior to Kumārajīva, the *Śūraṃgamasamādhisūtra* had already been translated into Chinese by Serindians or Chinese: Chih Ch'an (in 186 C.E.), one or several scholars from Ssŭ-chuan (between 220 and 265), Chih Ch'ien (between 222 and 229), Po Yen (in 258), Dharmarakṣa (in 291), Chu Shu-lan (in 291), Chang T'ien-hsi, Chih Shih-lun and Po Yen (in 373). These translations were already lost by the sixth century and we only know of them through their titles[5].

The full title of the Sūtra was *Śūraṃgamasamādhi*, transliterated in Chinese by *Shou-lêng-yen san-mei* 首楞嚴三昧, translated into Chinese as *Yung fu-ting* 勇伏定 'Concentration of Heroic Victory', and rendered

[1] C. Bendall edition, pp.8, *19-20*; 91, *8* - 92, *6*.

[2] Published in R. Hoernle, *Manuscript Remains of Buddhist Literature I*, Oxford 1916 (repr. Amsterdam 1970, Delhi 1988), pp.125-32 [† See also the author's Foreword, pp. xv sq.].

[3] *Shou-lêng-yen san-mei ching*, T[aishō] 642.

[4] *dPaḥ-bar-ḥgro-baḥi tiṅ-ṅe-ḥdzin*, Tib. Trip. vol.32, No.800.

[5] See below, Ch. Two of the Introduction.

in Tibetan by *dPaḥ-bar-ḥgro-baḥi tiṅ-ṅe-ḥdzin*. It is in this full form that it appears or is quoted in the translation by Dharmarakṣa (entitled *Yung-fu-ting*), in that by Kumārajīva (having the title of *Shou-lêng-yen san-mei*), in three places in the Upadeśa (T 1509, pp.92*b* 3; 134*b* 18; 349*c* 19 [† for details of translation of this work, see below p.54]), in the Nandimitrāvadanā (T 2030, p.14a 16) and in a section of the Śikṣāsamuccaya (ed. C. Bendall, p.91,*8*; T 1636, p.93*c* 23).

Conversely, it is abridged to the title of *Śūraṃgama* (transliterated in Chinese as *Shou-lêng-yen*) in all the Chinese versions except for those by Dharmarakṣa and Kumārajīva. It is equally in this abridged form that it is quoted in five places in the Upadeśa (T 1509, pp.249*c* 11; 273*b* 5; 303*b* 11; 312*a* 27; 586*b* 1), in one place in the Śikṣāsamuccaya (ed. Bendall, p.8,19; T 1636, p.77*a* 14) and once in the Bodhicaryāvatāra-pañjikā (ed. L. de La Vallée Poussin, p.24,*12*).

The titles of nearly all Mahāyāna sūtras display these discrepancies, but in the present case they had particularly serious consequences: a Chinese apocryphal work composed at the beginning of the eighth century, with the abridged title of Śūraṃgamasūtra (T 945), has often been confused in the past as well as the present with the authentic Śūraṃgamasamādhisūtra with which we are concerned here, and this confusion explains in part the considerable success that the forgery met with in China[6].

We do not know where or when the Indian Śgs was published. With regard to its date, we can say no more than that it preceded the first Chinese translation made in 186 C.E. On the other hand, it presupposes a very advanced elaboration of the early canonical writings of Buddhism. As far as its place of origin is concerned, the scant details supplied by the text itself regarding the location of its teaching, i.e. the Vulture Peak Mountain in Rājagṛha, have no historical value. The action does not take place on earth, but unfolds within the framework of the Buddha-fields and Pure Lands which, by definition, escape the confines of time and space.

Chih Ch'an, who was the first to translate the Śgs, was a Yuëh-chih, an Indo-Scythian from Central Asia. He translated other Buddhist texts in collaboration with Chu Shuo-fo or Chu Fo-shuo, an Indian who arrived in Lo-yang with the original texts or who knew the latter by heart. However, it does not seem as though Chu Shuo-fo participated in the translation of the Śgs, and we do not know how Chih Ch'an came into possession of this text.

[6] See below p.98.

II. SETTING AND PERSONS

Canonical sūtras begin with an introduction (*nidāna*) which briefly indicates the circumstances of the time, place and persons with which the sūtra is concerned. This tradition continued to be followed by the Mahāyāna sūtras with the difference that the assembly surrounding the Buddha is particularly numerous.

According to the introduction of the Śgs (§ 1–4), one day, the Buddha Śākyamuni was in Rājagṛha, on the Gṛdhrakūṭaparvata 'Vulture Peak Mountain' with a great assembly consisting of 32,000 bhikṣus, 72,000 bodhisattvas, all the gods and demi-gods of the Great Cosmos of which our small universe of four continents is part.

This assembly should be envisaged not according to the realist views of Sthaviravāda Buddhism but from the perspective particular to the Mahāyāna for which persons and things are absolutely non-existent.

Thus the Gṛdhrakūṭaparvata where the assembly gathers is not the most famous of the five mountains which dominate Rājagṛha, the ancient Magadhan capital, but an idealised place blessed by the presence of the dharmakāya of the Buddhas. It could be called *bodhimaṇḍa* on the understanding that it is not localised at Bodh-Gayā, where all the Buddhas attain enlightenment, but anywhere – Bodh-Gayā, Rājagṛha, Vaiśālī, Śrāvastī – where minds are edified by the expounding of the Buddhas (§ 118, n.242). The Gṛdhrakūṭaparvata concerned here is not part of the receptacle-world; it is derived from a Buddha-field (*buddhakṣetra*) or, as it will later be called, a 'Pure Land'. This is so true that, on the injunction of a bodhisattva, all its trees are transformed into 'Bodhi trees' each sheltering a bodhisattva (§ 168).

The Buddha Śākyamuni who appears in the Sūtra is not the Buddha of the sixth century B.C.E. whom we call 'historical' and whom the Mahāyānists term 'transformational', that Buddha who was born in the Lumbinī Park, attained enlightenment at Bodh-Gayā, expounded the Dharma for forty-five years, and passed into Nirvāṇa in Pāvā. This is Śākyamuni in Heroic Progress, a pure ray of wisdom and power, who manifests himself simultaneously in our little universe of four continents, in the Great Cosmos from which the latter derives, and in all the great cosmic systems as numerous as the sands of the Ganges; here, he repeats the feat of the historical Buddha; there, he is some divinity; there again, he is a banker, householder, minor king, great king, warrior, brahmin or śūdra (§§ 122–3). He is identical with the Buddha Sarvaguṇadharmasaṃdarśakavikurvaṇaprabhārāja who expounds the

Dharma in the Ekapradipā universe located at the zenith and separated from our world by universes as numerous as the sands of the Ganges (§§ 125–6). He is the same as the Buddha Vairocana who, on the borders of the East, rules over the Pratimaṇḍitā universe. Proof of this is that both Buddhas have an identical life-span of 700 incalculable periods (§§ 170–2).

But enough of these comparisons! This Śākyamuni is able, among other prodigies, to create through transformation 84,000 replicas of himself and to sit with these 84,000 fictitious Buddhas on the innumerable thrones that the devas offered him (§§ 15–16). The authentic Buddha and the fictitious Buddhas are equally 'real' (according to the Chinese version) or 'unreal' (according to the Tibetan version). Originally and spontaneously, they are not born; they are non-existent in the present and the future; they are the same and without difference, in the beginning, in the middle and at the end (§ 18).

Like things of illusion, things of mirage, we see them perform the classic feats of the Buddha: they are born, reach enlightenment, set turning the Wheel of the Dharma and enter Nirvāṇa. However, all this is only illusion: the appearance of a Buddha is the absence of arising, duration and destruction (§ 72); their Nirvāṇa is the fact that they are always and at all times in Nirvāṇa (§ 71). The world of the Buddha is no different from the world of Māra (§ 114).

The other persons in the assembly participate in this ineffable non-existence in some way. They can be classified into three categories: śrāvakas, devas and bodhisattvas.

The śrāvakas are the great disciples of Śākyamuni, the faithful followers of the Master during the forty-five years of his public life, the depositories of his Teaching and guardians of his Order after the Nirvāṇa. The Buddha solemnly recognised their pre-eminence: Śāriputra is the foremost of the wise; Mahākāśyapa, the foremost of those who observe the ascetic rules; Ānanda, the foremost of the learned; Subhūti, the foremost of those worthy of offerings, etc.

We would expect them to play in the Śgs the same role as they did in the past in the canonical sūtras. We would especially like them to defend their status of Arhat of which they are so proud, and the right to Nirvāṇa, the object of their ardent aspirations.

Nothing of the kind. Here they are represented as vanquished, disabused figures who have lost faith in their ideal. Ānanda humbly admits his erudition is nothing compared with that of the bodhisattvas (§ 136); he still agrees to memorise the sūtras, but these sūtras are no longer the authentic word of the Master; they are new theories devised by the Mahāyānist trend. Moreover, the protection that Ānanda is able to assure them is so weak that he has to be bolstered by Śakra Meruśikharadhara (§ 168).

Subhūti is no longer the foremost of those worthy of offerings; he admits that he does not fulfil any of the ten qualities needed to be a 'true field of merit' (§ 134).

The questions posed by Śāriputra again clearly call for clarification of the fictitious nature of entry into Nirvāṇa (§§ 141–2).

As for Kāśyapa, he is no longer the austere monk who, after the decease of the Buddha, convened the First Council and ruled the Community with a rod of iron. He no longer has that total and exclusive respect for the Master which he dedicated to him in the past; he considers all beings as being the Master in person and thus refutes his own authority (§ 102). Even more, he considers himself, as well as all the śrāvakas, as being like those blind from birth, not knowing the profound teachings of the Buddha, not knowing and not seeing the domain of the Blessed One (§ 132).

These nondescript beings no longer have anything in common with the glorious disciples described to us in the canonical texts. Let us say that they are bodhisattvas who, through skill in means and in order to win over beings, assume the role of a śrāvaka and make him as unpleasant as possible. Do we not know that the great bodhisattva Maitreya is present in the thousand million Jambudvīpas which constitute our cosmic universe? 'Here, he is the attendant of the Buddha like Ānanda, there the foremost of the sages like Śāriputra, there again like the foremost of the ascetics like Mahākāśyapa, etc.' (§ 156). One cannot help but feel that the śrāvakas who appear in the Śgs are nothing but bodhisattvas in disguise.

It is the same for the devas, gods and demi-gods of all kinds, who also have their part to play. Already the early canonical texts and the old Central Indian school of sculpture had associated them directly with the life and legend of Śākyamuni. Whether it is a question of the six classes of the gods of the world of desire – Caturmahādevas, Trāyastriṃśas, Tuṣitas, etc. – or of the seventeen classes of the Brahmā gods of the world of subtle form, all acknowledge the supreme dominion of the Buddha; they applaud his teachings and pledge him an attachment which is as humble as it is sincere. There is only one exception among them: Māra, the 'Buddhist Satan', supreme chief of the Kāmadhātu (the world of desire) and, because of this, the sworn enemy of the Buddha who destroyed desire. Throughout history Māra and his daughters, the devakanyās, intensify attacks on Śākyamuni and his disciples which are as ineffectual as they are incessant.

These devas also have their place in the Mahāyāna sūtras. The fact that in the past they adhered to the Four Truths in no way prevents them from rallying enthusiastically to the theories and doctrines of the Great Vehicle, which they consider to be the 'second turning of the Wheel of the Dharma' (*dvitīya dharmacakrapravartana*). In the Sūtra with which we are concerned here, the devas congratulate themselves on hearing the homily on Heroic Progress (§§ 11, 169); they offer thrones to the Buddha (§§ 12–14); they scatter flowers over Śākyamuni (§ 129), over the bodhisattvas Māragocarānupalipta (§ 89) and Mañjuśrī (§ 148); they praise the new teaching (§§ 67, 83) and go so far as to develop themselves revolutionary theories on the superiority of the offender over the holy one (§ 150).

However, the main point is the arousal of the thought of Bodhi (*cittotpāda*) to which the devas proceed one after the other (§§ 17, 90, 167): a step of cardinal importance which starts them on the bodhisattva career. The devakanyās are not slow to do this and seven hundred of them obtain the preparatory certainty on the spot (§ 90). Two hundred young goddesses are of a passionate nature and seek the favours of the bodhisattva Māragocarānupalipta as a preliminary; the latter creates through transformation two hundred replicas of himself and unites with each of them. Their desires thus satisfied, they arouse the *cittotpāda* (§§ 93–4) and the Buddha 'gives the prediction' to them: after their death they will change their feminine bodies, be reborn in the Tuṣita heaven and one day become a Buddha with the name of Vyūharāja (§§ 110–12).

There is, therefore, no clear demarcation between the devas and the bodhisattvas. Moreover, it is in the form of devas that the latter prefer to manifest themselves in the Śgs.

The bodhisattvas appear in great numbers and there would be no point in listing these elusive beings.

The introduction of the Śgs supplies, in § 3, a list of twenty-six bodhisattvas, all of them unknown except Maitreya. These are only names intended to enhance the innumerable qualities of these future Buddhas. The last one, Dṛḍhamati 'Firm Intelligence', will be the moving spirit of the Sūtra. It is he who questions Śākyamuni on the Concentration of Heroic Progress (§§ 5–7) and converses with his kind. The immense merit that he has accumulated in the past enables him to obtain the Śgs (§ 167).

Among the other great bodhisattvas on whom the literature of the Mahāyāna has conferred a semblance of reality, we must point out Maitreya, Mañjuśrī and Matyabhimukha who play a leading part here. There is no mention of Avalokiteśvara, nor of the Buddha Amitābha.

Maitreya already occupied a special position in the writings of the Small Vehicle. He was, along with Ajita, one of the sixteen disciples of the brahmanic ascetic Bāvari. Śākyamuni predicted to him that he would be the next Buddha and as a pledge gave him the gold tunic which his aunt Mahāprajāpati Gautamī had just presented to the Sangha. Under the name of Ajita-Maitreya, he plays the part of the Buddhist Messiah and will appear in the golden age when a human's life-span lasts for 80,000 years[7]. In the writings of the Great Vehicle which multiply the Buddhas in time and space, this privilege tends to be softened down, but Maitreya still continues to be a very great bodhisattva. Here, the Śgs shows him as being present everywhere at once in the Jambudvīpas of the Great Cosmos, a god among gods, a man among men, begging for his food, expounding the Dharma or plunged into solitary meditation (§ 156). Moreover, he is the authorised guardian of the Mahāyāna sūtras.

Mañjuśrī is a purely Mahāyānist creation, but he is the wisest and most zealous of the bodhisattvas[8]. He is in no hurry to attain enlightenment and will stay in the world of rebirth until the end, as long as a being remains to be saved. He moves from *buddhakṣetra* to *buddhakṣetra* to go and question the Buddhas and remove the doubts of the assembly (§§ 125–8). Gifted with unequalled intelligence and eloquence, he rethinks the old doctrines in the light of the Mahāyāna and supplies new definitions of the 'field of merit' and the learned disciple (§§ 133, 135). As a master of skilful means, his exploits can no longer be counted. During the Virocana kalpa, in the course of three hundred and sixty hundreds of thousands of existences, he entered Nirvāṇa through the Vehicle of the Pratyekabuddhas (§§ 142, 144–7). In the course of his long career he appears in turn as a bodhisattva of the present, a Buddha of the present, and even a Buddha of the past and already in Parinirvāṇa. It is thus that, in the remote past, the Buddha

7 Regarding the Maitreya of the Hīnayānist sources, see É. Lamotte, *History of Indian Buddhism*, tr. S. Boin-Webb, Louvain-la-Neuve 1988, pp.699-710. See also W. Baruch, 'Maitreya d'après les sources de Sérinde', *Revue de l'Histoire des Religions* CXXXII, 1946, pp.67-92.

8 Regarding Mañjuśrī, see my article 'Mañjuśrī', *T'oung Pao* XLVIII, 1960, pp.1-96, and the learned work by M.-T. de Mallman, *Étude iconographique sur Mañjuśrī*, Paris 1964.

Nāgavaṃśāgra appeared in the Samā universe separated from ours by a thousand Buddha-fields. He reached enlightenment, set turning the Wheel of the Dharma and won over an infinite number of beings to the three Vehicles. His life-span was 440 myriad years and, his work accomplished, he entered Nirvāṇa after having given the prediction to the bodhisattva Jñānaprabha. Well, that bygone Buddha Nāgavaṃśāgra is none other than Mañjuśrī (§§ 158–62). That immense work was carried out by Mañjuśrī without the least effort because, for him who has understood the emptiness of dharmas, nothing is difficult (§ 164).

However, the great find of the Sūtra which concerns us here is the invention of the devaputra Matyabhimukha or, according to the Tibetan version, Buddhamatyabhimukha 'Close to the Intelligence of a Buddha'. He is a great bodhisattva of the tenth stage, in possession of the Heroic Progress (§ 64). His supernormal power is such that he successively transforms all the members of the assembly into cakravartin kings, devendra Śakras, Brahmadevas, Kāśyapas, and, in culmination, Śākyamuni Buddhas (§ 65). He engages Dṛḍhamati in a long philosophical discussion (§§ 69–75) on the question of the Buddha attributes, absolutely the same as the qualities of worldlings (§ 69), the Heroic Progress which does not lead anywhere (§ 70), the Buddhas who do not go to Nirvāṇa because they undergo no real birth (§§ 71–2), the true eloquence which presupposes the previous eradication of all notions (§§ 74–5), and above all, the absence of a base (*apratiṣṭhāna*) upon which beings and things can lean (§ 73). As will be seen in the notes covering these paragraphs, these are theories dear to Vimalakīrti and which are developed at length in the Vimalakīrtinirdeśa. Might not the famous lay bodhisattva from Vaiśālī be one and the same as the devaputra Matyabhimukha? Just like Vimalakīrti, Matyabhimukha comes from the Abhirati universe occupied by the Buddha Akṣobhya (§ 77). Later, in the Sahāloka which will then bear the name of Prasannadarśanā, during the 63rd small kalpa of the period which will follow the present Bhadrakalpa, Matyabhimukha will become a Buddha with the name of Vimalaprabhākīrtirāja (§§ 78–9), a title of which 'Vimalakīrti' is only a variation (§ 78, n.181).

Alongside these great bodhisattvas, the Sūtra also brings on the scene a devaputra Vimalacandragarbha who, because he offered some precious parasols to Śākyamuni, is destined to become the Buddha Ekaratnacchattra in the Sarvaratnaracitā universe (§ 138). There is also the bodhisattva Nāmamati or Rājamati who sees the Heroic Progress as the source of all benefits (§ 157) and suspects Maitreya of possessing it (§ 155).

The Concentration of Heroic Progress places the bodhisattvas who possess it well above the gods of the world of desire (*kāmadhātu*) and the world of subtle form (*rūpadhātu*).

According to early Buddhist cosmography, partly coinciding with brahmanical cosmography, the Kāmadhātu is not only the receptacle of the hell-born, animals, pretas and mankind. It also contains the six classes of Kāmadevas, the second of which is that of the Trāyastriṃśa gods ruled by the devendra Śakra; the sixth is that of the Paranirmitavaśavartins over whom Māra holds sway.

To the devendra Śakra of the early texts, the Śgs here opposes Meruśikharadhara, a bodhisattva in possession of the Heroic Progress. He also occupies the summit of Mount Meru, but an idealised Meru, located outside the confines of the great cosmic system (§§ 50–1). He manifests himself in all Śakra's palaces, but Śakra has never seen him (§§ 52–3). At the Buddha's request, he displays his marvellous body to the assembly, and his precious jewels shine with a brilliance more vivid than those of the god Śakra (§§ 54–5). He vows to protect the Sūtra and, as witness of his good faith, transforms all the trees on the Gṛdhrakūṭaparvata into as many bodhivṛkṣas, each one sheltering a bodhisattva (§ 168).

Still on the subject of the Trāyastriṃśas, the Śgs skilfully exploits the case of a certain Gopā or Gopī. According to early canonical sources, she was a young girl of the Śākyan clan who lived in Kapilavastu and had known Śākyamuni before he left home. She took refuge in the Three Jewels, rejected all feminine thoughts and cultivated masculine thoughts. Because of this, after her death she was reborn in the Trāyastriṃśa heaven as the daughter of the devendra Śakra. Basing itself on this tradition, the Śgs brings on the scene a devaputra Gopaka whom it presents as once having been the wife of Śākyamuni and, above all, as a bodhisattva. Gopaka invites all the members of the assembly to arouse the thought of Bodhi (§ 57). A convinced supporter of sexual equality, he admits to having taken on a masculine body, but nonetheless without having lost his feminine form (§ 58). If he has not as yet obtained the Concentration of Heroic Progress, he nevertheless knows a small part of it and this enables him to make some interesting revelations (§§ 59–60).

Māra the Malign, whose aerial palaces (*vimāna*) dominate the whole of the Kāmadhātu, is compared by the Śgs with the bodhisattva Māragocarānupalipta who frequents Māra's dwelling without being defiled (§ 87). He manifests his marvellous body, and his radiance is so brilliant that it eclipses Māra, who becomes as black as a block of ink

(§ 93). A past master of skilful means, he unites by means of fictitious substitutes with two hundred devakanyās and thus causes them to arouse the *bodhicitta* (§ 94). All these exploits he accomplishes through the supernormal power of the Heroic Progress (§ 121).

Faced with this all-powerful bodhisattva, Māra the Malign is a lamentable figure. The sworn enemy of the Buddha, he wants to join the assembly in order to disrupt the teaching of the Heroic Progress, but immediately finds himself tied by five bonds (§ 82). The latter fall away when he renounces his plan (§ 88). After the goddesses in his entourage are converted, he pretends to arouse the *bodhicitta* in the hope of winning them back (§ 92). He goes to the assembly and begs the Buddha not to expound the Heroic Progress any more (§ 95). When his attempt fails, he wants to return to his paradise. He has not even started out when he finds himself in his palaces but, horror of horrors, these are occupied by the great assembly and Śākyamuni is expounding the Heroic Progress there (§ 115).

This unhappy figure no longer has anything in common with the fearful Māra of the canonical sources, that Māra who contended with Śākyamuni over the seat of Bodhi and brought about the Master's premature entry into Nirvāṇa. The Māra of the Śgs covers himself with so much ridicule that we can but suspect him of playing a voluntarily humiliating role. Might he not be one of those bodhisattvas who are 'established in inconceivable liberation and who, through skilful means, behave like Māra in order to ripen beings'? (Vkn, p.150) Anyway, the very fact of having heard the name of the Śūraṃgamasamādhi uttered, the very fact of having aroused the *bodhicitta* with a self-interested motive, will one day win him access to Buddhahood (§ 98).

We now leave the Kāmadhātu for the Rūpadhātu, the world of subtle form inhabited by the sixteen or seventeen classes of Brahmā gods; that world with which the practice of *dhyāna* can momentarily put us in contact. The effects of the Śūraṃgamasamādhi are felt there as well and, alongside the Brahmās Tudu, Nārada, Ghaṭikāra, Baka, Sanatkumāra and Sahaṃpati of whom the early sources speak, we now see the appearance of bodhisattva-Brahmās, fully won over to the teachings of the Great Vehicle. Here, it is the Brahmarāja Samatāvihārin 'Residing in Sameness' who persuades Śākyamuni to explain that there is no difference between a 'real' Buddha and an 'imaginary' Buddha and that if the non-existent Buddha still displays his wonderful physical body, this is only an illusion (§§ 18–19). There, it is the Brahmadeva Maitrīsaṃpanna 'Endowed with Goodwill' who remarks that the best way to train in the Heroic Progress is to travel through all the realms of foolish worldlings (§ 46).

The divisions set up here between śrāvakas, devas and bodhisattvas do not stand up to scrutiny. As Matyabhimukha declares, 'At present in the assembly, there are bodhisattvas in possession of the Heroic Progress who manifest themselves in the body of a devendra Śakra, in the body of a Brahmarāja or in the bodies of devas, nāgas, yakṣas, gandharvas, asuras, garuḍas, kiṃnaras and mahoragas. There are bodhisattvas in possession of the Heroic Progress who manifest themselves in the bodies of bhikṣus, bhikṣuṇīs, upāsakas and upāsikās. There are bodhisattvas in possession of the Heroic Progress with bodies adorned with the primary and secondary marks [† of a Buddha]. There are bodhisattvas who, in order to ripen beings, manifest the figure, colours and signs of a female body; others manifest the figure, colours and signs of a śrāvaka; and yet others, the figure, colours and signs of a pratyekabuddha' (§ 62). Also, the Venerable Mahākāśyapa makes the resolve of henceforth considering all beings as the same as the Buddha himself, all individuals whoever they are as being able to belong to the bodhisattva vehicle (§§ 102–3).

This is what later caused certain scholars to say that the personalities who come into the Mahāyāna sūtras are Buddhas and bodhisattvas of the pure lands and that particularly the śrāvakas and devas of the assembly are only supernormal creations of the Buddha or again transformations of the bodhisattvas who have entered the Bhūmis[9].

III. THE SUBJECT – CONCENTRATION

As its title indicates, the subject of the Sūtra is concentration, or to be more precise the Concentration of Heroic Progress. In order to understand the significance of this, it is indispensable to return to the early sources which already attributed an important role to the purification of thought through concentration of the mind.

1. *Samādhi in the Śrāvaka or Small Vehicle*

The path of Nirvāṇa, as it has been defined by the Buddha in the canonical sources, consists of three essential elements: morality (*śīla*), concentration (*samādhi*) and wisdom (*prajñā*). These three elements are inseparable and are practised concurrently.

[9] Cf. Bandhuprabha in the Buddhabhūmisūtraśāstra, T 1530, ch.1, p.292*b* and foll.; P. Demiéville, in *Journal Asiatique*, 1936, pp.653-4.

With a wholly scholastic precision, the early texts inform us about the preliminaries, stages and fruit of Samādhi[10].

The Preliminaries to Samādhi. These are the observance of morality, watching over the senses, mindfulness and awareness, absolute satisfaction, the choice of a secluded residence and the dispelling of the hindrances to meditation.

1. The observance of morality (*śīla)* consists of avoiding anything that could harm others: the three bad actions of body (destruction of living beings, theft and sexual misconduct), the four bad actions of speech (falsehood, slander, harsh speech and useless speech), and the three bad actions of the mind (animosity, covetousness and wrong views).

2. Watching over the senses (*indriyeṣu guptadvāratā*). When the ascetic has seen a form with his eyes, heard a sound with his ears, smelled an odour with his nose, tasted a flavour with his tongue, touched a tangible with his body, recognised a notion with his internal sense, he does not cling to outward signs, he does not cling to secondary features. He strives to protect himself from the object due to which wrong and baneful things, covetousness and suffering, assail the being who is not watchful over the senses.

3. Mindfulness and awareness (*smṛtisaṃprajanya*). The ascetic acts with awareness when he is going somewhere and returning, when he is looking ahead and to the side, when he is bending and stretching, when he is wearing his tunic, carrying his bowl and wearing his robe, when he is eating, drinking, chewing and tasting, when he is occupied in defecating or urinating, when he is walking, standing, sitting, sleeping,

[10] Here I follow the canonical sources which reproduce unchanged the old topic concerning the *dhyānas* and *samāpattis:* cf. Vin. III, p.4; D I, pp.37, 73, 172; II, p.313; III, pp.78, 131, 222, 265; M I, pp.21, 40, 89, 117. 159; II, pp.15, 204, 226; III, pp.4, 14, 25, 36; S II, pp.210, 216, 221; III, p.235; IV, pp.225, 236, 263; V, pp.10, 198, 213; A I, pp.53, 163, 182, 242; II, pp.126, 151; III, pp.11, 119; IV, pp.111, 176, 229, 410; V, pp.207, 343; Kathāvatthu II, p.484; Milinda, p.289. For the Sanskrit recensions, see Lalitavistara, p.129; Pañcaviṃśati, p.167; Daśasāhasrikā, pp.98-9; Kośavyākhyā, pp.665, 666, 673; Mahāvyutpatti, Nos 1478-81, 1492-5. Chinese version, e.g. Ch'ang-a-han, T 1, ch.8, p.50*c*; Chung-a-han, T 26, ch.47, p.720*a*; Tsa-a-han, T 99, ch.41, p.302*a*.

The passage has been translated by L. Renou, *Canon bouddhique pāli* I, Paris 1949, pp.63-75, and I have made wide use of this translation.

Concerning Samādhi, see the bibliography collated by J. May, *Candrakīrti,* Paris 1959, p.148, n.436.

awake, speaking or remaining silent.

4. Absolute satisfaction (*saṃtuṣṭi*). The ascetic is fully satisfied with a robe that protects his body and a begging bowl that protects his belly; wherever he goes, he goes with all his possessions.

5. The choice of a secluded residence (*vivikta senāsana*). The ascetic chooses a secluded residence, a solitary place, the foot of a tree, a mountain, a ravine, a cave, a cemetery, scrubland, an open area, a pile of straw. He sits there after his meal, when he returns from his begging round, crossing his legs under him, his body held straight, keeping his awareness alert.

6. The dispelling of the hindrances (*nīvaraṇa*) to meditation. The ascetic lives with a mind free from covetousness (*abhidhyā*), animosity (*vyāpāda*), torpor-languor (*styānamiddha*), frivolity-regret (*auddhatyakaukṛtya*) and doubt (*vicikitsā*). He does not covet anything; he is careful to be of benefit to all living beings; he is mindful and aware, his mind is inwardly pacified; he is unperplexed regarding good things. When he has freed himself from the five hindrances, he considers them as the discharge of a debt, as a cure, as the end of a detention, as the return to freedom, as a peaceful territory.

Stages of Samādhi. Buddhist cosmology posits a triple world (*traidhātuka*) consisting of:

1. The Kāmadhātu, the world of desire or of the five senses, comprising the destinies of the hell-born, animals, ghosts, human beings and some of the gods: the six classes of the gods of the world of desire.

2. The Rūpadhātu, the world of (subtle) form, containing celestial beings who have been reborn in the Brahmā world and are dispersed throughout the realms of the four absorptions (*dhyāna*). The first Dhyāna is in two or three stages, the second and third Dhyānas each have three stages and the fourth has eight. Although invisible to the human eye, these worlds are still made of form, being terraces or mansions inhabited by beings of subtle form.

3. The Ārūpyadhātu, the formless world, containing celestial beings who have been reborn in the form of a 'mental series' in the stages of the four attainments (*samāpatti*). These stages are: 1. the sphere of the infinity of space (*ākāśānantyāyatana*), 2. the sphere of the infinity of consciousness (*vijñānānantyāyatana*), 3. the sphere of nothingness

(*ākiṃcanyāyatana*), and 4. the sphere of neither perception nor non-perception (*naivasaṃjñānāsaṃjñāyatana*), also known as the Summit of Existence (*bhavāgra*).

A man is reborn in a sphere of attainment (one of the four Dhyānas or one of the four Samāpattis) – that is, he obtains an 'existence of an attained god' – because here in this world he obtained and practised a certain Samādhi. By Samādhi is meant the concentration of favourable thoughts on a single object (*śūbhānāṃ cittānām aikāgryam*): Samādhi properly so called always consists of non-craving (*arāga*), non-hatred (*adveṣa*) and non-delusion (*amoha*). We therefore need to distinguish between the Dhyānasamāpattis – 'existences' – and the Dhyānasamāpattis – 'concentrations': the latter are the cause of the former.

The candidate to attainment should free himself from the passions of the Kāmadhātu and eliminate craving, hatred and delusion. To this end, lengthy efforts are necessary and, among the recommended practices, we can quote: 1. the contemplation of the repulsive (*aśūbhabhāvanā*) or meditation on a decomposing corpse: the counteraction of craving; 2. the contemplation of goodwill (*maitrībhāvanā*) and other brahma practices: the counteraction of hatred; 3. the contemplation of causality (*pratītyasamutpādabhāvanā*): the counteraction of delusion; 4. mindfulness applied to breathing (*ānāpānasmṛti*): the counteraction of ratiocination; 5. the recollection of the Buddha (*buddhānusmṛti)*: the counteraction of the combination of the above.

The ascetic who is freed from the passions of the Kāmadhātu obtains, by means of the appropriate practices, the mental state called the first Dhyāna. When this first absorption comes to an end, he finds himself once again in a normal psychological state, in the state of a distracted mind with the feelings and ways of thinking of the Kāmadhātu. However, as long as he remains freed from the passions of the Kāmadhātu he stays in possession of the first Dhyāna and can easily return to it by concentrating his mind once more. After his death, he cannot be reborn in the Kāmadhātu, but will take on a new birth in the realm of the first Dhyāna – the 'existence'-Dhyāna – with a physical and mental organism in keeping with the existence of an 'attained' god of the first absorption: the absence of the organs of taste, smell and sex, and the incapacity for physical and mental suffering.

However, it is not necessary that a man die in order to reach the higher stages. As a rule, a being pertaining to one stage can practise the attainments which are higher than that stage: a human can practise all the attainments; a god born in the first Dhyāna can practise all the attainments of the second Dhyāna, and so on.

In order to get from one Dhyāna to another or from one Samāpatti to another, it is enough to free oneself from the passions which are inherent in the realm where one is. The path of the attainments consists in eliminating, one after the other, all the passions of the triple world which are susceptible to elimination through meditation. The attainments can only be acquired in the right order. Normally, the ascetic detaches himself from the passions of the Kāmadhātu, then from the passions inherent in the four Dhyānas and, finally, from the passions inherent in the four Samāpattis; which makes nine successive abodes (*navānupūrvavihāra*). The early canonical sources describe the ascetic's ascent in the following way:

1. When he considers the five hindrances, covetousness, etc., from which he has freed himself, joy (*prīti*) arises in him; from joy arises gladness; when his mind is glad his body is calm; when his body is calm, he feels happiness (*sukha*); when he is happy, his mind is absorbed. Detaching himself from desires, detaching himself from bad dharmas, he attains and dwells in the first Dhyāna, consisting of reasoning (*vitarka*) and deliberation (*vicāra*) and which, born of detachment, is joy (*prīti*) and happiness (*sukha*). He floods his body with this joy and happiness born of detachment.

2. Then having discarded reasoning and deliberation, he attains and dwells in the second Dhyāna which, being inward peace (*ādhyātmasaṃprasāda*) and one-pointedness of mind (*cetasa ekotibhāva*), excludes reasoning and deliberation and which, born of concentration, is joy and happiness. He floods his body with this joy and happiness born of concentration.

3. Then, having renounced joy (*prīti*), he dwells with equanimity (*upekṣaka*), mindful (*smṛtimat*) and fully aware (*saṃprajānan*); in his body he feels happiness (*sukha*), in such a way that the Noble Ones call him the one with equanimity, the mindful one, the happy man; thus he attains and dwells in the third Dhyāna. He floods his body with this happiness devoid of joy.

4. Then, through destroying happiness (*sukha*) and through destroying suffering (*duḥkha*), through the previous discarding of joy (*prīti*) and sorrow (*daurmanasya*), he attains and dwells in the fourth Dhyāna, free of suffering and happiness, purified by equanimity and

mindfulness (*upekṣāsmṛtipariśuddha*). He is seated there, permeating his body with an utterly pure, utterly cleansed thought, and there is no part of his body which is not touched by this utterly pure, utterly cleansed thought.

5. Having entirely gone beyond all notions of form (*rūpasaṃjñā*), having banished all notions of resistance (*pratighasaṃjñā*), having disregarded all notions of plurality (*nānātvasaṃjñā*), he exclaims: 'Infinite is space', and he attains and dwells in the sphere of the infinity of space (*ākāśānantyāyatana*).

6. Having entirely gone beyond the sphere of the infinity of space, he exclaims: 'Infinite is consciousness', and he attains and dwells in the sphere of the infinity of consciousness (*vijñānānantyāyatana*).

7. Having entirely gone beyond the sphere of the infinity of consciousness, he exclaims: 'Nothing exists', and he attains and dwells in the sphere of nothingness (*ākiṃcanyāyatana*).

8. Having entirely gone beyond the sphere of nothingness, he attains and dwells in the sphere of neither perception nor non-perception (*naivasaṃjñānāsaṃjñāyatana*).

Having reached this stage the ascetic is freed from desire in relation to the Kāmadhātu, from the four *dhyānas* and the first three *samāpattis*, but he is still bound to the nine categories of the passions connected with the fourth *samāpatti* which, as has been seen, constitutes the Summit of Existence (*bhavāgra*). In fact, the ascetic discards only one attainment through the desire for a higher attainment. In the mundane path (*laukikāmārga*) of the attainments, such as can be travelled by a worldling (*pṛthagjana*), there is no attainment higher than the fourth *samāpatti*.

If, therefore, one wishes to escape all the passions of the triple world and attain Nirvāṇa, then one must practise the transcendental path (*lokottaramārga*) of Nirvāṇa which consists not only of the path of meditation (*bhāvanāmārga*) as has just been described, but also the path of vision (*darśanamārga*) which penetrates the Four Noble Truths expounded by the Buddha. The path of vision eliminates the 'passions to be eliminated by the vision of the Buddhist truths' (*satyadarśanaheyakleśa*), namely, the delusion, the doubt that prevents the Noble Truths from being seen 'purely': 'All the pyscho-physical phenomena of existence are transitory (*anitya*), therefore painful (*duḥkha*); they are also impersonal (*anātman*) in the sense that they do not pertain to a self (*anātmya*) and are not a self (*anātman*). All the phenomena of existence spring from desire. The elimination of desire is the elimination of existence: this is peaceful Nirvāṇa. The Buddha discovered and expounded the path to it'.

Continued reflection on these truths suddenly culminates in an insight (*vipaśyanā*), an understanding (*abhisamaya*) of the 'Four Noble Truths': this is pure wisdom, the Prajñā which definitively dispels all delusion and transforms the candidate from the worldling (*pṛthagjana*) that he was into a Noble One (*ārya*), and places him in the stream of Nirvāṇa (*srotaāpanna*). Without this Prajñā, it is impossible for the ascetic to sever the passions connected with the fourth and last *samāpatti*.

However, this Prajñā, although it may dispel delusion, does not eliminate the desires related to the various realms of existence; the latter have to be eliminated through meditation (*bhāvanāheya*), through the four *dhyānas* and the four *samāpattis* described above. This is why the path of Nirvāṇa links Prajñā indissolubly with Samādhi.

When Śākyamuni sat on the seat of enlightenment he was still a worldling, but a worldling who had, by means of the way of attainment, eliminated all the passions inherent in the realms of existence with the exception of the last passion. During the night of enlightenment he saw, in sixteen moments, the Noble Truths and, this time, eradicated all delusions; then, in eighteen moments, he eradicated the desires connected to the highest realm of existence and became a holy one (*arhat*). At the same time, he became a Buddha because of his meritorious deeds.

However, according to the normal order, the candidate to Nirvāṇa travels the path in the following manner:

1. In the course of the stage of vision (*darśanamārga*) he sees, in sixteen moments, the Noble Truths and eliminates the passions to be eliminated through right view (*dṛgheya*), namely the perverted views of which the main one is the false view of self. In the first moment he obtains the state of Ārya; in the sixteenth, the state of Srotaāpanna, the first fruit of the spiritual life.

2. In the course of the stage of meditation (*bhāvanāmārga*) he eliminates, in 162 moments, the 81 categories of the passions to be eliminated through meditation (*bhāvanāheya*), passions which attach him to the nine realms of existence: the Kāmadhātu, the four Dhyānas

of the Rūpadhātu and the four Samāpattis of the Ārūpyadhātu. In the twelfth moment he obtains the second fruit of the spiritual life and becomes a Sakṛdāgāmin; in the eighteenth moment, he is freed from the last category of the passions of the Kāmadhātu, wins the third fruit of the spiritual life and becomes an Anāgāmin; in the 162nd and last moment he gains possession of the fourth fruit of the spiritual life: he is an Arhat 'holy one, worthy of respect from all', or an Aśaikṣa 'holy one, who has no more to learn with regard to the elimination of the corruptions'. He knows that all his impurities are destroyed and, if he remains unshakable (*akopya*), they will not recur again. After his death he will reach complete Nirvāṇa without any remainder of pyscho-physical conditioning (*nirupadhiśeṣanirvāṇa*).

This Nirvāṇa which is the end of suffering and the stopping of the round of rebirth can be reached by a holy one in this life. Having previously gone up to the fourth formless attainment, he enters the last of the nine successive abodes (*anupūrvavihāra*), namely the attainment consisting of the cessation of perception and feeling (*saṃjñā-vedayitanirodhasamāpatti*). This is the only attainment that does not have an existence as its fruit. The holy one reaches Nirvāṇa there, but in the absence of thought and feeling he reaches it only with his body (*kāyasākṣin*). On leaving this attainment, he thinks: 'Oh, this attainment of *nirodha* is as calm as Nirvāṇa!' We know that the Buddha practised this and that it is reserved for the great holy ones (the Anāgāmins) but that it in no way contributes to holiness[11].

We have only mentioned here the nine successive abodes, but Samādhi is also the basis of many other mental exercises which presuppose or require concentration of the mind. We will limit ourselves to pointing out three other Samādhis called doors to deliverance (*vimokṣamukha*) where the Small Vehicle borders on the Great Vehicle[12].

a) Concentration on emptiness (*śūnyatāsamādhi)*. This considers things under the aspects of non-self (*anātman*) and the empty (*śūnya*), and thus counteracts the belief in me and mine.

b) Concentration on signlessness (*ānimittasamādhi*). This considers Nirvāṇa, under the aspect of the calm (*śama*), as being devoid of all the

[11] On the path of Nirvāṇa sketched in outline here, see É. Lamotte, *History*, pp.611-20.

[12] Regarding these three Samādhis, see Vin. III, p.93; D III, p.219; S IV, p.360; Milinda, p.337; Atthasālinī, pp.179 sq., 222 sq., 290 sq.; Kośa VIII, p.184; Upadeśa in *Traité* I, pp.321-3; Sūtrālaṃkāra, p.148; Bodh. bhūmi, p.276.

characteristic signs of conditioned things.

c) Concentration on wishlessness (*apraṇihitasamādhi*). This relates to all conditioned dharmas while not forming any wish regarding them.

As is explained in the Kośa (VII, pp.184–6), these three Samādhis exhaust the sixteen aspects of the Noble Truths and thus constitute the doors to deliverance.

In brief, the path of Nirvāṇa which the Buddha defined to his disciples (*śrāvakas*) consists of three elements which are closely linked although of unequal value: 1. the observance of morality (*śīla*) which is an indispensable condition; 2. concentration (*samādhi*) which purifies the mind and without which wisdom cannot blossom; 3. wisdom (*prajñā*) which, pending the arrival of final Nirvāṇa, confers holiness, namely Arhatship free from delusions and defilements. It does not, however, give omniscience (*sarvajñāna*) which is reserved for the Buddhas alone by reason of their unique meritorious deeds.

As has been so aptly remarked by L. de La Vallée Poussin, 'Prajñā is not a gnosis, the apperception of a transcendental reality, as is, for the monist-pantheists of the Vedānta or Brahmanism, the knowledge of the Brahman or Absolute, the consciousness of the identity of the "I" and the Brahman. Prajñā is simply the knowledge of the laws which preside over the evolution of this world made of causes and effects (*pratītyasamutpāda*) and, at its highest level, the exact appreciation of the value of the world, the distinction of the general characteristics of things [impermanence, suffering and non-substantiality], with, furthermore, the affirmation of an incomprehensible Nirvāṇa'[13].

The close connection between Samādhi and Prajñā is clearly visible in the Abhijñās or superknowledges which are derived from attainment.

The Fruits of Samādhi. Attached to the possession of the attainments are certain great advantages of a worldly kind: the superior powers and knowledges.

When the mind of the ascetic is absorbed, utterly pure, utterly cleansed, unstained, free of impurity, become supple, ready to act, having reached impassibility, he gives an impulse to his mind (*cittam abhinirharati*) and directs it in the following manner:

1. He directs his mind towards the vision of knowledge (*jñāna-darśana*). He knows this: this body which is mine, having form, made

[13] [Tr. from] L. de La Vallée Poussin, *Morale bouddhique*, Paris 1927, p.102.

of the four great elements, born of father and mother, is a heap of boiled rice and gruel, an impermanent thing, which is subject to its own wear and tear, breakage and dissolution; and yet this consciousness which is mine is attached to it, bound to it.

2. He directs his mind towards the creation of a mind-made form (*manomaya abhinirmāṇa*). From his body he produces another body having form, but mind-made, with all its limbs and organs, its faculties intact.

3. He directs his mind towards the first Abhijñā: the supernormal powers (*ṛddhi*). Being one he becomes many, being many he becomes one; he becomes visible, invisible; goes through walls, ramparts and mountains without being impeded, just as through air; he immerses himself in the earth and emerges from it as if in water; he goes on water without breaking through it, as if on [solid] earth; he travels through the air crosslegged like a winged bird; he takes in his hands and touches the moon and the sun, those two wonderful, mighty beings, and with his body he extends his power as far as the Brahma world.

4. He directs his mind towards the second Abhijñā: the divine ear (*divyaśrotra*). On this purified plane of the divine ear, which transcends the human, he hears both sounds, divine and human, those that are far and those that are near.

5. He directs his mind towards the third Abhijñā: the knowledge of others' minds (*paracittajñāna*). He recognises the impassioned mind as an impassioned mind; he recognises the freed mind as a freed mind, etc.

6. He directs his mind towards the fourth Abhijñā: the recollection of former existences (*pūrvanivāsānusmṛti*) which he himself has lived. He recalls his various dwellings in his previous life: one existence, two existences and up to an hundred thousand existences... In such a way that he says to himself: at that time I had such-and-such a name, such-and-such a family, such-and-such a caste, such-and-such sustenance, I felt such-and-such a pleasure and such-and-such a suffering, I reached such-and-such an age. When I lost that existence I came to my present existence.

7. He directs his mind to the fifth Abhijñā: the knowledge of the passing away and rebirth of beings (*cyutyupapattijñāna*). With his purified divine eye (*divyacakṣus*), transcending the human, he sees beings leaving existence and being reborn. He realises that beings are

lowly or noble, lovely or ugly, happy or unhappy according to the actions they have carried out. On the breaking up of the body after death, those who are possessed of bad practices will be reborn to downfall, the wrong way, perdition, hell; those who are possessed of good practices will be reborn to good destinies, to the heavenly world.

According to the latest opinion, the first five Abhijñās can be possessed by persons who are not Buddhist holy ones, and therefore by the worldly, as long as they practise the meditational exercises according to the rules. Conversely, the sixth and last Abhijñā, which presupposes the understanding of the Noble Truths and the elimination of all the passions of the world, is the prerogative of the Buddhist holy one, the Arhat.

8. The ascetic directs his mind towards the sixth Abhijñā: the knowledge of the destruction of the defilements (*āsravakṣayajñāna*). He clearly acknowledges suffering (*duḥkha*), the origin of suffering (*duḥkhasamudaya*), the cessation of suffering (*duḥkhanirodha*) and the way that leads to the cessation of suffering (*duḥkhanirodhagāminī pratipad*). He clearly acknowledges the defilements (*āsrava*), their origin, their cessation and the way that leads to their cessation. When he knows that, when he sees that, his mind is liberated from the defilements of desire (*kāmāsrava*), the defilements of existence (*bhavāsrava*) and the defilements of ignorance (*avidyāsrava*). When he is liberated he understands that there is liberation. He acknowledges that rebirth is exhausted for him, that the brahma life has been lived, that the task is completed and that there will be no further returning here [for him].

Thus then, for early scholasticism, the path taught by the Buddha eliminates all delusions, eradicates the passions of the triple world, puts an end to painful existence and culminates in Nirvāṇa. It is a path that requires prolonged effort, is carefully graduated and in which arise morality, concentration and wisdom. Wisdom, or Prajñā, constitutes a decisive element in it, but there is no real wisdom without a minimum of concentration, or Samādhi, from which are derived those distinguished powers and knowledges known as the Abhijñās.

The path is defined in terms of precise philosophical concepts. Things (*dharma*) and in particular the aggregates (*skandha*) – form (*rūpa*), feeling (*vedanā*), perception (*saṃjñā*), volition (*saṃskāra*) and consciousness (*vijñāna*) – which constitute the pyscho-physical phenomena of existence are transitory (*anitya*), painful (*duḥkha*) and impersonal (*anātman*) in the sense that they are not a self and do not pertain to a self. However fleeting they may be, things do not arise by chance: they are the result of their causes and the cause of their effects; they are 'conditioned' (*saṃskṛta*). It must be acknowledged that they have a self-nature (*svabhāva*) and marks (*lakṣaṇa*): an arising (*utpāda*), a duration and modification (*sthity-anyathātva*) and a disappearance (*vyaya*).

The whole philosophy of early Buddhism is summarised in two theses: the thesis of the non-existence in itself of the individual or person (*pudgalanairātmyavāda*) and the thesis of the existence only of the conditioned aggregates (*skandhamātravāda*).

2. *Samādhi in the Great Vehicle*

During the last five hundred years of the ancient era, the śrāvakas were the only spokesmen for Buddhism. They specified the rules of the monastic order, codified the teachings of the Buddha and systematised them in the voluminous Abhidharmas. From the third century B.C.E. onwards, they spread throughout the whole of India and became firmly established in Ceylon. Eighteen schools formed among them, but they were only opposed on points of detail and they all remained faithful to the great theses of early Buddhism: the Pudgalanairātmya and the Skandhamātravāda.

However, towards the beginning of the Common Era, effected by influences that there is no room to go into here, a new form of Buddhism appeared: the Great Vehicle (*mahāyāna*) or Bodhisattva Vehicle as opposed to the Small Vehicle (*hīnayāna*) or Śrāvaka Vehicle.

Without supplanting the adherents of early Buddhism who imperturbably continued on their way, the protagonists of the Great Vehicle were inspired by a new ideal and professed more advanced philosophical theories.

By the means that we have already pointed out, the śrāvakas were inclined towards a Prajñā concerned with the general characteristics of things: impermanence, suffering and impersonality. That Prajñā constituted an 'awakening' (*bodhi*), but a limited awakening, only ensuring the personal benefit (*svārtha*) of the adherent through the acquisition of holiness (*arhattva*) and accession to Nirvāṇa.

The bodhisattva is also drawn towards a Prajñā, but a Prajñā infinitely higher, a Prajñāpāramitā or perfection of wisdom, an omniscience (*sarvajñāna*), knowing all things in all their aspects (*sarvākārajñatā*). This perfection of wisdom constitutes the awakening above all others, the 'supreme and right complete awakening' (*anuttarasamyaksaṃbodhi*) pertaining specifically to the Buddhas and ensuring not just the personal benefit (*svārtha*) of the adherent but above all the benefit of others (*parārtha*), the welfare and happiness of all beings (*sarvasattvahitasukha*). The most important step taken by the bodhisattva, an adherent of the Great Vehicle, is therefore the 'arousal of the thought of supreme and right complete Enlightenment' (*anuttarasamyaksaṃbodhicittotpāda*). In brief, the Cittotpāda: 'I, of such-and-such a name, after having confessed my faults and taken the threefold refuge, for the welfare and deliverance of the infinite world of creatures and in order to release them from the sufferings of the round of rebirth and establish them in the supreme omniscient knowledge; just as the bodhisattvas past, future and present, having aroused the thought of Bodhi, have attained, will attain and attain Buddhahood; just as all the Buddhas, through their Buddha knowledge, free of all obstacles, and their Buddha eye, know and see; just as they acknowledge the absence of the self-nature of things (*dharmāṇāṃ niḥsvabhāvatā*); so I, having such-and-such a name, before my teacher of such-and-such a name and in the presence of all the Buddhas and bodhisattvas, arouse the thought of supreme and right complete Enlightenment'[14]. This resolve conducts the adherent into the Great Vehicle; it makes him a bodhisattva certain to reach, after a longer or shorter period of time, the supreme and perfect enlightenment which gives rise to Buddhas.

Between the arousal of the thought of enlightenment (*cittotpāda*) and the reaching of this enlightenment (*abhisaṃbodhi*) stretches the whole career of the bodhisattva. The acquisition of omniscience, the knowledge of all things in all their aspects is, without the slightest doubt, an arduous task, but not in the sense that one might think. Omniscience is not concerned with an infinity of things but with the absence of their self-nature or their non-existence pure and simple. Not to see them any more is not within the reach of everyone, it is a privilege of the great bodhisattvas and Buddhas.

The ideal followed by the adherent of the Great Vehicle is on a par with revolutionary philosophical theories. The śrāvaka, as we have seen, professed the non-existence in itself of the individual, the personality (*pudgalanairātmya*), but accepted a self-nature and

[14] Bodhisattvaprātimokṣasūtra, ed. N. Dutt, *Indian Historical Quarterly* VII, 1931, p.274,*1-7*.

characteristics in dharmas arising from causes, in the psycho-physical phenomena of existence. Whereas the bodhisattva denies the existence both of the individual and things; in technical terms he professes the *pudgalanairātmya* and the *dharmanairātmya*.

The Dharmanairātmya completely overturned the meaning of the Noble Truths that Śākyamuni had taught in the discourse at Vārāṇasī: 1. All is suffering; 2. the origin of suffering is craving; 3. there is a cessation of suffering: Nirvāṇa; 4. the path that leads to it has been determined by the Buddha. The adherent of the Great Vehicle understands that all is suffering, but painful things do not exist. Suffering originates in craving, but non-existent things do not arise in any way: dependent origination (*pratītyasamutpāda*) is non-origination (*anutpāda*). There is a cessation of suffering, Nirvāṇa, but, being non-existent, things are originally 'in Nirvāṇa': Saṃsāra is no different from Nirvāṇa. There is a path to Nirvāṇa, but Nirvāṇa having already been acquired does not imply there is any path to be travelled along.

From this point of view, the Noble Truths are purely and simply dodged, and the grandiose edifice of the Abhidharma, so patiently and carefully built up by the śrāvakas over the centuries, crumbles.

Since beings and things do not exist and have never existed, the only eloquence of any value is silence, true wisdom is the stopping of thought. Faced with the universal emptiness that is itself not-something, the mind of the bodhisattva 'does not fear, does not tremble, does not take fright'.

However, the bodhisattva only aspires to this supreme and perfect enlightenment for the benefit of others. Immediately after having formulated the Cittotpāda he defines his intentions, which are exclusively altruistic: 'I, of such-and-such a name, who have thus aroused the thought of Bodhi, adopt the infinite world of beings as my mother, father, sisters, brothers, sons, daughters, relatives of whatever degree and kinsmen. Having adopted them, with all my power, with all my strength, with all my knowledge, I will implant good roots in them. Henceforth, the gift that I shall give, the morality I observe, the patience I maintain, the vigour I exert, the absorption I practise, the wisdom I develop, all of this will be for the interest, the benefit and the happiness of all beings'[15].

The Buddhas and bodhisattvas are not only great sages, they are also possessed of great compassion (*mahākāruṇika*). According to the

[15] *Ibid.*, p.275.

Vimalakīrtinirdeśa (Vkn, p.126), 'their wisdom is acquired through skilful means, and their skilful means are acquired through wisdom' (*upāyasahitā prajñā, prajñāsāhita upāyaḥ*). Through their wisdom they do not see anything, neither beings nor things; through skilful means they procure the welfare of beings in every way. The Śgs (§ 35) explains: 'The bodhisattva does not see the self-nature of beings but, in order to ripen them, he speaks of beings. He does not see either a living being or an individual, but he speaks of a living being and an individual. He does not see the self-nature of actions or the self-nature of fruition, but he teaches action and fruition to beings. He does not see the self-nature of the passions of Saṃsāra, but he teaches a clear knowledge of the passions of Saṃsāra. He does not see Nirvāṇa, but he talks of reaching Nirvāṇa. He does not see that dharmas admit of distinctive marks, but he speaks of good and bad dharmas'.

What is more, it is in so far as the bodhisattva no longer sees anything, that he carries out, spontaneously and effortlessly, his beneficial activity.

The bodhisattva career consists of the practice of six perfections: giving (*dāna*), morality (*śīla*), patience (*kṣānti*), vigour (*vīrya*), absorptive meditation (*dhyāna*) and wisdom (*prajñā*). The second, fifth and sixth correspond respectively to the three elements of the path of Nirvāṇa as conceived by the śrāvakas, namely, Śīla, Samādhi and Prajñā.

Nonetheless, from his point of view, there is no perfection for the bodhisattva to practise, or rather, he practises them while taking their futility into account. The Prajñāpāramitā (Pañcaviṃśatisāhasrikā, p.18; Śatasāhasrikā, p.56) is quite categoric in this respect: 'The bodhisattva dwells in the perfection of wisdom by not dwelling in it. He should fulfil the perfection of giving by refusing everything, by not seeing either a giver, a beneficiary or a thing given. He should fulfil the perfection of morality by no longer conceiving either a misdeed or a meritorious action. He should fulfil the perfection of patience by not being disturbed (by offences). He should fulfil the perfection of vigour by never relaxing his bodily and mental vigour. He should fulfil the perfection of absorptive meditation by not tasting the flavour (of the attainments). He should fulfil the perfection of wisdom by not making any distinction between true wisdom and false wisdom'.

This is what makes the Śgs say that 'the bodhisattva activates great vigour, but does not develop any activity of body, speech or mind'

(§ 30), or again that he has no dharma to practise and that he has passed beyond all practices (§ 37). In consequence, the bodhisattva does not act and, if he seems to act, this is only skilful means (*upāya*) aimed at ripening beings (*sattvaparipācanārtham*).

The main differences between the Śrāvaka Path and the Bodhisattva Path is that the former leads to the individual perfecting of the ascetic while the latter aims only at the welfare of others. The former is egotistic, the latter altruistic.

It ensues that the Samādhi of the bodhisattvas is not merely an exercise aimed at purifying the mind; it is also and above all a work of edification. The accent is no longer placed on the technique of concentration but on the supernormal power (*ṛddhibala*) which derives from it for the greatest good of beings.

The Prajñāpāramitā, in a passage which I shall quote further on (p.31), points out that the bodhisattva quickly reaches *saṃbodhi* by entering the concentration on the 'non-arising of all things' (*sarvadharmānutpāda*), but that in the wake of this there follows an infinity of other concentrations of which the Heroic Progress is only a variation.

When the bodhisattva has penetrated the emptiness of beings and things, no longer sees them, no longer speaks or thinks about them he has attained the summit of wisdom. By this very fact, he is 'in possession of the concentrations' (*samādhipratilabdha*) and he plays at will with the superknowledges which result from this (*abhijñāvikrīḍita*), for 'as many as there are functionings in the mind and mentations of beings to be won over are there functionings in this Samādhi' (Śgs, § 154).

The long lists of Samādhis found in the texts should not impress us. They are only modalities of the single Samādhi where the Buddhas and great bodhisattvas are always concentrated and, whether it is called Heroic Progress or something else, this Samādhi encompasses all the good dharmas (Śgs, § 25), contains all the perfections (§§ 26–38) and exercises them simultaneously (§§ 42–44). It has multiple aspects which coincide particularly with the ten powers of the Tathāgata (§ 21, n.45 and sq.). It is therefore quite correctly that the Mahāyānist Mahāparinirvāṇasūtra defines it as the self-nature of the Buddha.

Among the great Abhijñās that result from this Samādhi, it is particularly the first, the Abhijñā of supernormal power (*ṛddhi*), which is emphasised. In the Śgs and in all Mahāyāna sūtras in general, the Buddha does not stop 'manifesting' and then 'withdrawing' the bases of his supernormal power. In the Sūtra with which we are concerned here, wonders follow wonders: multiplication of the Buddhas (§ 15), manifestations of marvellous bodies (§§ 54 and 93), transformation of the assemblies (§ 65), capture and liberation of Māra (§§ 82 and 88), creation of imaginary bodhisattvas (§ 94), changes of location without displacement (§ 115), simultaneous manifestation of a Buddha or a bodhisattva in several places at once (§§ 122–7 and 156), appearance of the Buddhas of the ten regions (§ 165), transformation of an 'impure land' into a 'pure land' (§ 168), etc.

The Śgs does not have a monopoly on this wonder-working, all Mahāyāna sūtras are filled with it. A philosopher would be required to define correctly this Mahāyānist marvel which does not correspond to any other form of marvel. According to current acceptance, a miracle is a supernatural action contrary to the laws of nature, or again, the insertion of a free divine causality into natural causes. However, this idea of a miracle cannot be applied to the Mahāyānist marvel. Since beings and things do not exist, the supposed laws of nature only originate from erroneous imagination (*abhūtaparikalpa*), and no action, as astonishing as it may seem, can run contrary to laws which do not exist. Extraordinary actions are therefore as unreal as ordinary actions. If the Buddhas and bodhisattvas manifest them, this can only be through skilful means (*upāya*), in order to ripen beings who mistakenly believe they are involved in the world of becoming and the laws of nature. This is what brings Vimalakīrti to say that the Buddha-fields or Pure Lands where these wonders occur are essentially empty, calm, unreal and like space (Vkn, pp.133, 182, 210); confronted with all these splendours, the bodhisattva only experiences indifference (Vkn, p.226).

The scholars of the Great Vehicle took up all these ideas and explained them systematically in their śāstras.

The Upadeśa in *Traité* II, pp.1043–57, reveals no less than nineteen differences between the Samādhi of the śrāvakas and that of the bodhisattvas. Its somewhat involved explanation amounts to this:

Sectaries (*tīrthika*), śravakas and bodhisattvas can all practise the absorptions (*dhyāna*) and attainments (*samāpatti*), but the Samādhi of the sectaries is tainted by false views, particularly the belief in a self (*satkāyadṛṣṭi*); the śrāvakas, even in a state of concentration, only know the general characteristic marks of things (*sāmānyalakṣaṇa*), impermanence, suffering and impersonality. Only the bodhisattvas know the true mark of things (*bhūtalakṣaṇa*), namely, non-arising, non-cessation, original calm; in a word, emptiness. Thus, when he enters an absorption his mind enjoys perfect peace (*kṣema*). It is no longer disturbed by contingencies – by what could be seen, heard, thought or known (*dṛṣṭaśrutamatavijñāta*); it is devoid of that reasoning (*vitarka*) and discursive thought (*vicāra*) which, normally, makes language possible; it no longer makes any distinctions, to the point of not grasping any difference between distraction and absorption. People know the thought of entering absorption (*dhyānapraveśacitta*) and the thought of leaving absorption (*dhyānavyutthānacitta*) in a bodhisattva, but once a bodhisattva is absorbed neither gods nor humans know his thought any longer, that thought that has neither support (*āśraya*) nor object (*ālambana*). Differing from other ascetics, the bodhisattva is incapable of 'savouring' the absorptions and attainments; in vain would one seek to find in him that dangerous relishing (*āsvādana*) which only too often leads the meditative to confuse the blisses of the mystical spheres with true deliverance.

The śrāvaka who has entered the path of Nirvāṇa practises Samādhi in order to purify his mind, which is a legitimate but egotistical preoccupation. In contrast, the bodhisattva himself only practises absorption for the good of others (*parārtha*). Seeing people giving themselves unrestrainedly over to the pleasures of the senses, he experiences great feelings of compassion (*mahākaruṇācitta*) and makes the following aspiration: 'I shall act so that beings may avoid impure happinesses, so that they may obtain the internal happiness of the *dhyānas* and *samāpattis* and so that, by relying on these practices, they may finally reach the most excellent happiness, that of Buddhahood'. This is why his absorption is so beneficent. While his mind is no longer disturbed by any object or concept, the bodhisattva transforms his body in countless ways, enters the five destinies of the triple world and there he wins over beings by means of the teaching of the three vehicles.

Finally, the bodhisattva enjoys perfect mastery over the *dhyānas* and *samāpattis* as well as over the *abhijñās* which result from them.

In order to reach the first *dhyāna*, the ordinary ascetic must first free himself from all the passions of the world of desire (*kāmadhātu*). To do this, he enters the *anāgamya* which is like the entrance-hall of the first *dhyāna*, and it is there that he eliminates the coarse passions. Conversely, the bodhisattva, having cultivated the perfections for a long time, can enter the *dhyāna* with a thought of the Kāmadhātu.

The śrāvaka can traverse the nine successive abodes (*anupūrva-*

vihāra), which were mentioned earlier, in four different ways: by following the ascending order (*dhyānānulomatas*), the descending order (*dhyānapratilomatas*), the ascending then descending order (*dhyānānulomapratilomatas*) or by jumping from one abode to another (*dhyānotkrāntitas*)[16]. This last method is known as the attainment of jumping (*vyutkrāntakasamāpatti*)[17]. However, a bodhisattva who has mastered jumping can, on leaving the first *dhyāna*, jump to the third – which is normal – but he can also jump directly either to the fourth *dhyāna* or to one of the four *samāpattis* of the Ārūpyadhātu; sometimes he jumps over one abode, sometimes two, sometimes even over all nine.

According to the canonical sources, when the ordinary ascetic has purified his mind by means of the *dhyānas* and *samāpattis*, 'he gives an impulse to his mind and directs his mind towards the *abhijñās*' (*abhiññāya cittaṃ abhinīharati abhininnāmeti*), and by virtue of this effort he practises the six superknowledges, supernormal power, etc. In contrast the great bodhisattva, the bodhisattva of the eighth stage, without making any mental effort (*cittānābhogena*), plays at will with the superknowledges (*abhijñāvikrīḍana*). He proceeds at will and spontaneously to the Buddha-fields, but without grasping their signs; there, while remaining perfectly absorbed, he pays homage to the Buddhas of the ten regions and he expounds the Dharma to beings. This activity is unconscious; it can be compared to the lutes of the gods which play ceaselessly even though there is no-one to pluck them.

The Mahāyānasaṃgraha, Chapter VII (tr. É. Lamotte, Vol.II, pp.218–31), contains an even more systematic description. The author contrasts the three elements constituting the path of Nirvāṇa, morality (*śīla*), concentration (*samādhi*) and wisdom (*prajñā*) with the higher morality (*adhiśīla*) of the bodhisattva, his higher thought (*adhicitta*) and higher wisdom (*adhiprajñā*).

The Samādhi of the bodhisattva differs from that of the śrāvaka due to six superiorities:

1. Superiority in object (*ālambanaviśeṣa*). The Samādhi of the bodhisattva is concerned with the teaching of the Great Vehicle; that of the śrāvaka, with the teaching of the Small Vehicle.

16 Cf. Atthasālinī, p.187; Vism., ed. Warren, pp.314-15.

17 See Kośa II, p.210; VIII, p.173; J. Rahder, Introduction to the Daśabhūmikasūtra, p.xxii.

2. Superiority in variety (*nānātvaviśeṣa*). The *dhyānas* and *samāpattis* and some other meditations practised by the śrāvaka can be contrasted to the 108 Samādhis of the bodhisattva listed in the Prajñāpāramitā; in fact they are infinite in number.

3. Superiority as a counteractive (*pratipakṣaviśeṣa*). The Samādhi of the bodhisattvas eliminates all delusions and all passions.

4. Superiority in aptitude (*karmaṇyatāviśeṣa*). The Samādhi of the śrāvakas purifies the mind of the ascetic; but the bodhisattva, while remaining absorbed, takes on birth everywhere his presence may be of use to beings.

5. Superiority in results (*abhinirhāraviśeṣa*). The Abhijñās of the śrāvakas are limited; those of the bodhisattva do not encounter any opposition.

6. Superiority in actions (*karmaviśeṣa*). The supernormal powers of the śrāvakas described above (pp.20–1) are contrasted with the great supernormal powers (*maharddhi*) of the bodhisattva: causing trembling, blazing, illuminating, rendering invisible, transforming, coming and going across obstacles, reducing or enlarging worlds, inserting any matter into one's own body, assuming the aspects of those one frequents, appearing and disappearing, submitting everyone to one's will, dominating the supernormal power of others, giving intellectual clarity to those who lack it, giving mindfulness, bestowing happiness, and finally, emitting beneficial rays[18].

Regarding the practical applications of these great powers, the Vimalakīrtinirdeśa, Ch. V (Vkn, pp.141–8), may be consulted.

Apart from the Śgs, there are some references to the Concentration of Heroic Progress in the sūtras and śāstras. I shall point out the main ones here:

Aṣṭādaśasāhasrikā, T VII, No.220, ch.485, p.462*b* 1–12; Pañcaviṃśatisāhasrikā, ed. N. Dutt, p.142, *1–8* (cf. T 221, ch. 3, p.16*a* 27-*b* 6; T 222, ch.4, p.172*a* 20-*b* 3; T 223, ch.3, p.237*c* 11–22; T VII, No.220, ch.409, pp.50*c* 21–51*a* 4; Śatasāhasrikā, ed. P. Ghosa, p.825,*7–20* (cf.

[18] The same list is found in Bodh. bhūmi, pp.58-63. On supernormal power in general, see *Traité* I, pp.329-30.

T V, No.220, ch.41, p.229*c* 10–23.

Sanskrit text of the Śatasāhasrikā, p.825,*7–20*: *Sāpi khalu sarvākārajñatā advayā advaidhīkārā sarvadharmābhāvasvabhāvatām upādāyā, ayaṃ sarvadharmānutpādo (var. sarvadharmasvabhāvā-nutpattir) nāma samādhir bodhisattvānāṃ mahāsattvānāṃ vipulaḥ puraskṛto 'pramāṇaniyato 'saṃhāryaḥ sarvaśrāvakapratyekabuddhaiḥ. anena samādhinā viharan bodhisattvo mahāsattvaḥ kṣipram anuttarāṃ samyaksaṃbodhim abhisaṃbudhyate.*

[Śāriputra] āha. kiṃ punar, āyuṣman Subhūte, anenaiva samādhinā viharan bodhisattvo mahāsattvaḥ kṣipram anuttarāṃ samyak-saṃbodhim abhisaṃbudhyate athānyair api samādhibhiḥ.

Subhūtir āha. anyair apy, āyuṣman Śāriputra, samādhibhir viharan bodhisattvo mahāsattvaḥ kṣipram anuttarāṃ samyaksaṃbodhim abhisaṃbudhyate.

[Śāriputra] āha. katamaiḥ punar, āyuṣman Subhūte, 'nyaiḥ samādhibhir viharan bodhisattvo mahāsattvaḥ kṣipram anuttarāṃ samyaksaṃbodhim abhisaṃbudhyate.

Subhūtir āha. asti śūraṃgamo nāma samādhir yena samādhinā viharan bodhisattvo mahāsattvaḥ kṣipram anuttarāṃ samyak-saṃbodhim abhisaṃbudhyate. asti siṃhavikrīḍito nāma samādhir iti vistaro yāvad ākāśāsaṅgavimuktinirupalepo nāma samādhiḥ.

Author's translation: This knowledge of things in all their aspects is without duality and without division, by reason of the fact that all things have non-existence as their self-nature. This is the concentration called Non-arising-of-all-things (variation: Non-arousal-of-the-self-nature-of-all-things), a concentration proper to the bodhisattvas; it is vast, placed above everything, fixed in the infinite and not shared by the Listeners and Solitary Buddhas. Dwelling in this concentration, the bodhisattva rapidly reaches supreme and perfect enlightenment.

Śāriputra said: Venerable Subhūti, is it only when he dwells in this concentration that a bodhisattva reaches supreme and perfect enlightenment, or when he dwells in other concentrations as well?

Subhūti replied: Venerable Śāriputra, it is when he dwells in other concentrations as well.

Śāriputra asked: Venerable Subhūti, in what other concentrations does the bodhisattva [† dwell and] rapidly reach supreme and perfect enlightenment?

Subhūti said: There is a concentration called Heroic Progress and when he dwells in that concentration, the bodhisattva rapidly reaches supreme and perfect enlightenment. There is... [There follows the classical list of the 108 or 118 concentrations of the bodhisattva, but which not all the Chinese versions reproduce in full; this list is taken up by the Mahāvyutpatti, Nos 506–623].

Translation by Kumārajīva (T 223, ch.3, p.237*c* 10–14): The self-nature (*svabhāva*) of dharmas is non-existence (*abhāva*) because it does not follow the procedure (*hsing* = *saṃskāra, caritra, gamana*) of dharmas and does not assume the marks (*hsiang* = *lakṣaṇa*) of dharmas. This is what is called the Concentration on the Non-assuming of all dharmas (*sarvadharmāsamādāna*), a concentration proper to the bodhisattvas; it is vast in its uses and is not shared by the śrāvakas and pratyekabuddhas. The bodhisattva who practises this concentration and does not deviate from it rapidly attains supreme and perfect enlightenment. [The rest as above].

Translation by Hsüan-tsang (T V No.220, ch.41, p.229*c* 10–18): When the bodhisattva practises the Prajñāpāramitā, he is absolutely free of grasping (*upādāna*) and free of attachment (*abhiniveśa*) regarding dharmas and the Prajñāpāramitā. This is what is called the Concentration without grasping or attachment regarding dharmas, a concentration proper to the bodhisattvas. This concentration is beautiful (*cāru*), is above all else (*puraskṛta*), vast (*vipula*) and immense (*apramāṇa*); it reunites infinite (*ananta*) and unresisting (*apratigha*) actions (*kāritra*); it is not shared by any śrāvaka or pratyekabuddha. O Śāriputra, if the bodhisattva constantly dwells in this concentration and does not abandon it, he rapidly witnesses supreme and perfect enlightenment. [The rest as above].

Commentary in the Upadeśa (T 1509, ch.43, p.373*c* 4–17): *Q*. If the Buddha has said that the sole path of Nirvāṇa consists of [the three *samādhis*] called *śūnyatā, ānimitta and apraṇihita*, why does Śāriputra ask here if there are also other samādhis which enable a bodhisattva to attain Buddhahood rapidly?

A. When one is not yet near Nirvāṇa, there are many other paths, but when one is near Nirvāṇa, there is only a single path: *śūnyatā, ānimitta and apraṇihita*. The other *samādhis* all lead to these three doors to deliverance (*vimokṣamukha*). It is the same as for a great town: there are many gates and all allow entry. Or it is like the numerous rivers and the ten thousand watercourses that all lead to the sea. What are these other *samādhis*? There is the Śūraṃgamasamādhi, etc. The Buddha will speak of them himself in the Chapter on the Mahāyāna where he will explain things that are profound and difficult to understand. When the bodhisattva practises these 108 *samādhis* and *dhāraṇīmukhas*, the Buddhas of the ten regions give him the prediction (*vyākaraṇa*). And why? Even though the bodhisattva obtains these *samādhis*, he is really free from reflection (*manasikāra*) or notion (*saṃjñā*) concerning the idea of self. He does not say to himself: 'I am going to enter such-and-such a *samādhi*, I am entering it, I have entered it; I am going to dwell in this *samādhi*, it is my own *samādhi*'. Because of this purity of thought (*cittaviśuddhi*) and this marvellous detachment, the Buddhas give him the prediction...

Aṣṭādaśasāhasrikā, T VII, No.220, ch.488, p.481*a* 14-*c* 3; Pañcaviṃśatisāhasrikā, ed. N. Dutt, p.198,*11–14* (cf. T 221, ch.4, p.23*b* 15–18; T 222, ch.6, p.190*a* 18-*c* 11; T 223, ch.5, p.251*a* 8-*b* 14; T VII, No.220, ch.414, p.74*a* 9-*c* 4); Śatasāhasrikā, ed. P. Ghosa, pp.1412, *7*–1415,*3* (cf. T V, No.220, ch.52, p.292*a* -*c* 13):

Punar aparaṃ, Subhūte, bodhisattvasya mahāsattvasya mahāyānaṃ yad uta śūraṃgamo nāma samādhiḥ [The enumeration follows, more or less complete according to the sources, of the 108 *samādhis,* each of which is then taken up and briefly defined]: *tatra katamaḥ śūraṃgamo nāma samādhiḥ. yaḥ samādhiḥ sarvasamādhīnāṃ gocaram anubhavaty ayam ucyate śūraṃgamo nāma samādhiḥ.*

Author's translation: Besides, O Subhūti, the Great Vehicle of the bodhisattvas is the Concentration named Heroic Progress, etc... Which is this concentration? The concentration that embraces the domain of all the concentrations is named Concentration of Heroic Progress.

Translation by Hsüan-tsang (T V, No.220, ch.52, p.292*c* 11–13): When one dwells in this *samādhi*, one embraces the domain of all the samādhis; one achieves infinite and supreme Heroic Progresses (*chien-hsing* 健行); one is to the fore of all the *samādhis*.

Commentary in the Upadeśa (T 1509, ch.47, pp.398*c* 27–399*a* 2): Śūraṃgamasamādhi, in the language of the Ch'in, is called *Chien-hsing* 'Heroic Progress'. It knows in detail the domain (*gocara*) and marks (*lakṣaṇa*) of all the *samādhis*, their number and the degree of their depth. It is like a great general who knows the number of his soldiers.

Besides, when the bodhisattva has obtained this *samādhi,* neither the Kleśamāra nor the Māras can harm him. He is like a cakravartin king who possesses the jewel called 'The General's' (*pariṇāyakaratna*); wherever he goes, no-one can vanquish him.

Pañcaviṃśatisāhasrikā, ed. N. Dutt, p.23,*19–22* (cf. T 223, p.219*b* 23–25):

Punar aparaṃ, Śāriputra, bodhisattvena mahāsattvena sarva-sattvānāṃ manorathān paripūrayitukāmena anna-pāna-vastra-gandha-mālya-puṣpa-dhūpa-cūrṇa- vilepana-śayanāsana-gṛha-dhana-dhanyālaṃkāra-ratna-maṇi-muktā-vaiḍūrya-śaṅkha-śilā-pravāḍa-jātarūpa-rajatodyāna-rājyādibhir upakaraṇaiḥ prajñāpāramitāyāṃ śikṣitavyam.

Author's translation: Besides, O Śāriputra, the bodhisattva who wishes to fulfil the desires of all beings with food, drink, clothing, perfumes, garlands, flowers, incense, perfumed powders, unguents, couches and seats, houses, goods and riches, ornaments, jewels, pearls, necklets of pearls, beryls, shells, crystals, corals, gold, silver, gardens, kingdoms and other useful things, this bodhisattva, say I, should train himself in the Prajñāpāramitā.

Commentary in the Upadeśa (T 1509, ch.30, p.278*a* 8–24 = *Traité* IV, pp.1939–40): *Q*. When the Buddha was in the world, beings still suffered from hunger and thirst, the sky did not always shed rain and beings were distressed. If the Buddha himself could not fulfil the desires of all beings, why do you say here that the bodhisattva can fulfil them?

A. The bodhisattva who dwells in the tenth *bhūmi* and who has entered the Śūraṃgamasamādhi is to be found in the *tri-sāhasramahāsāhasralokadhātu* [† 3,000 great world systems], and there he sometimes arouses the *prathama cittotpāda* [† first thought of Bodhi] and practises the six *pāramitās*; he sometimes manifests himself as irreversible; he sometimes manifests himself as an *ekajātipratibaddha* [† separated from Buddhahood by one life only] and expounds the Dharma to the devas in the Tuṣita heavens; he sometimes descends from the Tuṣita heavens and is born in the palace of King Śuddhodana; he sometimes takes up the *pravrajyā*

[† homeless life] and becomes a Buddha; he sometimes appears in the midst of the great assembly, sets turning the Wheel of the Dharma and delivers innumerable beings; he sometimes manifests his entry into Nirvāṇa and seven precious stūpas are erected to him so that, everywhere in all the kingdoms, beings can honour his *śarīra* [† relics]; finally, his Dharma sometimes disappears completely. If the bodhisattva can render such services, what then can be said of the Buddha? The body of the Buddha is of two kinds: the true body (*bhūtakāya*); and the transformation body (*nirmāṇakāya*). When beings see the true body of the Buddha, all their desires are fulfilled. The true body of the Buddha fills space (*ākāśa*); his rays illuminate the ten regions; the sounds of his teaching of the Dharma equally, in the ten regions, fill countless universes as innumerable as the sands of the Ganges; all the members of the great assembly hear the Dharma simultaneously, and he expounds the Dharma without interruption; in the space of a moment each listener comprehends what he hears.

Lalitavistara, ed. S. Lefmann, p.442,*1–9* (cf. T 186, ch.8, p.537*b* 25-*c* 2; T 187, ch.12, p.616*c* 14–21):

Yaḥ kaścin, mārṣā, imaṃ Lalitavistaraṃ dharmaparyāyaṃ bhāṣyamāṇam avahitaśrotaḥ śroṣyati, so 'ṣṭau cittanirmalatāḥ pratilapsyate. katamā aṣṭau. tadyathā. yad uta maitrīṃ pratilapsyate sarvadoṣamirghātāya. karuṇāṃ pratilapsyate sarvavihiṃsotsargāya, muditāṃ pratilapsyate sarvāratyapakarṣaṇatāyai, upekṣāṃ pratilapsyate anunayapratighotsargāya, catvāri dhyānāni pratilapsyate sarvarūpadhātuvaśavartitāyai, catasra ārūpyasamāpattīḥ pratilapsyate cittavaśavartitāyai, pañcābhijñāḥ pratilapsyate anyabuddhakṣetragamanatāyai, sarvavāsanānusaṃdhisamudghātaṃ pratilapsyate śūraṃgamasamādhipratilambhāya. imā aṣṭau cittanirmalatāḥ pratilapsyate.

Friends, whoever, without turning their ear, will listen to this interpretation of the Dharma called Lalitavistara will obtain the eight purities of mind. Which are those eight? He will obtain goodwill so as to destroy all faults, compassion so as to eliminate all violence, joy so as to avoid all woes, equanimity so as to eliminate affection and aversion, the four absorptions so as to hold sway over the world of [subtle] form, the four formless attainments so as to hold sway over the mind, the five superknowledges so as to go to other Buddha-fields, the destruction of every connection regarding the pervasions [of the passions] so as to obtain the Concentration of Heroic Progress.

Chuang-yen p'u-t'i-hsin ching (T 307, pp.961*c* 28–962*a* 6; T 308, p.964*a* 3–12):

To the ten Pāramitās correspond ten Cittotpādas, and each of them is protected by one of the following ten Samādhis: 1. Dharmaratna-samādhi; 2. Sārasamādhi; 3. Āniñjyasamādhi; 4. Avaivartikasamādhi; 5. Ratnapuṣpasamādhi; 6. Sūryālokasamādhi; 7. Sarvārthasamādhi; 8. Jñānālokasamādhi; 9. Sarvabuddhasaṃmukhāvasthitasamādhi; 10. Śūraṃgamasamādhi.

Kuśalamūlasaṃparigrahasūtra (T 657, ch.6, p.166*a* 16-*c* 21):

The Buddha sees all the great assemblies gathered together and, remaining on his seat, he enters each of the fifty-seven Samādhis in turn, the first of which is the Śūraṃgamasamādhi, and the last, the Āniñjyasamādhi. Then the Śuddhāvāsika devas praise him with stanzas.

Mahāparinirvāṇasūtra (T 374, ch.27, pp.524*c* 19-525*a* 11; T 375, ch.25, p.769*b* 1–24):

Besides, O Kulaputra, the nature of the Buddhas is the Śūraṃgamasamādhi. This nature, like cream (*sāra*), is the mother of all the Buddhas. Through the power of the Śūraṃgamasamādhi, the Buddhas always delight in their own personal purity (*ātmaviśuddhi*).

All beings possess the Śūraṃgamasamādhi but, because they do not cultivate it, they are not able to see it. That is why they do not attain *anuttarā samyaksaṃbodhi*.

Kulaputra, the Śūraṃgamasamādhi has five kinds of names: 1. Śūraṃgamasamādhi, 2. Prajñāpāramitā, 3. Vajrasamādhi, 4. Siṃhanādasamādhi, 5. Buddhasvabhāva. Depending on its activities it sometimes takes one name and sometimes another, just as a single *samādhi* takes on various names and *dhyāna* indicates four dhyānas. *Indriya* designates the samādhīndriya; *bala,* the samādhibala; *saṃbodhi,* the saṃbodhyaṅga; *samyak*, the samyaksamādhi; and the saṃbodhi of the eighth-level holy one (*aṣṭamaka*) is called *samādhisaṃbodhi*. It is the same for the Śūraṃgamasamādhi.

Kulaputra, all beings are endowed with this *samādhi*, but to a higher, middling or lesser degree. The higher degree is the nature of the Buddhas; that is why it is said that all beings possess Buddha-nature. The middling degree is the fact that all beings possess the first *dhyāna*. When they possess the requisite causes and conditions (*hetupratyaya*) they can practise it, but if they do not possess those causes and conditions they cannot practise it. Those causes and conditions are of two kinds: the calamity of fire and the destruction of the fetters (*saṃyojana*) binding beings to the *kāmadhātu*. That is why it is said that all beings are endowed with the middling *samādhi*. The lesser *samādhi* is the concentration of the mind (*citta*) and mentations (*caitta*) in the course of the ten *bhūmis*; this is why it is said that all beings are endowed with the lesser *samādhi*.

All beings possess Buddha-nature but, as the passions (*kleśa*) hide this, they are not able to see it. Even though the bodhisattvas of the tenth stage see the single vehicle, they do not know that the Tathāgata is eternally existent.

[In the word Śūraṃgama], *śūram* means 'absolutely' (*atyanta*), and *gama* means 'solid' (*sāra*)[19]. That which acquires absolute solidity is termed Śūraṃgama. That is why it is said that the Śūraṃgamasamādhi is the nature of the Buddhas.

Mahāparinirvāṇasūtra (T 374, ch.30, p.546*a* 23–26; T 375, ch.28, p.791*c* 11–13):

At the moment when the Buddha is about to enter Nirvāṇa, Siṃhanāda says to him: 'I wish that the Great Compassionate One, as an adornment, would always remain in this grove of Śāla trees.' The Buddha answers him: 'All dharmas have non-abiding as their nature; how can you wish for the Buddha to remain somewhere? Non-abiding is the Śūraṃgamasamādhi; the Śūraṃgamasamādhi which

[19] This is a purely imaginary etymology.

knows all dharmas is devoid of attachment; having no point of attachment, it is called Heroic Progress. The Tathāgata being endowed with the Śūraṃgamasamādhi, how can you tell him to remain somewhere?'

Mahāyānasaṃgraha of Asaṅga (tr. É. Lamotte, p.219):

Compared with the Samādhi of the śrāvakas, the Adhicitta of the bodhisattvas proffers six superiorities and particularly a superiority in variety (*nānātvaviśeṣa*), for the variety of the concentrations like the Mahāyānaloka 'Brilliance of the Great Vehicle', the Sarvapuṇya-samuccaya 'Accumulation of Every Merit', the Samādhirājabhadrapāla 'King of Concentration, Auspicious Protector', the Śūraṃgama 'Heroic Progress', etc., is infinite.

The Tibetan Upanibandhana explains: The attainment where the whole teaching of the Great Vehicle shines is the Mahāyānāloka. The one where all the merits are accumulated and appropriated is named Sarvapuṇyasamuccaya. The Samādhirājabhadrapāla, like a king on earth, is named the chief of all the Samādhis. When it is there, the Bhagavat Buddhas of the present era and located in the ten regions are seen facing each other (*abhimukha*). The Śūraṃgama is the best of Samādhis; like a hero, head of an army, in the midst of his soldiers, it is capable of destroying the horde of Māra.

Buddhabhūmisūtraśāstra of Bandhuprabha (T 1530, ch.6, p.316*a* 7–10):

Samādhi is Adhicitta, is the *samādhis*, Śūraṃgama, etc. The Samādhi is so named because it takes precedence over all the worldly and transcendental *samādhis* and because others cannot surpass it. Moreover, it is so named because it is frequented by heroes, Buddhas and bodhisattvas; for only the bodhisattvas of the tenth stage and the Buddhas obtain this Samādhi.

The Dharmasaṃgraha, § 136 (ed. F.M. Müller, p.32), indicates a tetrad of Samādhis: Śūraṃgama, Gaganagañja, Vimalaprabha and Siṃhavikrīḍita.

IV. THE HISTORICAL BACKGROUND OF THE SŪTRA

It is difficult to place the Śgs in the enormous mass of Mahāyāna sūtras. Indian sources are silent on their dates and places of origin. We know more or less when they were translated into Chinese, but nothing proves that the chronological order in which these Chinese translations followed one another corresponds to the chronological order of the appearance of the Indian originals. Furthermore, there is nothing to enable us to fix the time which elapsed between the appearance of a text in India and the translation of this same text in China; the most diverse of circumstances could have accelerated or delayed the translation of a particular work.

On the basis of Japanese research, H. Nakamura has attempted a classification of the Mahāyāna sūtras[20]. He distinguishes thirteen classes of them and places the Śgs among the 'Meditation Sūtras' which are the foundation of Zen Buddhism.

The Mahāyāna sūtras devoted to a Samādhi are fairly numerous; among them we note the Pratyutpannabuddhasaṃmukhāvasthitasamādhi (T 416–419), the Tathāgatajñānamudrāsamādhi (T 632 and 633), the Caturdārakasamādhi (T 378 and 379), the Sarvapuṇyasamuccaya-samādhi (T 381 and 382), the Māyopamasamādhi (T 371 and 372), the Samādhirāja (ed. N. Dutt; T 639), the Praśāntaviniścayaprātihārya-samādhi (T 648), etc.

From another point of view, the Śgs can be placed among those ten-odd Mahāyāna sūtras which contributed to the implantation of the Great Vehicle in China and which were translated several times during the second and third centuries C.E. Here is a list, with the date of their first Chinese translation:

1. Akṣobhyatathāgatasya vyūha (T 313), sūtra in Ratnakūṭa, tr. in 147 by Chih Ch'an[21].
2. Aṣṭasāhasrikā Prajñāpāramitā or Small Prajñā (T 224), translated in 179 by Chih Ch'an.
3. Pratyutpannabuddhasaṃmukhāvasthitasamādhi (T 418), tr. in 179 by Chih Ch'an.
4. Kāśyapaparivarta (T 350), sūtra in Ratnakūṭa, tr. in 179 by Chih Ch'an.
5. Śūraṃgamasamādhi, tr. in 186 by Chih Ch'an (translation lost).

[20] 'A Critical Survey of Mahāyāna and Esoteric Buddhism', *Acta Asiatica* VI and VII, Tokyo 1964.

[21] Too early a date, see further on, p.64 sq.

6. Vimalakīrtinirdeśa (T 474) tr. between 222 and 229 by Chih Ch'ien.

7. Amitābhavyūha (T 362) or 'Larger Sukhāvatīvyūha', tr. between 222 and 229 by Chih Ch'ien[22].

8. Tathāgataguhyaka (T 312), sūtra in Ratnakūṭa, tr. in 280 by Dharmarakṣa.

9. Pañcaviṃśatisāhasrikā Prajñāpāramitā or Large Prajñā, partially translated in 286 by Dharmarakṣa and Gītamitra (T 222) and in full by Mokṣala and Chu Shu-lan in 291 (T 221).

10. Saddharmapuṇḍarīka (T 263), tr. in 286 by Dharmarakṣa.

11. Daśabhūmika (T 285), sūtra in Avataṃsaka, tr. in 297 by Dharmarakṣa.

Among these sūtras, the most important and perhaps the oldest are the Prajñāpāramitās (Nos 2 and 9; hereafter Prajñā). They are the main source of inspiration of the Madhyamaka or Śūnyavāda school founded by Nāgārjuna and his disciple Āryadeva. The exact date of these authors is not known but, according to Kumārajīva, the greatest authority on the subject, they would have lived during the third century C.E.[23]

Undoubtedly connected with their school is the Mahā-prajñāpāramitopadésa (abbrev. to Upadeśa), a voluminous commentary on the Pañcaviṃśati and most likely to have been compiled during the fourth century.

According to the Chinese catalogues, Kumārajīva translated, in 404, the Śatakaśāstra of Āryadeva with the commentary by the bodhisattva Vasu (T 1569); in 404–405 the Upadeśa (T 1509); in 409 the Dvādaśamukhaśāstra of Nāgārjuna (T 1568); in 409 the Madhyamakaśāstra of Nāgārjuna with the commentary by Piṅgala (T 1564); even later the Daśabhūmikavibhāṣā of Nāgārjuna (T 1521).

The sources noted here represent the first phase of Madhyamaka Buddhism. Having described its philosophical position elsewhere[24], I shall limit myself here to determining the place the Śgs occupies in it.

1. The essential aim of the Śgs is to inculcate into its listeners or readers the Pudgala- and Dharmanairātmya. Not only do beings not exist,

22 Regarding the Amitābhavyūha, supposedly translated by Chih Ch'ien (T 361), see P. Demiéville in Inde Classique II, p.414.

23 See the Vkn, pp.XCI-XCVIII. Regarding Nāgārjuna's date, G. Tucci (Minor Buddhist Texts II, Rome 1958, repr. Delhi 1986, p.284) draws attention to an inscription at Nāgārjunakoṇḍa where this scholar is mentioned. The Brāhmī characters used in this inscription would place it between 450 and 500 C.E.

24 See Vkn, pp.LX-LXXXI.

but things are empty of self-nature, unarisen, undestroyed, originally calm and naturally abiding in Nirvāṇa, free of marks and in consequence inexpressible and unthinkable, the same and devoid of duality.

Like all the sūtras of the Madhyamaka, the Śgs requires a certain mental disposition of its adherents: the *anutpattikadharmakṣānti* or certainty of the non-arising of dharmas (cf. § 48 and n.119); it is in this gradually acquired and firmly anchored certainty that the ascetic will purify his mind and attain his own deliverance even while working on that of others.

The Śgs, however, limits itself to affirming the non-arising of things and does not attempt to demonstrate it. It announces itself as the word of the Buddha which is and can only be a word of truth. It would rest with Nāgārjuna and his school to back up the Madhyamaka with a rational argumentation. This in no way constitutes a dogmatism, but a critique of the notions and categories of early Buddhism by the method of reduction to the absurd (*prasaṅga*) and the principle of the solidarity of opposites[25].

The sūtras only ask to be believed, remembered, repeated, expounded and put into practice (§ 11, 173, 175). They instigate a bibliolatry unknown to early Buddhism.

2. The first Mahāyāna sūtras – among them the Śgs – are not systematic and their literary treatment is inferior to that of the canonical sūtras which have a more pronounced scholastic character.

In vain would we search the Aṣṭa, the Pratyutpanna, the Śūraṃgama and the Vimalakīrti for a complete and coherent explanation of the Mahāyāna which they claim as their authority.

E. Conze, the foremost specialist of the Prajñās, encountered great difficulties in the analysis of the Prajñās. He states: 'The contents of this Sūtra are not easily summarized'[26], and again, 'In any case, such analytical studies of ancient writings are tedious to compose and unattractive to read, and when carried too far, they threaten to shatter and pulverize the very text which they set out to examine, as we have seen in the case of Homer and the New Testament'[27].

[25] On Nāgārjunian critique, see J. May, *Candrakīrti,* Paris 1959, pp.14-22; E. Frauwallner, *Die Philosophie der Buddhismus II*, Berlin 1956, pp.170-7; A. Bareau, 'Der indische Buddhismus' in *Religionen der Menschheit* 13, III, Stuttgart 1965, pp.155-60.

It should be noted that the *anutpattikadharmakṣānti* to which the Madhyamaka sūtras return obsessively is not even mentioned in the Kārikas by Nāgārjuna or the Vṛtti by Candrakīrti. This is because these authors no longer appealed to conviction but to reason.

[26] *The Prajñāpāramitā Literature*, The Hague 1960 (repr. Tokyo 1978), p.52.

[27] 'The Composition of the Aṣṭasāhasrikā Prajñāpāramitā', *Bulletin of the School of Oriental and African Studies* XIV, 1952, p.251.

The early exegetists had already come up against the same difficulties, and a work like the Abhisamayālaṃkāra has no other aim than to draw up a plan of the Large Prajñā. We can guess that this plan was not considered very satisfying since later more than forty sub-commentaries were needed to explain it.

The numerous notes that I have had to add to the translation of the Śgs show my awkward position well enough; and reference to later sources, far from clarifying the text, hardly does more than produce a list of contradictions. In fact, the Śgs represents a Mahāyāna in the course of formation, in revolt against the early Buddhist concepts but unable to break away from the traditional ways of thinking and formulas.

The doctrinal point that is best established is that of the six Pāramitās which are the essential of the bodhisattva career (§§ 26–38, 44), but this teaching had already been formulated in the Buddhism of the Small Vehicle, and the bas-reliefs of the old school of sculpture of Central India had copiously illustrated it[28].

In the Śgs we also find explanations and lists which seem systematic, but these are only adjuncts like the four *vyākaraṇas* (§§ 100–108) or tables without pertinence or link between each other, like the hundred aspects of Heroic Progress (§ 21), the twelve bonds of the *dṛṣṭis* (§ 84), the four qualities required for having faith (§ 130), the ten qualities needed in order to be a true *puṇyakṣetra* (§ 133), the ten *bodhisattvabalas* (§ 152), the eighteen motives which encourage the hearing of the Sūtra (§ 153), the twenty inconceivable virtues which result from hearing it (§ 174). More often than not we wonder whether the author drew up these lists himself or whether he borrowed them from elsewhere.

A more serious fault is the imprecision of the vocabulary. When is a bodhisattva irreversible (*avaivartika*): is it before his entry into the *bhūmis*, at the moment of entry or after? The indications supplied by the Śgs (§ 5, n.5; § 104, n.209) are not conducive to a decision. The same uncertainties come to mind when it is a question of the pre-destination (*niyāma, niyatipāta*) of the bodhisattva, parallel to the *samyaktvaniyāma* of the śrāvaka (cf. § 7, n.13; § 56, n.140; § 104, n.210 and 211; § 150). The most awkward problem is posed by *kṣānti,* sometimes 'perfection of patience' (§ 28, n.86), and sometimes 'certainty' regarding the non-arising of dharmas and susceptible to

[28] See A. Foucher, *Les Vies antérieures du Bouddha*, Paris 1955.

going through several stages (§ 19, n.42; § 48, n.119).

An urgent task fell on the promoters of the Great Vehicle: to fix the stages of the bodhisattva career. They did not succeed without much hesitation and wariness.

a) The Aṣṭasāhasrikā (ed. U. Wogihara, p.831) classes the bodhisattvas in four categories: 1. Those who are committed to the Vehicle (*prathamayānasaṃprasthita*); 2. those who are endowed with the practices (*caryāpratipanna*); 3. irreversible (*avinivartanīya*) bodhisattvas; 4. bodhisattvas separated from Buddhahood by only one existence (*ekajātipratibaddha*). This important text seems as yet not to know anything about the ten stages (*bhūmi*) of the bodhisattvas.

b) There is also no reference to them in the Vimalakīrtinirdeśa (cf. Vkn, p.xcviii), but attention should be drawn to a Khotanese fragment, 'Book of Vimalakīrti', where they are mentioned[29].

c) The Śgs knows of the ten stages (§ 21, n.44) and particularly emphasises the eighth and tenth (§ 48). Moreover, at § 149, it mentions an 'eighth-level holy one' (*aṣṭamaka*), which seems to imply that it was acquainted with the plan concerning the stages common (*sādhāraṇabhūmi*) to both vehicles (cf. § 149 and n.299).

d) In the Large Prajñā we find a clear, systematic and complete description of the Bhūmis. The bodhisattva stages form the subject of a whole chapter (Pañcaviṃśati, ed. Dutt, pp.214–25; Aṣṭādaśa, T 220, ch.490–1, pp.490*b*-497*b*; Śatasāh., ed. Ghosa, pp.1454–73). As for the stages common to both vehicles, they are listed in the same sources (Pañcaviṃśati, pp.225,*16–18*; 235,*18–19*; Aṣṭadaśa, ed. E. Conze, pp.183,*24–26*; 197,*4–8*; Śatasāh., pp.1473,*11–16*; 1520,*20–22*).

e) The merit of having given a name (Pramuditā, etc.) to the ten bodhisattva stages is undoubtedly due to the Daśabhūmika of the Avataṃsaka. This nomenclature was to become indispensable to the sūtras and śāstras of the Great Vehicle.

The enormous progress shown by the Large Prajñā over earlier sūtras must be generally emphasised. The Aṣṭasāh., the Pratyutpanna, the Śūraṃgama, the Vimalakīrti and the Sukhāvatī do not give a complete or coherent idea of the Great Vehicle; these texts represent a Mahāyāna in the course of formation. It is in the Large Prajñā (Pañcaviṃśati, etc.) that, for the first time, we find a good definition of the bodhisattva and a systematic explanation of Mahāyānist teachings.

Here, with references given to the N. Dutt edition, is a summary of a

[29] Edited by Sir H.W. Bailey, *Khotanese Buddhist Texts*, London 1951, pp.104-13.

particularly important section of the Pañcaviṃśati[30]:

I. Definition of the bodhisattva, with a classification of dharmas (pp.160–9).

II. Definition of the bodhisattva as a Mahāsattva (pp.169-94):

1. He leads a great number of beings to the summit (pp.169-72).
2. He eliminates all false views (pp.172–3).
3. He is detached even from the Bodhicitta (pp.173–5).
4. He puts on the great armour of the perfections (pp.175–9).
5. He commits himself to the Great Vehicle (pp.180–3).
6. He has mounted the Great Vehicle (pp.183–5).
7. He is neither bound nor liberated (pp.185–94).

III. Definition of the Mahāyāna (pp.194–242).

1. Its constituent elements.
   a. The six *pāramitās* (pp.194–5).
   b. The twenty kinds of *śūnyatā* (pp.195–8).
   c. The one hundred and twelve *samādhis* (pp.198–203).
   d. The twenty-one practices (pp.203–12): 1. Four *smṛtyupasthānas*, 2. four *samyakprahāṇas*, 3. four *ṛddhipādas*, 4. five *indriyas*, 5. five *balas*, 6. seven *bodhyaṅgas*, 7. the *aṣṭāṅgamārga*, 8. three *samādhis*, 9. eleven *jñānas*, 10. three *indriyas*, 11. three *samādhis*, 12. ten *anusmṛtis*, 13. four *dhyānas*, 14. four *apramāṇas*, 15. four *samāpattis*, 16. eight *vimokṣas*, 17. nine *anupūrvavihāras*, 18. ten *tathāgatabalas*, 19. four *vaiśāradhyas*, 20. four *pratisaṃvids*, 21. eighteen *āveṇika buddhadharmas*.
   e. The forty-three *dhāraṇīmukhas* (pp.212–14).
   f. The ten *bhūmis* (pp.214–25).
2. The Mahāyāna counteracts notions of subject and object (pp.225–31).
3. The greatness of the Mahāyāna (pp.231–42).

3. Whether they originate in the Small or Great Vehicle, Buddhist sūtras are not exempt from a certain ambiguity, and their correct interpretation requires a large amount of dexterity. It is therefore not without reason that, in the Catuṣpratisaraṇasūtra[31], recognised by both vehicles, the Buddha fixes exegetical rules and recommends in

[30] Passage translated and annotated by E. Conze, *The Large Sūtra on Perfect Wisdom*, London 1961, pp.96-180; repr. Berkeley 1975, pp.117-87.

[31] See the references in the Vkn, pp.262-3 in the notes, and add the Vikurvaṇarājaparipṛcchā, T 420, ch.1, p.927*a-b*.

particular that one should rely on the meaning (*artha*) and not on the letter (*vyañjana*), on sūtras of explicit meaning (*nītārtha*) and not on sūtras whose meaning needs interpreting (*neyārtha*).

Ambiguity is most obvious in the oldest Mahāyāna sūtras and, among others, in the Śgs. Thus one of the hundred aspects of the Heroic Progress consists of the second power of the Tathāgata: *karma-vipākajñānabala* 'the power consisting in knowing the fruition of actions' (§ 21, No.5), but it is said that 'the bodhisattva does not see either the self-nature of actions or the self-nature of fruition' (§ 35).

In a comparison which has become famous, the Buddha explains to Dṛḍhamati that a bodhisattva should train himself gradually in the practice of Heroic Progress, in the manner of an archer who practises drawing on ever smaller targets (§§ 47–8), but elsewhere it is said that, in the cultivation of good dharmas, there is nothing which the bodhisattva cultivates and nothing that he does not cultivate (§28, at the end); if he activates great vigour in the search for good dharmas, he nevertheless does not develop any activity of body, speech or mind (§ 30). In fact, all the activities of the bodhisattvas are equivocal and contradictory (§§ 30, 31 and 35)[32].

The Śgs devotes several paragraphs to the *vyākaraṇas* and describes the circumstances under which the Buddha predicts to such-and-such a person his future accession to supreme Bodhi (§§ 100–109). Conversely, in the Vimalakīrtinirdeśa (Vkn, pp.86–90), Vimalakīrti explains to Maitreya, the Buddha of the future, that supreme Bodhi, free from the beginning and by right, is possessed by everyone and that in consequence any prediction concerning it is null and void.

We hasten to add that all these contradictions are desired and intentional; they are aimed at purifying the mind of all prejudice. Also, in looking through Mahāyāna sūtras, the reader should always ask him/herself on what level the author is placed: is it on that of convention (*saṃvṛti*) or on that of absolute truth (*paramārtha*)? Saṃvṛti hides the true nature of things (*svabhāvāraṇa*); it causes the appearance of the false (*anṛtaprakāśana*) because it presupposes a self-nature for things which does not belong to them (*asatpadārtha-svarūpāropikā*) and veils the view of the true nature (*svabhāvadarśanā-varaṇātmikā*). Reality itself is *asaṃskṛta,* immutable and beyond all expression and all instruction. But how can it be approached without having recourse to Saṃvṛti?

32 See also Vkn, pp.LVII-LX, 29-30, 55-8, 128-33, 173-6, 234-6; Avataṃsaka, T 279, ch.56, pp.296*c* 22-297*a* 3.

The theory of the two truths has been widely exploited by Buddhists of both vehicles[33].

Sammuti, mahārāja, esā: ahan-ti mamāti, na paramattho eso [† It is, great king, conventional opinion that 'this is I, this is mine'; it is not absolute truth], Nāgāsena had already said to the Indo-Greek king Menander!

However, if the oldest Mahāyāna sūtras apply it tacitly, they do not give it full or formal status. I can find no trace of it in the Aṣṭasāh., the Śgs or the Vimalakīrti. One of the first to mention it, it seems, is the Pañcaviṃśati (T 223, ch.22, p.378*c* 8–23; ch.24, p.397*b* 16-*c* 2; ch.25, p.405*a* 15–18). However, the most remarkable formulation is in the Pitāputrasamāgama of the Ratnakūṭa (T 310, ch.66, p.378*b* 17 sq.) and is a famous passage often reproduced by scholars (Śāntideva in Śikṣāsamuccaya, p.256,*4*; Prajñākaramati in Pañjikā, pp.367,*3*; 593,*2*; Candrakīrti in Madhyamakāvatāra, pp.175–8, and *Le Muséon*, 1910, pp.356–7). Unfortunately the Pitāputrasamāgama, unlike other sūtras involved in the compilation of the Ratnakūṭa, seems to be of quite late a date; it was translated for the first time into Chinese by Narendrayaśas, in the fourth *t'ien-t'ung* year or 568 C.E.[34]

Nāgārjuna, in his Kārikās (XXIV, 8–10), condensed into a few words the exact implication of the two truths: 'The Buddhas teach the Dharma on the basis of two truths: conventional worldly truth and absolute truth. Those who do not discern the distinction between these two truths do not discern the profound reality in the Buddha's teaching. Without relying on experience, reality cannot be taught; without having understood absolute truth, Nirvāṇa cannot be reached'. That is why, comments Candrakīrti, conventional truth must necessarily be admitted, at least to start with, since it is the method of attaining Nirvāṇa in the same way that he who wants to draw water makes use of a receptacle.

As might be expected, the theory was the object of subsequent elaborations, e.g. in the Upadeśa (*Traité* I, p.27 sq.), and in the Siddhi (pp.549-53).

4. Unlike the Lokottaravādins, the Sarvāstivādins and above all the Yogācārins, the Madhyamaka does not dwell in long considerations on the nature and bodies of the Buddha. Its Tathāgata does not escape the verdict of the Pudgalanairātmya, does not exist in any way and ultimately

[33] See the bibliography on the subject in Siddhi, pp.547-53; L. de La Vallée Poussin, 'Les deux, les quatre, les trois vérités', *Mélanges chinois et bouddhiques* V, 1937, pp. 159-87; *Traité* I, pp.27-47; J. May, *Candrakīrti,* pp.224-9.

[34] Cf. *Li*, T 2049, ch.9, p.87*b* 24; *K'ai*, T 2154, ch.6, p.543*c* 10.

amounts to a body of teaching (*dharmakāya*).

For the Aṣṭasāh. (p.160), 'the supreme Buddha himself is only an illusion, is only a dream; and supreme Buddhahood itself is also only an illusion, is only a dream'. According to the Pañcaviṃśati (p.146), 'the bodhisattva does not grasp the ātman, does not grasp dharmas and does not grasp the categories of holy ones or pratyekabuddhas, or bodhisattvas, or Buddhas. If he does not grasp them, it is because of their absolute purity (*atyantaviśuddhitā*). What is this purity? Non-arising (*anutpāda*), non-manifestation (*aprādurbhāva*), imperceptibilty (*anupalambha*) and inactivity (*anabhisaṃskāra*)'.

In the sūtra that bears his name (Vkn, pp.238–42), Vimalakīrti goes to the Āmrapālīvana in Vaiśālī to see the Buddha. 'How do you see the Tathāgata?' the latter asks him. Vimalakīrti replies: 'O Blessed One, now that I see the Tathāgata, I see him as if there was nothing to see... The Tathāgata is neither seen, nor heard, nor thought, nor known... He has achieved the non-distinction of all things (*sarvadharmanirviśeṣa*)'.

This point of view, or rather absence of view, is shared by the Śgs. Śākyamuni and the imaginary Buddhas created by him with salutary intent are the same and without difference: equally real or equally unreal (§ 18). The feats of the Buddhas which unfold before our eyes – conception, birth, teaching, Nirvāṇa – are only a phantasmagoria (§ 21, Nos 96–100; §§ 123 and 163): 'There is for the Tathāgata no real arising, no real cessation' (§ 71). Between the world of the Buddhas and the world of the Māras, there is neither duality nor difference (§ 114).

The narrow-minded will cry shame and accuse the Mādhyamikas of nihilism. However, it would be the former who would be in the wrong for, as Nāgārjuna explains (Kārikās XXII, 13), whoever believes that the Tathāgata exists must also believe that once having entered Nirvāṇa he no longer exists. It is because his self-nature is non-arising (*anutpādasvabhāvāt*) that the Buddha is imperishable (*avyaya*) and transcends all definition (*prapañcātīta*). A sūtra[35] puts it very well:

'The Tathāgata always constitutes non-arising, and all dharmas are like the Sugata. By grasping marks in non-existent dharmas, puerile minds drift in this world.

'For the Tathāgata is only the reflection of the good and pure teaching. Therein there is truly no suchness (*tathatā*) nor Tathāgata: this is a reflection that appears to all persons'.

Looking more deeply into this problem, the Madhyamaka is still very

[35] Sūtra quoted in Madh. vṛtti, pp.449,*5-12*; 540,*1-4*.

close to early Buddhism, but it introduces onto the ontological level that which the early Buddhists had founded on an historical level.

Referring to Śākyamuni or his rare predecessors, the early exponents had predicted: 'However long his body lasts, so long shall gods and mankind see him; but, on the dissolution of his body, when his life departs, gods and mankind shall no longer see him' (Dīgha I, p.46). 'Just as a flame blown out by a puff of wind, goes from sight, disappears, so the wise man, discarding the *nāma-rūpa* (physical and mental aggregates of existence) disappears, goes from the sight of all. None can measure him; to speak of him, there are no words; what the mind could conceive vanishes and every path is closed to discussion' (Suttanipāta, v.1074 sq.).

Agreed, the Mādhyamikas might say, save, however, with the nuance that disappearance, instead of being acquired with time, is acquired at all times and by all things.

Hence the dialogue between Dṛḍhamati and Matyabhimukha in the Śgs (§ 71):

Dṛḍhamati: 'The Buddhas, where do they go?'

Matyabhimukha: 'The Buddhas, because of the suchness of things *(tathatā),* do not go anywhere'.

Dṛḍhamati: 'Do not the Buddhas go to Nirvāṇa?'

Matyabhimukha: 'All dharmas are [already] absolutely in Nirvāṇa; that is why the Tathāgatas do not go to Nirvāṇa. Because of the very nature of Nirvāṇa, one does not go to Nirvāṇa'.

If the śrāvakas and bodhisattvas differ over the meaning, they agree over the letter. This explains how the old canonical formulas could be adapted and reproduced practically without change by the Mādhyamikas. Here, for example, is a stanza from the Udānavarga XXII, 12 (ed. F. Bernhard, p.288) taken up with some variation by the Aṅguttara II, p.71,*15–16,* and the Theragāthā, v.469:

Ye me rūpeṇa minvanti, ye me ghoṣeṇa cānvagāḥ, chanda-rāgavaśopetā, na māṃ jānanti te janāḥ.

'Those who measure me as a material form and who are guided by my voice, being subjected to the dominion of desire and passion, do not know me'.

We can also add another canonical formula, taken from the Saṃyutta III, p.120,*27–31*:

Alaṃ, Vakkali, kiṃ te iminā pūtikāyena diṭṭhena. Yo kho, Vakkali, dhammaṃ passati so maṃ passati, yo maṃ passati so dhammaṃ passati. Dhammaṃ hi, Vakkali, passanto maṃ passati, maṃ passanto dhammaṃ passati.

'Enough, Vakkali, what good is there in seeing this body of filth? Whoever sees the Dhamma sees me, whoever sees me sees the Dhamma. Seeing the Dhamma he sees me, seeing me he sees the Dhamma'.

This is how these two texts are exploited in the sūtras and śāstras of the Madhyamaka (Vajracchedikā, pp.56–7; Madh. vṛtti, p.448,*11–15*; Pañjikā, p.421,*10–11*):

Ye māṃ rūpeṇa adrākṣur, ye māṃ ghoṣeṇa anvayuḥ,
mithyāprahāṇaprasṛtā na māṃ drakṣyanti te janāḥ,
dharmato buddhā draṣṭavyā dharmakāyā hi nāyakāḥ,
dharmatā cāpy avijñeyā na sā śakyā vijānitum.

'Those who have seen me as a material form and who have been guided by my voice, those persons, involved in false and ruinous views, will not see me. It is through the Dharma that the Buddhas should be seen, for the Leaders are Dharma-Bodies. The nature of things itself being unknowable cannot be discerned'.

5. The least one can say is that Mādhyamika radicalism is hardly conducive to devotion (*bhakti*). Although justified from the viewpoint of Saṃvṛti, an offering (*pūjā*) makes no sense on the Paramārtha level. In the Śgs there is indeed a matter of offerings of thrones (§ 12), of meals and vihāras (§§ 116–120) of parasols (§ 138): all these gifts are of equal value. Rather than practise the six *pāramitās* for an hundred thousand kalpas it is better to hear the Sūtra, take it, remember it, repeat it and expound it to others: this is making an offering of the truth (§ 175).

As it appears in the most characteristic of its sūtras, the Madhyamaka represents a Mahāyāna which is rather in defiance of devotion. The fact is all the more astonishing in that there existed at the time a strong current of devotion; turning away from Nirvāṇa, some followers of both the Small and Great Vehicles aspired to rebirth in impure lands, in the Tuṣita heavens, in the paradise of Maitreya, from whence they would redescend to become Buddhas; others, being exclusively Mahāyānist, vowed to be reborn in a pure land, in the Sukhāvatī heaven of Amitābha. This devotional movement has been examined in detail by P. Demiéville in his learned study on the 'Yogācārabhūmi de Saṅgharakṣa' (*Bulletin de l'École française d'Extrême-Orient* XLIV, 1954, pp.339–436). It is impossible that the authors of the Aṣṭasāh., the Pañcaviṃśati, the Śūraṃgamasamādhi and the Vimalakīrti could not have known about it.

In § 48, No.4, the Śgs mentions the *pratyutpannabuddha-*

saṃmukhāvasthitasamādhi 'concentration during which the Buddhas appear face to face in (one's) immediate presence'. In fact a sūtra bearing this title (T 418) was translated into Chinese by Chih Ch'an on 24 November 179, the same day as the Aṣṭasāh. (T 224), and eight years before the Śgs. It is an Amidist sūtra singing the praises of the recollection – that is, the mental vision of the Buddhas (*buddhānusmṛti*); it is the basis of the contemplative mystique linked to the cult of Amitābha which, activated by Hui-yüan, developed in the fourth century at the Lu-shan into the Association of the White Lotus.

As for the Amitābhavyūha (or Amitāyuḥsūtra, or Sukhāvatīvyūha), which is like a breviary of Amidism, it was translated twelve times into Chinese on dates that are still being discussed, but there is no doubt that the Indian original was already in circulation by the end of the first century C.E., and by the second at the latest.

If the authors of the Aṣṭasāh., etc., certainly knew of the Maitreyan and Amidist movement, they do not seem to have been influenced by it except perhaps with regard to those particular aspirations (*viśeṣapraṇidhāna*) by means of which the bodhisattva prepares his future Buddha-field. Some solemn aspirations are clearly formulated in the Aṣṭasāh. (748,*2*) and especially in the Pañcaviṃśati (ed. Dutt, p.34,*16–17*, corresponding to T 223, ch.1, p.221*a* 18; *ibid.,* T 223, ch.17, pp.347*b*-349*b*); in the Śgs (§ 110), the devakanyās wish to obtain the prediction; however, according to the Vimalakīrti (Vkn, pp.21–2), the bodhisattva 'purifies' his Buddha-field by purifying his own mind, and this is fully in line with the Madhyamaka.

In the sūtras with which we are concerned, Maitreya appears as the acknowledged guardian of the Mahāyāna sūtras, but nowhere is there mention of his paradise. As for Amitābha and the two great bodhisattvas – Avalokiteśvara and Mahāsthāmaprāpta – who are associated with him[36], there is hardly any mention of them, and they are not singled out in any way from the mass of other Buddhas and bodhisattvas. So therefore, it is clear that, to begin with, the Madhyamaka did not nourish hopes of paradise in pure or impure lands. We hasten to add that it would not always be so and that the great Mahāyānist dharmācāryas would succumb to the temptation of the realms of light and infinite longevity. Nāgārjuna, the author of the Madhyamakaśāstra, also wrote a Daśabhūmikavibhāṣā (T 1521) in which he proposes an 'easy way' to reach the Sukhāvatī. Vasubandhu,

[36] Cf. Sukhāvatīvyūha, § 34, p.114.

the author of the Vijñaptimātratāsiddhi, is also responsible for a Sukhāvatīvyūhopadeśa (T 1524) where, with all his heart, he takes refuge in the Tathāgata of Infinite Light and hopes to be reborn in the land of the Sukhāvatī[37]. For the authors of the Upadeśa, the 'Sūtra of the Buddha Amitābha' was an authoritative work (cf. T 1509, ch.9, p.127*a* 11 = *Traité* I, p.556; ch.92, p.708*c* 10).

6. If the Śgs displays no devotion concerning Amitābha, it nevertheless invokes, according to accepted usage, great contingents of bodhisattvas. The majority are only names, albeit very often names of inordinate length. However, certain of them, through having been mentioned in the texts, ended by acquiring a semblance of personality.

So, what do these bodhisattvas represent in the eyes of those Mahāyānists and why do the latter show a preference for one or another bodhisattva?

Bodhisattvas are creatures of great wisdom who, filled with compassion, multiply skilful means in order to win over beings. According to the formula in the Vimalakīrti (Vkn, pp.126–8), their wisdom is acquired through skilful means (*upāyopāttaprajñā*) and their skilful means are acquired through wisdom (*prajñopāttopāya*). Their wisdom penetrates in depth the twofold *nairātmya,* the non-existence of beings and things: they no longer see anything, say anything or think anything. Nevertheless, through compassion for non-existent beings, they evolve a whole range of skilful means, according to the circumstances and needs of beings to be won over. Sometimes they reproduce the twelve actions of the Buddhas' historical feats (Śgs, § 21, Nos 96–99, §§ 123 and 163); sometimes they indulge in unbridled wonder-making: they insert Mount Sumeru into a mustard-seed, they pour the waters of the four oceans into a pore of their skin, they cast the great cosmos beyond universes as manifold as the sands of the Ganges and then return them to their place, they deposit all the beings in the palm of their hands and travel through all the universes but without moving, they insert the cosmic fires into their bellies, they shrink or stretch time at will, etc. (Vkn, pp.141–8). Occasionally and always for the benefit of beings, they do not hesitate to make use of means of doubtful taste; in order to demonstrate to Śāriputra the perfect equality of the sexes, a bodhisattva-goddess changes him into a woman while she herself is transformed into a man (Vkn, pp.170–1); in order to win over two hundred lustful devakanyās, the bodhisattva Māragocarānupalipta creates two hundred

[37] Cf. S. Yamaguchi, *Muryōjukyō Upadaisha ganshōge no shikai,* Kyoto 1962.

doubles of himself and unites with them (Śgs, § 94). The goodwill and compassion of the bodhisattvas place them above the rules of morality: the latter are only of provisional and relative value and, from a certain point of view, the offender is superior to the holy one (Śgs, § 150; Vkn, pp.55, 180). We cannot doubt that the bodhisattvas are highly virtuous, even if all their behaviour occurs under the sign of fiction, contradiction and ambiguity (Śgs, §§ 30, 31, 35; Vkn, pp.29–30, 44–8, 55–8, 128–33, 171–6, 234–7; Avataṃsaka, T 279, ch.56, pp.296*c* 22–297*a* 3).

Among the crowd of holy ones that the Śgs presents, it seems to display what I would call, if not a predilection, a particular interest in certain Buddhas and bodhisattvas.

Among these, the foremost is the Buddha Akṣobhya who rules over the Abhirati universe in the eastern region. He appears in practically all the Mahāyāna sūtras: Akṣobhyatathāgatasya vyūha, supposedly translated in 147 C.E. by Chih Ch'an (T 313), Aṣṭasāh. (pp.745, 853, 874–5), Śgs (§ 77), Vimalakīrtinirdeśa (Vkn, pp.168, 243–9), Smaller Sukhāvatīvyūha (p.204), Pañcaviṃśati (pp.91–2), Saddharmapuṇḍarīka (pp.160-85), Karuṇāpuṇḍarīka (T 157, p.194*b*), Suvarṇabhāsa (p.152), etc.

The Akṣobhyavyūha and Vimalakīrtinirdeśa describe at length the splendours of the Abhirati universe where Akṣobhya reigns. According to the Vimalakīrtinirdeśa (Vkn, pp.243–5), the bodhisattva Vimalakīrti comes from this universe; according to the Śgs (§§ 77–79), the devaputra Matyabhimukha has the same origin and he is destined one day to become the Buddha Vimala[prabhā]kīrtirāja in the Sahāloka. The Mahāsaṃnipāta (T 397, ch.31, pp.216–17; ch.35, p.239) also places Vimalakīrti in the universes of the eastern region: in the Apramāṇa, he will be the bodhisattva Sūryaguhya, and in the Niṣparidāha, the bodhisattva Sūryakośagarbha. The perfect identity of beings and things allows all these identifications.

Mañjuśrī is passed over in silence in the Aṣṭasāh.; the Large Prajñā (Pañcaviṃśati, pp.5,*10*; 17,*18*; Śatasāh., pp.7,*3*; 55,*13*), as well as the Sukhāvatī (p.194,*9*), only mention him in passing. It is strange that these texts remained outside the strong Mañjuśrian current which swept through Mahāyāna literature. Mañjuśrī plays a leading role in the Vimalakīrti[38] and his part in the Śgs (§§ 140–148) is not negligible. He was also the inspiration for quite a few other sūtras, some of which had already been translated into Chinese under the Late Han in the second century: Lokānuvartana (T 807), Ajātaśatrukaukṛtyavinodana (T 626)

38 See the Index to the Vkn, *s.v.* Mañjuśrī.

and Mañjuśrīparipṛcchā (T 458).

To conclude, we can note a curious point of contact between the Śgs and the Lotus. The former (§ 170–172) mentions, in the Pratimaṇḍitā universe in the eastern region, a Buddha Vairocanaraśmi-pratimaṇḍitavikurvaṇarāja whom the latter, in Ch.25, brings into a long jātaka. Both discover affinities veering on identity between this Vairocana of the east and the Śākyamuni of the Sahāloka. This is the skeleton of esoteric Buddhism for which Mahāvairocana is the historical Śākyamuni idealised in the *dharmakāya* 'which is not born and does not die'.

V. THE SOURCES OF THE SŪTRA

The author of the Śgs was fully acquainted with the early canonical texts and he makes wide use of their formulas and stock phrases. However, considering himself also as a spokesman of the Buddha, he felt no need to invoke the authority of other sūtras. I have therefore not been able to make out more than a few precise references to canonical sources:

1. Aṅguttara I, p.22,*1–4* (Ekottara, T 125, ch.3, p.561*a* 8–12): *Ekapuggalo bhikkhave loke uppajjamāno*... (quoted in § 71).

2. Saṃyukta, T 99, ch.35, p.258*a* 23–25, *c* 7–8 (cf. Aṅguttara III, pp.350,*4–8*; 351,*13–16*; V, pp.140,*18–22*; 143,*16–20*): *Mā bhikṣavaḥ pudgalena pudgalaṃ pravicetavyam*... (quoted in § 103).

3. Aṅguttara I, p.23 sq. (Ekottara, T 125, ch.3, p.557*a*): *Etad aggaṃ bhikkhave mama sāvakānaṃ bhikkhūnaṃ*... (quoted in §§ 133–134, 136, 156).

Furthermore, the author was not unaware of the additions made by the paracanonical texts to the golden legend of Buddhism. So, as against the Nikāyas-Āgamas, but in conformity with the separate biographies of the Buddha and the Vinaya of the Mūlasarvāstivādins, he makes Gopā a wife of the bodhisattva Śākyamuni (cf. § 56, n.138; § 58, n.143). He mentions the *saṃcodana* [† exhortation] of the devas inviting the bodhisattva Śākyamuni to leave his father's palace – an episode which, to my knowledge, is only related in the paracanonical sources (cf. § 59, n.147).

Nowhere in the Śgs can I find a reference to any Abhidharma [† however, is there not a hint of it when Māra quotes the Buddha in

§ 99?]. It is true that in § 149, it distinguishes in the manner of the Abhidharmas a whole category of holy ones, but it could have borrowed them from 'scholastic' sūtras such as those we find in the Canon (cf. § 149, n.299).

The same statement can be made regarding the Aṣṭasāh., the Vimalakīrti and the Pañcaviṃśati, etc.: it is impossible to say whether they were inspired by one or other of the Abhidharmas. In contrast, the Upadeśa frequently uses and discusses the Abhidharma, but only that of the Sarvāstivādins: Jñānaprasthāna, Ṣaṭpādābhidharma and Vibhāṣā[39]. This is one of the many indications of its northern origins.

The Śgs was considered authoritative among the Mādhyamika scholars who quite often quote it:

1. Mahāprajñāpāramitopadeśa (T 1509), translated by Kumārajīva between 402 and 404 C.E.:

ch.4, p.92*b* 3–6 [† tr. in *Traité* I, p.293] = § 100 of the Śgs.
ch.10, p.134*b* 18–19 [† *Traité* I, pp.602–3] = § 162.
ch.26, p.249*c* 11–12 [† *Traité* III, p.1647] = § 171.
ch.29, p.273*b* 5–8 [† *Traité* IV, p.1907] = § 147.
ch.33, p.303*b* 11–12 [† *Traité* V, pp.2235–6] = §147.
ch.34, p.312*a* 27–29 [† *Traité* V, p.2340] = §§ 171–172.
ch.40, p.349*c* 19–21 [† not translated in *Traité*] = § 101.
ch.75, p.586*b* 1–2 [† not translated in *Traité*] = § 147.

2. Nandimitrāvadāna, translated in 654 by Hsüan-tsang (T 2030, p.14*a* 16–17).

3. Śikṣāsamuccaya of Śāntideva (seventh century C.E.). A Chinese translation (T 1636) was made in Pien-liang, in the first half of the eleventh century, by Dharmarakṣa of the Sung.

a. Ed. C. Bendall, p.8,*19–20* (T 1636, ch.1, p.77*a* 14–16): *Śūraṃgamasūtre 'pi śāṭhyotpāditasyāpi bodhicittasya buddhatva-hetutvābhidānāt, kaḥ punar vādaḥ kiṃcid eva kuśalaṃ kṛtvā* [† tr. in C. Bendall and W.H.D. Rouse, *Śikshā-Samuccaya*, Delhi, repr. 1971, 1990, p.9]. This quotation, also reproduced in the Bodhi-caryāvatārapañjikā of Prajñākaramati (ed. L. de La Vallée Poussin,

39 See, e.g., *Traité* I, pp.109-11, 245-83.

p.24,*12–13*), seems to be a free reference to § 97 of the Śgs.

b. Ed. C. Bendall, pp.91,*8–92,6* (T 1636, ch.6, pp.93*c* 23–94*a* 9) [† tr. Bendall and Rouse, p.93] = § 101 and 102 of the Śgs.

4. In the Chinese records of the Council of Lhasa (*Le Concile de Lhasa*, tr. P. Demiéville), the Śūraṃgamasamādhisūtra is quoted twice: on page 73 (reference to § 47) and on pages 141–2 (reference to § 100), and the apocryphal Śūraṃgamasūtra is quoted once, on page 43 (reference to T 945, ch.6, p.131*a*). If I am not mistaken, the Śgs is not invoked in the three Bhāvanākramas published, about 795 C.E., by Kamalaśīla at the close of the Council.

CHAPTER TWO

THE CHINESE AND TIBETAN VERSIONS

The information we have at our disposal is taken from Chinese catalogues and biographies:

Ch'u = *Ch'u san-tsang chi chi* (T 2145) 'Selection of notes taken from the Three Baskets', in fifteen chüan, compiled in Chien-yeh (Nanking) by Sêng-yu (435–518), published for the first time in 515 and revised by the author shortly before his death. He gleaned his information from various earlier biographies, particularly from the *Tsung-li chung-ching mu-lu* compiled in 374 in Hsiang-yang, in northern Hu-pei, by Tao-an (312–385) and subsequently completed by the author. Conversely, the *Ch'u*, written in the south, does not mention the catalogues drawn up in the north, such as the *Han lu* by Chu Shih-hsing (about 260), the *Chung-ching lu* by Nieh Tao-chên (about 300), and the *Ching-lun tu-lu* by Chih Min-tu (between 325 and 342).

Kao = *Kao-sêng chuan* (T 2059) 'Biographies of eminent monks', in fourteen chüan, published around 530 by Hui-chiao (497–554), in the Chi-hsiang ssŭ of Hui-chi (in the Chê-chiang). The *Ch'u san-tsang chi chi* is one of his main sources.

Chung A = *Chung-ching mu-lu* (T 2146) 'Catalogue of sūtras', in seven chüan, compiled in Ch'ang-an in 594 by Fa-ching and other śramaṇas of the Ta Hsing-shan ssŭ.

Li = *Li-tai san-pao chi* (T 2034) 'Chronicle of the Three Jewels', in fifteen chüan, composed in Ch'ang-an in 597 by the lay scholar Fei Chang-fang, a native of the Ssŭ-chuan. This compilation often refers to the *Ch'u san-tsang chi chi*, but also quotes several ancient catalogues which it lists (T 2034, ch.15, p.127*b-c*). These catalogues had already been lost in Fei Chang-fang's time, but he was able to quote them secondhand, probably from the *Li-tai chung-ching mu-lu* finished in 518 by Pao-ch'ang (cf. T 2034, ch.11, p.94*b* 16).

Chung B = *Chung-ching mu-lu* (T 2147), in five chüan: Ch'ang-an edition compiled in 602, on the order of Wei-ti of the Sui, by the bhadanta Yen-ts'ung and other monks from the Ta Hsing-shan ssŭ in Ch'ang-an, who were joined by lay scholars.

Chung C = *Chung-ching mu-lu* (T 2148), in five chüan: Lo-yang edition compiled in 666 by Shih Ching-t'ai and the monks of the Ta

Ching-ai ssŭ in Lo-yang.

Nei = *Ta T'ang nei tien lu* (T 2149), in ten chüan, compiled in 664 by Tao-hsüan (596–667), then Superior of the Hsi-ming ssŭ in Ch'ang-an. This catalogue borrows widely from the *Li-tai san-pao chi*.

T'u = *Ku chin i ching t'u chi* (T 2151), 'Descriptive memoirs concerning ancient and modern translations', in four chüan, compiled in 664–5, in Ch'ang-an, by the śramaṇa Ching-mai, a collaborator of Hsüan-tsang since 645.

Wu = *Wu* (or *Ta*) *Chou k'an ting chung-ching mu-lu* (T 2153) 'Catalogue of sūtras drawn up under the Chou dynasty of the Wu family', in fifteen chüan, compiled in Ch'ang-an in 695, on the order of the empress Wu, by Ming-ch'üan and others.

K'ai = *K'ai-yüan shih-chiao mu-lu* (T 2154) 'Buddhist catalogue of the *k'ai-yüan* period', in twenty chüan, compiled in 730 by the śramaṇa Chih-shêng of the Hsi Ch'ung-fu ssŭ in Ch'ang-an.

Hsü-k'ai = *Ta T'ang chêng-yüan hsü k'ai-yüan shih chiao lu* (T 2156) 'Buddhist catalogue of the *chêng-yüan* period of the T'ang', in three chüan, compiled in 795 by Yüan-chao of the Hsi-ming ssŭ in Ch'ang-an.

Chêng = *Chêng-yüan hsin-ting shih-chiao mu-lu* (T 2157) 'Newly drawn up Buddhist catalogue of the *chêng-yüan* period', in thirty chüan, compiled on imperial order in 799-800 by Yüan-chao of the Hsi-ming ssŭ in Ch'ang-an.

These catalogues contain lists of the Chinese translations of the Śgs made in the course of time with the titles of *Shou-lêng-yen ching* or *Yung-fu-ting ching*:

1. *Ch'u*, T 2145, p.14*a* 15–18: *Shou-lêng-yen ching*: 1. *Shou-lêng-yen* by Chih Ch'an, two chüan; 2. *Shou-lêng-yen* by Chih Ch'ien, two chüan; 3. *Shou-lêng-yen* by Po Yen, two chüan; 4. Chu Fa-hu also translated the *Yung-fu-ting* in two chüan: this is a new translation of the *Shou-lêng-yen;* 5. *Shou-lêng-yen* by Chu Shu-lan, two chüan; 6. New translation of the *Shou-lêng-yen* by Kumārajīva, two chüan; 7. The *Chiu lu* (or an ancient catalogue) mentions a *Shu* 蜀 *Shou-lêng-yen* in two chüan, but does not say who translated it. Seven men translated this one and only sūtra, but the name of one of the translators is lost.

2. *Li*, T 2034, p.78*a* 12–13: The *Shou-lêng-yen ching* [by Kumārajīva], in two chüan, is the seventh translation. With the *Shou-*

lêng-yen by 1. Chih Ch'an, 2. Chih Ch'ien, 3. Po Yen, 4. Fa-hu, 5. Shu-lan, and 6. the *Yung-fu-ting* [by Fa-hu], these are different versions of the same original. There are also [after the translation by Kumārajīva which is the seventh] two works: 8. the *Shu* [*Shou-lêng-yen*] and 9. the *Hou-ch'u* [*Shou-lêng-yen*]: altogether nine translations constituting different versions.

3. *K'ai*, T 2154, pp.631*c* 29-632*a* 18: 1. *Shou-lêng-yen ching*, in two or three chüan, translated by the Yüeh-chean trepiṭa Chih Lou-chia-ch'an of the Hou Han: this is the first translation; 2. *Fang-teng Shou-lêng-yen ching*, in two chüan, translated by the Yüeh-chean upāsaka Chih Ch'ien of the Wu: this is the second translation; 3. *Shu Shou-lêng-yen ching*, in two chüan, seemingly from the Shu territory; translation lost under the Ts'ao Wei: this is the third translation; 4. *Hou-ch'u Shou-lêng-yen ching*, in two chüan; translation lost under the Ts'ao Wei: this is the fourth translation; 5. *Shou-lêng-yen ching*, in two chüan, translated by the trepiṭa from the Western Countries, Po Yen of the Ts'ao Wei: this is the fifth translation; 6. *Yung-fu-ting ching,* in two chüan. [Tao]-an says that this is yet another translation of the *Shou-lêng-yen ching*. It is ascribed to the trepiṭa Chu Fa-hu of the Hsi Chin: this is the sixth translation. According to the catalogues by Sêng-yu (T 2145), Chang-fang (T 2034), etc., Chu Fa-hu should be credited with a *Shou-lêng-yen ching* in two chüan. However, between *Shou-lêng-yen* and *Yung-fu-ting*, the titles [respectively] in Sanskrit and Chin Chinese are the only things to differ; the two sūtras do not differ. The colophon of the *Yung-fu-ting ching* says: 'On the ninth day of the fourth month of the first *yüan-k'ang* year (23 May 291), the bodhisattva from Tun-huang, Chih Fa-hu, holding the Indian sūtra in his hands, orally translated the *Shou-lêng-yen ching*; the upāsaka Nieh Ch'eng-yüan took it down with his brush'. Hence we know for a fact that the *Shou-lêng-yen ching* and the *Yung-fu-ting* are not two different things. 7. *Shou-lêng-yen ching*, in two chüan, translated by the upāsaka from the Western Countries, Chu Shu-lan of the Hsi Chin: this is the seventh translation. 8. *Shou-lêng-yen ching*, in two chüan, translated by the Yüeh-chean upāsaka Chih Shih-lun of the Ch'ien Liang: this is taken from the colophon of this *Shou-lêng-yen ching*. It is the eighth translation and has recently been inserted in the catalogue. These eight sūtras represent a single original. There was later a ninth translation: [that by Kumārajīva]; this ninth translation is extant (T 642), the eight previous ones are all lost. According to the catalogues by [Sêng]-yu

(T 2145), [Chang]-fang (T 2034), etc., under the Hui-ti of the Chi Chin the śramaṇa Chih Min-tu assembled the four earlier translations by the two Chih [Chih Ch'an and Chih Ch'ien] and the two Chu [Chu Fa-hu and Chu Shu-lan] and combined them into a single edition of eight chüan. This is not a separate translation of a Sanskrit original and it does not appear in the correct enumeration of the authentic translations.

These lists agree in the main. The *K'ai* has noted that only one translation of the Śgs with the title of *Yung-fu-ting* can be attributed to Chu Fa-hu. According to the extract we have just given, it seems that the *Ch'u* was equally aware of this; however, as will be seen further on in its summary of the works of Chu Fa-hu, it attributes to the latter two distinct translations of the Śgs with the titles of *Shou-lêng-yen* and *Yung-fu-ting*. The *Li* makes the same mistake.

The *K'ai* is the only catalogue to have taken account of the translation by Chih Shih-lun, but the *Ch'u*, which reproduces its colophon, had already encountered it.

I shall examine each of the translations concerned.

I

Shou-lêng-yen ching **首楞榜經, 2 chüan, translated in Lo-yang on 16 January 186 C.E. by Chih Ch'an 支讖 of the Late Han.**

Chih Ch'an or Chih Lou-chia ch'an (Lokakṣema[?] of the Yüeh-chih) is credited with twelve translations by Tao-an (*Ch'u*, T 2145 p.6*b* 29), fourteen by the *Ch'u*, (T 2145, p.6*b* 27), twenty-one by the *Li*, the *Nei* and the *T'u* (T 2034, p.53*a* 18; T 2149, p.224*a* 4; T 2151, p.348*c* 17), and twenty-three by the *K'ai* (T 2154, p.479*a* 7).

His translation of the Śgs is part of a small number of translations by Chih Ch'an which are authenticated by old colophons and records dating back to the third century and the beginning of the fourth century C.E. These are translations of the following works: Aṣṭasāhasrikā Prajñāpāramitā, Pratyutpannabuddhasaṃmukhāvasthitasamādhi, Śūraṃgamasamādhi, Ajātaśatrukaukṛtyavinodana and Drumakiṃnararājaparipṛcchā.

Chih Ch'an made the first two in collaboration with the Indian Chu Fo-shuo (or Chu Shuo-fo); for all five he seems to have been assisted by the Chinese laymen Mêng Fu 孟福, cognomen Yüan-shih 元士, from Lo-yang; Chang Lien 張蓮, cognomen Shao-an 少安, from Nan-yang (Ho-nan), and Tzŭ-pi 子碧 from Nan-hai (Canton). The names of two of these collaborators were discovered by T'ang Yung-t'ung on two inscriptions from the Han period dating from 181 and 183 C.E., where they are mentioned as followers of a local Taoist cult in Yüan-shih hsien (in Hu-pei)[1].

Here, in chronological order, are the colophons and records concerning these translations:

1. *Ch'u* (T 2145, p.47*c* 4–9). Colophon of the *Tao hsing ching* (T 224: *Tao hsing pan-jo ching* = Aṣṭasāhasrikā p.p.). Author unknown. [Colophon dating from 24 November 179].

On the eighth day of the tenth month of the second *kuang-ho* year (24 November 179), Mêng [Fu], cognomen Yüan-shih, from Lo-yang in Ho-nan, gave it orally[2]. The bodhisattva from India, Chu Shuo-fo 竺朔佛, at that very moment, transmitted the word. The translator was the bodhisattva of the Yüeh-chih, Chih Ch'an. At that time the assistants were Chang [Lien], cognomen Shao-an, from Nan-yang (in Ho-nan) and Tzŭ-pi from Nan-hai (Canton). The helpers were Sun-ho 孫和 and Chou T'i-li 周提立. On the fifteenth day of the ninth month of the second *chêng-kuang* year (correct to *chêng-yüan*: 1 November 255), in the town of Lo-yang, at the Hsi p'u-sa ssŭ, the śramaṇa Fo-ta 佛大 copied it down.

2. *Ch'u* (T 2145, p.48*c* 9–16). Record of the *Pan-chou san-mei ching* (T 417 and 418: Pratyutpannabuddhasaṃmukhāvasthitasamādhi). Author unknown. [Colophon dating from 5 November 208].

Pan-chou san-mei ching. On the eighth day of the tenth month of the second *kuang-ho* year (24 November 179), the Indian bodhisattva Chu Shuo-fo recited it in Lo-yang. [The bodhisattva Fa-hu.] He who at that time transmitted the word was the Yüeh-chean bodhisattva Chih Ch'an; he gave it to Mêng Fu, cognomen Yüan-shih from [the commandery in] Lo-yang in the prefecture of Ho-nan, who was then assistant to the bodhisattva. Chang Lien, cognomen Shao-an, took (it) down with his brush, so that afterwards (this book) became universally disseminated.

In the thirteenth *chien-an* year (208), collated and accepted as

[1] See E. Zürcher, *The Buddhist Conquest of China*, Leiden 1959, repr. 1972, pp.35 and 332, n.91.

[2] This information is incorrect: it is probable that Chu Shuo-fo 'recited' or 'orally transmitted' the sūtra, either by reciting the Indian text from memory or by reading the manuscript out loud. Then Chih Ch'an 'transmitted the word', i.e. explained orally in Chinese, and 'gave the sūtra' to Mêng Fu. The latter, being pure Chinese, was quite incapable of 'giving' it. See the next colophon.

complete at the temple of the Buddha. May all those who recopy it in the future succeed in paying homage to the Buddha.

It is also said: in the third (read thirteenth) *chien-an* year, on the eighth day of the eighth month (5 November 208), collated at the temple of Hsü-ch'ang[3].

3. *Ch'u* (T 2145, p.49*a* 16–21). Record of the combined Śūraṃgamasūtras. Author Chih Min-tu. [Date of edition: 301 C.E.]

This [Śūraṃgamasamādhi-]sūtra originally had a notice saying that it had been translated by Chih Ch'an. [Chih] Ch'an was a Yüeh-chih. In the reigns of Huan (146–168) and Ling (168–189), he came to settle in China. His wide knowledge was profound and wonderful; his talents and mind probed the subtle. All the sūtras that he translated are of a profound and mysterious kind. He aimed at precision above all, but was not preoccupied with embellishments of style. The *Hsaio p'in* (T 224: *Tao hsing pan-jo ching* = Aṣṭasāhasrikā p.p.), the *A-chê-shih* (T 626: *A-chê-shih wang ching* = Ajātaśatru-kaukṛtyavinodana), the *Tun-chên* (T 624: *Tun-chên t'o lo so wen ju-lai san-mei ching* = Drumakiṃnararājaparipṛcchā) and the *Pan-chou* (T 417 and 418: *Pan-chou san-mei ching* = Pratyutpannabuddha-saṃmukhāvasthitasamādhi) existing at present were all translated by [Chih] Ch'an.

4. *Ch'u* (T 2145, p.49*a* 14–15), quoting a passage from the catalogue by Tao-an composed in Hsiang-yang (in Hu-pei) in 374:

[Tao]-an kung in his catalogue of sūtras says: The sūtra translated by Chih Ch'an on the eighth day of the twelfth month of the second *chung p'ing year* (16 January 186) begins by saying: 'Thus have I heard: the Buddha was residing in Rājagṛha, on the Gṛdhra-kūṭaparvata'.

The date of 16 January 186 established by Tao-an is adopted by the *Ch'u* (T 2145, p.6*b* 11) in its list of works by Chih Ch'an.

Also to be found in the *Ch'u* (T 2145, pp.95*c* 22–97*a* 7) is an account of Chih Ch'an and his collaborator Chu Shuo-fo who took part in the translation of the Aṣṭasāhasrikā p.p. and the Pratyutpannasamādhi:

Chih Ch'an was a native of the kingdom of the Yüeh-chih. His

3 The translation here is based on that by H. Maspero, 'Les origines de la Communauté bouddhiste de Lo-yang', *Journal Asiatique*, 1934, p.94. As the author has rightly noted, the mention of the bodhisattva Fa-hu is a gloss mistakenly inserted in the text. Chu Fa-hu, who worked from 284 to 297, could not have played any part in a translation undertaken in 179.

conduct was pure and profound, his character open and lively. He was renowned for his faithfulness to the religious precepts (*dharmaśīla*) and for his energy (*vīrya*). He recited the sūtras and was resolved to protect and expound the Dharma. At the end of the reign of Huan-ti (circa 168) of the Han, he went to Lo-yang and, under Ling-ti, during the *kuang-ho* (179–184) and *chung-p'ing* (184–189) periods, he transmitted and translated the Indian texts. He published three sūtras: the *Pan-jo tao hsing p'in* (T 224: Aṣṭasāhasrikā p.p.), the *Shou-lêng-yen* (Śūraṃgama) and the *Pan-chou san-mei* (T 417 and 418: Pratyutpannasamādhi).

There are also ten sūtras: the *A-chê-shih wang* (T 626: Ajātaśatrurājasūtra), the *Pao-chi* (T 350: Kāśyapaparivarta), etc. For a long time they were not catalogued, but [Tao]-an kung who has collated and reviewed the old and modern (translations) and carefully examined the styles says that these translations resemble those by [Chih] Ch'an. All these translations discerningly render the tenor of the (Indian) original, but without adding any embellishment. It can be said that the translator skilfully expounded the message of the Dharma and propagated the Path. Afterwards it is not known when he died.

As for the śramaṇa Chu Shuo-fo, he was an Indian. Under Huan-ti (146–168) of the Han, also bringing[4] with him the *Tao hsing ching* (Aṣṭasāhasrikā p.p.), he arrived in Lo-yang and immediately translated it from Indian into Chinese. The interpreter hesitating often, there was a loss of literal import but, with the exception of the style, the essential was preserved and the spirit of the sūtra was deeply penetrated.

Furthermore, in the second *kuang-ho* year (179) under Ling-ti, [Chu] Shuo-[fo], in Lo-yang, translated the *Pan-chou san-mei ching* (T 417 and 418: Pratyutpannasamādhi). At that time [Chih] Ch'an transmitted the word. Mêng Fu, from Lo-yang in the prefecture of Ho-nan, and Chang Lien took (it) down with the brush.

The *Kao sêng chuan* (T 2059, p.324*b* 13–25) textually reproduces this notice with the difference that it places the arrival in Lo-yang of Chih Ch'an and Chu Shuo-fo, not in the reign of Huan-ti (146–168), but in that of Ling-ti (168–189).

Later, Chih-shêng 智昇 (668–740), in his 'History of old and modern

[4] The character *chi* 齎 'to bring' lacks precision; it could be a matter of material manuscripts or memorised texts.

controversies between Buddhists and Taoists' (T 2105, pp.401*c* 27–402*a* 4) places Chih Ch'an's arrival in Lo-yang in the year five of the *hsing-p'ing* period (176–177), and Chu Fo-shuo's in the year two of the *kuang-ho* period (179–180) of the emperor Ling.

All the sources examined up to now represent the old tradition concerning the activity of Chih Ch'an and Chu Shuo-fo, the Yüeh-chean and Indian bodhisattvas, who purportedly introduced the Mahāyāna into China. The tradition amounts to this:

1. Towards the end of the reign of Huan-ti in 168, or at the beginning of the reign of Ling-ti in 176, the bodhisattva of the Yüeh-chih named Chih Ch'an (Lokakṣema) arrives in Lo-yang.

2. In 179 he is joined by the bodhisattva from India, Chu Shuo-fo. The two bodhisattvas together translate, on 24 November 179, the Aṣṭasāhasrikā p.p. (T 224) and the Pratyutpanna... samādhi (T 417 and 418). Chu Shuo-fo 'recites' or 'orally transmits' the Sanskrit text which he delivers from memory or the manuscript of which he reads. Chih Ch'an 'transmits the word', that is, he explains it orally in Chinese. Mêng Fu, Chang Lien and Tzŭ-pi 'take down with the brush' (colophons of the *Tao hsing ching* and the *Pan-chou san-mei ching*).

3. On 16 January 186, Chih Ch'an on his own translates the Śūraṃgamasamādhi (according to the catalogue by Tao-an).

4. Chih Ch'an's activity takes place between 179 and 189, in the reign of the emperor Ling of the Han. He also translated the Ajātaśatrukaukṛtyavinodana (T 626) and the Drumakiṃnararājaparipṛcchā (T 624) (according to the account by Chih Min-tu). Basing himself no longer on the old colophons but on the study of style, Tao-an attributes to him ten further old translations (according to the *Ch'u*).

A more recent literary tradition, codified by the *Li*, modifies the dates proposed up to now:

1. *Li*, T 2034, pp.33*a* 23; 52*c* 23: The first *chien-ho* year (147), Chih Ch'an translated the *A-ch'u fo kuo ching* (T 313: Akṣobhyatathāgatasya vyūha). See Chu Shih-hsing, *Han-lu*.

2. *Li*, T 2034, pp.34*a* 5; 53*c* 8: The first *hsi-p'ing* year (172), Chu Fo-cho, having arrived in Lo-yang, translated the *Tao hsing ching* (Aṣṭasāhasrikā p.p.). See Chu Shih-hsing, *Han lu*.

3. *Li*, T 2034, pp.34*d* 6; 52*c* 16: On the eighth day of the tenth (variant: seventh) month of the second *kuang-ho* year (24 November 179), Chih Ch'an translated the *Pan-jo tao-hsing p'in* (T 224: Aṣṭasāhasrikā p.p.). This is the first translation. See the *Chih Min-tu lu*.

4. *Li*, T 2034, pp.34*a* 7; 52*c* 27: On the eighth day of the tenth month of the second *kuang-ho* year (24 November 179), Chih Ch'an translated the *Pan-chou san-mei ching* (T 417 and 418: Pratyutpannasamādhisūtra). This is the first translation. See the *Nieh Tao-*[*chên*] *lu*, etc.

5. *Li*, T 2034, p.53*c* 7: On an undetermined date, Chu Fo-shuo translated the *Pan-chou san-mei ching* (Pratyutpannasamādhisūtra). This is the second translation.

6. *Li*, T 2034, pp.34*e* 8; 52*c* 18: On the eighth day of the second month of the third *chung-p'ing* year (16 March 186), Chih Ch'an translated the *Shou-lêng-yen ching* (Śūraṃgamasūtra). This is the first translation. See Chu Shih-hsing, *Han lu*.

These dates will be taken up again by catalogues postdating the *Li*. See, for that of the Śgs, *Nei* (T 2149, p.223*c* 10), *T'u* (T 2151, p.348*c* 10), *Wu* (T 2153, p.397*c* 18–19, *K'ai* (T 2154, p.479*a* 1).

These calculations led to modifications in the record devoted to Chih Ch'an. According to the *Li* (T 2034, p.53*a* 19 sq.) and the *K'ai* (T 2154, p.479*a* 11–12), Chih Ch'an worked in Lo-yang from the first *chien-ho* year (147) under Huan-ti until the third *chung-p'ing* year (186) under Ling-ti.

It appears that the whole of this new tradition regarding Chih Ch'an should be rejected.

Firstly, it makes use of suspect documents. It is known that Fei Chang-fang, the author of the *Li*, refers to some fifteen catalogues already lost by his time but which he could quote at secondhand, probably from the catalogue by Pao-ch'ang. Here he bases himself on an indication in the *Han lu* by Chu Shih-hsing (220–264) in order to date the translation of the *A-ch'u fo kuo ching* in 147 and, hence, Chih Ch'an's arrival in Lo-yang. But this *Han lu* is a late and none too trustworthy work, compiled to replace a lost original from the third century; it is never mentioned in the catalogues prior to the *Li* and the author himself of the latter work declares that he has never seen it. It probably never existed as an independent work[5].

[5] Cf. Zürcher, *Buddhist Conquest*, p.324, n.2.

Secondly, the new tradition claims that the Aṣṭasāhasrikā p.p. and the Pratyutpannasamādhi were each the object of a dual translation, one by Chu Fo-shuo, the other by Chih Ch'an. It therefore goes directly against the old colophons of the third century, by the terms of which the two texts were translated simultaneously and conjointly by the two masters.

Finally, the new tradition contains some improbabilities. It is unlikely that Chih Ch'an, after having translated the Akṣobhya-tathāgatasya vyūha in 147, should then have waited thirty-two years before resuming his activity and translating, in 179, the Aṣṭasāhasrikā p.p. and the Pratyutpannasamādhi.

In conclusion, the old tradition represented by the *Ch'u* and followed by the *Kao* is to be preferred to the new one. It has the merit of relying on the colophons of the third century and the authority of two great masters of the fourth: Chih Min-tu and Tao-an.

II and III

Shu Shou-lêng-yen ching 蜀首楞嚴經 and *Hou-ch'u Shou-lêng-yen ching* 後出首楞嚴經, translated in Ssŭ-chuan, under the Ts'ao Wei (220–265 C.E.), by one or several persons unknown.

These two translations are mentioned for the first time in the *Ch'u* and later catalogues:

1. *Ch'u*, T 2145, p.32*b* 2–3: *Shu Shou-lêng-yen ching*, two chüan. Mentioned in the *Chiu lu*. Seems to come from Shu (Ssŭ-chuan) territory. *Hou-ch'u Shou-lêng-yen ching*, two chüan. Mentioned in the *Chiu lu*: it is said that it contains ten gāthās.

2. *Chung* A, T 2146, p.119*c* 8–9: *Shu Shou-lêng-yen ching*, two chüan. *Hou-ch'u Shou-lêng-yen ching*, two chüan.

3. *Li*, T 2034, p.78*a* 12–13: [After having listed the seven translations of the Śgs, including that by Kumārajīva, the *Li* adds]: There are two further works, the *Shou* and the *Hou-ch'u*.

4. *Nei*, T 2149, p.231*a* 14–15 (see also p.252*c* 22): *Shu Shou-lêng-yen ching*, two chüan. See the *Chiu lu*. Seems to come from Shu (Ssŭ-chuan) territory. *Hou-ch'u Shou-lêng-yen ching*, two chüan. See the *Chiu lu*; it is said that it contains ten gāthās.

5. *T'u*, T 2151, p.352*c* 10: *Shu Shou-lêng-yen ching*, two chüan. *Hou-ch'u Shou-lêng-yen ching*, two chüan.

6. *Wu*, T 2153, p.398*a* 13–16: *Shu Shou-lêng-yen ching*, a work in two chüan. *Hou-ch'u Shou-lêng-yen ching*, a work in two chüan. Translated under the Wei (220–265) and Ch'i dynasties.

7. *K'ai*, T 2154, p.491*c* 11–12: *Shu Shou-lêng-yen ching*, two chüan. See the *Chiu lu*. Seems to come from Shu (Ssŭ-chuan) territory. It is the third translation. *Hou-ch'u Shou-lêng-yen ching*, two chüan. See the *Chiu lu*; it is said that it contains ten gāthās. It is the fourth translation.

8. *Ch'êng*, T 2157, p.789*a* 7–8: repeats the above. *Ibid*., p.965*c* 18–19: *Shu Shou-lêng-yen ching*, two chüan. Seems to come from Shu (Ssŭ-chuan) territory. Under the Ts'ao Wei (220–265), the translation was lost. It is the second translation. *Hou-ch'u Shou-lêng-yen ching*, two chüan. Under the Ts'ao Wei the translation was lost. It is the second translation.

Obviously, the authors of these catalogues never had access to these two translations. They got their information from the *Chiu lu* 舊錄; this is undoubtedly a matter of an 'old catalogue', not otherwise defined, and not that *Chiu lu* which would have been the catalogue of Buddhist books prior to Ch'in Shih-huang-ti, seen by Liu Hsiang in the first century C.E. In reality this *Chiu lu* was drawn up in its final form in the fifth century, after 435, and was lost by the end of the sixth century (cf. *Li*, T 2034, p.127*c* 1; *Nei,* T 2149, p.336*b* 14–17; *K'ai,* T 2154, p.572*c* 8–11).

According to the old catalogue mentioned here, these two translations contained ten gāthās. However, no stanzas appeared in the Sanskrit original of the Śgs translated in the fifth century by Kumārajīva. Notwithstanding, the Tibetan version executed in the ninth century by Śākyaprabha and Ratnarakṣita contains two long series of stanzas (see below, § 21, n.43, and § 178, n.356).

IV

Shou-lêng-yen ching or *Fang-têng* 方等 *Shou-lêng-yen ching* 'Śūraṃgamasamādhisūtra of the Vaipulya class', re-issue of the version by Chih Ch'an revised in Wu-ch'ang between 222 and 229 C.E. by Chih Ch'ien 支謙 (alias Kung-ming 恭明, or Chih Yüeh 支越) of the Eastern Wu.

This is not a new translation but merely a revision of the translation by Chih Ch'an. Chih Min-tu is categorical on this point. I have already mentioned above (p.61) his 'Record of the combined Śūraṃgamasūtras' dating from 301 C.E. and reproduced in the *Ch'u*. After having pointed out the old translation of the Śgs by Chih Ch'an, it continues (*Ch'u,* T 2145, ch.7, p.49*a* 22-*b*8):

> [After Chih Ch'an], there was also [Chih Ch'ien] or Chih Yüeh, cognomen Kung-ming. He was a Yüeh-chih as well. His father had also, in the reign of Ling-ti (168–189) of the Han, come to China to pay tribute, and Yüeh was born in China. It appears he did not see [Chih] Ch'an. But there was still Chih Liang 支亮, known as Chi-ming 紀明, who had studied under [Chih] Ch'an; it is thus that Yüeh could receive his instruction from [Chih] Liang.
>
> The talent and knowledge of Yüeh were profound and perspicacious; he completely penetrated Buddhist and non-Buddhist texts. At that time, style was esteemed and, sometimes, conciseness was appreciated. This is why in the sūtras he translated he follows the elegance of style quite well. Nevertheless, in the composition and analysis of ideas, although elegant, he does not go beyond the original and, although concise, he renders the ideas with truth. It can be said that he penetrates the text deeply.
>
> On the fall of the Han, troubles broke out and he fled to the Wu in the south. From the *huang-wu* period (222–229) until the *chien-hsing* period (252–254), the sūtras he translated together make up several tens of chüan. There is a catalogue with a separate biography which also says that [Yüeh] translated this [*Shou-lêng-yen*] *ching*, but at present we do not see that this could have been a different text [from the old translation by Chih Ch'an]. The *Shou-lêng-yen* [by Yüeh] does indeed present some small peculiarities with regard to the prolixity or concision of sentences, the Chinese or barbaric character of expression. I have compared and examined [the two translations]: one cannot say that these are two distinct translations ascribed to different men. I think that Yüeh condemned a mode of expression full of barbaric terms in the translation by [Chih] Ch'an. The divergencies [between the two translations] are deletions or corrections [due to Yüeh]; the points they have in common are a reproduction without change [of the version by Chih Ch'an]. The two texts each have a preface. The version which, among all the others, has the simplest and easiest terminology, uses the least barbaric terms and is widespread throughout the world, is the revised version by Yüeh.

So for Chih Min-tu, Yüeh, otherwise known as Chih Ch'ien, limited himself to revising the old translation of the Śgs by Chih Ch'an. However, later catalogues classified this revision as if it were a new translation:

1. *Ch'u*, T 2145, p.7*a* 17: *Shou-lêng-yen ching*, two chüan. Mentioned in the *Pieh lu*. The catalogue by [Tao]-an does not have it. Lost at present.

2. *Ch'ung* A, T 2146, p.119*c* 2: *Shou-lêng-yen ching*, two chüan. Translated by Chih Ch'ien of the Wu dynasty.

3. and 4. *Li*, T 2034, p.57*b* 7; *Nei,* T 2149, p.228*a* 9: *Fang-têng Shou-lêng-yen ching*. This is the second translation dating from the *huang-wu* years (222–229). Differs a little from the translation by Chih Ch'an of the Late Han. See the *Wu lu* by Chu Tao-tsu. The catalogue by [Tao]-an does not have it. [Sêng]-yu (T 2145) refers to the *Pieh lu*.

5. *T'u*, T 2151, p.351*b* 28–29: *Fang-têng Shou-lêng-yen ching*, two chüan.

6. *K'ai*, T 2154, p.488*c* 23: *Fang-têng Shou-lêng-yen ching*, two chüan. Translated during the *huang-wu* years (222–229). It is the second translation. The original was identical to that already translated by Chih Ch'an of the Late Han. See the *Wu lu* by Chu Tao-tsu. It does not appear in the catalogue by [Tao]-an. [Sêng]-yu (T2145) does not have the characters *Fang-têng* [in the title]; he refers to the *Pieh lu*.

This translation cites two old catalogues, already lost by the time of the *Li-tai san-pao chi*:

1. The *Pieh lu*. The *Pieh lu* in question could be an abbreviation of *Chung ching pieh lu*, a catalogue which was considered to date from the Sung between 420 and 478 (cf. *Li*, T 2034, p.125*b* 28), but the title more probably refers to the second of two catalogues compiled by Chih Min-tu at the monastery of Yü-chang shan (in Chiang-hsi) in the reign of Ch'êng-ti (326–342), namely the *Ching lun tu lu* in one chüan, and the *Pieh lu*, equally in one chüan (cf. *Li*, T 2034, p.74*a* 8–9; *Nei*, T 2149, p.336*c* 23–25; *K'ai*, T 2154, p.573*a* 14–17).

2. The *Chung ching mu lu*, a catalogue, or rather series of catalogues, classed according to various periods or regions (Wei,

Wu, Chin and Ho-hsi), begun on Mount Lu by a disciple of Hui-yüan, Tao-liu, and after the premature death of the latter, completed in 419 by the disciple Tao-tsu (cf. *Kao*, T 2059, p.363*a* 11–12; *Li*, T 2034, p.127*c* 4; *Nei*, T 2149, p.336*c* 16–22; *K'ai*, T 2154, p.573*a* 11–13).

It is quite believable that the version of the Śgs revised by Chih Ch'ien appeared in the bibliographical lists by Chih Min-tu. Tao-an, who was still living in the north when these were compiled, does not seem to have known of them. This is why Chih Ch'ien's version is not mentioned in his *Tsung-li chung-ching mu lu*, compiled, in 374, in Hsiang-yang in northern Hu-pei.

Chih Ch'ien, grandson of the Yüeh-chean Fa-tu, was born in China. A Buddhist layman (*upāsaka*), he received his religious instruction in Lo-yang from Chih Liang, himself a disciple of Chih Ch'an (Lokakṣema). In 220 C.E., the collapse of the Old Empire of the Han led to the formation of the Three Kingdoms (220–280): the Empire of the Wei (220–264) in the Yellow River basin, the Empire of the Shu (221–263) in Ssŭ-chuan and the Empire of the Wu (222–280) in the Blue River basin. The troubles which broke out in Lo-yang about 219 led Chih Ch'ien to seek refuge in the south; he crossed the Yang-tzê and went to the court of the Marquis of Wu, Sun Ch'üan, then in conflict with the Wei. During the *huang-wu* period (222–229), he stayed in Wu-ch'ang. There he met the Sogdian monk K'ang Sêng-hui and, in 224, the two Indian masters Wei-ch'i-nan (Vighna) and Chu Chiang-yen (variant, Lü-yen). During this period, Chih Ch'ien translated the Vimalakīrtinirdésa and the Śūraṃgamasamādhi. In 229 the Marquis of Wu, Sun Ch'üan, took the title of emperor and moved his capital to Chien-yeh (Nanking). Chih Ch'ien followed him there and, in his capacity as *po-shih* 'master of immense knowledge', was charged with the instruction of the imperial heir Sun Têng, in collaboration with the head preceptor Wei Yao (or Wei Shao). On the death of his pupil in 241, Chih Ch'ien retired to Mount Ch'iung-lu, in Chiang-su, where he met the monk Chu Fa-lan. Begun in 222, his literary activity continued until 253 and was prolific. The *Ch'u* attributes to him 27 or 36 translations (T 2145, pp.97*c* 11, and 7*a* 23); the *Kao*, 49 (T 2059, p.325*b* 2); the *Li* and the *Nei*, 129 (T 2034, p.58*c*

14; T 2149, p.229*b* 27); the *K'ai*, 88 (T 2154, p.489*b* 1); only the rich obtain credit! Chih Ch'ien also composed three books of Sanskrit hymns in praise of the Bodhisattva, as well as a commentary upon the Śālistambasūtra. He died on Mount Ch'iung-lu, aged sixty. When this occurred the Wu emperor, Sun Liang, sent a letter of condolence to the monks.

The details given here are taken from the notice on Chih Ch'ien included in the *Ch'u* (T 2145, ch.13, p.97*b* 13-*c* 18). Here is its translation, completed here and there by the *Kao-sêng chuan* (T 2059, pp.325*a* 18–326*b* 4):

> Chih Ch'ien 支謙, cognomen Kung-ming 恭明 and also called Yüeh 越, was a great Yüeh-chih. His paternal grandfather Fa-tu 法度, in the reign of Ling-ti (168–189) of the Han, had brought several hundreds of his compatriots to embrace the Chinese civilisation, and the emperor had named him *Shuai-shan chung-lang-chiang* 率善中郎將 'Colonel leading the good'.
>
> When he was seven years old, Yüeh was playing astride a bamboo horse at a neighbours. He was bitten by the dog and a bone in his leg was broken. The neighbour wanted to kill the dog and take its liver to dress the wound. Yüeh said: 'Heaven produced this being for men, so as to guard them and bark. If I had not come to your house, the dog would not have bitten me. In all this, the fault devolves on me and does not concern the dog. To kill it would be a mistake. Not only is it forbidden, but it would be futile and you would be uselessly committing a grave offence. Furthermore, animals are deprived of reasoning, so how could one reprimand them through arguments?' As a result of that, several tens of villagers, moved by his words, stopped killing living beings.
>
> At the age of ten he learned to write, and his co-disciples deferred to the liveliness of his intelligence. At the age of thirteen, he learned the barbarian writings and completely mastered the tongues of the Six Countries.
>
> To begin with, in the reigns of Huan (146–168) and Ling (168–189), Chih Ch'ien translated religious texts. Then Chih Liang 支亮, cognomen Chi-ming 紀明, studied under [Chih] Ch'an. Finally, [Chih] Ch'ien received his instruction from [Chih] Liang and read the classical texts widely. There was nothing he had not examined in depth. He was practised in the secular professions and arts.
>
> He was a slender, tall, dark and slight man. His eyes were very

white and his pupils yellow. His contemporaries said of him: 'Mister Chih has yellow pupils; although he is slight in build, he is a bagful of knowledge'. From the very beginning, he revered the Great Dharma and skilfully mastered the import of the texts.

At the end of the reign of Hsien-ti (190–219), the Han family underwent great confusion. Along with several tens of villagers, Yüeh fled to the Wu. On the day of his departure he had only one coverlet. A guest who was very cold and had no coverlet followed him. Yüeh invited the guest to sleep with him. On the dot of midnight, the guest took the coverlet and went off. Next day Yüeh's companions asked where the coverlet was. Yüeh replied: 'Last night it was taken from me by the guest'. His companions said to him: 'Why not denounce him?' Yüeh replied: 'If I denounce him, the villagers will certainly accuse him of theft. Would it be just to kill a man for a single coverlet?' From far and near, those who heard him all admired him.

Later, the sovereign of the Wu, Sun Ch'üan (229–252), heard of his immense knowledge, capabilities and wisdom; immediately, he summoned him to his court. He questioned him on the profound and hidden meaning (in certain passages) of the sūtras. Answering on each occasion, Yüeh explained the difficult points and there was no doubt that he was unhesitating. Most satisfied, [Sun] Ch'üan named him *po-shih* 博士 'master of immense knowledge', charged him with the instruction of the imperial heir and covered him with favours and high position. [With Wei Yao 韋曜 (alias Wei Chao 韋昭 (200–273), the head preceptor) and others, Yüeh thus rendered services to the kingdom of the Wu. However, because of his foreign origin, he was not registered in the Wu Annals.]

Yüeh knew that, despite the progress of the Great Teaching, the sūtras were mostly in a foreign language and that nobody understood them. Since he knew Chinese and Sanskrit, he assembled some works and translated them into the language of the Han. From the first *huang-wu* (222–229) year until the middle of the *chieng-hsing* period (252–254), the texts translated by him – *Wei-mo-chieh* (T 474: Vimalakīrtinirdeśa), *Ta pan-ni-yüan* (Mahāparinirvāṇa), *Fa-chü* (T 210: Dharmapada), *Jui-ying-pên-ch'i* (T 185: *Kumārarāja-pūrvanimmittāvadāna), etc. – number twenty-seven (forty-nine, according to the *Kao-sêng chuan*). He renders the sacred meaning deftly; the terms and tenor are elegant.

Furthermore, on the basis of the *Wu-liang-shou* (T 362: Sukhāvatīvyūha) and the *Chung-pên-ch'i ching* (T 196), he composed three books of Sanskrit hymns in rhythmic phrases in praise of the Bodhisattva. He commented upon the *Liao pên shêng ssŭ ching* (T 708: Śālistambasūtra). All these books are in circulation at present.

Later, the imperial heir [Sun] Têng 孫登 died (241), and Yüeh retired to Mount Ch'iung-lung 穹隆 (to the south-west of Wu-hsien 吳縣 in Chiang-su) where he joined the monk Chu Fa-lan 竺法蘭 and continued to practise the five precepts (of laymen). All those he frequented were śramaṇas. Then, he died on the mountain, aged sixty years.

The sovereign of the Wu, Sun Liang 孫亮 (252–258), in a letter addressed to the monks, wrote: 'Chih Kung-ming did not cure diseases, but his actions were of undiluted purity; from the beginning until the end, he was great. The regret we have for him is unbearable'. Such was the sadness that was felt at the time.

V

Shou-lêng-yên ching, two chüan, translated in Lo-yang, at the Po-ma ssŭ, in 258 C.E. by Po Yen 白 [variant 帛] 延 of the Wei.

The information is fragmentary and contradictory.

1. *Ch'u*, T 2145, p.7*b* 2–6: *Shou-lêng-yen ching*, in two chüan: lost; *Hsü-lai ching* (T 328: Surataparipṛcchā), in one chüan: lost; *Ch'u-tsai-huan ching* 'Sūtra averting calamities', in one chüan: lost. These three works together forming four chüan were translated by Po Yen at the time of Kao Kuei-[hsiang] kung (254–260) of the Wei. They are mentioned in the *Pieh lu*. The catalogue by [Tao]-an kung, previously, did not have this name.

Ibid., p.96*a* 27–28 (notice on An Hsüan): As for Po Yen, it is not known who he was. At the end of the *chêng-shih* period (240–249) of the Wei, he again translated the *Shou-lêng-yen* and, furthermore, the *Hsü-lai* and the *Ch'u-tsai-huan ching*: in all, three works.

2. *Kao*, T 2059, p.325*a* 10–12 (notice on Dharmakāla): There was also the śramaṇa Po Yen. It is not known who he was. He too possessed talent and profound and penetrating intelligence. In the middle of the *kan-lu* period (256–260) of the Wei, he translated the *Wu liang ching ch'ing p'ing têng chüeh ching*, etc.: in all, six works.

Nothing is known of his death.

3. *Chung* A, T 2146, p.119*c* 3: *Shou-lêng-yen ching*, two chüan, translated by Po Yen of the Wei Dynasty.

4 and 5. *Li*, T 2034, p.56*c* 8; *Nei*, T 2149, p.227*a* 12, noting six translations: *Shou-lêng-yen ching*, in two chüan. This is the second (variant: third) translation. Compared with the translation by Chih Ch'an of the Han dynasty, the [Sanskrit] original was the same, but the translation differs slightly. See the *Chin shih tsa lu* by Chu Tao-tsu and the *Chu san tsang chi* (T 2145)... The six translated works make up eight chüan. In the reign of Kao Kuei-hsiang kung (254–260), the śramaṇa Po Yen of the Western Countries embraced the Path and departed on a tour of conversion. During the *kan-lu* years (256–260), he reached Lo-yang and stayed at the Po-ma ssŭ where the Saṃgha invited him to translate.

6. *T'u*, T 2151, p.351*b* 8–10: The śramaṇa Po Yen, a native of the Western Countries, in the reign of Kao Kuei-hsiang kung (254–260) in the year three of the *kan-lu* period, *ting-sh'ou* (error for *wu-yin*: 258) cycle, in Lo-yang, at the Po-ma ssŭ, translated the *Shou-lêng-yen ching* in two chüan... : in all, six works in eight chüan.

7. *Wu*, T 2153, p.397*c* 21–23: *Shou-lêng-yen ching*, a work in two chüan. This is the second translation. Translated during the *kan-lu* years (256–260) of the Ts'ao Wei by Po Yen, in Lo-yang, at the Po-ma ssŭ. Extract from the catalogue by [Fei] Chang-fang (T 2034).

8. *K'ai*, T 2154, pp.487*a* 20, 632*a* 6: Notes five translations among which is the *Shou-lêng-yen ching*, in two chüan. This is the fifth translation. Compared with the translation by Chih Ch'an of the Han, etc., the Sanskrit original was the same but the translation is different. See the *Chih shih tsa lu* by Chu Tao-tsu and the catalogue by Sêng-yu (T 2145). These five works in seven chüan are lost. The śramaṇa Po Yen, a native of the Western Countries, during the reign of Kai Kuei-hsiang kung (254–260) in the year three of the *kan-lu* period, *wu-yin* cycle (258), departed on a tour of conversion, reached Lo-yang and settled at the Po-ma ssŭ.

As his name indicates, Po Yen must have been a Kuchean and have belonged to the royal family. We know in fact that the royal dynasty of Kucha was called Po from the beginning of the Common Era. The sources, as we have just seen, hesitate over the exact date of his literary activity: the *chêng-shih* period (240–249) or the *kan-lu* period (256–260) of the Wei.

His translation of the Śgs, if it ever existed, had no influence, as will be seen later (p86) and in contradiction to the assertion by certain catalogues, Chih Min-tu did not use it in his combined edition of the Śgs in 301, and Tao-an does not mention it at all in his catalogue from 374. The catalogues from the sixth and seventh centuries which have come down to us learned of his existence from two catalogues from the fifth century: the *Chin shih* by Chu Tao-tsu from 419, and the *Pieh lu* of the Sung (420–478), already lost by their time. Obviously, all these bibliographers never had access to the three, six or seven translations which they attribute to Po Yen and which they all declare to be lost. However, in T 328 we find a translation of the Surataparipṛcchā attributed to Po Yen. There is perhaps a confusion between the Po Yen of the Wei of the third century and the Po Yen of the Ch'ien Liang of the fourth who will be mentioned below (p.90).

VI

***Yung-fu-ting ching* 勇伏定經 'Sūtra of the Concentration (*samādhi*) of Heroic Victory (*śūraṃgama*)', two chüan, translated, probably in Ch'ang-an, on 23 May 291 C.E. by Chu Fa-hu 竺法護 (Dharmarakṣa) of the Hsi Chin.**

In this work, the title of the sūtra, *Śūraṃgamasamādhi,* instead of being transcribed as *Shou-lêng-yen* as previously, is translated by *Yung-fu-ting* 'Concentration of Heroic Victory'[6].

The translation by Dharmarakṣa is accompanied by a notice (*chi*) or a colophon (*hou chi*) which Chih Min-tu reproduces in the preface to his combined edition of the Śgs dating from 301 (cf. *Ch'u*, T 2145, p.49*b* 15–17) and which the *K'ai* (T 2154, p.632*a* 11–12) also quotes:

> The notice on the *Yung-fu-ting* says: On the ninth day of the fourth month of the first *yün-k'ang* year (23 May 291), the bodhisattva from Tun-huang, Chih Fa-hu (Dharmarakṣa) held the foreign text in his hands and orally translated the Śūraṃgamasamādhi. Nieh Ch'êng-yüan took it down with his brush.

In the same preface (*Ch'u*, T 2145, p.49*b* 7–9), Chih Min-tu also says:

[6] The Lalitavistara (ed. S. Lefmann, p.442, *8-9*) mentions the Śūraṃgamasamādhi. In his Chinese translation of the Lalitavistara (T 186, ch.8, p.537*c* 2), Dharmarakṣa renders *śūraṃgamasamādhi* by *yung-fu-ting*. Divākara, in another translation of the same text (T 187, ch.12, p.616*c* 21) transcribes *shou-lêng-yen san-mei*.

At the beginning of the Great Chin dynasty (265–316), the śramaṇa Chih Fa-hu (Dharmarakṣa) and the upāsaka Chu Shu-lan again translated this [Śūraṃgamasamādhi]-sūtra. For whoever seeks the meaning, the two translations clarify each other.

Here now is the information supplied on this *Yung-fu-ting* by the catalogues of the sixth and seventh centuries:

1. *Ch'u*, T 2145, p.9*a* 1: *Yung-fu-ting ching*, two chüan. [Tao]-an kung says that it is another translation of the *Shou-lêng-yen,* made on the ninth day of the fourth month of the first *yün-k'ang* year (23 May 291).

Ibid., p.14*a* 15: Chu Fa-hu once again translated the *Yung-fu-ting* in two chüan which is a new translation of the *Shou-lêng-yen.*

2. *Chung* A, T 2146, p.119*c* 5: *Yung-fu-ting*, two chüan. Translated by Chu Fa-hu during the [first] *yün-k'ang* year (291) of the Chin.

3 and 4. *Li*, T 2034, p.62*c* 11; *Nei,* T 2149, pp.233*b* 16 and 240*c* 24: *Yung-fu-ting,* two chüan. Translated on the ninth day of the fourth month of the first *yün-k'ang* year (23 May 291). This is the fourth translation. Compared with the *Shou-lêng-yen ching* translated by Chih Ch'an, Chih Ch'ien and Po Yen, the original was the same, but the title is altered and the translation slightly different. See the catalogue by Nieh Tao-chên.

5. *T'u*, T 2151, p.353*b* 17: *Yung-fu-ting ching*, two chüan.

6. *Wu*, T 2153, p.398*a* 2: *Yung-fu-ting ching*, a book in two chüan. It is the fourth translation.

7. *K'ai,* T 2154, p.495*c* 2: *Yung-fu-ting ching*, two chüan. [Tao]-an kung says that it is another translation of the *Shou-lêng-yen* made on the ninth day of the fourth month of the first *yün-k'ang* year (23 May 291). Nieh Ch'êng-yüan received it with his brush. It is the sixth translation. See the two catalogues by [Nieh] Tao-chên and Sêng-yu (T 2145). The two catalogues by [Sêng]-yu (T 2145) and [Chang]-fang (T 2034) also mention a *Shou-lêng-yen* [which would have been translated by Chu Fa-hu], but it is a mistake.

The *Yung-fu-ting* by Dharmarakṣa is therefore fully authenticated: it is mentioned in the notice dated 291 which was added to it, in the preface by Chih Min-tu to the combined edition of the Śūraṃgamasamādhi dating from 301, in the catalogue by Nieh Tao-chên compiled between 307 and 312 and in the catalogue by Tao-an completed in 374.

Dharmarakṣa published it on 23 May 291 in Ch'ang-an, a few years before his translation of the Vimalakīrtinirdeśa which dates from the first day of the fourth month of the second *t'ai-an* year, i.e. 3 May 303 (cf. *Li,* T 2034, p.63*c* 9; *K'ai,* T 2154, p.495*b* 16–17).

The life of Chu Fa-hu (Dharmarakṣa) is known through two biographical notices contained in the *Ch'u* (T 2145, ch.13, pp.97*c* 19-98*a* 20) and the *Kao-sêng chuan* (T 2059, ch.1, p.326*c* 2–27). Here is the translation:

> Chu Fa-hu. His ancestors were Yüeh-chih and, for generations, had inhabited the cantonment of Tun-huang.
>
> At the age of eight, he left home and took as his master a foreign śramaṇa, an Indian of high class (*chu kao-tsu*). He recited the sūtras at the rate of ten thousand words a day and understood them at first sight. His character was good and his conduct ascetic. He sincerely and resolutely liked studying and sought his teachers within a radius of ten thousand li. He widely read the (Confucian) Six Classics and was fully conversant with the words of the Hundred Schools (of Chinese philosophy). [*Kao*: he widely read the Six Classics and mastered the Seven Books]. Even if people criticised him, he attached no importance to it.
>
> This was then during the reign of Wu-ti (265–290) of the Chin. Monasteries, temples, stūpas and images were in fashion in the capital (Lo-yang), but the profound Vaipulya sūtras were confined to the Western Countries [*Kao*: beyond the Mount of Onions]. Fa-hu deplored this and was much grieved by it. He resolved to propagate the Great Dharma. [*Kao*: he followed his masters to the Western Countries], and travelled through all the kingdoms one by one. Altogether, he studied the thirty-six tongues of the foreign Countries as well as their books; he understood and penetrated them. Phonetics, semantics, forms of characters, there was nothing he did not know fully. Bringing foreign texts in great numbers, he returned to China.
>
> From Tun-huang to Ch'ang-an, all along the way, he transmitted, translated and wrote in the language of the Chin.
>
> The sūtras of the Great and Small Vehicles which he had procured – *Hsien-chieh* (T 425: Bhadrakalpika), *Ta-ai* (T 398: Tathāgatamahākaruṇānirdésa), *Fa-hua* (T 263: Saddharmapuṇḍarīka), *P'u-yao* (T 186: Lalitavistara), etc. – in all numbered 149 works. [*Kao*: the

texts which he obtained and read – *Chêng-fa hua* (T 263: Saddharmapuṇḍarīka), *Kuang tsan* (T 222: Pañcaviṃśatisāhasrikā p.p.), etc., – numbered 165 works.] He devoted himself assiduously to this task in order to know them in depth. All his life he translated and wrote, without sparing any effort. If the teaching of the sūtras was widespread throughout China, this is due to [Fa]-hu.

At the end of the reign of Wu (265–290) of the Chin, he retired to a high mountain. On this mountain there was a limpid stream. He regularly took water from it in order to wash. One day someone who was collecting fuel impolitely fouled the bank, and the water immediately dried up. [Fa]-hu, walking up and down, sighed and said: '[*Kao*: If man is without virtue, the limpid spring stops flowing.] The water has definitely dried up and I will find no more of it. I shall have to go elsewhere'. He had just finished speaking when the spring again began to run to overflowing. Such were the consequences of his deep sincerity.

[*Kao*: This is why Chih Tun 支遁, on drawing his portrait, addressed him with the following eulogy:

> The noble [Fa]-hu is serene and tranquil;
> His teaching and virtues are of profound beauty.
> A gentle sigh from the lofty vale,
> And the dried-up spring gushes with water.
>
> Oh! Admirable [Fa]-hu;
> His bearing is as exalted as Heaven:
> He bathes his feet in the Shifting Sands,
> But his head has pierced the sublimities of the Mysterious.]

Later, he founded a monastery in Ch'ang-an, outside the Ch'ing Gate, and there he practised the Way assiduously. Thence his virtues and wonders spread in the four directions and his reputation covered the distances. Several thousands of disciples came to revere him.

At that time, there was the śramana Chu Fa-ch'êng 竺法乘[7]. Aged eight, he was intelligent and wise. He took [Fa]-hu as his master. Now there was in Kuan-chung a noble family who, on the point of embracing the Great Dharma, wanted to test [Fa]-hu's teaching and virtues. The head of the family went to him with the purpose of

[7] After having lived in Ch'ang-an with his master, Fa-ch'eng went to Tun-huang, Dharmarakṣa's native land, and founded a monastery there. It is thanks to him that Buddhist civilisation reached the west of China: 'He changed the hearts of wolves and taught the rites to the Barbarians' (cf. Ch'u, T 2145, p.98a; Kao, T 2059, p.347b-c).

> asking him urgently for 200,000 sapeks. [Fa]-hu had not yet answered when [Fa]-ch'êng, then aged thirteen, and who was at his master's side, immediately said to the visitor: 'My upādhyāya has already consented mentally'. The visitor having withdrawn, [Fa]-ch'êng said: 'Considering the expression of that man, he did not really come to look for money but to examine the degree of the teaching and virtues of the upādhyāya'. [Fa]-hu said: 'I think so too'. The next day the visitor, bringing all his family of more than one hundred persons with him, came in search of [Fa]-hu and asked to be given the Five Precepts. He thanked him for being open to the request for money. Then the literati and the people of the four corners of the world, learning the news, came and assembled. He taught the Buddha's new teaching for more than twenty years.
>
> When Hui-[ti] (290–307) of the Chin fled to the west, disorder reigned in Kuan-chung and the whole population moved away. Then [Fa]-hu and his disciples withdrew and went down to the east as far as Min-ch'ih 澠池 (near Lo-yang). He fell ill and died at the age of seventy-eight years.

Dharmarakṣa left behind him a considerable number of works: 154 translations according to Tao-an (*Ch'u*, T 2145, p.9*b* 28), 149 according to the notice in the *Ch'u* (T 2145, p.98*a* 2), 165 according to the *Kao* (T 2059, p.326*c* 13), 210 according to the *Li* (T 2034, p.64*c* 14), and 175 according to the *K'ai* (T 2154, p.496*c* 7).

Some colophons added to these translations have been reproduced by the *Ch'u* (T 2145) in chüan eight and nine. E. Zürcher (*Buddhist Conquest*, p.343, n.221) has analysed them in detail and shown that the periods of Dharmarakṣa's greatest activity were from 284 to 288 and from 291 to 297 C.E. Of the sixteen translations that the colophons enable us to locate and date, nine were made in Ch'ang-an during the years 266, 286, 291, 297, 300 and 308; two in Tun-huang in 284; three in Lo-yang in 289 and 290; and finally, two in Chiu-ch'uan 酒泉 (in central Kan-su) in 294.

The passage from the *Ch'u* (T 2145, p.14*a* 15–18) translated above (p.57) clearly shows that its author Sêng-yu only attributed to Dharmarakṣa a single translation of the Śūraṃgamasamādhi, a translation entitled *Yung-fu-ting* and not *Shou-lêng-yen* like those of his predecessors. However, in his list of the works of Dharmarakṣa, Sêng-yu attributes to the latter two translations of the Śūraṃgamasamādhi, one entitled *Shou-lêng-yen* (T 2145, p.7*c* 5) and the other *Yung-fu-ting* (p.9*a* 1). This is only an inadvertent mistake and quite excusable if one thinks of the many documents that Sêng-yu had to check. Unfortunately, this mistake was reproduced in subsequent catalogues which, with one exception, credit Dharmarakṣa with a *Shou-lêng-yen* along with a *Yung-fu-ting*. Here are the references :

1. *Ch'u*, T 2145, p.7*c* 5: *Shou-lêng-yen ching*, two chüan. Another translation entitled *A-nan yen* 'Words of Ānanda'.

2. *Chung* A, T 2146, p.119*c* 4: *Shou-lêng-yen ching*, two chüan. Translated by Chu Fa-hu of the Chin dynasty.

3 and 4. *Li,* T 2034, p.62*c* 1; *Nei,* T 2149, pp.233*b* 6 and 240*c* 15: *Shou-lêng-yen ching*, two chüan. Another translation also exists. *Shou-lêng-yen* known as *A-nan yen* 'Words of Ānanda'.

5. *T'u,* T 2151, p.353*b* 14: *Shou-lêng-yen ching*, two chüan.

6. *Wu*, T 2153, p.397*c* 29: *Shou-lêng-yen ching*, a work in two chüan. Translated by Chu Fa-hu of the Chin Dynasty. Extract from the catalogue by Chang-fang (T 2034).

It was only in 795 that the error was corrected by Chih-shêng in his particularly carefully compiled catalogue from the *k'ai-yüan* era:

> *K'ai,* T 2154, p.632*a* 10–14: Between *Shou-lêng-yen* 'Śūraṃgama' and *Yung-fu-ting* 'Concentration of Heroic Victory', the titles, respectively in Sanskrit and the Chinese of the Chin, alone differ; there are not two different sūtras. The colophon of the *Yung-fu-ting* says: 'On the ninth day of the fourth month of the first *yüan-k'ang* year (23 May 291), the bodhisattva from Tun-huang, Chu Fa-hu, held the Sanskrit text in his hands and orally translated the *Shou-lêng-yen ching*. The upāsaka Nieh Ch'êng-yüan took it down with his brush'. Hence it is proved that the *Shou-lêng-yen* and the *Yung-fu-ting* are not two separate things.

I think we must side with this verdict, but another explanation is possible. Dharmarakṣa himself could have drafted a translation of the Śūraṃgamasamādhi with the title of *Shou-lêng-yen* and then have submitted it to his many Chinese friends, particularly his devoted collaborator Nieh Ch'êng-yüan. The latter, a fine scholar, could not only have taken it down with his brush but could also have reviewed and corrected it and given it a new title, no longer transcribed from the Indian but translated into Chinese: *Yung-fu-ting.*

This is more or less what happened with the Sūryaprabhāsamatikrāntasamādhi which, with the title of *Ch'ao jih-ming ching*, was translated by Dharmarakṣa (*Ch'u*, T 2145, p.8*c* 15) then revised by Nieh Ch'êng-yüan (*ibid.*, p.9*c* 5–7). Only the revised translation has come down to us (T 638). The notices concerning Dharmarakṣa in the *Ch'u* (T 2145, p.98*a* 23) and the *Kao* (T 2059, p.327*a* 1) explain:

> There lived at the time of [Fa-hu], the upāsaka Nieh Ch'êng-yüan 聶承遠, an intelligent and gifted man who was resolved to serve the Dharma. When the venerable [Fa-]hu translated sūtras, Ch'êng-yüan suggested many phrases in correct style to him. Thus, in the first translation of the *Ch'ao jih-ming* there was a certain amount of repetition and clumsiness. Ch'êng-yüan clarified and corrected the style and the gāthās and condensed the translation into two chüan; this is the two-chüan edition which is circulating at present. The other revisions carried out by him are all of the same type.

Commentary on the *Yung-fu-ting*, compiled in Ch'ang-an between 291 and 306 C.E. by Po Yüan 帛遠, cognomen Po Fa-tsu 帛法祖, of the Western Chin.

Whether revised or not by Nieh Ch'êng-yüan, the *Yung-fu-ting* by Dharmarakṣa was highly successful and was soon commented upon by the scholar-monk Po Yüan (cf. *Ch'u*, T 2145, p.107, note 37; *Kao*, T 2059, p.327*b* 28).

Po Yüan[8] was the son of a Confucian scholar Wan Wei-ta 萬威達, a native of Ho-nei 河內, in northern Ho-nan. Having entered the Buddhist Order, Po Yüan founded a monastery and a school in Ch'ang-an to which flocked nearly a thousand disciples, both monks and laymen. His literary activity took place during the reign of the emperor Hui-ti (290–307): he published a commentary upon the *Yung-fu-ting* by Dharmarakṣa, with whom he was undoubtedly acquainted, and he made about twenty translations of which five have come down to us (T 5, 144, 330, 528 and 777).

In 304, the prince of Ho-chien 河間 and prime minister, Ssŭ-ma Yung 司馬顒, expelled the puppet emperor Hui-ti and entrenched himself in Ch'ang-an with members of the high aristocracy. Po Yüan

8 Regarding Po Yüan, cognomen Fa-tsu 法祖, see E. Zürcher, *Buddhist Conquest*, pp.76-7.

became a friend of his and, in the quiet of the evenings, the two men discussed 'the Way and Virtue' together.

As the political situation continued to worsen, Po-Yüan, like so many others, particularly Dharmarakṣa, was forced to leave the capital. He fled to the west in the company of Chang Fu 張輔 who was appointed governor of Ch'in-chou 秦州, a town located to the east of Tun-huang. The governor, who very much admired him, requested him to leave the robe and enter his service. Po Yüan refused absolutely. The quarrel became aggravated and, once they had reached the sub-prefecture of Ch'ien 汧, Po Yüan was thrown into prison and died under the lash.

A legend set down in the *Kao* (T 2059, p.327*b* 16–18) throws light on Po Yüan's devotion to the Śūraṃgamasamādhi:

> A short while after [Po Yüan's death], there was a man whose family name was Li 李 and first name T'ung 通 who died and came back to life. He said he had seen the dharmācārya [Fa]-tsu (alias Po Yüan) in the dwelling of Yama, king [of the hells], expounding the Śūraṃgamasūtra to the king. Po Yüan declared that after giving this teaching he had to go to the Trāyastriṃśa gods.

VII

Shou-lêng-yen ching, two chüan, translated in Lo-yang in 291 C.E. by the upāsaka Chu Shu-lan 竺叔蘭 of the Western Chin.

This is again a matter of a translation made in the north, not by Serindians like Chih Ch'an, Chih Ch'ien, Po-yen and Fa-hu, but by a highly sinicised layman of Indian origin.

This translation is mentioned, in 301, by Chih Min-tu in the preface to his combined edition of the Śūraṃgamasamādhi (cf. *Ch'u,* T 2145, p.49*b* 8) and it is listed in all the catalogues that have come down to us:

> 1. *Ch'u*, T 2145, p.9*c* 13–15: *Shou-lêng-yen ching*, two chüan. It is recorded in the *Pieh lu*, but was previously missing in the catalogue by [Tao]-an. The *Chiu lu* mentions the *Shou-lêng-yen* by Chu Shu-lan in two chüan. [With the Vimalakīrtinirdeśa], this sūtra was translated under Hui-ti (290–307) of the Chin in the first *yüan-k'ang* year (291).

> 2. *Chung* A, T 2146, p.119*a* 6: *Shou-lêng-yen ching*, two chüan. Translated by Chu Shu-lan in the reign of Hui-ti of the Chin.

> 3 and 4. *Li,* T 2034, p.65*b* 28; *Nei,* T 2149, p.236*b* 29: *Shou-lêng-*

yen ching, two chüan, translated in the first *yüan-k'ang* year (291). It is the fifth translation. In relation to the translations by the two Chih [Chih Ch'an and Chih Ch'ien], Po-[yen] and Chu [Fa-hu], the translation is different but the original was the same. See the catalogue by Nieh Tao-chên. [With the Vimalakīrtinirdeśa], this sūtra was translated under Hui-ti (290–307) by the śramaṇa[9] from the Western Countries, Chu Shu-lan, in Lo-yang.

5. *T'u,* T 2151, p.354*b* 16: *Shou-lêng-yen ching*, two chüan.

6. *Wu,* T 2153, p.398*a* 8–10: *Shou-lêng-yen ching*, two chüan and thirty-six folios. Translated during the *yüan-k'ang* period (291–299) of Hui-ti of the Chin by Chu Shu-lan, in Lo-yang.

7. *K'ai,* T 2154, p.498*a* 11: *Shou-lêng-yen ching*, two chüan. Translated in the first *yüan-k'ang* year (291). It is the seventh translation. In relation to the translations by Chih Ch'an, Chih Ch'ien, Po-yen and Fa-hu the original was the same but the translation differs. See the catalogue by Nieh Tao-chên and the catalogue by Sêng-yu (T 2145).

Ka'i (T 2154, p.632*a* 13) and the *Chêng* (T 2157, pp.795*b* 3–4, 965*c* 29) insist on the fact that Chu Shu-lan was indeed an upāsaka and not a śramaṇa.

We can consider the reference to the *Chiu lu* as worthless, but Chu Shu-lan's translation is well enough guaranteed by Chih Min-tu's testimony that he used it in his combined edition of 301, and by the mention of Nieh Tao-chên who lists it in his catalogue, the *Chung Ching lu*, compiled between 307 and 312[10]. And if it is true that Tao-an passed over it in silence in his catalogue of 374, it appeared in the *Pieh lu* of the Sung.

The *Ch'u* (T 2145, p.98*b* 3–*c* 15) contains a notice on Chu Shu-lan which the *Kao-sêng chuan* (T 2059, p.346*c* 1–6) summarises in a few lines. This biography is strongly tinted with legend and partially apocryphal, but it describes the mentality and manners of the golden youth of the period so vividly that I think it worthwhile to give a translation of it:

Chu Shu-lan was of Indian origin. His grandfather Lou-t'o 婁陀

9 'Śramaṇa' is a mistake, Chu Shu-lan was an upāsaka.

10 Nieh Tao-chên was the son of Nieh Ch'êng-yüan, friend and collaborator of Dharmarakṣa. On his catalogue, the *Chung Ching lu*, see *Li*, T 2034, p.127*c* 2; *Nei*, T 2149, p.336*b* 27-29; *K'ai*, T 2154, p.572*c* 22-24.

(Rudra) sincerely and resolutely loved to study. He was of proven honesty and chaste conduct.

At that time the king of the country had no principles, and the whole population was disposed to rebel. A treacherous minister, at the head of the army, committed an offence. Afraid of being killed, he called on the nobles of the country to revolt with him. Rudra, displeased, said to him: 'You were born in a humble and lowly family but you are fulfilling an important duty. You seem unable to respond to this favour with valour. Are you planning to revolt and rebel? As for me, I prefer to die while remaining faithful than live in revolt'. The rebel, fearing that his plan would be given away, killed Rudra and started the revolution.

Rudra's son Ta-mo-shih-lo (Dharmaśira) – in Chinese 'Head of the Dharma' – was at first in another country. The two older brothers of his wife were śramaṇas. Learning that his father had just been killed and that great disorder reigned in the country, he fled to China with the two śramaṇas and took up residence in Ho-nan (Lo-yang). There it was that he fathered Shu-lan.

From childhood Shu-lan was intelligent and eloquent. He accompanied his two maternal uncles and, by consulting them, received the teaching of the sūtras. As soon as he heard, he understood. He knew foreign tongues and Chinese, and he was well read in literature and history. However, he was fickle and violent by nature, and he hunted in an unrestrained way.

One day, when out riding alone, he was chasing a stag when he encountered a tiger and fell off his horse. He broke his right arm and took a long time to recover. Later he again took up his incessant galloping, for which his mother reproached him often, but he would not mend his ways. She subjected him to a vegetarian diet and then he stopped.

He, of course, loved wine, and had to drink up to five or six *shêng* to be happy. One day, when he was completely drunk, he lay down at the side of the road; he then went into the palace of the cantonment in Ho-nan and shouted. The police sent him to the Ho-nan prison. At that time the Prefect of Ho-nan, Lo Kuang 樂廣, was getting drunk with his guests. Already tipsy, he said to [Shu]-lan: 'You are a foreigner who is staying with us. Why do you imitate those of us here who drink wine?' Shu-lan said: 'Tu K'ang made the wine, and the whole Chinese empire drinks it. Why put this question to someone who has been living here so long?' Lo Kuang said: 'To drink wine is permissable. But why get into a rage and cause disorder?' Shu-lan answered: 'The people, even in a rage, do not cause disorder, and you, esteemed Prefect, even when wined, do not get into a rage'. At which Lo Kuang burst into laughter.

Then a fellow guest said: 'You are a foreigner, why are you so white-faced?' Shu-lan answered: 'In Ho-nan certain people are black-faced, but you do not doubt them. If I, your servant, have a white face, why resent me?' Then the guests and the host, admiring his skill and eloquence, released him.

Shortly afterwards Shu-lan, without being ill, died suddenly. Three days later he came back to life. He told how he had entered a dwelling whose doors were painted red and whose rooms were in gold and silver. There he saw a man who told him: 'I am your grandfather', and continued: 'I did good for years and now I am enjoying this reward. You, wrong-doer, how did you get here?' Upon which, the door-keeper ejected him with blows from a stick. Shu-lan entered a bamboo wood and there he saw his hunting companions; bitten by eagles and dogs, they dripped with blood and called on Shu-lan to help them. Shu-lan continued on his way, covering several tens of steps. He met a man with an ox's head who tried to gore him. Shu-lan said: 'For several generations we have been disciples of the Buddha and I have continually supported two śramaṇas. For what fault do you want to punish me?' The ox-headed man replied: 'For that you have deserved happiness, but this in no way affects your hunting crimes'. Suddenly he saw his two maternal uncles and the latter said to the ox-headed man: 'As for us, we have always enjoyed his support. His faults are few but his good works are numerous. You can let him go'. Shu-lan returned in the wake of the two monks and, finally, came back to life.

From then on he mended his ways and cultivated goodwill (*maitrī*). He devoted himself especially to the teaching of the sūtras. In the first *yüan-k'ang* year (291) of the Chin he translated the *Fang kuang ching* (Pañcaviṃśatisāhasrikā p.p.) and a new *Wei-mo-chieh* (Vimalakīrtinirdeśa): more than ten myriad words. Since he knew both the foreign tongue and Chinese, the sense of his translations is perfectly correct.

Later he lost his mother and, after three months, wished to bury her. A neighbour said to him: 'The present year and month are not appropriate. You should wait until next year'. Shu-lan answered: 'Whoever is born must necessarily die, and whoever is dead cannot again be born. Man and spirit follow two different ways, that is quite normal. If I act so that my dead mother has a place to rest her spirit, the greed of the crows and birds will be brought to an end. If I wait until next year, I am afraid of having to flee and of no longer finding anywhere [to bury her]. How would I have time to look for a tomb?' Upon which he immediately buried her.

The next year, in fact, Shih Lê 石勒 rebelled, and brigands abounded everywhere. Shu-lan left [Ho-nan] and fled to Chin-chou 荆州 [in present-day Hu-pei].

Later, without being ill, he said to a friend: 'I am going to die', and a few days later he died. Those who knew him held him to be a man 'knowing the decrees of Heaven'.

VIII

Ho 合 *Shou-lêng-yen ching* 'The combined Śūraṃgamasūtras', eight chüan, probably undertaken in Ch'ang-an in 301 C.E. by Chih Min-tu 支愍度 of the Western Chin.

This is not a question of a new Chinese translation but of a combined or synoptic edition of three Chinese translations made earlier.

This edition, which is lost today, was accompanied by a notice compiled by Chih Min-tu himself and which has come down to us (cf. *Ch'u,* T 2145, p.49*a* 16). Its title is:

> Record of the combined Śūraṃgamasūtras. This strange term signifies, in the tongue of the Chin, *Yung-fu-ting* 'Concentration of Heroic Victory'. [The author] is Chih Min-tu. These three [combined] sūtras were commented upon by Hsieh Fu 謝敷 in four chüan.

Chih Min-tu first supplies some interesting information on the Chinese translations by Chih Ch'an, Chih Ch'ien, Chu Fa-hu and Chu Shu-lan (see above, pp.61, 67–8, 74–5); he then speaks of his own work (cf. *Ch'u,* T 2145, p.49*b* 9–17):

> To make a choice between the three works [namely, the revised translation by Chih Ch'an, alias Yüeh, the translation by Chu Fa-hu and that by Chu Shu-lan] was both laborious and difficult. Wishing that students should have a concordance of these versions at their disposal, I have taken here the revised translation by Yüeh as the basic text, the translation by [Chu Fa]-hu as the secondary text and that by [Chu Shu]-lan as a supplement. I have immediately noted and distinguished what was not to be found in one or other of these

versions. Sometimes the style and meaning were the same; sometimes the meaning was similar but the style varied very slightly. It was not worthwhile recopying them and I have blended the texts in considering them as alike. Although this may not add to the interest, I have divided the work into chapters and sentences so that they can be clearly seen.

[After having reproduced the notice on the *Yung-fu-ting* by Fa-hu (see p.74 above), Chih Min-tu concludes]: I would like the Four Communities to examine [these translations] and propagate them, while distinguishing the different and similar meanings.

It appears clear from this notice that Chih Min-tu took only three earlier translations into consideration: the translation by Chih Ch'an revised by Chih Ch'ien, the *Yung-fu-ting* by Fa-hu and the translation by Shu-lan. However, certain catalogues from the sixth and seventh centuries claim that he also collated the translation, much lacking in authentication, by Po Yen. This is a mistake that the *Ch'u* does not make and which the *K'ai* contested:

1. *Ch'u,* T 2145, p.10*a* 12: *Ho Shou-lêng-yen ching*, eight chüan. Combines into a single work the four *Shou-lêng-yen* translated by Chih Ch'an, Chih Ch'ien, Chu Fa-hu and Chu Shu-lan. Sometimes in five chüan. Compiled by the śramaṇa Chih Min-tu under Hui-ti (290–307) of the Chin.

2. *Chung* A, T 2146, p.125*a* 2: *Ho Shou-lêng-yen ching*, eight chüan.

3 and 4. *Li,* T 2034, p.66*c* 6; *Nei,* T 2149, p.237*c* 17: *Ho Shou-lêng-yen ching*, five works in eight chüan. It is the sixth translation. It combines into a single work the five works by the two Chih [Chih Ch'an and Chih Ch'ien], the two Chu [Fa-hu and Shu-lan] and Po Yen. See the catalogue by Chih Min-tu.

5. *Wu,* T 2153, p.398*a* 5–6: *Shou-lêng-yen ching*, a work in eight chüan. It is the sixth translation. During the *yung-ning* year (301–302) of the Western Chin, Chih Min-tu combined into a single work the five works by the two Chih, the two Chu and Po Yen. See the catalogue by Chih Min-tu.

6. *K'ai,* T 2154, p.501*b* 13–16: In the reign of Hui-ti (290–307), the śramaṇa Chih Min-tu combined the four works by the two Chih and the two Chu. The catalogue by [Fei Chang]-fang (T 2034) also

adds the work by Po [Yen], which would make five works. However, according to the catalogue by [Sêng]-yu (T 2145) and the colophon of the combined edition [by Chih Min-tu], four works only were combined; they do not mention Po Yen.

The sources are mostly silent on Chih Min-tu, but his social background is well known and has been admirably described by E. Zürcher (*Buddhist Conquest* I, pp.81–110).

Chih Min-tu was a scholar-monk who came from a cultured background. At first he lived in the north, most probably in Ch'ang-an, in the reign of Hui-ti (290–307) and he was in personal contact with the civil and military aristocracy as well as the great Dharma masters such as Dharmarakṣa, Po Yüan, Chu Shu-lan, etc.

For the use of the Chinese who did not know Sanskrit he published combined editions of the Śūraṃgamasamādhi and the Vimalakīrtinirdeśa, in which the Chinese versions of these works were assembled and collated.

According to the *Wu* (T 2153, p.398*a* 5–6), his 'Combined Śūraṃgamas' appeared in the 301. They encompass the translation by Chih Ch'an revised by Chih Ch'ien between 222 and 229, and the very recent translations by Dharmarakṣa and Chu Shu-lan, both of which appeared in 291. The same year Po Yüan had already commented upon the one by Dharmarakṣa.

Later Chih Min-tu published his 'Combined Vimalakīrtis', of which only the preface has come down to us (cf. *Ch'u,* T 2145, p.58*b* 21). This edition encompassed the versions by Chih Ch'ien, Dharmarakṣa and Chu Shu-lan. Since the one by Dharmarakṣa was completed on 3 May 303 (cf. *Li,* T 2034, p.63*c* 9), Chih Min-tu could not have undertaken his work until after that date.

The explanations supplied by the prefaces on this kind of editing are lacking in clarity. Properly speaking, it is neither a matter of synopses nor of 'translations blended into a single one' but more of what the Chinese at present call a *Fo-t'u ho-pên tsu-chu* 佛徒合本子注, namely a 'commentary upon a synthetic edition of the Buddhists'[11]. In the particular case of the Śgs, Chih Min-tu took Chih Ch'an's version as the 'basic text' (*mu* 母); he divided it into chapters and paragraphs and, after each paragraph, he reproduced, in the guise of a commentary, the corresponding passages from the versions by Dharmarakṣa and Chu Shu-lan qualified respectively as 'secondary text' (*tzŭ* 子) and

[11] See Weng Tung-wen in *T'oung Pao* XLVIII, 1960, pp.488-9.

'supplementary text' (*hsi* 繫). Nonetheless, the minimal differences between the versions were not noted.

Such a method has its inconveniences. A synthetic edition in fact consisted of an indigestible mass abounding in repetitions. That of the Śgs took up six chüan, as many as three separate versions together. Even more, the quotations taken from the 'secondary text' and the 'supplementary text' were still not noted in small characters; hence the difficulty of distingushing between the 'basic text' and the 'secondary texts' which were meant to clarify the former.

Chih Min-tu was not, however, the inventor of this method. During the second half of the third century Chih Ch'ien, the translator of the *Wei-mi ch'ih* 微密持, 'Dhāraṇī of the Subtle Secret' (T 1011), had also produced a synthetic edition of it based upon the comparison of three distinct versions (*Ch'u*, T 2145, p.51*c* 17–19).

After Chih Min-tu, but still in the fourth century, Tao-an (312–385) and Chih Tun 支遁 (314–366) applied the same method to the Prajñāpāramitā.

In his *Ho Fang-kuang Kuang-tsan lüeh chieh* 'Brief explanation of the combined *Fang-kuang* and *Kuang-tsang',* of which the preface has been preserved *(Ch'u,* T 2145, p.47*c* 29), Tao-an instituted the synthesis of two Chinese versions of the Pañcaviṃśatisāhasrikā p.p., namely:

a. The *Fang-kuang ching* 放光經 (T 221). The Sanskrit original, discovered in 260 in Khotan by Chu Shih-hsing 朱士行, had reached China through the good offices of his Khotanese pupil Puṇyadhana(?) and had been translated in Ts'ang-Yüan (Ho-nan) between 28 June and 31 December 291 by the Khotanese Mokṣala and the sinicised Indian Chu Shu-lan, and this translation had been revised, on the basis of a Sanskrit original and five Chinese copies, by Chu Shu-lan between 10 December 303 and 22 May 304.

b. The *Kuang-tsan ching* 光讚經 (T 222). The Sanskrit manuscript had been brought from Khotan by a certain Gītamitra and translated, by Dharmarakṣa and Gītamitra, in Ch'ang-an on 27 December 286. Tao-an obtained a copy of this version in Liang-chou (Kan-su) in 376.

With regard to Chih Tun (314–366), also called Chih Tao-lin, he published some *Ta-Hsiao p'in tui-pi yao-ch'ao* 'Synoptic extracts from the Large and Small Prajñās', the preface of which has been preserved (*Ch'u*, T 2145, p.55*a* 13). In this he compared the Pañcaviṃśatisāhasrikā and the Aṣṭasāhasrikā.

The Prajñāpāramitās, the Vimalakīrti and the Śūraṃgamasamādhi are closely related; objectively they posit a universal emptiness (*śūnyatā*) while avoiding hypostatising it; subjectively they extol mental adherence to the non-existence and non-arising of all things (*anutpattikadharmakṣānti*). Of all the Mahāyāna sūtras that were studied in Ho-nan and Kan-su under the Western Chin, these were the ones that aroused the most interest; not content with translating and re-translating them, combined editions were made of them. Even more, these sūtras directly inspired the first Buddhist school of philosophy to arise in China, the *Hsin-wu-i* 心無義 'Theory of the non-existence of the mind', the founder of which was precisely Chih Min-tu. It is not certain that he interpreted his Indian sources correctly, since his *śūnyatā* is less an ontological idea than a subjective state: the void of the mind of the sage. However, the Chinese were fully aware that the three sūtras exploited the same philosophical vein and that this was not without its similarities to Confucian and Taoist speculations concerning the connections between name (*ming* 名) and reality (*shih* 實), between substance (*t'i* 體) and function (*yung* 用), speculations known as the Doctrine of Names (*ming-chiao* 名教) and Dark Learning (*hsüan-hsüeh* 玄學).

Another text which, at the same time and in the same situation, held the attention of the Chinese was the Saddharmapuṇḍarīka. Among specialists on the *Lotus* can be cited Chu Tao-ch'ien 竺道潛, cognomen Fa-chên 法深 (286–374), and his disciple Chu Fa-i 竺法義 (307–380). Contrary to what his name might seem to indicate, the former was a pure Chinese and related to the Wang family who were very powerful at the Chin court. The two masters were in contact with two monks, who were either of distant Sogdian origin or followed a Sogdian master, K'ang Fa-ch'ang 康法暢 and K'ang Sêng-yüan 康僧淵, specialists in Pure Conversation (*ch'ing-t'an* 清談) and Characterisation of Persons (*mu* 目).

During the first quarter of the fourth century revolutions at the palace, swiftly followed by invasions by the Hsiung-nu who ravaged Ch'ang-an in 311 and 316, led to a mass exodus of the population. K'ang Fa-ch'ang, Chih Min-tu and K'ang Sêng-yüan crossed the Yang-tsê river and reached the capital of the Eastern Chin, Chien-k'ang, present-day Nanking. This was in the reign of the emperor Ch'êng, between 325 and 342 (cf. *Kao,* T 2059, pp.346*c* 28–347*a* 2). In Ch'ien-k'ang the fugitives enjoyed the protection of the powerful Wang family, particularly Wang Tao 王導 (276–339). However, the situation changed when the Yü 庾, rivals of the Tao, seized effective power. Faced with the anti-Buddhist attitude taken by Yü Ping 庾冰 in 340, several scholar-monks deserted the capital and reached the coastal regions of Chiang-su or Chê-chiang in the south-east. Chu Tao-ch'ien and his disciples established their vihāra in the Shan 剡 massif (*Kao*, T 2059, p.348*a* 29); Chih Tun and his followers settled provisionally in Wu-hsien 吳縣 before reaching Shan themselves (*Kuang hung ming chi*, T 2103, p.350*a* 18); as for K'ang Sêng-yüan, he retired to the Yü-chang 豫章 mountains and founded a monastery there (*Kao*, T 2059, p.347*a* 13). It is probable that Chih Min-tu followed the last. In any case, it is in the Yü-chang mountains that, in the reign of Ch'êng-ti (325–342), he compiled his two catalogues entitled *Ching-lun tu-lu* and *Pieh-lu*, each in one chüan (*Nei*, T 2149, p.336*c* 23–25; *K'ai*, T 2154, p.573*a* 14–17). We have just seen that his combined editions of the Śūraṃgama and the Vimalakīrti were mentioned in them.

Commentary in four chüan, composed by Hsieh Fu 謝敷 of the Eastern Chin, upon the '*Combined Śūraṃgamas*' by Chih Min-tu.

We know of the existence of this commentary through a note by Sêng-yu added to the preface by Chih Min-tu (cf. *Ch'u*, T 2145, p.49*a* 17).

Hsieh Fu was a native of K'uai-chi, in present-day Chê-chiang, and belonged to those families of literati who sought in both Buddhism and Taoism the secret of the Supreme Truth (*chih-li*), a truth which cannot be illustrated by words or symbols. For more than ten years he withdrew to the T'ai-p'ing mountains and underwent prolonged fasting. He was in contact with Chih Tun and his powerful protector Hsi Ch'ao 郄超 (336–377). He also composed a commentary upon the Mahānāpānasmṛtisūtra, a sūtra of the Small Vehicle translated into Chinese by An Shih-kao (T 602). This text was of particular interest to the Chinese because it dealt with breathing exercises which were also cultivated in Taoism. Of the commentary by Hsieh Fu, only the preface has come down to us (*Ch'u*, T 2145, p.43*c* 25 sq.).

IX

***Shou-lêng-yen ching*, two chüan, translated in Liang-chou (in Kan-su) in 373 C.E. by the prefect Chang T'ien-hsi 張天錫, the upāsaka Chih Shih-lun 支施崙 and Po Yen 帛延 of the Ch'ien Liang.**

This translation is furnished with a colophon by an unknown hand, and is preserved in the *Ch'u* (T 2145, ch.7, p.49*b* 18–19):

During the third *hsien-ho* (correct to *hsien-an*) year, *kuei-yu* cycle (373), the prefect of Liang-chou 涼州 (in Kan-su), Chang T'ien-hsi translated this *Shou-lêng-yen ching* in the prefecture. At that time there was a Yüeh-chih upāsaka, Chih Shih-lun, who held the foreign original in his hands. Chih [Shih-lun] had read the sūtras widely; he was particularly versed in the developed (*vaipulya*) sūtras and the concentrations (*samādhi*), and gave himself over resolutely to the study of the Mahāyāna. He translated the *Shou-lêng-yen* (Śūraṃgamasamādhi), the *Hsü-lai* (T 329: Surataparipṛcchā), the *Chang-chin-kuang-shou* (Mañjuśrīvikrīḍita) and the *Ju-huan san-mei* (Māyopamasamādhi or Susthitamatiparipṛcchā).

At that time, they were assembled at the local seat of the prefecture in Liang-chou, on the porch of the pavilion. The translator then was the son of the king of Kucha, Po Yen, who knew Chinese and the barbarian tongue. [Po] Yen thoroughly penetrated the texts and understood both Buddhist and non-Buddhist works.

Those who took it down [by brush] were: 1. the 'functionary constantly at the disposition of the prince', Chao Hsiao 趙瀟, from Hsi-hai 西海; 2. the sub-prefect from Hui-shui 會水, Ma I 馬亦; 3. the 'head of the intendancy of the Inner Palace', Lai Kung-chêng 來恭政. These three men were all of noble virtue and possessed a sense of justice.

At the time, there were present the śramaṇas Shih Hui-ch'ang 釋慧常, and Shih Chin-hsing 釋進行.

The prefect of Liang-chou himself chose the terms [for the translation]. Their tenor conformed to the original and did not add stylistic ornaments. Stylistic ornament verges on the naïve; accuracy attains the truth. Only saints can achieve this linking of style and accuracy.

The śramaṇas Shih Hui-ch'ang and Shih Chin-hsing who assisted in this translation were probably disciples of Tao-an (312–385). Wishing to go to India, they had stopped on the way in Liang-chou and from there, in 373, sent five texts to Tao-an who was then in Hsiang-yang 襄陽 (on the river Han in northern Hu-pai). These five texts were:

1. *Kuang-tsan ching* (T 222), a translation of the Pañcaviṃśatisāhasrikā p.p. made by Dharmarakṣa and Gītamitra on the twenty-fifth day of the eleventh month of the seventh *t'ai-kang* year (27 December 286); cf. *Ch'u,* T 2145, p.48*a* 3.

2. *Chien-pei ching* (T 285), a translation of the Daśabhūmika made by Dharmarakṣa on the twenty-first day of the eleventh month of the seventh *yüan-k'ang* year (21 December 297); cf. *Ch'u,* T 2145, p.7*b* 22.

3. *Shou-lêng-yen ching*, a translation of the Śūraṃgamasamādhi made in Liang-chou in 373 by Chang T'ien-hsi, Chih Shih-lun and Po Yen.

4. *Hsü-lai ching* (T 329), a translation of the Suratapariprcchā made in Liang-chou in 373 by Chih Shih-lun.

5. *Wu-po chieh* 'The Five Hundred Precepts'.

The texts, which were sent from Liang-chou in 373, arrived in Hsiang-yang in a different order in 376. The fifth did not reach its destination.

The above information is culled from two contemporary documents by Tao-an himself:

1. Preface by Tao-an to his *Ho Fang-kuang Kuang-tsan lüeh chieh* (*Ch'u*, T 2145, p.48*a* 20–23):

> Then Hui-ch'ang, Chin-hsing, Hui-pien 慧辯, etc., wishing to go to India, passed through Liang-chou on their route. They copied and forwarded [the *Kuang-tsan ching*] and, crossing the Ch'in and the Yung, the text reached Hsiang-yang on the twenty-fourth day of the fifth month of the first *t'ai-yüan* year (27 June 376). I have examined and checked it and I have had the joy of profiting from it. I immediately took note of it and have used it widely in the present 'Brief Explanation' [of the combined *Fang-kuang* and *Kuang-tsan*]'.

2. Letter by an unknown writer (probably Tao-an) concerning the *Chien-pei* or Daśabhūmika (*Ch'u*, T 2145, p.62*c* 4–17):

> On the twenty-fourth day of the fifth month of the first *t'ai-yüan* year, *ping-tzŭ* cycle (27 June 376), this [*Kuang-tsan*] *ching* reached Hsiang-yang. Shih Hui-ch'ang, in the year *kuei-yu* (373), had sent this sūtra and charged a man in the Exchange Market, K'ang-êrh 康兒, to have it conveyed to Ch'ang-an. In Ch'ang-an the messenger An Fa-hua 安法華 had sent it to the Exchange Market and the Exchange Market man had transported it to Hsiang-yang and handed it to the śramaṇa Shih Tao-an. At that time the assembled community in Hsiang-yang numbered three hundred members. Shih Sêng-hsien

釋僧顯 was ordered to copy this sūtra and take it to the Yang-chou monk, Chu Fa-t'ai 竺法汰 (320–387).

The *Chien-pei* (Daśabhūmika) reached Hsiang-yang on the third day of the tenth month of the first *t'ai-yüan* year (31 October 376). It had also been sent by Hui-ch'ang, etc., and it had left with the *Kuang-tsan,* but the inhabitants of Nan-hsiang had retained it briefly to copy it. That is why it did not arrive with the *Kuang-tsan.*

The *Shou-lêng-yen* (Śūraṃgama translated by Chang T'ien-hsi, Chih Shih-lun and Po Yen) and the *Hsü-lai* (Surata translated by Chih Shih-lun) arrived together with the *Chien-pei* (Daśabhūmika). Shih Hui-ch'ang, the monk from Liang-chou, in the year *jên-shên* (372–373) had copied these sūtras at the Nei-Yüan ssŭ. He forwarded them in the year [*kuei*]-*yu* (373–374) and it was on the twenty-third day of the fourth month of the [*ping*]-*tzŭ* year (27 May 376) that they reached Hsiang-yang. This *Shou-lêng-yen ching* is, in all respects, richer than previous [translations]; this is not the case for the first, second and ninth. Its chapters are very numerous and approach three or four hundred words. As for the style and sentences, it is very useful.

The *Hsü-lai ching* (Surata) is also a little longer and can contain some lovely passages.

It is said that there was also a *Wu-po chieh* 'The Five Hundred Precepts'. It is not known why it did not arrive [in Hsiang-yang]. Nevertheless it is urgently needed; the fourfold Community is imperfect and for the great Dharma it is a deficiency.

The translation of the *Shou-lêng-yen* by Chang T'ien-hsi, Chih Shih-lun and Po Yen was only entered in the large catalogues much later. The *K'ai* (T 2154, pp.519*a* 24-b3; 632*a* 15) was the first to index it. It attributes it to the Yüeh-chean upāsaka Chih Shih-lun along with the translations of three other works: the Suratapariprcchā which has come down to us (T 329), the Māyopamasamādhi and the Mañjuśrīvikrīḍita. However, the *K'ai* reproduces in full the colophon to the *Shou-lêng-yen* translated above, while correcting the date: third *hsien-an* year, *kuei-yu* cycle (373). According to it, this translation of the Śgs is the eighth, and it is newly included in the catalogue.

The information supplied by the *K'ai* is repeated by the *Chêng*, T 2157, p.816*a* 3–4.

X

Hsin Shou-lêng-yen san-mei ching 新首楞嚴三昧經, 'New Śūraṃgama-samādhisūtra', two chüan, translated, either in Liang-chou between 385 and 402 C.E. or in Ch'ang-an between 402 and 409 C.E., by Chiu-mo-lo-shih 鳩摩羅什 (Kumārajīva) of the Late Ch'in. Translation preserved (T 642).

With regard to this 'new' translation, the oldest attestation is supplied by a preface *(hsü)* to the *Hsin-ch'u Shou-lêng-yen ching* compiled in 458 by Shih Hung-ch'ung 釋弘充. It is preserved in the *Ch'u,* T 2145, ch.7, p.49*c*. We read (lines 12–14):

> From his childhood, the Dharma master Lo-shih (Kumārajīva) expounded the Way, meditated and penetrated the teachings of the Dharma. Formerly, finding himself in Kuan-yu 關右 (a region located to the west of Han-ku-kuan), he translated this [Śūraṃgama-samādhi]-sūtra. From the moment of its publication, this work was distributed in the course of time, causing joy and good fortune; the joys of the world prospered. While its dissemination was at its greatest, the sun and the moon were even more active.

Captured in Kucha in 384 by Lü Kuang 呂光, general of the emperor Fu Chien 苻堅 (357–385) of the Early Ch'in, Kumārajīva was taken to Liang-chou 涼州 (in Kan-su) in 385. The following year Lü Kuang, breaking away from the Early Ch'in, announced his independence and in Ku-tsang 姑臧 (in Kan-su) inaugurated the dynasty of the Late Liang, which lasted from 386 to 404. A plaything for the fantasies of these Turko-Mongols, Kumārajīva remained in Liang-chou for seventeen years, from 385 to 402. He does not seem to have worked much there: 'He kept his profound teaching to himself and did not expound it'.

In the meantime, one of the old lieutenants of Fu Chien, Yao Ch'ang 姚萇, undoubtedly of Tibetan race, had founded in Ch'ang-an the dynasty of the Late Ch'in, destined to last from 384 to 417. His son Yao Hsing 姚興 (394–416) engaged in hostilities against Kan-su and, in 401, obtained the capitulation of Lü Lung 呂隆, the nephew and third successor of Lü Kuang. Yao Hsing invited Kumārajīva to come and live in his capital. According to the information supplied by the oldest records, Kumārajīva reached Ch'ang-an on the twentieth day of the twelfth month of the third *hung-shih* year, i.e. 8 February 402 (cf. *Ch'u,* T 2145, p.101*b* 12–13; *Kao*, T 2059, p.332*a* 24–25); he worked there until his death which occurred on the twentieth day of the eighth month of the eleventh *hung-shih* year, i.e. 15 September 409 (cf. *Kao,* T 2059, p.333*a* 4)[12].

If we can believe the preface by Shih Hung-ch'ung quoted above, Kumārajīva would have translated the Śgs between 385 and 402, during his enforced stay in Kuan-yu, that is, Liang-chou. But such is not the opinion of the large catalogues from the sixth and seventh centuries which allege that all Kumārajīva's activity as a translator evolved in Ch'ang-an from 402 on. Hence, after having listed thirty-five translations, the *Ch'u* (T 2145, p.11*a* 25–27) observes:

> These 35 works forming 294 chüan were translated by Kumārajīva, the śramaṇa from India. During the time of An-ti (396–419) of the [Eastern] Ch'in, Kumārajīva, in the year three of the *hung-shih* period (402) of Yao Hsing of the usurping Ch'in, arrived in Ch'ang-an, and it was in the Ta ssŭ and the garden of Hsiao-yao that he translated.

The catalogues, however, do not give the exact date of the translation of the Śgs by Kumārajīva, but limit themselves to a vague suggestion: the *hung-shih* period, which ran from 399 to 415. Kumārajīva's version was chronologically the sixth translation of the Śgs (*Ch'u*, T 2145, pp.10*c* 23, 14*a* 15), the seventh (*Li*, T 2034, p.78*a* 12; *Wu*, T 2153, p.398*a* 11–12) or the ninth (*K'ai*, T 2154, p.512*c* 18).

More precise dates are supplied concerning other works closely connected to the Śgs by their ideas and which Kumārajīva also translated:

1. The Pañcaviṃśatisāhasrikā p.p. translated with the title of *Mo-ho pan-jo po-lo-mi ching*, in twenty-seven chüan (T 223). The same translation is mentioned in the *Ch'u* (T 2145, p.10*c* 16) with the title of *Hsin Ta-p'in ching*, in twenty-four chüan. Begun in the garden of Hsiao-yao on the twenty-second day of the fourth month of the fifth *hung-shih* year (28 May 403), it was finished on the twenty-third day of the fourth month of the sixth year (18 May 404).

2. The Vimalakīrtinirdeśa, translated in the eighth *hung-shih* year (406) with the title of *Hsin Wei-mo-chieh ching*, in three chüan (T 475); cf. *Ch'u,* T 2145, p.10*c* 22.

3. The Aṣṭasāhasrikā p.p., translated with the title of *Mo-ho-pan-jo*

[12] The notice in the *Kao-sêng chuan* on Kumārajīva has been translated by J. Nobel, 'Kumārajīva' in *Sitzungsberichte der Preussischen Akademie der Wissenschaft* XX, 1927, pp.206-33.

po-lo-mi ching, in ten chüan (T 227). The same translation is mentioned in the *Ch'u* (T 2145, p.10*c* 18) with the title of *Hsin Hsiao-p'in ching*, in seven chüan. Begun on the sixth day of the second month of the tenth *hung-shih* year (18 March 408), it was completed on the twentieth day of the fourth month of the same year (30 May 408).

However it may be, Kumārajīva's translation of the Śgs was so superior to its predecessors that it was enough to eliminate them all. The seven earlier versions made respectively by Chih Ch'an, the anonymous translator(s) from Ssŭ-chuan, Chih Ch'ien, Po Yen, Dharmarakṣa, Chu Shu-lan and Chih Shih-lun had already disappeared by the beginning of the sixth century and Sêng-yu, in his *Ch'u san-tsang chi chi* published in 515, already records them as lost.

Kumārajīva's translation of the Śgs is therefore the only one to have come down to us. The translation which follows is based wholly on it.

Kumārajīva's methods are known to us. He aimed above all at making himself understood by the Chinese, but he was not preoccupied with details. His translations are rigorously accurate, with the slight nuance that he was not always consistent in his way of rendering technical terms and that the numerous stock phrases with which the Sanskrit originals were studded obviously irritated him. He therefore usually only translated their opening words, except where he gave only a brief summary of them.

Even for the fastidious this is not a serious inconvenience, especially since we have the Tibetan version at our disposal as is the case with the Śgs. Thanks to this, we are free to restore the technical terms which Kumārajīva somewhat decimated, the stock phrases which he reduced or summarised and also some sentences which he left out. These omissions can, moreover, be blamed as much on the copyists as the translator.

Assisted, if not hampered, by a large number of collaborators (hundreds, even thousands), Kumārajīva commented upon the texts as he translated them. Often explanations of his own invention slipped into his translations as, for example, in that of the *Ta-chih-tu lun* (T 1509: Upadeśa). This, however, is not the case here since a comparison with the Tibetan version shows that, in relation to the Indian original, Kumārajīva's translation sins more through omission.

Commentary composed in 458 C.E., in Chien-k'ang (Nanking), by Shih Hung-ch'ung 釋弘充 of the Sung, upon the *Hsin Shou-lêng-yen ching* by Kumārajīva.

We have just seen that Hung ch'ung was the author of a preface to the new translation of the *Shou-lêng-yen* by Kumārajīva. It also appears from this preface (*Ch'u*, T 2145, p.49*c* 14–19) that Hung-Ch'ung composed a commentary upon this translation as well:

> The prime minister, prince of Chiang-hsia 江夏 (in Hu-pei), knows the texts well and examines them with depth and perspicacity. Each time he reads the scrolls (of this *Hsin Shou-lêng-yen*) he is particularly and profoundly moved.
>
> I, [Hung]-ch'ung, a foolish and obscure person, have attempted to approach the Mysterious, and already I have met old craftsmen who have opened and explained the 'core' of the text for me. Consulting with and listening to these sages, I have worked hard at the style and meaning. In the second *ta-ming* year, *yen-mou* cycle (458), under the Imperial Sung, at the monastery of Fa-yen 法言, I made a commentary in brief so that the text can be easily propagated. I have dared to recopy what I have heard. As there are certainly some mistakes, I await the sages (to correct me).

The *Kao-sêng chuan* (T 2059, p.376*a* 10–19) devotes a short notice to Hung-ch'ung of which this is a translation:

> Shih Hung-ch'ung was a native of Liang-chou (in Kan-su). In his youth, he possessed strength of will. He comprehended Chuang-[tzŭ] and Lao-[tzŭ], and understood Sūtra and Vinaya. At the end of the *ta-ming* period (457–464), he crossed the [Yang-tzê] river and at first stayed at the To-pao ssŭ. He excelled in posing objections, and the sages were put to confusion for the most part. Later, he inaugurated a 'Festival of the Dharma', and debate raged furiously. Since [Hung]-ch'ung penetrated the subtleties of the Mysterious in meditation and since his eloquence was supernormal, he comprehended doubtful things and explained difficulties. Each time he expounded the Saddharmapuṇḍarīka and the Daśabhūmika, the listeners filled the auditorium. The prime minister of the Sung, [Liu] I-kung 劉義恭, prince of the literati, from Chiang-hsia (in Hu-pei), esteemed him greatly.
>
> When Ming-ti (466–472) mounted the throne, he built the Hsiang-kung ssŭ and begged [Hung]-ch'ung to become its Superior. [Hung]-

ch'ung changed his residence forthwith.

At that time in the Hsiang-kung, there was the bhikṣu Fa-hsien 法鮮. Intelligent and wise, he also possessed the power of reflection and equalled [Hung]-ch'ung in renown.

[Hung]-ch'ung died in the middle of the *yung-ming* period (483–494) of the [Nan] Ch'i, aged seventy-two years. He made a commentary upon the *Wên-shu wên pu-t'i ching* (T 464: Gayaśīrṣa) and upon the Śūraṃgamasūtra (T 642).

The catalogues from the sixth and seventh centuries record a Catalogue by Shih Hung-ch'ung, in one chüan, already lost by their time (cf. *Li,* T 2034, p.127*c* 7; *Nei,* T 2149, p.337*a* 8; *Kai,* T 2154, p.573*a* 21).

XI

[Additional Note]

The Śūraṃgamasamādhisūtra, often referred to in the abridged form of Śūraṃgamasūtra, is a text of certain authenticity undoubtedly based upon an Indian prototype.

It should not be confused with another Śūraṃgamasūtra composed in Chinese with the title of *Ta-fo-ting-ju-lai mi-yin hsiu-chêng liao-i chu p'u-sa wan hsing shou-lêng-yen ching*, abbreviated to *Shou-lêng-yen ching* (T 945). This is a Chinese apocryphal work composed at the beginning of the eighth century, probably by Fang Jung 房融, a minister of the empress Wu of the T'ang. Although its Indian origin was quickly contested, it is at present still one of the most widespread of Buddhist works in China. P. Demiéville (*Le Concile de Lhasa*, Paris 1952, pp.43–52, in the notes) devoted to this counterfeit a substantial study in which all the desired information can be found; the first four chüan were adapted and summarised in English by S. Beal (*Catena of Buddhist Scriptures from the Chinese*, London 1871, repr. Taipei 1971, pp.286–369), [† Chapter I was translated by Joseph Edkins in *Chinese Buddhism* (London 1893, repr. San Francisco 1976)], and the complete work has now been translated into English by Charles Luk (Lu K'uan Yü) with the title of *The Śūraṅgama Sūtra*, London 1966, repr. New Delhi 1985.

Because of the similarity of titles, modern authors often confuse the authentic Śūraṃgamasamādhi with the apocryphal Śūraṃgama. Among others, see C. Bendall, ed. of the Śikṣāsamuccaya, p.8, n.2; L. de La Vallée Poussin, Siddhi, p.633.

XII

***ḥPhags-pa dPaḥ-bar ḥgro-baḥi tiṅ-ṅe-ḥdzin ces-bya-ba theg-pa-chen-poḥi mdo*: Āryaśūraṃgamasamādhir nāma Mahāyānasūtram, in five bamp-po, translated at the beginning of the ninth century C.E. by the Indian pandit Śākyaprabha and the (Tibetan) corrector-interpreter Ratnarakṣita.**

This translation is included in the Narthang Kanjur (vol. Ta 6°, fol. 407*b* 5–510*a*) and the Peking Kanjur (*Tibetan Tripiṭaka*, ed. D.T. Suzuki, Tokyo-Kyoto 1958, vol.32, No.800, pp.71–98, fol.276*a* 4–344*a* 5). It is this latter edition which I have used for the present work.

The *Inventaire des Manuscrits Tibétains de Touen-houang conservés à la Bibliothèque Nationale* published by M. Lalou (3 vols, Paris 1939, 1940, 1961) and the *Catalogue of the Tibetan Manuscripts from Tun-huang in the India Office Library* compiled by L. de La Vallée Poussin (Oxford 1962) do not note any manuscript or fragment of such of the Śūraṃgamasamādhi in Tun-huang. This fact is all the more surprising in that Tun-huang has yielded several Tibetan translations of the Prajñāpāramitās and the Vimalakīrtinirdeśa (cf. M. Lalou, 'Les manuscrits tibétains des grandes Prajñāpāramitā trouvés à Touen-houang', *Silver Jubilee Volume of the Zinbun-Kagaku-Kenkyusyo*, Kyoto 1954, pp.257–61; 'Les plus anciens rouleaux tibétains trouvés à Touen-houang', *Rocznik Orientalistyczny* XXI, 1957, pp.149-52; É. Lamotte, Vkn (English version), pp.xxxviii-xliii). With the reservation that further discoveries are always possible, we can conclude that the only Tibetan version of the Śgs which was ever made is that by Śākyaprabha and Ratnarakṣita as it appears in the Kanjur. Selections from this version have been translated into English by Thubten Kalsang Rimpoche and Bhikkhu Pāsādika in *Excerpts from the Śūraṅgama Samādhi Sūtra*, Dharamsala 1975.

It differs from Kumārajīva's version on the following two points:

1. It contains two long, partially versified, passages which are not found in the Chinese version: fol.286*b* 5–289*a* 3 following § 21 of my translation; fol.338*b* 8–344*a* 1 following § 177 of my translation.

2. It is, according to Tibetan usage, divided into five bam-po (a roll or scroll):

bam-po I, fol.276*a* 5 (§ 1 of my translation).

bam-po II, fol.289*b* 5 (§ 26).
bam-po III, fol.304*b* 5 (§ 67).
bam-po IV, fol.317*a* 8 (§ 109).
bam-po V, fol.329*b* 5 (§ 150).

There is no doubt that the Indian original of the Śgs underwent successive enlargements in the course of time, as is confirmed by the Chinese and Tibetan versions. The two Chinese translations made in Ssŭ-chuan between 220 and 265 contained ten stanzas (cf. above, p.66); the one by Chih Shih-lun, dating from 373, was longer than its predecessors according to Tao-an's certification (cf. above, p.93). The Tibetan version, which is the most recent, marks the final point of this evolution by including in the text some long series of stanzas.

The oldest Mahāyāna sūtras, such as the Aṣṭasāhasrikā, Pañcaviṃśatisāhasrikā, Aṣṭādaśasāhasrikā and Śatasāhasrikā p.p., were entirely in prose. Later, when literary taste had evolved, sūtras appeared in prose interpolated with verse. It also happened that earlier productions had stanzas added to them at a later date. We have already noted (Vkn, p.11) a certain fluctuation in the number of stanzas put into the mouth of Ratnākara in Chapter One of the Vimalakīrtinirdeśa.

The authors of the Tibetan version, Śākyaprabha and Ratnarakṣita, are not unknown to us. They worked as a team and have also left us versions of the Ratnakaraṇḍa (*Otani Kanjur Cat.*, No.785), Pratyutpannasamādhi (No.801), Brahmaviśeṣacintiparipṛcchā (No.827), Saṃvṛtiparamārthasatyanirdeśa (No.846), Aṅgulimālīya (No.879), Tathāgatagarbha (No.924) and Akāśagarbha (No.926).

They witnessed, to some degree at least, the great events that marked the glorious reign of Khri-sroṅ-lde-btsan (755–797)[13]: the fortunes of the Tibetan campaigns in Bengal (755) and in China marked by the fleeting occupation of Ch'ang-an (763) and the expulsion of the Chinese from Beshbalik in Turkestan (788–790); the declared sympathy of the king towards Buddhism despite the opposition of the clans who remained attached to Bon (755); the mission of two Nepalese monks to Tibet; the Dharma master Śāntarakṣita and the wonder-worker Padmasambhava;

[13] On his reign, see G. Tucci, 'The Validity of Tibetan Historical Tradition' in *India Antiqua*, Leiden 1947, pp.309-22; *The Tombs of the Tibetan Kings*, Serie Orientale Roma I, 1950, pp.5-20; *Minor Buddhist Texts*, Serie Orientale Roma IX, 2, pp.1-68; P. Demiéville, *Le Concile de Lhasa*, Paris 1952, Index, s.v. Khri-sroṅ-lde-bcan; L. Petech, *A Study of the Chronicles of Ladakh*, Calcutta 1939; 'Tibet' in *Le Civiltà dell'Oriente* I, Rome 1955, pp.1123-40; 'Tibet' in *Storia Universale*, Rome, pp.269-72; M. Lalou, *Les Religions du Tibet*, Paris 1957, pp.25-35; R.A. Stein, *La civilisation tibétaine*, Paris 1962, pp.43-7.

the erection at Bsam-yas [† Lhasa] of a large collection of Buddhist temples and monasteries (erection begun in 775?), modelled on the Indian temple at Odantapurī or Nālandā; the ordination of the first Tibetan monks, the Seven Elect (*sad-mi*), chosen from among the nobility (779?); the thirteen years' abbacy of Śāntarakṣita in Bsam-yas (775–788); the arrival in Tibet, on the king's invitation, of two Chinese Buddhist monks destined to be replaced every two years (781); the royal edict elevating Buddhism to a state religion (791); the doctrinal controversy which, in Tibet, opposed the 'sudden way' of the Chinese Buddhists (represented by the *hva-śaṅ* Mahāyāna) to the 'gradual way' of the Indian Buddhists (led by Kamalaśīla, a disciple of Śāntarakṣita); the triumph of the latter at the Council of Bsam-yas (792–794); the publication by Kamalaśīla of the three Bhāvanākramas in which he defined the Indian position; and finally, the assassination of Kamalaśīla (795), soon followed by the death of the king (797).

Khri-sroṅ-lde-btsan's death was followed by a period of troubles; one or two of his sons, Mu-ne-btsan-po and Mu-tig-btsan-po, perished in the palace revolutions. Finally (in 804?), his youngest son Khri-lde-sroṅ-btsan, alias Sad-na-legs, ascended the throne which he occupied until 817[14].

It was indeed he, and not his son Khri-tsug-lde-btsan, alias Ral-pa-can (817–841), as Bu-ston[15] claims, who initiated several important ventures from the Buddhist point of view: he sanctioned a new method in the translation of Buddhist texts; he had an inventory of Tibetan translations extant in Tibet drawn up; and finally, he ordered the compilation of a Sanskrit-Tibetan lexicon, the Mahāvyutpatti.

We read in Bu-ston (fol.130; tr. E. Obermiller, *Buston, History of Buddhism* II, Heidelberg 1932, repr. Delhi 1986, pp.196–7)[16]:

> In the past, at the time of [Khri-sroṅ-lde-btsan], the bodhisattva master Jñānendra, Źan-rgyal-ñen-ña-bzaṅ, Blon-khri-bźir-saṅ-śi, the translators Jñānadevakośa, Khyi-ḥbrug from Lce, the brahmin Ananta and others created a religious language *(dharmabhāṣā)* with some words not in common use in Tibet. Since they were translating out of various tongues, Chinese, languages of Li [† Khotan] and Lahore, etc., it was difficult to study the Dharma because of the great number of dissimilar words (*viṣamanāman*).
>
> Seeing this, the king [Khri-lde-sroṅ-btsan, and not Ral-pa-can]

14 See G. Tucci, 'The Validity…', p.321; *Tombs…*, p.20 (see previous note).

15 Id., *Tombs…*, p.18.

16 This passage had been edited by A. Ferrari, 'Arthaviniścaya', in *Atti della Reale Accademia d'Italia, Memorie, Classe sc. mor. e stor.*, Serie VII, vol.IV, 1944, p.539.

issued a threefold decree: 1. [† For the sake of] the masters from the Aparāntaka 'Western Continent' Jinamitra, Surendrabodhi, Śīlendrabodhi and Bodhimitra the Tibetan masters Ratnarakṣitā and Dharmatāśīla, the able translators Jñānasena [the famous Ye-śes-sde], Jayarakṣita, Mañjuśrīvarman, Ratnendraśīla, etc., translating the works of the Great and Small Vehicles [directly] from Sanskrit into Tibetan, let there be written in an index (*dkar-chag = sūcipattra*) [namely, the Mahāvyutpatti] the [Tibetan equivalents] attached to the [Sanskrit] terms; 2. while never deviating from the holy text *(gźuṅ-lugs = samaya),* let this be made suitable for study by all, 3. finally, let the texts translated earlier (*pūrvapariṇata*) be re-edited (*punar upadiṣṭa*) in the new language.

By means of these measures, Khri-lde-sroṅ-btsan was not only setting up a programme for the future; he wanted above all to sanction the remarkable activity undertaken by the Indian masters and Tibetan lotsabas of his generation, among whom figured Śākyaprabha and Ratnarakṣita, the translators of the Śgs.

The work accomplished was already considerable. In the year of the Dragon (812, according to G. Tucci[17]), Dpal-brtsegs and Nan-mkhaḥi-sñiṅ-po had compiled an inventory of the translations of the āgamas and śāstras in the palace of Ldan kar ma, in Stoṅ-thaṅ. In doing this they were responding to a royal order, doubtless emanating from Khri-lde-sroṅ-btsan: 'Let there be written an index of titles (*byaṅ*) and names of sections (*ḥtshal*) of the Saddharma, 'Prajñāpāramitā in a hundred thousand', etc., translated in the kingdom of Tibet'. This inventory, which appears in the Tanjur, Mdo ḥgrel, vol.CXXVII, fol.352*a*-373*a* of the Peking edition, has been published by S. Yoshimura, *The Denkar-ma, an oldest Catalogue of the Tibetan Buddhist Canon*, Ryukoku University, Kyoto 1950, and by M. Lalou, 'Les textes bouddhiques au temps du roi Khri-sroṅ-lde-bcan', *Journal Asiatique*, 1953, pp.313–53.

The inventory, which is divided into thirty sections, lists 736 translations indicating for each of them the total number of ślokas which make up the work, then the number of bam-po and also that of the ślokas. Mention is made therein of works by authors as late as Śubhagupta (c.720–780), Arcata (c.730–790), Kamalaśīla (c.740–795)

[17] *Minor Buddhist Texts* II, pp.47-8 in the notes: the inventory postdates the Council and was compiled in the time of Khri-lde-sroṇ-btsan, probably in 812. In an article published earlier, E. Frauwallner, 'Zu den buddhistischen Texten in der Zeit Khri-sroṇ-lde-btsan's, *Wiener Zeitschrift für die Kunde Süd- und Ost-asiens I*, 1957, p.11, dates the inventory in the year 800.

and Dharmottara (c.750–810)[18]. It therefore ensues that the inventory was compiled in the reign of Khri-lde-sroṅ-btsan (804?–817) and not in that of Khri-sroṅ-lde-btsan (755–797) as Bu-ston claims (E. Obermiller, II, p.191).

As M. Lalou[19] has remarked, the number of bam-po attributed by the inventory to a given work does not always correspond to the number of bam-po appearing in the classical editions of the Kanjur and Tanjur. Between the inventory and the classical editions there were modifications which sometimes led to the enlarging, sometimes to the diminution of the text.

This was not the case for the Śgs, which appears in the inventory under the number 111 with the mention: *dpaḥ bar ḥgro baḥi tiṅ ṅe ḥdzin*, 1,500 ślokas, 5 bam-po; these are exactly the same measurements as those of the Śgs which appears in the Kanjur (*Otani Cat.*, No.800) with Śākyaprabha and Ratnarakṣita as translators.

To return to the Mahāvyutpatti, its colophon, reproduced with some variations by Padma dkar po (1562–1592) in his *Chos-ḥbyuṅ* (fol.101*b*) and summarised by the fifth Dalai Lama (fol.42*a*)[20], clearly shows that it was initiated in the year of the Horse (814, according to G. Tucci[21]) by the king Khri-lde-sroṅ-btsan in his palace at ḥOn caṅ do. Begun in 814, this protracted work could not have been finished for several years, namely in the reign of Khri-tsug-lde-btsan Ral-pa-can (817–841). The sixty-fifth section of the Mahāvyutpatti lists the titles of one hundred and five holy texts (*saddharmanāmāni*): the thirty-first is precisely the Śūraṃgamasamādhinirdeśa, in Tibetan *dpaḥ-bar ḥgro-baḥi tiṅ-ṅe-ḥdzin btsan pa*[22].

18 I have taken these dates from E. Frauwallner, 'Landmarks in the History of Indian Logic', *Wiener Zeitschrift für die Kunde Süd-und Ost-asiens* V, 1961, pp.146-8.

19 'Les textes bouddhiques…' *Journal Asiatique*, 1953, p.314.

20 See A. Ferrari, 'Arthaviniścaya', pp.538-40.

21 *Minor Buddhist Texts* II, p.48, in the notes.

22 Collaterally and doubtless prior to the Chinese and Tibetan versions, a Khotanese translation of the Śgs should be noted. A long fragment discovered in Khadaliq near Khotan has been published by Sir H.W. Bailey, *Khotanese Buddhist Texts*, London 1951, pp.1-7, and this has been translated into English and analysed by R.E. Emmerick, *The Khotanese Śūraṅgamasamadhisūtra*, Oxford 1970 [† for more details see the author's Foreword above]. See also R.E. Emmerick, *A Guide to the Literature of Khotan* (Studia Philologica Buddhica, Occasional Papers Series II), Tokyo 1979, esp. p.32. On Khotan, a centre of Buddhist studies much frequented by the Chinese, see also Sir H.W. Bailey, 'Gaustama: The Kingdom of the Sakas in Khotan' in *Indo-Scythian Studies*: *Khotanese Texts* IV, Cambridge 1961, pp.1-18. The small neighbouring kingdom of Karghalik (in Chinese Chê-chü-chieh, in Tibetan Ca-ko-ka or Cu gon[pan]) possessed a store of Mahāyāna sūtras in their long recensions; cf. É. Lamotte, 'Mañjuśrī', *T'oung Pao*, 1960, p.65, n.156.

CONCORDANCE OF THE TRANSLATIONS OF THE ŚŪRAṂGAMASAMĀDHISŪTRA

§ refers to the paragraphs of my translation. Ch. = Chinese translation by Kumārajīva (T 642), the page numbers of which are embedded in my translation in square brackets. Tib. = Tibetan translation of the Peking Kanjur (ed. D.T. Suzuki, volume 32, No.800).

§	Ch.	Tib.	§	Ch.	Tib.
1	629*b* 11	276*a* 6	30	632*b* 5	290*b* 6
2	629*b* 13	276*a* 8	31	632*b* 24	291*b* 3
3	629*b* 21	276*b* 6	32	632*c* 12	292*b* 3
4	629*c* 6	277*b* 4	33	632*c* 17	292*b* 7
5	629*c* 10	277*b* 6	34	632*c* 24	293*a* 5
6	629*c* 18	278*a* 6	35	632*c* 29	293*a* 8
7	629*c* 21	278*b* 3	36	633*a* 7	293*b* 4
8	630*a* 9	279*b* 3	37	633*a* 12	293*b* 7
9	630*a* 16	280*a* 1	38	633*a* 21	294*a* 5
10	630*a* 21	280*a* 6	39	633*a* 29	294*b* 2
11	630*b* 5	280*b* 5	40	633*b* 5	294*b* 5
12	630*b* 12	281*a* 2	41	633*b* 9	294*b* 7
13	630*b* 16	281*a* 4	42	633*b* 20	295*a* 6
14	630*b* 23	281*b* 1	43	633*b* 23	295*b* 1
15	630*b* 28	281*b* 4	44	633*b* 28	295*b* 6
16	630*c* 5	282*a* 2	45	633*c* 6	296*a* 3
17	630*c* 8	282*a* 5	46	633*c* 11	296*a* 6
18	630*c* 19	282*b* 5	47	633*c* 17	296*b* 2
19	631*a* 11	283*b* 4	48	633*c* 25	297*a* 1
20	631*a* 16	283*b* 8	49	634*a* 20	298*a* 5
21	631*a* 18	284*a* 1	50	634*a* 28	298*b* 1
–	–	286*b* 5	51	634*b* 3	298*b* 3
22	631*c* 27	289*a* 3	52	634*b* 16	299*a* 2
23	632*a* 1	289*a* 5	53	634*b* 19	299*a* 4
24	632*a* 2	289*a* 7	54	634*b* 24	299*a* 7
25	632*a* 7	289*b* 3	55	634*c* 2	299*b* 4
26	632*a* 9	289*b* 5	56	634*c* 21	300*b* 1
27	632*a* 15	290*a* 1	57	634*c* 26	300*b* 3
28	632*a* 23	290*a* 5	58	635*a* 3	300*b* 7
29	632*a* 28	290*b* 1	59	635*a* 16	301*a* 7

§	Ch.	Tib.	§	Ch.	Tib.
60	635*a* 22	301*b* 3	97	638*b* 25	314*b* 1
61	635*a* 29	301*b* 8	98	638*c* 2	314*b* 4
62	635*b* 12	302*a* 6	99	638*c* 8	314*b* 8
63	635*b* 25	302*b* 8	100	638*c* 12	315*a* 3
64	635*c* 2	303*a* 5	101	638*c* 17	315*a* 6
65	635*c* 6	303*a* 8	102	638*c* 29	315*b* 5
66	635*c* 24	304*b* 3	103	639*a* 4	315*b* 7
67	635*c* 29	304*b* 5	104	639*a* 9	316*a* 2
68	636*a* 13	305*a* 7	105	639*a* 16	316*a* 5
69	636*a* 19	305*b* 5	106	639*a* 22	316*b* 2
70	636*a* 28	306*a* 3	107	639*a* 25	316*b* 5
71	636*b* 6	306*b* 1	108	639*b* 2	317*a* 2
72	636*b* 19	307*a* 1	109	639*b* 12	317*a* 8
73	636*b* 16	307*a* 6	110	639*b* 26	318*a* 1
74	636*c* 4	307*b* 4	111	639*c* 1	318*a* 4
75	636*c* 15	308*a* 4	112	639*c* 4	318*b* 2
76	636*c* 22	308*b* 1	113	639*c* 9	318*b* 5
77	636*c* 26	308*b* 4	114	639*c* 13	318*b* 7
78	637*a* 3	309*a* 3	115	639*c* 21	319*a* 5
79	637*a* 8	309*a* 8	116	640*a* 1	319*b* 3
80	637*a* 17	309*b* 8	117	640*a* 3	319*b* 5
81	637*b* 3	310*a* 4	118	640*a* 5	319*b* 6
82	637*b* 5	310*a* 6	119	640*a* 9	319*b* 8
83	637*b* 16	310*b* 5	120	640*a* 12	320*a* 1
84	637*b* 19	310*b* 8	121	640*a* 16	320*a* 4
85	637*b* 27	311*a* 6	122	640*a* 23	320*a* 8
86	637*c* 7	311*b* 2	123	640*b* 14	321*a* 5
87	637*c* 12	311*b* 4	124	640*b* 25	321*b* 6
88	637*c* 20	312*a* 3	125	640*c* 3	322*a* 1
89	638*a* 2	312*b* 1	126	640*c* 15	322*b* 1
90	638*a* 7	312*b* 4	127	640*c* 22	322*b* 5
91	638*a* 17	313*a* 3	128	640*c* 26	322*b* 7
92	638*a* 24	313*a* 6	129	641*a* 2	323*a* 3
93	638*b* 3	313*b* 2	130	641*a* 16	323*b* 2
94	638*b* 7	313*b* 6	131	641*a* 24	323*b* 6
95	638*b* 13	314*a* 1	132	641*a* 27	323*b* 8
96	638*b* 22	314*a* 6	133	641*b* 14	324*b* 1

§	Ch.	Tib.	§	Ch.	Tib.
134	641*b* 24	325*a* 1	157	643*c* 20	332*b* 6
135	641*c* 8	325*b* 1	158	644*a* 29	333*a* 3
136	641*c* 16	325*b* 7	159	644*a* 3	333*a* 6
137	642*a* 1	326*a* 7	160	644*a* 9	333*b* 3
138	642*a* 13	326*b* 8	161	644*a* 16	333*b* 8
139	642*a* 21	327*a* 4	162	644*a* 18	334*a* 3
140	642*a* 26	327*a* 7	163	644*a* 20	334*a* 5
141	642*b* 6	327*b* 4	164	644*a* 24	334*a* 7
142	642*b* 9	327*b* 6	165	644*b* 7	334*b* 4
143	642*b* 16	328*a* 3	166	644*b* 16	335*a* 4
144	642*b* 23	328*a* 6	167	644*b* 19	335*a* 5
145	642*c* 2	328*b* 2	168	644*b* 25	335*b* 2
146	642*c* 7	328*b* 6	169	644*c* 7	336*a* 1
147	642*c* 10	328*b* 8	170	644*c* 16	336*a* 6
148	642*c* 14	329*a* 2	171	644*c* 24	336*b* 4
149	642*c* 20	329*a* 6	172	645*a* 5	337*a* 4
150	643*a* 3	329*b* 5	173	645*a* 13	337*b* 2
151	643*a* 11	330*a* 1	174	645*a* 22	338*a* 1
152	643*a* 18	330*a* 7	175	645*b* 7	338*a* 8
153	643*b* 4	330*b* 6	176	645*b* 12	338*b* 2
154	643*b* 21	331*b* 2	177	645*b* 15	338*b* 4
155	643*c* 6	332*a* 4	–	–	338*b* 8
156	643*c* 10	332*a* 7	178	645*b* 22	344*a* 1

ŚŪRAṂGAMASAMĀDHISŪTRA

translated by the

TRIPIṬA KUMĀRAJĪVA

from the Land of Kucha under the Late Ch'in

[*Introduction*]

1. Thus have I heard. At one time the Buddha was in Rājagṛha on the Gṛhdrakūṭaparvata, with a great assembly of bhikṣus, thirty-two thousand bhikṣus, and Mahāsattva-bodhisattvas numbering seventy-two thousand.

2. These last were universally known (*abhijñānābhijñāta*); they possessed the *dhāraṇīs*; they were gifted with eloquence (*pratibhāna*) and delighted in expounding ceaselessly; well established in concentration (*samādhisupratiṣthita*), they never strayed from it; they were skilled in knowledge (*jñānakuśala*) and of inexhaustible wisdom (*akṣayaprajñā*); they possessed the certainty concerning the profound teachings (*gambhīradharmakṣānti*) and had penetrated the profound expositions of the Dharma (*gambhīradharmamukha*); for innumerable incalculable periods (*asaṃkhyeyakalpa*) they had cultivated good dharmas (*kuśaladharma*) and still recalled them all; they had overcome Māra and adversaries (*nihatamārapratyarthika*)[1]; they had secured perfectly adorned Buddha-fields (*buddhakṣetra*); they possessed great goodwill (*mahāmaitrī*) and great compassion (*mahākaruṇā*), and their bodies were adorned with all the marks (*lakṣaṇa*); they had reached the other shore of great vigour (*mahāvīryapāramiṃgata*); they were acquainted with all languages (*nirukti*) and other skilful means (*upāya*); their practices (*caryā*) and bodily attitudes (*īryāpatha*) were perfectly consummate (*saṃpanna*); they were all determined as to the three doors to deliverance (*vimokṣamukha*); through unobstructed knowledge (*apratihatajñāna*), they had penetrated the triple world (*traidhātukaniryāta*); they had formed the resolve (*niścaya*) never to abandon anyone; they were gifted with mindfulness (*smṛti*), intelligence (*mati*) and understanding (*saṃkalpa*), as well as patience (*kṣānti*) and knowledge (*jñāna*).

3. The bodhisattvas endowed with such virtues (*guṇa*) were:

the bodhisattva Avaivartikadharmacakrapravartaka 'Setting turning the irreversible Wheel of the Dharma'

1 A traditional expression; cf. Saddharmapuṇḍ., p.430, *1*; below, § 8, 129.

the bodhisattva Utpāditacittadharmacakrapravartaka 'Setting turning the Wheel of the Dharma after having aroused the thought of Bodhi',

the bodhisattva Anāvaraṇadharmacakrapravartaka 'Unobstructedly setting turning the Wheel of the Dharma',

the bodhisattva Vimalaśuddhi 'Unstained Purity',

the bodhisattva Sarvaparyutthānaviṣkambhin 'Eliminating all the veils of passion',

the bodhisattva Viśudderyāpathasaṃdarśananandin[2] 'Delighting in adopting pure bodily attitudes',

the bodhisattva Varalakṣaṇavyūharājamati 'Royal intelligence adorned with marvellous marks',

the bodhisattva Sarvasattvāvisaṃvādin, 'Not wronging any being',

the bodhisattva Anantaguṇasamudramati 'Intelligence like the sea of infinite virtues',

the bodhisattva Sadāsamāhitāvikṣiptendriya 'Of senses ever concentrated and undistracted',

the bodhisattva Bhūtasvara 'Of truthful sounds',

the bodhisattva Sarvadevastuti 'Praise of all the gods' [**629c**],

the bodhisattva Dhāraṇīśvararāja 'Sovereign king of *dhāraṇīs*',

the bodhisattva Pratibhānālaṃkāra 'Adornment of eloquence',

the bodhisattva Mañjuśrī kumārabhūta 'Of gentle majesty and crown prince of the Dharma',

the bodhisattva Maitreya, 'Good-willed',

the bodhisattva Sumerukūṭarāja 'King of the summit of Sumeru',

the bodhisattva Guṇaratnavyūhasamudramati[3] 'Intelligence like the sea adorned with the jewels of the virtues',

the bodhisattva Mahāvyūha 'Of great adornments',

the bodhisattva Mahālakṣaṇa 'Of great marks',

the bodhisattva Prabhālakṣaṇa 'Mark of light',

the bodhisattva Prabhāśrī 'Majesty of light',

the bodhisattva Viśuddhamati 'Pure intelligence',

the bodhisattva Prāmodyarāja 'King of joy',

the bodhisattva Dṛḍhasthāma 'Firm might',

the bodhisattva Dṛḍhamati[4] 'Firm intelligence'.

[2] A doubtful reconstruction; in Tib. we find *Dgaḥ ba daṅ dad paḥi spyod lam ston pa = Nandaprasāderyāpathasaṃdarśaka.*

[3] In Tib. *Yon tan rin po che bkod pa rgya mtsho blo gros.*

[4] Chien-i 堅意, in Tib. *Blo gros brtan pa*, which gives the Skt Dṛḍhamati. This name is confirmed in a fragment of the Śgs from Central Asia published by A.F. Hoernle, *Manuscript Remains of Buddhist Literature found in Eastern Turkestan* I, Oxford 1916, p.126,*2*, and in an extract from the Śgs quoted in the Śikṣāsamuccaya, p.91,*9* sq. Here Dṛḍhamati is the main

These and other Mahāsattva-bodhisattvas numbering seventy-two thousand.

4. In addition, all those who existed in the trichiliomegachiliocosm (*trisāhasramahāsāhasralokadhātu*) by way of Śakras, Brahmās, Lokapāla Kings of the gods, devas, nāgas, yakṣas, gandharvas, asuras, garuḍas, kiṃnaras, mahoragas, manuṣyas, amanuṣyas, universally known (*abhijñānābhijñāta*), having planted good roots (*avaropitakuśalamūla*) and resolutely intent on the sublime teaching (*udārādhimuktika*), were present in that assembly (*tasminn eva parṣatsaṃnipāte saṃnipatitā abhūvan saṃniṣaṇṇāḥ*).

[*The Most Excellent Concentration*]

5. Then the bodhisattva Dṛḍhamati, present in that great assembly, had this thought: I would now like to ask the Tathāgata a question which would be such as to protect (*parirakṣaṇa*) the lineage of the Buddha (*buddhavaṃśa*), the lineage of the Dharma (*dharmavaṃśa*) and the lineage of the Community (*saṃghavaṃśa*), obscure and eclipse (*dhyāmīkaraṇa*) the dwellings of Māra (*mārabhavana*) and confound (*nigrahaṇa)* proud people (*abhimānika*). Thus, those who have not yet planted good roots (*anavaropitakuśalamūla*) will plant them immediately. Those who have already planted good roots will add to (*vardhana*) them. Those who have not yet aroused the thought of supreme and perfect enlightenment (*anutpāditānuttara-samyaksaṃbodhicitta*) will arouse that thought (*cittotpāda*). Those who have already aroused that thought will become irreversible (*avaivartika*) [bodhisattvas][5]. Irreversible bodhisattvas will rapidly (*kṣipram*) attain *anuttarasamyaksaṃbodhi*. Beings speculating on objects (*sālambana*) and attached to false views (*dṛṣṭyabhiniviṣṭa*) will arouse the thought of eliminating them. Beings attached to inferior teachings (*hīnādhimuktika*) will become resolutely attached to the sublime teaching (*udārādhimuktika*). Those who are resolutely intent on the sublime teaching will experience great joy (*pramuditā*).

interlocutor of the Buddha; he will obtain the Concentration of Heroic Progress at the end of the sūtra (§ 167). [† see the Foreword, p.xv for the list of these bodhisattvas as it appears in the Khotanese version of the Śgs.]

[5] This concerns absolutely irreversible bodhisattvas (bss) in possession of an irreversible certainty (*avaivartikakṣāntipratilabdha*: cf. Saddharmapuṇḍ., p.259,*13*). They obtain this virtue in the eighth stage, the Acalā, also called 'Irreversible Stage' (*avivartyabhūmi*) in the Daśabhūmika, p.71,*12*; *avaivartikabhūmi* in Bodh. bhūmi, p.235,*18*). It is generally in this full sense that the texts use this expression (cf. Vkn, pp.61, 141, 222, 265, 291). However, as we shall see further on, § 104, n.209, two or even three kinds of *avaivartika* can be distinguished.

6. Having had this thought, Dṛḍhamati rose from his seat and, having arranged his upper robe on one shoulder, having placed his right knee on the ground and having extended his joined hands towards the Bhagavat, he said to him (*atha khalu Dṛḍhamatir bodhisattva utthāyāsanād ekāṃsam uttarāsaṅgaṃ kṛtvā dakṣiṇaṃ jānumaṇḍalaṃ pṛthivyāṃ pratiṣṭhāpya yena bhagavāṃs tenāñjaliṃ praṇamya bhagavantam idam avocat*): Bhagavat, I would like to question the Bhagavat Tathāgata on a small point if the Bhagavat gives me leave to ask a question (*pṛccheyam ahaṃ bhagavantam arhantaṃ samyaksaṃbuddhaṃ kaṃcid eva pradeśaṃ sa cen me bhagavān avakāśaṃ kuryāt pṛṣṭapraśna-vyākaraṇāya*)[6].

The Buddha said to Dṛḍhamati: Question the Tathāgata on whatever you wish, and I, in answering all these questions, will delight your mind (*evam ukte bhagavān Dṛḍhamatiṃ bodhisattvam āmantrayate sma pṛccha tvaṃ tathāgatam arhantaṃ samyaksaṃbuddhaṃ yad yad evākāṅkṣasi. ahaṃ te tasya tasya praśnasya vyākaraṇena cittam ārādhayiṣye*)[7].

7. The bodhisattva Dṛḍhamati said to the Buddha: Bhagavat, what is the *samādhi* through which a bodhisattva:

rapidly attains *anuttarasamyaksaṃbodhi*,

is never apart from frequentation by the Buddhas,

illuminates with his own light (*avabhāsa*) all the ten regions,

acquires a wondrous wisdom (*vikurvitaprajñā*) so as to destroy Māras (*mārāṇāṃ nigrahāya*),

obtains mastery in knowledge (*jñānavaśitā*) and wins spontaneous knowledge (*svayaṃbhūjñāna*)[8],

obtains the untaught knowledge (*anupadiṣṭajñāna*)[9] and does not depend on others (*aparapraṇeya*)[10],

possesses indestructible eloquence (*anācchedyapratibhāna*) up to the

6 Stock phrase: cf. Dīgha I, p.51, *3-5*; Majjhima I, p.229, *35-37*; III, p.15, *23-25*; Aṅguttara V, p.196, *12-14*; Samādhirāja I, p.10, *15-17*; II, p.217, *10-12*; III, p.487, *3-5*; Karmavibhaṅga, p.29, *22-23*.

7 Stock phrase liable to variations; cf. Samādhirāja, I, pp.10, *18* - 11, *2*; II, p.217, *13-15*; III, p.487, *7-9*.

8 In Tib. *raṅ byuṅ gi chos thob paḥi phyir ye śes la dbaṅ du ḥgyur ba*.

9 Read *te wu chiao chih* 得無教智, with the Tib. *ma bstan paḥi ye śes daṅ ldan paḥi phyir*. The 'untaught' (*anupadiṣṭa*) virtues form part of the *āveṇikadharmas* of the bodhisattva (bs); cf. Mahāvyutpatti, Nos.787-92.

10 In Tib. *gźan gyi driṅ la ḥjog par mi ḥgyur ba*, giving the Sanskrit *aparapratyaya* or *aparapraṇeya* (cf. Mahāvyutpatti, Nos.2396 and 2398).

final limit (*aparāntakoṭi*)[11],

obtains the bases of supernormal power (*ṛddhipāda*) and thus ensures himself of an incalculable life-span (*aprameyāyus*)[12],

expounds the Śrāvakayāna to adherents of the Śrāvakas (*śrāvakādhimukta*),

expounds the Pratyekabuddhayāna to adherents of the Pratyekabuddhas,

expounds the Mahāyāna to adherents of the Mahāyāna,

penetrates the teaching (*dharma*) of the Śrāvakas, but without entering into the predestination of the Śrāvakas (*śrāvakaniyāma*)[13],

penetrates the teaching of the Pratyekabuddhas, but without entering into the *pratyekabuddhaniyāma* [**630a**],

penetrates the teaching of the Buddhas, but without entering into complete cessation (*atyantanirodha*)[14],

manifests (*saṃdarśayati*) the figure (*saṃsthāna*), colours (*varṇa*) and bodily attitudes (*īryāpatha*) of a Śrāvaka, but without ever straying inwardly from the thought of enlightenment (*bodhicitta*)[15],

manifests the figure, colours and bodily attitudes of a Pratyekabuddha, but without ever straying inwardly from the thought of great compassion (*mahākaruṇācitta)* of the Buddhas[16],

manifests, through an illusionary concentration (*māyopamasamādhi*), the figure, colours and bodily attitudes of a Tathāgata,

[11] In Tib. *phyi maḥi mthaḥi bskal pa bye bar ston paḥi phyir spobs pa rgyun mi ḥchad par ḥgyur ba.*

[12] Possession of the four *ṛddhipādas* allows of prolongation of life at will; cf. Skt. Mahāparinirvāṇa, p.204: *yasya kasyacic catvāra ṛddhipādā āsevitā bhāvitā bahulīkṛtā ākaṅkṣamānaḥ sa kalpaṃ vā tiṣṭhet kalpāvaśeṣaṃ vā.* Corresponding Pāli passage in Dīgha II, p.103, *1-4*.

[13] Here *tao* corresponds to the Tib. *ṅes par gyur ba = niyāma*. Regarding the respective *niyāmas* of a śrāvaka and a bodhisattva, see Vkn, p.19, n.65, and below, § 56, n.140, § 104, n.210, § 133, n.268, § 150. As from his entry into the path of vision (*darśanamārga*), the śrāvaka is himself predestined as to his future acquisition of the absolute good (*samyaktva*), namely Nirvāṇa; the bs is himself predestined as to his future reaching of Saṃbodhi. The *niyāma* of the bs constitutes his second predestination (*niyatipāta*); see below, § 104, n.211.

[14] For the Śgs, entry into Nirvāṇa by the bodhisattvas and Buddhas is not real cessation, merely skill in means. All beings, all dharmas are essentially and eternally in Parinirvāṇa. Hence there can be no question of entry into Nirvāṇa (cf. §§ 71-2).

[15] In the guise of a śrāvaka, the bs does not aspire to the Bodhi of the śrāvakas or of the arhats, a Bodhi consisting of the knowledge of the destruction of the impurities (*āsravakṣayajñāna*) and the knowledge of their non-arising (*anutpādajñāna)*, the bs aims essentially for the *anuttarasamyaksaṃbodhi* of the Buddhas. Cf. Vkn, pp.298-303.

[16] In theory, if a Pratyekabuddha does not teach the Dharma, it is due to timidity or lack of courage; see Kośa III, p.196; below, § 133.

manifests, through the power of his own good roots (*kuśalamūla)*, the presence among the Tuṣita gods, the assuming of the last existence (*antimajātyādāna*), the entry into the womb (*garbhāvakrānti*), the birth (*jāti*), the renunciation of the world (*abhiniṣkramaṇa*) and the occupation of the seat of enlightenment (*bodhimaṇḍaniṣīdana*)[17],

manifests, through the power of profound wisdom (*prajñā*), the turning of the Wheel of the Dharma (*dharmacakrapravartana*),

manifests, through the power of skilful means (*upāya*), the entry into Nirvāna,

manifests, through the power of concentration (*samādhi*), the distribution of the relics (*śarīravibhāga*),

manifests, through the power of his previous aspiration (*pūrvapraṇidhāna*)[18], the disappearance of the Saddharma (*saddharmavipralopa*),

What then, O Bhagavat, is this *samādhi* through which a bodhisattva manifests such virtues (*guṇa*), but without definitively entering Parinirvāṇa?

8. The Buddha said to the bodhisattva Dṛḍhamati: Excellent, excellent (*sādhu sādhu*), O Dṛḍhamati, you question the Tathāgata on this subject *(artha*) for the welfare and happiness of many beings (*bahujanahitāya bahujanasukhāya*), through pity for the world (*lokānukampāyai*), for the benefit, welfare and happiness of the great body of beings, humans and gods (*mahato janakāyasyārthāya hitāya sukhāya devānāṃ ca manuṣyānāṃ ca*), for the protection of present and future bodhisattvas (*pratyutpānnāṃ cānāgatānāṃ ca bodhisattvānāṃ parigrahāya*).

Know this. You have planted good roots (*avaropitakuśalamūla*), you have honoured and served innumerable hundreds of thousands of koṭinayutas of Buddhas of the past; you have trodden all the paths (*mārga*)[19]; you have overcome Māra and adversaries (*nihatamārapratyarthika*); you have obtained an independent knowledge (*svatantrajñāna*) regarding all the Buddhadharmas; you have won over and protected throngs of bodhisattvas; you know the treasure (*kośa*) of all the teachings (*dharma*) of the Buddha; that is why you have come to ask me

17 A bs in the tenth stage magically carries out the exploits of an 'historical' Buddha. See more below, § 21, Nos.96-100, §§ 123, 163.

18 At the moment of his *cittotpāda*, a bs can, through an aspiration, determine the duration of the Saddharma which he will expound as a Buddha.

19 In Tib. *theg pa thams cad kyi ṅes par ḥbyuṅ baḥi lam rnams su ṅes par byuṅ ba* = *sarvayānaniryāṇamārganiryāta*, 'You have trodden the paths of release of all the Vehicles'.

a question (*praśnavyākaraṇa*) already asked in the past of Buddhas as numerous as the sands of the Ganges (*gaṅgānadī-vālukopama*).

9. Dṛḍhamati, in this assembly (*parṣad*), the Tathāgata does not see a single deva, nāga, yakṣa, gandharva, a single Śrāvaka or Pratyekabuddha who would be capable of formulating this question. Only a man as eminent as yourself is able to approach such a question. Listen well then, and engrave it on your mind (*tena hi śṛṇu sādhu ca suṣṭhu ca manasikuru*). I will tell you of that *samādhi* with which bodhisattvas must be endowed (*saṃpanna*) in order to obtain the virtues (*guṇa*) of which you speak and of even greater ones (*bahvantaraviśiṣṭa*).

Dṛḍhamati said to the Buddha: Excellent, O Bhagavat, and he began to listen (*sādhu bhagavann iti pratyaśrauṣīt*).

[*The Heroic Progress*]

10. The Buddha said to Dṛḍhamati: It is a *samādhi* called 'Concentration of Heroic Progress' [*Śūraṃgamasamādhi*; abbr. to Śgs]. Bodhisattvas who have obtained this *samādhi* can, since you ask about it, manifest Parinirvāṇa, but without definitively ceasing to be.

They manifest (*saṃdarśayanti*) figures (*saṃsthāna*) and colours (*varṇa*), but without harming the suchness of form (*rūpatathatā*)[20].

They circulate (*saṃcaranti*) through all the *buddhakṣetras*, but do not conceive (*na vikalpayanti*) of the *buddhakṣetras*[21].

They come close (*saṃyuñjanti*) to all the Buddhas, but do not see any distinction (*viśeṣa*) in the basic sameness (*samatā*) and the fundamental element (*dharmadhātu*)[22].

They perform all the practices (*caryā*), but clearly understand the method of purifying the practices (*caryāpariśodhana*).

They possess sovereignty (*ādhipatya*) over all the gods and mankind (*devamanuṣya*), but do not fall into pride (*māna*), pretension (*stambha*) or negligence (*pramāda*).

They possess the supreme power (*aiśvarya*) of all Māras, but abstain

20 In Tib. *gzugs su ston pa thams ca kyaṅ ston la gzugs kyi de bźin ñid las chos rnams ḥkhrugs par yaṅ mi byed*: 'Even while displaying themselves in all manifestations of form, they do not strip away the dharmas from the suchness of form (*rūpatathatā*)'. In other words, even while manifesting themselves by appearing in forms, the bss know that the suchness (*tathatā*) of form is empty and non-existent: *Rūpam eva śūnyatā śūnyataiva rūpam* (cf. Vkn, p.LXIX, n.19).

21 In fact the *buddhakṣetras* are empty and non-existent (cf. Vkn, pp.133, 182, 210).

22 *Fa hsing* 法性 corresponds to the Tib. *chos kyi dbyiṅs* = *dharmadhātu*. Non-existent like the rest, the Buddhas resort to the *dharmadhātu*, the fundamental element which is non-existence pure and simple (cf. Vkn, pp.LXX-LXXII). From this absolute point of view, everything is the same (*sama)* as everything else.

from the works of cruel[23] Māras (*mārakarman*).

They circulate through the triple world (*traidhātuka*), but do not swerve from the fundamental element (*dharmadhātu*)[24].

They are born [**630b**] in all the destinies (*gati*) but do not conceive (*na vikalpayanti*) of there being various destinies.

They skilfully pronounce (*vyākurvanti*) all the utterances of the Dharma (*dharmapada*) and, in various languages (*nirukti*), they clarify its meaning (*arthaṃ saṃprakāśayanti*), but they know (*adhigacchanti*) that syllables (*akṣara*) spring from sameness (*samatā*) and that there exist no differences (*viśeṣa*) between languages[25].

They are always recollected (*samāhita*), but they ripen (*paripācayanti*) beings.

They possess the certainty of universal destruction (*kṣayakṣānti*) and the certainty of the non-arising of dharmas (*anutpattikadharmakṣānti*), but they speak of dharmas as having arising (*utpāda*) and cessation (*nirodha*) as their marks (*lakṣaṇa*)[26].

They go alone (*ekacārin*) and without fear (*viśārada*) like a lion (*siṃha*).

[*The Offering of a Throne*]

11. Then, in the assembly, the Śakras, Brahmās, Lokapāla Kings of the gods and the whole assembly (*sarvāvatī parṣad*) had this thought: We have never before heard the name of this *samādhi*, even less the explanation of its meaning (*arthavibhaṅga*). Today, when we have come and seen the Buddha, it is of advantage (*lābhā naḥ sulabdhāḥ)* to hear the name of the Śūraṃgamasamādhi pronounced. The son of good family (*kulaputra*) or daughter of good family (*kuladuhitā*) seeking [perfect] Buddhahood (*samyaksaṃbuddhatva*)[27] and who, after having heard the explanation (*vibhaṅga*) of the Śūraṃgamasamādhi, believes it

[23] Read *mung* 猛 instead of *i* 猗.

[24] *Fa hsiang* 法相 corresponds here to the Tib. *chos kyi dybiṅs = dharmadhātu.*

[25] Cf. Vkn, p.203; below, § 74.

[26] They profess the *dharmanairātmya* even while adopting the language of the Sthaviras and Sarvāstivādins who speak of the three or four marks of the conditioned (*saṃskṛtalakṣaṇa*): arising, duration, modification and disappearance (cf. Kośa II, p.222).

[27] Kumārajīva usually renders by *fo-tao* 佛道 the Skt *samyaksaṃbuddhatva* (compare Pancaviṃśati, ed. Dutt, p.25, *16*, and the trans. by Kumārajīva, T 223, ch.1, p.220*a* 18). Further on (T 642, ch.2, p.638*c* 7), the four characters *ch'eng-chiu fo-tao* 成就佛道 have as their correspondence in the Tibetan version (Tib. trip., Vol.32, p.86, fol.314*b* 8), *bla na med pa yaṅ dag rdzogs paḥi byaṅ chub mṅon par rdzogs par ḥtshaṅ rgya bar ḥgyur ba*, equivalent to the Skt *anuttarāyāṃ samyaksaṃbodhāv abhisaṃbuddhaḥ* (cf. Mahāvyutpatti, No.6355).

(*adhimucyate*) and does not doubt, that son or daughter of good family will never stray from Buddhahood (*buddhatvān na vivartsyati*). Even more so, if after having believed it (*adhimucya*), he or she grasps it (*udgṛhṇāti*), remembers it (*dhārayati*), repeats it (*vācayati*), expounds it to others (*parebhyaḥ saṃprakāśayati*) and, conforming to what it says, applies his or her effort to it (*bhāvanāyogena prayunakti*)[28].

12. Then the Śakras, Brahmās and Lokapāla Kings of the gods had this thought: We should now present (*prajñāpayitum*) to the Tathāgata a lion-throne (*siṃhāsana*), a throne of the Good Dharma (*saddharmāsana*), a throne worthy of a great personage (*satpuruṣāsana*), a throne of great splendour (*mahāvyūhāsana*), a throne for a great turning of the Wheel of the Dharma (*mahādharmacakrapravartanāsana*), so that the Tathāgata, seated on this throne of ours, will expound the Śūraṃgamasamādhi.

Among themselves, each one said to himself: It is I alone who offer this *siṃhāsana* to the Buddha, no-one else can do so.

13. Then the Śakras, Brahmās and Lokapāla Kings of the gods each separately offered (*prajñāpayanti sma*) to the Tathāgata a *siṃhāsana* which was adorned (*alaṃkṛta*), pure (*viśuddha*), admirable (*darśanīya*) and very high (*unnata*), strewn with innumerable precious fabrics (*apramāṇaratnavastrāstīrṇa*), its top covered with canopies (*vitāna*), banners (*dhvaja*) and wonderful precious parasols (*ratnacchattra*), [surrounded] by a balustrade (*vedikā*) of all kinds of precious jewels (*ratna*), [set] to the right and left with innumerable precious trees (*ratnavṛkṣa*) with branches and leaves on which rows of pearls (*muktāvali*) were carefully arranged, hoisted with banners and flags (*samucchritadhvajapatāka*)[29], draped with great precious canopies (*mahāratnavitānavitata*)[30], adorned with interlacings of jewels and hung with precious bells (*ratnakiṅkiṇī*), the top scattered with all kinds of wonderful flowers (*nānāvidhapuṣpābhikīrṇa)*, perfumed with all kinds of celestial incenses (*divyadhūpavāsita*), embellished with gold (*hema*), silver (*rūpya*), jewels (*ratna*) of precious stones (*maṇi*) and pearls (*muktikā*): indeed, of the most varied of ornaments, none was missing from that seat.

14. At that precise moment (*etasminn eva kṣaṇalavamuhūrte*), there were before the Tathāgata 84,000 koṭinayutas of precious *siṃhāsanas*, but no discomfort (*āvaraṇa*) resulted from this for the assembly[31].

[28] Commonplace stock phrase; cf. Vkn, p.250, n.16.

[29] Cf. Mahāvyutpatti, No.6120.

[30] Cf. *ibid.*, No.6119.

[31] A commonplace wonder, cf. Vkn, pp.139, 211.

Taken one by one, the devaputras did not see the seats of the others and each one said to himself: I alone have offered a *siṃhāsana* to the Buddha, and it is on that throne that I have offered him that the Buddha will expound the Śūraṃgamasamādhi.

Then the Śakras, Brahmās and Lokapāla Kings of the gods, having completed the offering of the thrones, each said to the Buddha: May the Buddha sit on my throne and expound the Śūraṃgamasamādhi.

[*The Multiplication of the Buddhas*]

15. Then the Bhagavat performed such a supernormal action (*evaṃrūpaṃ ṛdhhyabhisaṃskarām abhisaṃskaroti sma*)[32] that he sat everywhere at the same time on the 84,000 koṭinayutas of *siṃhāsanas* [**630c**], but each deva only saw the Buddha seated on the throne that he had set out and did not see the other thrones. One Śakra devendra said to another Śakra: 'Just look at the Tathāgata seated on my throne'.

Similarly, the Śakras, Brahmās and Lokapāla Kings of the gods said to each other: 'Just look at the Tathāgata seated on my throne'. And the other Śakra replied: 'Now the Tathāgata is seated only on my throne; he is not on yours'.

16. Then the Tathāgata considered that those Śakras, Brahmās and Lokapāla Kings of the gods fulfilled the requisite conditions (*pūrva-pratyaya*) for being delivered and, desiring to demonstrate a little of the potency (*prabhāva*) of the Śūraṃgamasamādhi and have the practices (*caryā*) of the Mahāyāna adopted, the Tathāgata, say I, acted so that all the assemblies saw the Tathāgata present everywhere on the 84,000 koṭinayutas of precious *siṃhāsanas*.

17. The whole assembly experienced great joy (*prītiprāmodyajāta*) and was filled with wonder (*adbhutaprāpta*). They all rose from their seats (*utthāyāsanāt*) and, joining their hands (*pragṛhītāñjali*), bowed to the Buddha and said to him: Excellent, excellent! Immense is the power [of the Tathāgata] who is able to gratify the desires (*āśayaparipūraṇa*) of all the devaputras. All the devaputras who have offered a seat to the Tathāgata, having thus witnessed the supernormal might (*ṛddhi-prātihārya*) of the Buddha, aroused the *anuttarasamyaksaṃbodhicitta*. Together they addressed the Buddha and said to him: Bhagavat, it is in order to pay homage (*pūjana*) to the Tathāgata, calm the suffering of all beings (*sarvasattvaduḥkhapraśamana*), protect the Good Dharma (*saddharmaparigrahaṇa*) and not interrupt the lineage of the Buddhas (*buddhavaṃśānupaccheda*) that we arouse the *anuttarasamyak-*

[32] A traditional expression: cf. Vkn, pp.139, 204, 237, 247.

saṃbodhicitta. May we, in future time (*anāgate 'dhvani*), become Buddhas gifted with such supernormal might and accomplish wonders (*vikurvaṇa*) such as those that the Tathāgata accomplished today.

Then the Buddha congratulated (*sādhukāram adāt*) the devaputras: Excellent, excellent! It is exactly as you say (*evam etad yathā vadatha*): to arouse the *anuttarasamyaksaṃbodhicitta* for the welfare and happiness of all beings (*sarvasattvānāṃ hitāya sukhāya*) is the supreme homage (*paramapūjā*) rendered to the Tathāgata.

[*Unreality and Identity of the Tathāgatas*][33]

18. Now, in the assembly of Brahmās, there was a Brahmā god named Samatāvihārin[34] 'Residing in Sameness'. He said to the Buddha: Bhagavat, which then are the real (*bhūta*) Tathāgatas, the one seated on my throne or those who are on the thrones of the others?

The Buddha said to Samatāvihārin: All dharmas are empty (*śūnya*), like an illusion (*māyopama*). Born of the complex [of causes and conditions] (*sāmāgryutpanna*), they are inactive (*niśceṣṭa*). All spring from mental illusion and imagination (*viṭhapanaparikalpapratyupasthita*)[35] and, not being independent (*asvāmika*), they are born as one thinks of them[36].

All these Tathāgatas are real (*bhūta*)[37]. And why are they real?

These Tathāgatas, originally and spontaneously, are not born: hence they are real.

These Tathāgatas are non-existent in the present and in the future: hence they are real.

The Tathāgatas are not composed (*saṃgṛhīta*) of the four great elements (*mahābhūta*): hence they are real.

33 Śākyamuni, multiplying himself infinitely, is seated on the 84,000 koṭinayutas of thrones. How can the true Śākyamuni be distinguished from his countless doubles? Each devaputra would like the true Buddha to be the one to occupy the throne he has offered. In fact, all these Buddhas are equally 'real' (*chen shih* 眞實) according to the Chinese version by Kumārajīva, equally 'unreal' (*yaṅ dag pa ma yin pa*) according to the Tibetan translation. However, reality and unreality intermingle in one and the same non-existence, in one and the same emptiness. The ideas raised here can also be found in several parts of the Vkn, especially pp.227-8, 238-42. The sameness of all dharmas is one of the main theses of the Madhyamaka (see *ibid.*, pp.LXVIII-LXIX).

34 In Tib. *Mñam pa ñid la gnas pa*.

35 However, the traditional expression is *viṭhapanapratyupasthānalakṣaṇa*, in Tib. *rnam par bsgrub pa ñe bar gnas paḥi mtshan ñid* 'Having as their mark having been created by mental illusion': cf. Vkn, p.26, n.89.

36 In Tib. *de dag ni ji lta ji ltar ḥdod pa de lta de ltar rnam par sgrub po.*

37 As was pointed out in n.33, the Tibetan translation says 'unreal' instead of 'real'.

These Tathāgatas are not composed of the aggregates (*skandha*), bases of consciousness (*āyatana*) or elements (*dhātu*): hence they are real.

These Tathāgatas are the same (*sama*) and without difference (*nirviśeṣa*) at the beginning (*ādau*), in the middle (*madhye*) and at the end *(paryavasāne*): hence they are real.

O Brahmā, these Tathāgatas are the same and without difference. And why?

They are the same because of the suchness of form (*rūpatathatā*)[38]; the same because of the suchness of feeling (*vedanā*), of perception (*saṃjñā*), of volition (*saṃskāra*) and of consciousness (*vijñāna*): hence they are **[631a]** the same.

These Tathāgatas are the same because of the suchness of past time (*atītādhvatathatā*), the same because of the suchness of future time (*anāgatādhvatathatā*), the same because of the suchness of present time (*pratyutpannādhvatathatā*).

They are the same in that they are like the dharmas of illusion (*māyādharmopama*)[39], like the dharmas of mirage (*marīci-dharmopama*), non-existent (*asat*), free of coming (*āgamana*) and free of going (*nirgama*). That is why these Tathāgatas are said to be the same.

All dharmas are the same, and it is equally so for these Tathāgatas. All beings (*sattva*) are the same, and it is equally so for these Tathāgatas. All the Buddhas of all the universes (*lokadhātu*) are the same, and it is equally so for these Tathāgatas. All the universes are the same, and it is equally so for these Tathāgatas. That is why the Buddhas are said to be the same.

O Brahmarāja, these Tathāgatas do not deviate from the suchness of all dharmas (*sarvadharmāṇāṃ tathatāṃ nātikrāmanti*)[40]; this is why they are said to be the same. Understand it well, O Brahmarāja, the Tathāgatas know that all dharmas are hence the same; that is why the Tathāgatas give the name of sameness to all dharmas[41].

[38] Kumārajīva renders *tathatā* by the single character *ju* 如, whilst Hsüan-tsang translates it by *chen-ju* 眞如. See the Sanskrit list of the *asaṃskṛtadharmas* in Pañcaviṃśati, ed. Dutt, p.168, *16-17*, and the respective translations by Kumārajīva (T 223, ch.4, p.243*b* 2-3) and Hsüan-tsang (T 220, ch.486, p.469*a* 15-17).

[39] In Tib. *de bźin gśegs pa ḥdi dag ni sgyu maḥi chos kyi de bźin ñid kyis mñam.*

[40] Same expression in Vkn, p.72. Cf. Madhyāntavibhāga, p.221, *24*; Āloka, p.297, *20*: *dharmadhātuvinirmukto yasmād dharmo na vidyate.*

[41] In Tib. *de lta bas na de ltar de bźin gśegs pas chos thams cad mñam par mṅon par rdzogs par saṅs rygas te*: 'That is why the Tathāgatas are enlightened (*abhisaṃbuddha*) in sameness (*samam*) regarding all dharmas'.

19. The brahmarāja Samatāvihārin said to the Buddha: Bhagavat, it is astonishing (*adbhuta*) that the Tathāgata who thus penetrates the sameness of all dharmas (*sarvadharmasamatā*) also manifests his wonderful physical body (*pariniṣpanna rūpakāya*) to beings.

The Buddha replied: Brahmarāja, this is due to the potency (*prabhāva*) of the Śūraṃgamasamādhi as it was practised previously (*pūrvacarita*). For this reason the Tathāgata, even after having penetrated the sameness of all dharmas, also manifests his wonderful physical body to beings.

This having been said, the brahmarāja Samatāvihārin and ten thousand brahmadevas obtained the preparatory certainty (*anulomikī kṣānti*) concerning dharmas[42].

20. Then the Bhagavat withdrew his supernormal power (*ṛddhy-abhisaṃskāraṃ punar eva pratisaṃharati sma*); thereupon, the Buddhas and the thrones disappeared, and the whole assembly saw no more than a single Buddha.

[*The Hundred Aspects of the Heroic Progress*][43]

21. Then the Buddha said to the bodhisattva Dṛḍhamati: The Śūraṃgamasamādhi is not obtained by the bodhisattvas of the first, second, third, fourth, fifth, sixth, seventh, eighth and ninth stages (*bhūmi*); it is only the bodhisattva dwelling in the tenth *bhūmi* who can obtain this Śūraṃgamasamādhi[44]. What then is this Śūraṃgamasamādhi?

[42] This is the second *kṣānti*, the first being the *ghoṣanugā kṣānti*, and the third the *anutpattikadharmakṣānti*; cf. Vkn, pp.25, n.84, 290; below, § 48, n.119.

[43] The numbering of these hundred aspects is due to Chinese initiative; it does not appear in the Tibetan translation which gives more than a hundred of them. Among those which do not appear in the Chinese, there should be pointed out, in fol.285*a* 7, *zuṅ gi rim pa daṅ snrel źiḥi rgyud brtan pa śes pa = yamakavyatyastāhārajñāna* 'Knowledge consisting of the production of paired and inverted sounds'. Regarding this subject, see Vkn, pp.LVI-LX.

In the Tibetan translation, § 21 is followed by a partly versified passage going from folios 286*b* 5 – 289*a* 3. These stanzas probably did not appear in the original Sanskrit used by Kumārajīva as he certainly would not have omitted to translate them. In its oldest form, the Śgs was probably a prose work like the Aṣṭasāhasrikā, the Pañcaviṃśatisāhasrikā, the Aṣṭādaśasāhasrikā and the Śatasāhasrikā Prajñāpāramitā. However, in the course of time, literary taste having evolved, a certain number of stanzas may have been added. The Chinese translations made in Ssŭ-chuan, in the third century, include, it seems, ten *gāthās* (see above, p.65). At the end of the sūtra the Tibetan version introduces a further partly versified passage (Tib. Trip., vol.32, pp.96-8, folios 338*b* 8 - 344a 1) which does not appear in the translation by Kumārajīva.

[44] It will be noted that the ten stages of the bs are not yet designated by their traditional titles: Pramuditā, etc. (cf. Mahāvyutpatti, Nos 886-895). They are still anonymous as in the *bhūmiparivartas* of the large Prajñāpāramitās (Pañcaviṃśati, pp.214-25; Śatasāhasrikā, pp.1454-73; Aṣṭādaśa, T 220, ch.490-91, pp.409*b*-497*b*), chapters which E. Conze considers to be

1. Purifying the mind [and making it pure] like space (*ākāśavac cittaparikarman*).

2. Examining and bringing to the fore the minds of all beings (*sarvasattvacittānāṃ pratyavekṣā saṃmukhīkaraṇam*).

3. Knowing the strength and weakness of the spiritual faculties in beings (*sarvasattvānām indriyaparāparajñānam*)[45].

4. Determining (*avadhāraṇa*) and understanding (*parijñāna*) the [mechanism of] the cause and the fruit (*hetuphala*) in beings.

5. Knowing the fruition of action in beings (*sattvānāṃ karmavipākajñānam*)[46].

6. Penetrating the various aspirations of beings (*nānādhimuktipraveśa*)[47] and, after having penetrated them, not forgetting them (*asaṃpramoṣa*).

7. Knowing the multiple and various tendencies acquired by beings (*anekanānādhātusākṣātkāra*)[48].

8. Being at ease with the sounds of Brahmā[49] and the concentrations (*brahmasvarasamādhivikrīḍana*), teaching beings the diamond-like concentration (*vajropamasamādhisaṃprakāśana*)[50] and mastering at will the absorptions (*dhyāna*) and attainments (*samāpatti*)[51].

enlargements of the original edition. In fact, there is still no reference to the *bhūmis* in the Aṣṭasāhasrikā, the oldest known Prajñāpāramitā text.

45 This is the fifth tathāgatabala: *indriyaparāparajñānabala* (Mahāvyut., No.124). In the lines that follow, the Śgs will mention another eight tathāgatabalas, omitting only the *sthānasthānajñānabala*. See the list of the ten *balas* in Majjhima I, pp.69-71; Aṅguttara V, p.32 sq.; Patisaṃbhidā II, pp.174-6; Vibhaṅga, p.335 sq.; Mahāvastu I, pp.159-60; Kośa VII, pp.66-71; Kośavyākhyā, p.641, *14* sq.; Pañcaviṃśati, p.210; Mahāvyut., Nos 120-9; Arthaviniścaya, p.577; Dharmasaṃgraha, Ch.76.

46 The text is faulty; read *chih yeh pao* 知業報 instead of *chih wu yeh pao* 知無業報, with the Tib. *las kyi rnam par smin pa la ḥjug pa śes pa*. This is the second tathāgatabala: *karmavipāka-jñānabala* (Mahāvyut. No.121). See Kośa VII, p.69.

47 This is the third tathāgatabala *nānādhimuktijñānabala* (Mahāvyut., No.122). See Kośa VII, p.70.

48 This is the fourth tathāgatabala: *nānādhātujñānabala* (Mahāvyut., No.123). See Kośa VII, p.70.

49 *Hua-yin* 華音, a free translation of *fan yin* 梵音, in Tib. *tshaṅs paḥi dbyaṅs*. The *brahma-svara* is the psalmodised recitation of sacred texts; cf. Hōbōgirin, s.v. *Bombai*, pp.93-113, and P. Demiéville, 'Notes on the Buddhist Hymnology in the Far East' in *Buddhist Studies in Honour of Walpola Rahula*, London 1980, pp.44-61.

50 By means of the *vajropamasamādhi* the ascetic abandons the final passion of the highest sphere of existence: the *naivasaṃjñānāsaṃjñāyatana*. This *samādhi* is immediately followed by accesssion to arhatship; cf. Lamotte, *History*, p.617.

51 This is an allusion to the seventh tathāgatabala: *dhyānavimokṣasamādhisamāpattijñānabala* (Mahāvyut., No.126). There are four *dhyānas*, eight *vimokṣas*, three *samādhis*, two *samāpattis* and nine *anupūrvavihārasamāpattis*; cf. Kośa VII, p.69.

9. Discerning the paths which lead to the various destinies (*sarvatragāminīpratipadvyavalokana*)[52].

10. Knowing the former abodes without encountering any impediments (*anāvaraṇaṃ pūrvanivāsajñānam*)[53].

11. Possessing an unobstructed heavenly eye (*apratighaṃ divyacakṣus*)[54].

12. Obtaining the knowledge of the destruction of defilements (*āsravakṣayajñāna*)[55], but without attaining it inopportunely (*akālam*).

13. Obtaining the knowledge which penetrates the sameness of the world of form and the formless world (*rūpārūpyasamatāpraveśajñāna*). **[631b]**

14. Manifesting and being at ease with all forms (*sarvarūpasaṃdarśanavikrīḍana*).

15. Knowing that all sounds (*svaraghoṣa*) are the same as an echo (*pratiśrutkāsama*).

16. Successively penetrating mindfulness and wisdom (*smṛtiprajñānupraveśa*).

17. Delighting beings with good words (*subhāṣitaiḥ sattvasaṃtarpaṇam*).

18. Expounding the Dharma as circumstances require (*yathāpratyarhaṃ dharmadeśanā*).

19. Distinguishing between the opportune and the inopportune time (*kālākālavyavalokana*).

20. Being able to change one's sex (*indriyaparāvṛttijñānam*).

21. Giving instructions that are never in vain (*anirarthakā dharmadeśanā*).

22. Penetrating the limit of reality (*bhūtakoṭyanupraveśa*)[56].

23. Being skilful at winning over the various categories of beings (*sattvajātasaṃgrahaṇakuśala*).

24. Fulfilling all the perfections (*sarvapāramitāparipūri*).

25. Having bodily attitudes and a bearing precluding all peculiarity

52 This is the sixth tathāgatabala: *sarvatragāminīpratipajjñānabala* (Mahāvyut., No.125). See Kośa VII, p.70.

53 This is the eighth tathāgatabala: *pūrvanivāsānusmṛtijñānabala* (Mahāvyut., No.127). See Kośa VII, p.71.

54 This is the ninth tathāgatabala: *cyutyupapādajñānabala* (Mahāvyut., No.128). This understanding of the death and rebirth of beings arises from the heavenly eye (*divyacakṣus*). See Kosa VII, pp.68-9, n., and Vkn, p.67, n.57.

55 This is the tenth tathāgatabala: *āsravakṣayajñānabala* (Mahāvyut., No.129). See Kośa VII, p.71.

56 In Tib. *yaṅ dag paḥi mthaḥ la ḥjug pa*.

(*anadbhutā īryāpathavikramāḥ*).

26. Eliminating all reflection, discrimination and imagination (*sarvakalpavikalpaparikalpaprahāṇa*)[57].

27. Not harming the fundamental element (*dharmadhātu*), but exhausting it to the very end (*prāntakoṭi*)[58].

28. In a single instant, manifesting one's body in the presence of all the Buddhas.

29. Remembering the instructions of all the Buddhas (*sarva-buddhadharmadeśanādhāraṇa*).

30. In all the universes (*lokadhātu*), performing bodily transformations (*kāyavikurvaṇa*) like mirages (*marīcisama*).

31. Skilfully expounding all the Vehicles (*yāna*), delivering beings and always ensuring the uninterruption of the Triple Jewel (*triratnāsamuccheda*).

32. Producing great adornments up to the final limit (*aparāntakoṭi*) of Saṃsāra, and doing so without experiencing the slightest feeling of tiredness (*parikheda*).

33. Always manifesting oneself in all places of birth (*jātisthāna)*, and doing so opportunely and uninterruptedly.

34. Manifesting one's activity in all places of birth.

35. Being skilful at ripening beings (*sarvasattvaparipācanakauśala*).

36. Skilfully keeping up acquaintance with all beings.

37. Being unfathomable to all [adepts] of the two Vehicles[59].

38. Clearly understanding the pronunciation of all sounds (*svarāṅga*).

39. Causing all dharmas to be burnt (*pradīpta*)[60].

40. Causing an ordinary kalpa to become an incalculable kalpa (*asaṃkhyeyakalpa*).

41. Causing an *asaṃkhyeyakalpa* to be reduced to an ordinary kalpa[61].

[57] In Tib. *rtog pa daṅ rnam par rtog pa daṅ yoṅs su rtog pa thams cad yaṅ dag par bcom pa.*

[58] In Tib. *chos kyi dbyiṅs tha mi dad pa mñam paḥi ṅos la ḥjug pa śes pa*: 'Penetrating and knowing the depths (*tala*) of the undifferentiated (*asaṃbhinna*) and equalised (*sama*) *dharmadhātu*'. Even while manifesting himself in the world of beings and things, the bs never loses sight of the fundamental element, namely, the emptiness (*śūnyatā*) of beings and things. However, he is careful not to hypostatise it into a nature of things. Cf. Vkn, pp.LXIX-LXXII.

[59] In Tib. *ñan thos daṅ raṅ saṅs rgyas thams cad kyi ye śes kyis gtiṅ dpag dkaḥ ba*: 'Being difficult to fathom (*duravagāha*) by the knowledge (*jñāna*) of all the Śravakas and Pratyekabuddhas'.

[60] At the moment of the kalpa of disappearance (*saṃvartakalpa*), beings and the receptacle-world are destroyed by fire; cf. Vkn, pp.146 and n., 183, stanza 19.

[61] A *mahākalpa* includes four *asaṃkhyeyakalpas* and each *asaṃkhyeyakalpa* numbers twenty *antarakalpas* or small kalpas (cf. Vkn, p.146, n.). However, the bs, through his *acintyavimokṣa*, wields his dominance over time and, in the minds of those he wins over, can cause a very long period to appear as very short, and vice versa. See Vkn, pp.144-5.

42. Causing an ordinary field (*kṣetra*) to expand into innumerable fields (*asaṃkhyeyakṣetra*).

43. Causing innumerable fields to be reduced to an ordinary field.

44. Placing immense *buddhakṣetras* into a single pore of skin (*romakūpa*)[62].

45. Placing all beings into a single body[63].

46. Understanding that all *buddhakṣetras* are the same as space (*ākāśasama*).

47. Extending one's own body to all the *buddhakṣetras* without exception.

48. Placing all bodies into the fundamental element (*dharmadhātu*) so that there are no longer any bodies.

49. Understanding that all dharmas are free of marks (*alakṣaṇa*).

50. Being fully acquainted with all skilful means (*upāya*).

51. With a single vocal pronouncement (*ekavāgudāhāreṇa*), being able to express all the natures of things (*sarvadharmasvabhāva*).

52. In uttering only one phrase (*ekapada*), speaking for innumerable *asaṃkhyeyakalpas*.

53. Skilfully studying all the chapters of the expositions of the Dharma (*sarvadharmamukhaprakaraṇa*).

54. Fully recognising resemblances and differences, and expounding the Dharma briefly (*peyālam*) or at length (*vistareṇa*).

55. Withdrawing skilfully from all the paths of Māra (*sarvamāramārgātikramaṇa*).

56. Emitting the ray of great skilful means, of knowledge and of wisdom (*mahopāyajñānaprajñāraśmipramocana*)[64].

57. Causing actions of body, speech and mind to be preceded by knowledge (*kāyavāṅmanaskarmāṇi jñānapūrvaṃgamāni*)[65].

58. Without making any [special] effort (*anabhisaṃkāram*), always having the superknowledges (*abhijñā*) at one's disposal[66].

59. Using the four penetrating knowledges (*pratisaṃvijjñāna*)[67] so

62 Cf. Vkn, pp.145-6.

63 In Tib. *sems can gcig gi lus la sems can thams cad kyi lus yaṅ dag par ḥdu źiṅ ḥjug pa*: 'Concentrating and inserting the bodies of all beings into the body of a single being'.

64 In Tib. *thabs chen po la mkhas pas śes rab daṅ ye śes kyi ḥod zer gtoṅ ba*: 'Through ability in great skilful means, emitting the ray of wisdom and knowledge'.

65 These are the *āveṇikadharmas* Nos 13-15 of the Buddha: *sarvakāyakarma jñānapūrvaṃgamaṃ jñānānuparivarti*, etc. (cf. Mahāvyut., Nos 148-50).

66 Cf. Vkn, p.67, n.59.

67 Cf. Vkn, p.260, n.

that all beings experience great gladness (*saṃtuṣṭi*)[68].

60. Manifesting transformations (*vikurvaṇa*) to the limit of the fundamental element (*dharmadhātu*)[69].

61. Using the means of winning over (*saṃgrahavastu*)[70] to secure beings (*sattvaparigrahaṇa*).

62. Understanding all the languages (*vyavahāra*) used by all beings in the various universes (*lokadhātu*). **[631c]**

63. Not calling into question that dharmas are like an illusion (*māyopameṣu dharmeṣu niḥsaṃśayaḥ*).

64. In all places of birth, practising widely all the sovereign powers (*sarvajātisthāneṣu vaśitāparipūriḥ*).

65. [Obtaining] willingly and tirelessly all necessary things.

66. Showing oneself as a master (*adhipati*) among all beings.

67. Being a field of merit (*puṇyakṣetra*) equally profitable to the good and the bad.

68. Obtaining and penetrating all the secrets (*guhya*) of the bodhisattvas.

69. Always emitting rays (*raśmipramocana*) over all the universes without exception.

70. Possessing a knowledge (*jñāna*) which is profound (*gambhīra*) and unfathomable (*duravagāha*).

71. Having a mind (*citta*) like earth (*pṛthivī*), water (*ap*), fire (*tejas*) and wind (*vāyu*).

72. In every teaching (*nirdeśa*), statement (*pada*) and discourse (*nirukti*), skilfully causing the turning of the Wheel of the Dharma (*dharmacakrapravartana*)[71].

73. Unimpededly (*anāvaraṇam*) [penetrating] the Tathāgata stage (*tathāgatabhūmi*).

74. Spontaneously (*svarasena*) obtaining the *anutpattikadharma-kṣānti*.

75. Acquiring a mind conforming to the truth and not being defiled by the stains of the passions (*kleśamala*)[72].

[68] In Tib. *so so yaṅ dag rig pa bźis sems can gi khams thams cad tshim par byed pa*: 'Through the four *pratisaṃvids* delighting all the *sattvadhātu*'.

[69] In Tib. *chos kyi dbyiṅs thams cad kyis klas par rnam par ḥphrul pa ston pa* = *sarvadharmadhāthuparyantaṃ vikurvaṇasaṃdarśanam*.

[70] See Vkn. p.19, n.67.

[71] An early Mahāsāṃghika thesis: 'In all their words, the Tathāgatas set turning the Wheel of the Dharma'. Cf. A. Bareau, *Les Sectes bouddhiques*, p.58.

[72] In Tib. *ma bstan par raṅ gis bzod pa daṅ ye śes thob pa daṅ rin po che lta buḥi sems bskyed pas kun nas ñon moṅs pa thams cad kyi dri mas mi gos pa*: 'Untaught (*anupadésam*) and by

76. Inserting all the waters into a single pore (*ekasmin romakūpe*), but without disturbing the aquatic creatures (*jalastha*)[73].

77. Accumulating immense merit (*puṇya*) and good roots (*kuśalamūla*).

78. Clearly understanding the applications of skilful means (*upāyapariṇāmana*).

79. Excelling in wonders (*prātihārya*) and everywhere carrying out all the practices (*caryā*) of the bodhisattvas.

80. Finding security (*kṣema*) in all the Buddhadharmas.

81. After having found it, escaping from original existences [conditioned] by previous actions (*pūrvakarman*)[74].

82. Penetrating the hidden Dharma treasures of the Buddhas (*buddhānāṃ gūḍhadharmakośapraveśaḥ*).

83. Manifesting a dissolute life completely given over to pleasure[75].

84. Hearing quantities of teachings (*dharma*) and being able to remember them all.

85. Seeking out all dharmas (*sarvadharmaparyeṣaṇa*) without ever tiring.

86. Conforming to worldly conditions (*lokadharmānuvartana*)[76], without being defiled by them.

87. Expounding the Dharma to mankind for immense kalpas, but giving them the impression that the expounding lasted for only a morning (*pūrvāhṇa*)[77].

88. Manifesting all kinds of infirmities, making oneself lame (*khañja*), deaf (*badhira*), blind (*andha*) and mute (*mūka*) in order to ripen beings (*sattvaparipācanārtham*)[78].

89. Having an hundred thousand Guhyakādhipati Vajrapāṇi-Mallas

oneself (*svataḥ*), obtaining patience (*kṣānti*) and knowledge (*jñāna*) and, by means of a jewel-like (*ratnopama*) *cittotpāda*, not being defiled by the stains of the defilements (*saṃkleśamala*)'.

The *cittotpāda* 'like a jewel' (*ratnākaropama*) is accompanied by the perfection of morality (*śīlapāramitā*). It occupies the sixth place in the traditional list of the twenty-two *cittotpādas*; cf. Abhisamayālaṃkāra I, v.19; Āloka, p.25, *26-27*; Pañcaviṃśati, p.22, *1-2*; Sūtrālaṃkāra, p.16, *23*.

73 Cf. Vkn, p.143, § 11.

74 An obscure sentence, with no correspondence in Tibetan.

75 In Tib. *rtse ba daṅ dgaḥ ba daṅ loṅs spyod thams cad kun tu ston pa daṅ sems źi źiṅ rab tu źi la ñe bar źi ba*: 'Giving oneself over to games (*krīḍana*), pleasures (*nandana*) and delights (*upabhoga*), but resting, calming and stilling the mind'.

76 Regarding the eight *lokadharmas*, see Vkn, p.11, n.50.

77 In Tib. *bskal pa graṅs med pa sṅa dro gcig tu byin gyis rlob ciṅ chos ḥchad pa* = *asaṃkhyeyakalpaṃ pūrvāhṇam adhiṣṭhāya dharmadeśanā*. Cf. Vkn, p.144, § 13.

78 Cf. Vkn, p.183, stanza 18.

as permanent assistants (*nityānubaddha*)[79].

90. Seeing and discovering spontaneously (*svarasena*) all the states of Buddhahood (*buddhatva*).

91. Being able, in an instant, to manifest a life-span (*ayuṣpramāṇa*) being prolonged for innumerable *asaṃkhyeyakalpas*.

92. Seeming to adopt all the bodily attitudes (*īryāpatha*) of the first two Vehicles, but without inwardly renouncing the practices (*caryā*) of the bodhisattvas.

93. With a perfectly calm (*praśānta*) mind, [dwelling] on emptiness (*śūnyatā*) and signlessness (*ānimitta*).

94. Even while disporting oneself with female musicians, inwardly retaining the concentration on the recollection of the Buddhas (*buddhānusmṛtisamādhi*).

95. Whether seeing (*dṛṣṭe*), hearing (*śrute*), touching (*spṛṣṭe*) or co-existing (*saṃsthite*)[80], ripening innumerable beings (*apramāṇasattva-paripācana*).

96. From moment to moment, manifesting the acquisition of complete enlightenment (*abhisaṃbodhi*) and, by conforming with beings to be disciplined (*vaineya*), causing them to obtain deliverance (*vimukti*).

97. Manifesting the entry into the womb (*garbhāvakrānti*) and the birth (*janman*).

98. [Manifesting] the renunciation of the world (*abhiniṣkramaṇa*) and the acquisition of Buddhahood [or complete enlightenment] (*abhisaṃbodhana*).

99. Setting turning the Wheel of the Dharma (*dharmacakra-pravartana*).

100. Entering great Nirvāṇa, but without attaining complete cessation[81].

79 In Tib. *Lag na rdo rje ḥbum rtag tu phyi bźin du ḥbraṅ ba*. This concerns the yakṣa Vajrapāṇi 'Thunderbolt-in-hand'. His epithet of *Guhyakādhipati* can be interpreted as 'Great Master of the Guhyaka yakṣas' or 'Great Master of the three-fold Mystery (of the body, speech and mind of the Tathāgata)'. The epithet of *Malla* is not found in the Chinese versions; it can be a common name meaning 'athlete', or a proper name designating the Mallas of Northern Bihar where the Buddha entered Nirvāṇa. For the Mahāyāna, the bodhisattva Vajrapāṇi belongs to the close entourage (*abhyantaraparivāra*) of Śākyamuni and is, together with Ānanda, one of his *upasthāyakas* or attendants (cf. Nāgārjuna, *Traite* V, p.2236 and n.); he is 'permanently attached' (*nityānubaddha*) to the person of the Buddha and the great bodhisattvas (Lalitavistara, p.66, *5-7*; Daśabhūmika, p.71, *22*; Laṅkāvatāra, p.240, *10*). On the astonishing career of this mythical character, see my article 'Vajrapāṇi en Inde' in *Mélanges de Sinologie, Bibliothèque de l'Institut des Hautes Études Chinoises* XX, Paris 1966, pp.113-59.

80 Regarding this sequence of verbal adjectives in *ta-* in the locative, see Vkn, p.98, n.118.

81 This is how the Tib. (fol.286*b* 1-5) gives Nos.96 to 100: *sems can mthaḥ yas pa / tshad*

O Dṛḍhamati, the Śūraṃgamasamādhi is so infinite (*apramāṇa*) that it reveals all the marvellous power of the Buddha and innumerable beings benefit from it.

[*The Heroic Progress and Good Dharmas*]

22. Dṛḍhamati, this Śūraṃgamasamādhi is not understood in the light of a single statement (*ekapada*), a single object (*ekālambana*), a single meaning (*ekārtha*): all the absorptions (*dhyāna*), attainments (*samāpatti*), liberations (*vimokṣa*), concentrations (*samādhi*), superknowledges (*abhijñā*), supernormal powers (*ṛddhi*) and penetrating knowledges (*pratisaṃvijjñāna*) are included (*saṃgṛhīta*) in **[632a]** the Śūraṃgamasamādhi.

23. Just as springs, streams, rivers, tributaries and water courses flow into the great sea (*mahāsamudra*), so all the bodhisattva possesses in the way of *dhyānas* and *samāpattis* is to be found in the Śūraṃgamasamādhi.

24. Just as a noble Cakravartin king is accompanied everywhere by an heroic general (*śūrasenāpati*) and four army companies (*caturaṅgabala*), so, O Dṛḍhamati, all the *samādhimukhas*, *samāpattimukhas*, *pratibhānamukhas*, *vimokṣamukhas*, *dhāraṇīmukhas*, *abhijñāmukhas*, *vidyāvimuktimukhas* and *dharmamukhas* are included in the Śūraṃgamasamādhi, and everywhere that bodhisattvas practise the Śūraṃgamasamādhi they are accompanied by all the *samādhis*.

med pa yoṅs su smin par byed pa daṅ / sems kyi skad cig sems kyi skad cig la dul baḥi sems can ji ltar yoṅs su smin pa la / mṅon par rdzogs par byaṅ chub pa daṅ / rnam par grol ba ston pa daṅ / byaṅ chub sems dpaḥ dag mṅal du ḥjug pa daṅ / btsas pa daṅ / mṅon par ḥbyuṅ ba daṅ / dkaḥ ba spyod pa daṅ byaṅ chub kyi sñin por ḥgro ba daṅ / bdud ḥdul ba daṅ / byaṅ chub mṅon par rdzogs par ḥtshaṅ rgya ba daṅ / chos kyi ḥkhor lo bskor ba daṅ / mya ṅan las ḥdaḥ pa chen po daṅ / lus ḥjig pa yaṅ ston la byaṅ chub sems dpaḥi chos ñid de yaṅ mi gtoṅ źiṅ śin tu phuṅ po med par yaṅ mya ṅan las mi ḥdaḥ pa ḥdi ni blo gros brtan pa dpaḥ bar ḥgro baḥi tiṅ ṅe ḥdzin ces bya ste /: Ripening an infinite and countless number of beings and ripening them from moment to moment according to the requirements of beings to be disciplined (*vaineyasattva*); manifesting the attainment of enlightenment (*abhisaṃbodhi*) and deliverance (*vimukti*); manifesting the Bodhisattva's entry into the womb (*garbhāvakrānti*), the birth (*janman*), the leaving of the world (*abhiniṣkramaṇa*), the practice of the austerities (*duṣkaracaryā*), the going to the seat of enlightenment (*bodhimaṇḍagamana*), the victory over Māra (*māradharṣaṇa*), the attaining of enlightenment (*abhisaṃbodhana*), the turning of the Wheel of the Dharma (*dharmacakrapravartana*), the great Nirvāṇa and the destruction of the body (*kāyavināśa*), and all that while not abandoning the dharma-nature (*dharmatā*) of a bodhisattva and not definitively entering Nirvāṇa-without-a-remainder (*nirupadhiśeṣanirvāṇa*): this, O Dṛḍhamati, is what is called Śūraṃgamasaṁadhi'.

The feats of the Tathāgata (*tathāgatakārya*) are recapitulated in more or less the same terms by the Daśabhūmika, pp.14, *20-24*; 90, *12-15*. Also see above, § 7, n.17; further on, §§ 123, 163.

25. Dṛḍhamati, just as a noble Cakravartin king, while travelling, is followed by his seven jewels (*saptaratna*)[82], so, O Dṛḍhamati, the Śūraṃgamasamādhi is always followed by all the auxiliary dharmas of enlightenment (*bodhipākṣikadharma*). That is why this *samādhi* is named 'Heroic Progress' (*śūraṃgama*).

[*The Heroic Progress and the Perfections*]

1. *Dānapāramitā*

26. The Buddha said to Dṛḍhamati: The bodhisattva in Śūraṃgamasamādhi has no need to seek riches (*bhoga*) to give away. All precious substances (*ratnadravya*) to be found in the *mahāsāhasralokadhātu*, the great seas (*mahāsamudra*), the palaces of the gods (*devabhavana*) and the world of mankind (*manuṣyaloka*) – food (*anna*), drink (*pāna*), clothing (*vastra*), elephants (*hastin*), horses (*aśva*), vehicles (*yāna*) – these he has majestically at his disposal. They come to him by reason of his previous merit (*pūrvapuṇya*) and, furthermore, they are voluntarily created by his supernormal power (*ṛddhibala*). Such is the special fruit (*phalaviśeṣa*) of the perfection of giving (*dānapāramitā*) which characterises the bodhisattva in Śūraṃgamasamādhi.

2. *Śīlapāramitā*

27. The Buddha said to Dṛḍhamati: The bodhisattva in Śūraṃgamasamādhi does not pledge himself to morality, but does not avoid it (*śīlaṃ na samādadāti na tu śīlād vicalati*)[83]. In order to discipline beings (*sattvavinayanārtham*) he seems to pledge himself to morality (*śīlasamādāna*), comply with its bodily attitudes (*īyryāpatha-parigrahaṇa*)[84], confess his shortcomings, if he has any, and abhor his faults, but inwardly (*adhyātmam*) he is pure (*viśuddha*) and always faultless (*anāpattika*). [Conversely], in order to ripen beings (*sattvaparipācanārtham*), he is born in the world of desire (*kāmadhātu*), becomes a Cakravartin king, surrounds himself with an harem and a body of servants (*antaḥpurasevakakāyaparivṛta*), seems to have a wife

[82] Cf. Dīgha I, p.89, *1-4*, Mahāvyutpatti, Nos.3621-8, etc.

[83] In theory, the morality of commitment (*saṃvaraśīla*) – that of the monk who commits himself through vows – is superior to simple and natural honesty. Even if he does not commit himself, the bs practises a superior morality (*adhiśīla*), for all his activity is in the service of beings. As a monk, even if he does not abide by the rules, he is pure; as a layman, even if he leads a dissolute life, he is recollected. His altruism sanctifies all his actions. See Saṃgraha, pp.212-27, and the notes, pp.41*-43*.

[84] We have in Tib. *bslab pa yaṅ yoṅs su ḥdzin par byed* = *śikṣāparigrahaṇa*: 'observing the rules (of the religious life)'.

(*bhāryā*) and children (*putra*) and gives himself over to the five objects of desire (*pañcakāmaguṇaparicaraṇa*), but inwardly he is always established in concentration (*samādhistha*), of pure morality (*viśuddhaśīla*) and perfectly aware of the defects of the threefold existence (*bhavatrayadoṣadarśin*)[85]. Such is, O Dṛḍhamati, the special fruit of the perfection of morality (*śīlapāramitā*) which characterises the bodhisattva in Śūraṃgamasamādhi.

3. *Kṣāntipāramitā*

28. The Buddha said to Dṛḍhamati: The bodhisattva in Śūraṃgamasamādhi cultivates patience (*kṣāntiṃ bhāvayati*) to the end and completely[86]. 'Beings are not born', and thus he cultivates patience. 'Dharmas do not arise', and thus he cultivates patience. 'The mind (*citta*) is devoid of shape or colour (*saṃsthānavarṇa*)', and thus he cultivates patience. 'There is neither another (*para*) nor a self (*ātman*)', and thus he cultivates patience. 'Saṃsāra does not merit attention (*manyanā*)', and thus he cultivates patience. 'The self-nature of things (*svabhāvatā*) does not allow of destruction (*abhedya*)', and thus he cultivates patience. While the bodhisattva is thus cultivating patience, there is nothing that he cultivates and there is nothing that he does not cultivate.

29. In order to ripen beings (*sattvaparipācanārtham*), he is born in the world of desire (*kāmadhātu*); he shows himself to be angry (*sakrośa*), but inwardly he is serene (*abhiprasanna*); he shows himself to be unapproachable (*durāsada*), but he is neither distant (*dūre*) nor close (*antike*). In order to purify beings **[632b]**, he upsets accepted attitudes (*īryāpathān vikṣipati*), but he never upsets the fundamental element (*dharmadhātu*)[87]. He speaks of things to be endured, but there is no eternal (*nitya*), stable (*dhruva*), immutable (*avipariṇāma*) dharma to be endured. Endowed with such patience, it is in order to destroy the hatred (*dveṣa*) and animosity (*vyāpāda*) of beings that a bodhisattva always sings the praises (*varṇana*) of the merits of patience

85 Defects of the *kāma-, rūpa- and ārūpya-bhavas.*

86 Theorists distinguish three kinds of patience: patience in bearing insults (*apakāramarṣaṇa-kṣānti*), patience in accepting suffering (*duḥkhādhivāsanākṣānti*) and patience in contemplating the Dharma (*dharmanidhyānakṣānti*), that is, the profound and vast teachings of the Buddhist doctrine (cf. Saṃgraha, p.191). These profound teachings are notably the Summaries of the Dharma (*dharmoddāna*): 'Impermanent are all formations, painful are all formations, impersonal are all dharmas, calm is Nirvāṇa' (cf. Vkn, p.63, n.51). It is this patience concerning the Buddhist doctrine which is involved here. The subject is studied at length in *Traité* II, p.912 sq.

87 In Tib. *chos kyi dbyiṅs.*

(*kṣāntipuṇya*); however, for him there is neither animosity (*vyāpāda*) nor patience (*kṣānti*). Such is, O Dṛḍhamati, the special fruit of the perfection of patience (*kṣāntipāramitā*) which characterises the bodhisattva in Śūraṃgamasamādhi.

4. *Vīryapāramitā*

30. The Buddha said to Dṛḍhamati: The bodhisattva in Śūraṃgamasamādhi activates great vigour in the search for good dharmas (*kuśaladharmaparyeṣaṇārthaṃ mahāvīryam ārabhate*), but does not develop any activity of body, speech or mind (*kāyavāṅmanaḥsamudācāra*). It is for the idle (*kusīda*) that he seems to activate vigour, 'so that', he says, 'beings may imitate my exercises (*śikṣā*)', but no activism (*ārambha*), no grasp (*ādāna*) [can be exerted] on dharmas. And why is this? A bodhisattva knows that all dharmas rest eternally on the fundamental element (*dharmadhātu*) without coming (*āgamana*) or going (*nirgama*)[88]. Thus, even while remaining apart from all activity of body, speech and mind, he seems to activate his vigour (*vīryam ārabdhum*), but he does not see any dharma to acquire. Even though he seems to activate his vigour in this world, he is inwardly (*adhyātmam*) and outwardly (*bahirdhā*) free of exerting any activism (*ārambha*).

He ceaselessly traverses innumerable *buddhakṣetras*, but confronted with bodily forms, he remains the same (*sama*) and immovable (*acala*)[89].

He seems to bring into play all the good dharmas (*kuśaladharma*), but does not distinguish between either good or bad dharmas.

He seems to seek the truth (*dharmaparyeṣaṇa*) and initiate discussions but, with regard to Buddhahood (*abhisaṃbodhi*), he in no way depends on instruction from others (*aparapratyaya*).

He seems to seek a teacher (*ācārya*) and a preceptor (*upādhyāya*), but he is the master of gods and mankind (*śāstā devamanuṣyāṇām*).

He seems to enquire laboriously, but he possesses in himself an unobstructed eloquence (*apratihatapratibhāna*).

He seems to show respect (*satkāra*), but he is himself venerated by gods and mankind.

He seems to descend into a womb (*garbham avakrāntum*), but he is not defiled (*kliṣṭa*) by any stain (*mala*).

[88] In Tib. *byaṅ chub sems dpaḥ des chos kyi dbyiṅs gnas pa ñid ma ḥoṅs ma soṅ ba rtogs paḥi phyir ro.*

[89] In Tib. *lus kyi chos ñid las kyaṅ mi gyoḥo* = *kāyadharmatāyā na vicalati*: 'He does not swerve from the nature of the body'. Even while travelling through countless *buddhakṣetras*, the bs does not lose sight of the very nature of bodies and form, non-existent in themselves.

He seems to come into the world (*prasūta*), but he does not see any dharma arising or perishing.

He appears in the form of a boy (*dāraka*), but all the organs of his body are fully developed (*paripūrṇendriya*).

He seems to study the professions (*śilpasthāna*), medicine (*cikitsāvidyā*), magic (*mantravidyā*), writing (*lipi*), numeration (*saṃkhyā*), calculation (*gaṇanā*) and the manual arts (*karmasthāna*), but he knows all this perfectly in advance.

He appears ill (*glāna*), but he is free from all the diseases of the passions (*vigatakleśavyādhi*).

He appears old (*jīrṇa*), but all his organs are intact (*anupahatendriya*) in advance.

He appears to die, but he is beyond birth (*jāti*), death (*maraṇa*) and passing on (*cyuti*).

Such is, O Dṛḍhamati, the special fruit of the perfection of vigour (*vīryapāramitā*) which characterises the bodhisattva in Śūraṃgamasamādhi.

5. *Dhyānapāramitā*

31. The Buddha said to Dṛḍhamati: The bodhisattva in Śūraṃgamasamādhi, even though he knows that all dharmas are eternally concentrated (*sadāsamāhita*), teaches the various kinds of absorptions (*dhyānaviśeṣa*). He shows himself absorbed in order to win over the distracted (*vikṣiptacitta*), but he does not see any dharma that could be 'distracted', all dharmas being, like the fundamental element (*dharmadhātu*), [eternally concentrated]. In order to subdue the mind (*cittadamanārtham*), he never strays from absorption (*dhyānād na vicalati*).

He takes up the [four] bodily attitudes: he walks, stands[90], sits or lies down *(caturvidham īryāpathaṃ kalpayati tadyathā caṅkramyate tiṣṭhati niṣīdati śayyāṃ kalpayati*), but he is always calm (*śānta*) and concentrated (*samāhita*).

He holds conversations (*pralāpa*) with beings, but he does not abandon [**632c**] the state of concentration (*samādhidharmatāṃ na parityajati*).

Through goodwill (*maitrī*) and compassion (*karuṇā*) for beings, he enters the villages (*grāma*), towns (*nagara*), districts (*nigama*), capitals (*rājadhānī*) and kingdoms (*rāṣṭra*), but he always remains concentrated.

90 Read *chu* 住 in place of *ch'ü* 去.

When, for the welfare and happiness of beings (*sattvānāṃ hitāya sukhāya*), he seems to take food, he is always concentrated.

His body (*kāya*) is hard (*dṛḍha*), diamond-like (*vajrasama*), real, infallible (*amogha*) and indestructible (*abhedya*). It does not contain either a belly (*pakvāśaya*), or stomach (*āmāśaya*), or excrement (*viṣ*), or urine (*mūtra*), or bad odours (*durgandha*) or impurity (*aśuci*).

He seems to take food, but nothing penetrates into him, or it is only through compassion (*karuṇā*), for the welfare and happiness of beings (*sattvānāṃ hitāya sukhāya*). In all circumstances he is blameless (*sarvatrānavadya*). If he seems to exercise the practices of the worldly (*pṛthagjanacaryā*), he is really free of practice and he transcends all practices (*sarvacaryāḥ samatikrāmati*).

Dṛḍhamati, regarding this bodhisattva in Śūraṃgamasamādhi, when he appears in a forest (*araṇya*), it is exactly as if he were in a village (*grāma*); when he appears among the laity (*gṛhastha*), it is exactly as if he were among the religious (*pravrajita*). If he appears in white clothing (*avadātavasana*), he does not have the dissipation (*pramāda*) of a layman; and if he appears as an ascetic (*śramaṇa*), he does not have the arrogance (*manyanā*) of a monk.

He takes up the religious life in an heretical order (*pāsaṇḍikeṣu pravrajati*) in order to win over beings[91], but he does not really take it up (*pravrajyā*), he is not defiled (*kliṣṭa*) by all the false views (*mithyādṛṣṭi*) which prevail there and does not give any credence (*prasāda*) to them. He seems to adopt the bodily attitudes (*īryāpatha*) of the heretics (*pāsaṇḍika*), but does not conduct himself in accordance with them.

32. Dṛḍhamati, just as a guide (*pariṇāyaka*), placing himself at the head of a group of people, helps them to make their way along a steep path, then goes back to help other persons pass along, so, O Dṛḍhamati, the bodhisattva in Śūramgamasamādhi, taking into account the aspirations of beings – śrāvakayānikas, pratyekabuddhayānikas or buddhayānikas – indicates the appropriate path (*yathāpratyarhaṃ mārgaṃ deśayati*) to them and, after having helped them make their way, goes back to help others along. That is why this worthy man (*satpuruṣa*) is called a guide (*pariṇāyaka*).

33. Just as a good ship (*nau*), leaving this shore (*apāra*), conveys innumerable beings (*apramāṇasattvāṃs tārayati*) to the other shore (*pāra*)

[91] It is thus that Mañjuśrī took up the religious life with the Nirgranthas of Vaiśālī and became a disciple of Satyaka Nirgranthīputra; cf. Ratnakāraṇḍa, T 462, ch.2, pp.475*c*-476*b* (trans. 'Mañjuśrī', *T'oung Pao* XLVIII, 1960, p.40).

and, having reached the other shore, goes back (*pratinivartate*) to convey other beings, so too, O Dṛḍhamati, the bodhisattva in Śūraṃgamasamādhi: he sees beings being carried off by the fourfold flood (*caturogha*)[92] of Saṃsāra; he wishes to rescue them (*uttāraṇa*) and enable them to find the way out (*niḥsaraṇa*). He takes into account the degree of ripeness (*pakvatā*)[93] of the good roots (*kuśalamūla*) planted by those beings: if he sees beings destined to be rescued by the [Vehicle of the] Pratyekabuddhas, he shows himself to them and manifests Mahāparinirvāṇa; if he sees beings destined to be rescued by the [Vehicle of the] Śrāvakas, he expounds peacefulness (*śānti*) to them and, in front of them, enters Nirvāṇa. Then, through the power of his Śūraṃgamasamādhi, he returns to a new birth (*punarjanman*) in order to rescue other beings. That is why this worthy man (*satpuruṣa*) is called captain of the ship (*nāvikapati*).

34. O Dṛḍhamati, just as an illusionist (*māyākāra*), in the presence of a great gathering of people (*mahato janakāyasya purataḥ*), shows himself in the form of a corpse (*mṛtaśarīra*), swollen (*vyādhmātaka*), putrid (*vipūyaka*), burnt by fire (*vidagdhaka*) and devoured by animals (*vikhāditaka*)[94], then, when he has received money from the crowd, rises again because he fully understands illusionary wiles, so the bodhisattva in Śūraṃgamasamādhi, in order to ripen beings (*sattva-paripācanārtham*), appears [being born], old, [sick] and dead[95], but he is not subject to birth (*jāti*), old age (*jarā*), sickness (*vyādhi*) or death (*maraṇa*).

Such is, O Dṛḍhamati, the special fruit of the perfection of absorption (*dhyānapāramitā*) which characterises the bodhisattva in Śūraṃgama-samādhi.

6. *Prajñāpāramitā*

35. The Buddha said [**633a**] to Dṛḍhamati: The bodhisattva in Śūraṃgamasamādhi cultivates wisdom (*prajñāṃ bhāvayati*) and his faculties are sharp (*tīkṣṇendriya*).

He never sees the self-nature of beings (*sattvasvabhāva*) but, in order to ripen them, he speaks of beings. He does not see either a

[92] A traditional expression (Lalitavistara, p.195, *18*; Divyāvadāna, p.95, *15*; Avadānaśataka I, p.16, *11*; Gaṇḍavyūha, p.492, *1*) to designate the fourfold defilement (*āsrava*): defilement of desire (*kāma*), existence (*bhava*), false views (*dṛṣṭi*) and ignorance (*avidyā*). Besides *caturogha*, we also find *caturyoga*); cf. Dīgha III, pp.230 and 276.

[93] Adopt the variant *shu* 熟 instead of *chiu* 就.

[94] An allusion to the various stages of the meditation on repulsiveness (*aśubhabhāvanā*); cf. Mahāvyut., Nos.1159, 1163, 1161.

[95] In Tib. *skye ba daṅ / rga ba daṅ / na ba daṅ ḥchi ba yaṅ ston la.*

living being (*jīva*) or an individual (*pudgala*), but he speaks of a living being and an individual. He does not see[96] the self-nature of actions (*karmasvabhāva*) or the self-nature of fruition (*vipāka-svabhāva*), but he teaches action and fruition to beings. He does not see[96] the self-nature of the passions (*kleśasvabhāva*) of Saṃsāra, but he teaches a clear understanding of the passions of Saṃsāra (*saṃsārakleśaparijñā*). He does not see Nirvāṇa, but he talks of reaching Nirvāṇa. He does not see that dharmas admit of distinctive marks (*viśiṣṭalakṣaṇa*), but he speaks of good (*kuśala*) and bad (*akuśala*) dharmas.

36. Having already reached the other shore (*pāra*) of unobstructed knowledge (*apratihatajñāna*), he seems to be born in the world of desire (*kāmadhātu*), but he is not attached (*na sajjate*) to the world of desire. He seems to practise the absorptions (*dhyāna*) of the world of form (*rūpadhātu*), but he is not attached to the world of form. He seems to enter the attainments (*samāpatti*) of the formless [world] (*ārūpyadhātu*), but he is born in the world of form. He seems to practise the absorptions of the world of form, but he is born in the world of desire. He appears in the world of desire, but does not exercise the practices (*caryā*) of the world of desire. He knows all the absorptions (*dhyāna*) and limbs of absorption (*dhyānāṅga*); he can voluntarily enter an absorption (*dhyānapraveśa*) and withdraw from an absorption (*dhyānavyutthāna*). In order to ripen beings (*sattvaparipācanārtham*), he is born wherever he wishes and, in all the places of birth (*sarveṣu jātisthāneṣu*), he assumes an individual existence (*ātmabhāvaṃ parigṛhṇāti*).

37. Being endowed with profound and marvellous wisdom (*gambhīraprajñāsamanvāgata*), he eliminates all the practices of beings (*samucchinnasarvasattvacaryā*); in order to ripen beings, he seeems to exercise the practices, but in truth he has no dharma to practise, and he has transcended all practices (*sarvacaryā-samatikrānta*).

He has long since eliminated the 'grasp' [that is, the belief] concerning me and mine (*ātmātmīyagrāha*), but he 'grasps' (*gṛhṇāti*) things which he needs[97].

For a bodhisattva endowed with this knowledge (*jñāna*) and this wisdom (*prajñā*), all actions (*karman*) that he undertakes are consistent

96 Read *pu chien* 不見 instead of *pu tê* 不得, conforming with the Tib. *mi dmigs*.

97 In Tib. *de ni ṅar ḥdzin pa daṅ ṅa yir ḥdzin pa dag daṅ bral ba yin la len pa daṅ gtoṅ par yaṅ snaṅ ṅo.*

with knowledge and wisdom (*jñānaprajñānuparivartin*) and he is not defiled (*kliṣṭa*) by the fruits of actions (*karmaphala*)[98].

In order to ripen beings, he professes to be mute (*mūka*), but in truth he possesses a wonderful Brahmā voice (*brahmasvararutaravitā*)[99].

He has reached the other shore (*pāra*) of speaking (*nirukti*) and writing; he does not reflect in advance about what he should say; in all the assemblies where he goes, his word is well-spoken (*subhāṣita*); it provokes joy (*muditā*), and minds are strengthened. It is exactly as it should be (*yathāpratyarham*) that he expounds the Dharma, and the knowledge and wisdom of the bodhisattva do not undergo the slightest diminution (*apacaya*).

38. O Dṛḍhamati, let us imagine, for example, some men (*nara*) and women (*narī*), large or small, who, with all kinds of receptacles (*bhājana*), go to a source of water: stream (*udbhida*), lake (*taḍāga*), reservoir (*vilva*), river (*nadī*) or great sea (*mahāsamudra*). Each person, having filled the receptacle, large or small, which is at his or her disposal, returns home. Well now! The waters have not undergone the slightest diminution (*apacaya*). In the same way, O Dṛḍhamati, the bodhisattva in Śūraṃgamasamādhi goes to all kinds of assemblies: assembly of Kṣatriyas, assembly of Brāhmaṇas, assembly of Gṛhapatis, assembly of Śakras or assembly of Brahmās. Having reached those assemblies, he does not expend any mental effort (*cittābhoga*)[100]; with his good words (*subhāṣita*) he provokes delight (*saṃtoṣayati*), and it is exactly as it should be (*yathāpratyarham*) that he expounds the Dharma. However, his knowledge (*jñāna*) and eloquence (*pratibhāna*) do not undergo the slightest diminution. Such is, O Dṛḍhamati, the special fruit of the perfection of wisdom (*prajñāpāramitā*) which characterises the bodhisattva in Śūraṃgamasamādhi.

[*Liberating Action of the Heroic Progress*]

39. The Buddha said to Dṛḍhamati: Beings who see the bodhisattva in Śūraṃgamasamādhi [**633b**] are all liberated (*parimucyante*); those

[98] In Tib. *de śes rab daṅ ye śes daṅ ldan pas ye śes kyis byas paḥi las thams cad spyad kyi / ṅa rgyal gyis byed pa yaṅ ma yin la las daṅ rnam par smin par brjod pa yaṅ ma yin no /* 'Being endowed with wisdom (*prajñā*) and knowledge (*jñāna*), he accomplishes all the actions resulting from knowledge; but, by not acting through egoism (*ahaṃkāra*), for him there is no question of action (*karman*) or fruition (*vipāka*)'.

[99] In Tib. *tshaṅs paḥi sgra daṅ skad daṅ dbyaṅs* (cf. Mahāvyut., No.482). See *Hōbōgirin*, pp.133-5, s.v. 'Bonnon'.

[100] In Tib. *lhun gyis grub* = *anābhoga*. On the meaning of this expression, see the notes by L. de La Vallée Poussin in Siddhi, p.617.

who hear his name (*nāman*), see his bodily attitudes (*īryāpatha*), hear his instructions (*dharmadeśanā*) or see his silence (*tūṣṇīṃbhāva*)[101], are all liberated.

O Dṛḍhamati, it is like the great king of medicaments (*mahābhaiṣajyarāja*) tree called Darśanīya[102], 'Pleasant to behold': persons who see it find the cure for their sickness (*vyādhi*). So it is with the bodhisattva in Śūraṃgamasamādhi: beings who see him find the cure for craving (*rāga*), hatred (*dveṣa*) and delusion (*moha*).

40. It is like the great king of medicaments (*mahābhaiṣajyarāja*) called Vipravāsa[103], 'Dispersion': in time of battle (*saṃgrāma*) the drums (*dundubhi*) are coated with it; as soon as the wounded, hit by an arrow (*śalya*) or struck by a lance (*śūla*), hear the sound (*svara*) of those drums, the arrows come out [of their wounds] and the poisons (*viṣa*) are eliminated. So it is, O Dṛḍhamati, with the bodhisattva in Śūraṃgamasamādhi: for those who hear his name, the arrows (*śalya*) of craving (*rāga*), hatred (*dveṣa*) and delusion (*moha*) are pulled out of their own accord (*svataḥ*), the poisons of all the false views (*sarvadṛṣṭigataviṣa*) are eliminated and no more passion (*kleśa*) arises.

41. O Dṛḍhamati, it is like the medicament tree (*bhaiṣajyavṛkṣa*) called Saṃpanna[104], 'Complete': those who use its root (*mūla*) find the cure to their sickness (*vyādhi*); its trunk (*gaṇḍa*), knots (*saṃdhi*), pith (*sāra*), bark (*tvac*), branches (*śākhā*), leaves (*pattra*), flowers (*puṣpa*) and fruit (*phala*) can also cure sickness; whether it is standing (*samucchrita*), dried out (*śuṣka*) or cut into pieces (*khaṇḍaśaś chinna*), it can cure all the sicknesses of beings. So it is with the bodhisattva in Śūraṃgamasamādhi: there is not one moment when he is not benefiting beings; he always dispels their torment (*upadrava*); he expounds the Dharma to them and practises the four means of winning over (*saṃgrahavastu*) and the perfections (*pāramitā*) so that they can obtain liberation. Whether people respect him or not, whether they benefit him or not, the bodhisattva uses every means to bring them to security (*kṣema*). Even those who, until their dying day, ate flesh (*māṃsāda*): animals (*tiryagyoni*), bipeds (*dvipad*), quadrupeds (*catuṣpada*), birds (*pakṣin*), wild beasts (*mṛga*), belonging or not to human kind (*manuṣyāmanuṣya*), all these beings, by virtue of the morality (*śīla*) and previous aspirations (*pūrvapraṇidhāna*) of that bodhisattva, will be

[101] Vimalakīrti's silence continues to be famous; cf. Vkn, p.202.

[102] In Tib. *Blta na sdug pa;* cf. Mahāvyut., No.5214.

[103] In Tib. *Ḥbral ba*; cf. Mahāvyut., Nos 8386, 8413.

[104] *Chü-tsu* 具足 . The corresponding Tibetan is missing.

reborn after their death among the gods (*paraṃ maraṇād deveṣūpatsyante*); they will always be free of sickness and will escape torment (*upadrava*). Dṛḍhamati, the bodhisattva in Śūraṃgamasamādhi is exactly like the medicament tree (*bhaiṣajyavṛkṣa*).

[*Instantaneous and Simultaneous Practice of the Perfections*]

42. The Buddha said to Dṛḍhamati: The bodhisattva in Śūraṃgamasamādhi, in the course of all his births (*sarveṣu janmeṣu*), comprehends for himself the six perfections (*pāramitā*) without learning them from anyone. Whether he raises his foot (*caraṇotkṣepaṇe*) or lowers his foot (*caraṇanikṣepaṇe*)[105], whether he inhales (*āśvāse*) or exhales (*praśvāse*), at every instant (*kṣaṇe kṣaṇe*) he always possesses the six *pāramitās*. And why? O Dṛḍhamati, the body (*kāya*) of that bodhisattva consists of the self-nature of things (*dharmasvabhāva*) and his domain (*vihāra*) consists of things[106].

43. Dṛḍhamati, let us suppose that a king (*rājan*) or his ministers (*amātya*) grinds with a pestle an hundred thousand different kinds of perfumes (*gandha*) and reduces them to a fine powder (*cūrṇa*), and let us suppose that a certain man comes looking for a single kind of perfume to the exclusion of all the other kinds mixed with it. Then, O Dṛḍhamati, from this fine powder containing an hundred thousand kinds of perfumes, would it be possible to extract a single kind which has not been mixed with the others?

[Dṛḍhamati replied]: Certainly not, O Bhagavat.

[The Buddha went on]: Equally, O Dṛḍhamati, that bodhisattva having [long since][107] perfumed his body (*kāya*) and mind (*citta*) with all the *pāramitās*, it is at every instant (*kṣaṇe kṣaṇe*) that he arouses the six *pāramitās*.

44. How then, O Dṛḍhamati, does the bodhisattva arouse the six *pāramitās* at every instant?

1. The bodhisattva has renounced everything (*parityaktasarvasva*), and his mind is devoid of greed (*lobha*) and attachment (*abhiniveśa*): such is **[633c]** his *dānapāramitā*.

2. His mind is wholesome (*kuśala*), stilled (*praśānta*) and absolutely flawless: such is his *śīlapāramitā*.

[105] The same expressions are found in Vkn, p.98.

[106] In Tib. *byaṅ chub sems dpaḥ deḥi lus ni chos kyi raṅ bźin no / gnas pa ni chos kyi raṅ bźin no.*

[107] According to the Tib. *yun riṅ po nas.*

3. His mind is essentially indestructible (*akṣaya*)[108] and is not injured by any object (*sarvaviṣayair akṣata*): such is his *kṣāntipāramitā*.

4. Attentively he considers and analyses the mind (*cittaṃ vibhāvayati pravicinoti*) and recognises its mark of discernment (*cittasya viveka-lakṣaṇaṃ vijānāti*): such is his *vīryapāramitā*.

5. He is absolutely stilled (*atyantopaśānta*) and controls his mind (*cittaṃ damayati*): such is his *dhyānapāramitā*.

6. He examines the mind, knows the mind and penetrates the nature of the mind: such is his *prajñāpāramitā*.

Dṛḍhamati, it is thus that the bodhisattva in Śūraṃgamasamādhi possesses the six *pāramitās* at every instant.

45. Then the bodhisattva Dṛḍhamati said to the Buddha: It is wondrous (*adbhuta*), O Bhagavat. The domain (*vihāra*) acquired by the bodhisattva in Śūraṃgamasamādhi is inconceivable (*acintya*). O Bhagavat, bodhisattvas who wish to dwell in the domain of the Buddhas (*buddhavihāreṇa viharitukāma*) should train themselves in the Śūraṃgamasamādhi. And why? Because then, O Bhagavat, even if they travel through the domains (*vihāra*) of all the foolish worldlings (*bālapṛthagjana*), the bodhisattvas are free from craving (*rāga*), hatred (*dveṣa*) and delusion (*moha*).

46. Now there was in the assembly a great Brahmadeva named Maitrīsaṃpanna[109], 'Endowed with Goodwill'. He said to the Buddha: Bhagavat, if a bodhisattva wishes to travel through the domains of all the foolish worldlings, he should train himself in the Śūraṃgama-samādhi. And why? Because, even while travelling through the domains of all the foolish worldlings, his mind is free from craving, hatred and delusion.

The Buddha said: Excellent, excellent. O Maitrīsaṃpanna, it is exactly as you say (*evam etad yathā vadasi*). A bodhisattva who wishes to travel through the domain of all the foolish worldlings should train himself in the Śūraṃgamasamādhi, but without thinking of any training (*sarvaśikṣāṇām amanyanayā*).

[*Gradual Training in the Heroic Progress*]

47. The bodhisattva Dṛḍhamati said to the Buddha: Bhagavat, if a bodhisattva wishes to train himself in the Śūraṃgamasamādhi, how

[108] Corrupt text: read *hsin pu chin hsiang* 心不盡相 instead of *chih hsin chin hsiang* 知心盡相. The Tib. has *gaṅ sems kyi mi zad paḥi chos ñid daṅ / yul thams cad kyis smas par mi ḥgyur de ni deḥi bzod paḥi pha rol tu phyin paḥo.*

[109] In Tib. *Byams pa mchog.*

should he train himself?

The Buddha said to Dṛḍhamati: It is like training oneself in archery (*āvedha*). First of all, you aim at a large mound of earth[110]. When you have hit the large mound of earth, you learn to aim at a small mound of earth. When you have hit the small mound of earth, you learn little by little to aim at a target (*lakṣya*)[111]. When you have learnt to hit the target, you then learn to aim at a stick (*daṇḍa*). When you have learnt to hit the stick, you learn to aim at an hundred hairs (*roman*). When you have hit those hundred hairs, you learn to aim at ten hairs. When you have hit those ten hairs, you learn to aim at a single hair. When you have hit that single hair, you learn to aim at an hundredth fraction of a hair: once capable of hitting that, you are reputed to be a good archer (*niryāta iṣvastrācārya*); wherever you wish to aim, you do not strike emptiness; if you want to, you can effortlessly (*anābhogena*) reach any being, human (*manuṣya*) or non-human (*amanuṣya*), the sound of which is heard in the night (*rātri*) or darkness (*andhakara*).

48. Equally[112], O Dṛḍhamati,

[110] Adopt the variant *tui* 堆.

[111] The Tibetan version differs slightly: *ḥdi lta ste dper na ḥphoṅ gi slob dpon nam / ḥphoṅ gi slob ma ni thog mar ba laṅ gi ko ba la phog par byed do // gaṅ gi tshe na ba laṅ gi ko ba la lobs ba deḥi tshe / śiṅ leb la phog par byed do // gaṅ gi tshe śiṅ leb la lobs pa deḥi tshe ḥben pa la phog par byed do /* 'It is like a master archer (*iṣvastrācārya*: cf. Mahāvyut., No.3744) or his pupil (*antevāsin*) who aims first at an oxskin (*gocarman*); when he has hit the oxskin, he then aims at a plank of wood (*phalaka*); when he has hit the plank, he then aims at a target (*lakṣya*: cf. Mahāvyut., No.5090)'.

The Chinese records produced at the Council of Lhasa are close to this reading: 'When you learn archery, you first aim at bamboo matting as thick as an ox's body...' (cf. P. Demiéville, *Le Concile de Lhasa*, p.74).

[112] This paragraph, which I have divided into six sections, contains an outline of the career of the bs in the preparatory stages (*bhūmi*) and the stages proper. As in the *bhūmiparivartas* of the larger Prajñāpāramitās, these stages are as yet unidentified and do not bear the name of Pramuditā, etc., which will come to define them later.

The account in the Śgs is still incomplete but contains elements which will be taken up by later sūtras and śāstras and will finally culminate in a comparatively coherent system. The fundamentals of this can be found in the preface by J. Rahder to his edition of the Daśabhūmika and in other more systematic works, such as N. Dutt, *Aspects of Mahāyāna Buddhism*, London 1930, pp.238-89; L. de La Vallée Poussin, 'Bodhisattva' in *Encyclopaedia of Religion and Ethics* II, pp.743-8; 'La carrière de Bodhisattva' in Siddhi, pp.721-42.

I will limit myself here to indicating the still undecided position of the Śgs.

1. The first section concerns the bs's career before the *bhūmis*: the bs trains himself in good intentions (*āśaya*) and effort (*prayoga*); he arouses high resolve (*adhyāśaya*), develops the four infinite states (*apramāṇacitta*), also called Brahmavihāras, and undertakes the practice of the first five Abhijñās.

The bs is still at the beginner's level (*ādikarmika*) where his *cittotpāda* is merely associated with wishing (*chanda*), good intentions (*āśaya*) and high resolve (*adhyāśaya*) to bring about the welfare and happiness of creatures. Then he devotes himself to effort and his *cittotpāda*, flame-like, is 'associated with effort' (*prayogasahāgata*).

This preliminary phase will later be called Adhimukticaryābhūmi 'Stage of the Practice of Adherence'. It consists of two spheres: 1. the sphere of the accumulation of merits (*saṃbhārāvasthā*), 2. the sphere of effort (*prayogāvasthā*). The former consists in the cultivation of good roots leading to deliverance (*mokṣabhāgīya kuśalamūla*); the latter in the cultivation of good roots leading to the penetration of the truths (*nirvedhabhāgīya kuśalamūla*), namely, heat (*uṣmagata*), summits (*mūrdhan*), patience (*kṣānti*) and supreme worldly dharmas (*laukikāgradharma*).

Even though the *mokṣa-* and *nirvedhabhāgīyas* are mentioned by both Vehicles, the Śgs passes over them in silence. Conversely, it refers to the Brahmavihāras and Abhijñās, practices and mental powers whose origins are lost in the mists of time, but which have their place in the canonical writings of Buddhism and which the Prajñāpāramitā introduces into the bs's career (see Pañcaviṃśati, pp.181-2 and 184-5).

2. The second section in the Śgs is very brief: 'Having learnt the Abhijñās, he can then complete the six *pāramitās*'. This completing of the six *pāramitās* is a characteristic of the sixth stage: the Abhimukhī (cf. Pañcaviṃśati, p.216, *1-2*). In the course of the first six stages – Pramuditā, Vimalā, Prabhākarī, Arciṣmatī, Sudurjayā and Abhimukhī – the bs cultivates all six *pāramitās* at the same time, but especially giving (*dāna*) in the first, morality (*śīla*) in the second, patience (*kṣānti*) in the third, vigour (*vīrya*) in the fourth, absorptive meditation (*dhyāna*) in the fifth, and wisdom (*prajñā*) in the sixth. The Śgs gives sufficient allowance to this state of affairs by assigning the completing of the six *pāramitās* to the sixth *bhūmi*.

What it does not say, however, is that the first *bhūmi*, the Pramuditā, constitutes the path of vision (*darśanamārga*) of the bs, the sphere of his penetration of the truths (*prativedhāvasthā*), while the other nine *bhūmis* form his path of meditation (*bhāvanāmārga*). This assertion enables us to estabish a parallel between the Path of the śrāvakas and that of the bodhisattvas. We can take it that, at the time of the Śgs, no approximation between them had yet been made, or at least not markedly.

Other definitions were to follow later (cf. Bodh. bhūmi, p.367; Sūtrālaṃkāra, p.179):

a. The first *bhūmi*, the Pramuditā, is the stage of pure high resolve (*śuddhādhyāśaya*).

b. The following six *bhūmis* form the stage of the accomplishing of the practices (*caryā-pratipatti*): 1. the second *bhūmi*, the Vimalā, is the abode of higher morality (*adhiśīlavihāra*); 2. the third *bhūmi*, the Prabhākarī, is the abode of higher thought (*adhicittavihāra*); 3. the fourth, fifth and sixth *bhūmis* – namely, Arciṣmatī, Sudurjayā and Abhimukhī – form the abode of higher wisdom (*adhiprajñāvihāra*), being respectively associated with the auxiliaries of enlightenment (*bodhipākṣya*), the noble truths (*satya*), and dependent origination (*pratītyasamutpāda*); 4. the seventh *bhūmi*, the Dūraṃgamā, is the abode where 'not without action or effort, the bs no longer perceives objects' (*sābhisaṃskāraḥ sābhogo nirmittavihāraḥ*).

c. A close link unites *bhūmis* 2 to 7 (cf. Madhyāntavibhāga, p.190, 15-18): they aim at destroying attachment to objects (*nimittābhiniveśa*) by means of meditation (*bhāvanā*) and, to this effect, increase efforts (*ābhogaprayoga*): taken together, they constitiute the 'sphere of overcoming' (*niryāṇāvasthā*).

The preceding considerations seem to be totally unknown to the Śgs.

3. The third section in the Śgs evidently concerns the seventh *bhūmi*, the Dūraṃgamā, since 'the bs understands and penetrates skilfulness in means' and because, according to general opinion, the seventh *bhūmi* is particularly associated with the *upāyakauśalyapāramitā* (see Daśabhūmika, p.60, *6-7*; Saṃgraha, p.207; Siddhi, p.623).

Immediately after *upāyakauśalya*, the Śgs mentions the successive acquisition of two *kṣāntis*: 1. the second certainty called preparatory (*dvitīyānulomikī kṣānti*); 2. the certainty of the non-arising of dharmas (*anutpattikadharmakṣānti*). Once the latter is acquired, the Buddha gives the bs the great prediction (*mahāvyākaraṇa*) and announces to him that he will one day reach Saṃbodhi.

However, this classification will not be retained; as will be seen later on, in n.119, the *dvitīyānulomikī kṣānti* is a characteristic of the sixth *bhūmi* and not the seventh, while the *anutpattikadharmakṣānti*, followed immediately by the *mahāvyākaraṇa*, is definitively obtained in the eighth.

4. The fourth section in the Śgs concerns the eighth *bhūmi*, the Acalā. According to our author, it is characterised by the 'Concentration consisting of always being in the presence of the Buddhas of the present' (*pratyutpannabuddhasaṃmukhāvasthitasamādhi*), the requirements necessary for acquiring the Buddha attributes and, finally, the securing of a Buddha-field (*buddhakṣetra*).

However, by placing the *pratyutpannasamādhi* in the eighth *bhūmi*, the author contradicts himself, for he will assert in section 6 that all the concentrations of the bs are obtained in the tenth *bhūmi*, and we know from the Daśabhūmika (p.82, *14-15*) that the *pratyutpannasamādhi* is no exception. Conversely, it is indeed in the eighth *bhūmi* that the bs practises the vision (*darśanatā*), realisation (*pariniṣpādanatā*) and purification (*viśodhanatā*) of his *buddhakṣetra*. Here the Śgs agrees with the Pañcaviṃśati, p.217; the Śatasāhasrikā, p.1458, the Daśabhūmika, p.66, *10-16*, etc.

The Śgs, however, does not seem to have given much consideration to the importance of the eighth *bhūmi*, which later sources emphasize emulously:

a. The eighth *bhūmi* is characterised by the definitive acquisition (*pratilābha, pratilambha, pratilambhatā*) of the *anutpattikadharmakṣānti* (see the references below, n.119).

b. The acquisition of the *kṣānti* is accompanied by the great prediction (*mahāvyākaraṇa*) concerning the final triumph of the bs; cf. Lalitavistara, p.35, *21*; Daśabhūmika, p.71, *24*; Saddharmapuṇḍ., p.266, *1-2*; Sūtrālaṃkāra, pp.20, *15*; 141, *27*; 166, *12*; Madhyāntavibhāga, pp.190, *18*; 192, *1*.

c. From then on, the bs is predestined as to his future Buddhahood: *niyatipatito bhavati buddhatve* (Madhyāntavibhāga, p.190, *20*); *niyato bhavaty anuttarāyāṃ samyaksaṃbodhau* (Sūtrālaṃkāra, p.83, *24*); *tṛtīyaniyatipātapatito bhavati* (Bodh. bhūmi, p.367, *12*). He is an irreversible (*avaivartika*) bs, in possession of an irreversible certainty (*avaivartika-kṣāntipratilabdha*; cf. Saddharmapuṇḍ., p.259, *13*). Besides, the eighth *bhūmi*, the Acalā, is also called Niyatabhūmi 'Predestined Stage' (Bodh. bhūmi, p.367, *11*), Avivartyabhūmi, Avinivartanīyabhūmi, Avaivartikabhūmi 'Irreversible Stage' (Daśabhūmika, p.71, *12*; Sūtrālaṃkāra, p.176, *22*; Bodh. bhūmi, p.235, *18*). It marks the beginning of the irreversible career (*avivartacaryā, avivartanacaryā*), the infallible career (*abandhyacaryā*) which will carry on through the last three *bhūmis* (cf. Mahāvastu I, pp.1, *3*; 63, *13-14*; Bodh. bhūmi, p.290, *21*).

d. Finally and above all, in the eighth *bhūmi*, the activity of the bs is carried out spontaneously, without action or effort, for it is no longer distracted by objects or notions; that is why it is called Anabhisaṃskārānābhogavihāra or Anābhoganirmittavihāra (cf. Madhyāntavibhāga, p.105, *18-21*; Sūtrālaṃkāra, p.178, *3*; Bodh. bhūmi, p.367, *11*; Saṃgraha, p.202).

5. The fifth section in the Śgs concerns the ninth *bhūmi*, the Sādhumatī. The author mentions only five accomplishments (*saṃpad*) characterising the bs from his descent from the Tuṣita heaven until his reaching Saṃbodhi. It is therefore not as complete as the Prajñāpāramitā (Pañcaviṃśati, pp.217, *11-16*; 224, *10* - 225, *7*; Śatasāhasrikā, pp.1458, *11-18*; 1470, *16* - 1472, *7*), the Abhisamayālaṃkāra (I, vv.68-9) and the Āloka (p.103, *19-26*), which attribute up to twelve accomplishments to the ninth *bhūmi*, while not interpreting them in exactly the same

1. A bodhisattva who wishes to train himself in the Śūraṃgamasamādhi should first train himself in good intentions (*āśaya*). [Having learnt good intentions, he should learn effort (*prayoga*)[113]].[Having learnt effort], he should learn high resolve (*adhyāśaya*)[114]. Having learnt high resolve, he should learn great goodwill (*mahāmaitrī*). Having learnt great goodwill, he should learn great compassion (*mahākaruṇā*). Having learnt great compassion, he should learn the four Noble Brahmā Abodes (*ārya brahmavihāra*), that is, goodwill (*maitrī*), compassion

way. Certain accomplishments indicated by the Śgs – accomplishment of birth (*janman*), family (*kula*), clan (*gotra*), conception (*garbhāvakrānti*) – are partly inspired by the biographies of the Buddha Śākyamuni; cf. Majjhima III, pp.119-23; Aṅguttara II, p.130; Mahāvastu I, pp.142-8; Nidānakathā in Jātaka I, pp.48-9.

Here again, however, the Śgs is silent on the particularly mystical value of the ninth *bhūmi*, the stage of assured practice and the abode of the four analytical knowledges (*niyatacaryābhūmi* and *pratisaṃvidvihāra*; cf. Bodh. bhūmi, p.367, *13*), having as its main virtue the power (*bala*) of the *pratisaṃkhyāna* and *bhāvanā* (Saṃgraha, p.208; Siddhi, p.624). It is pre-eminently the sphere of the instructor (*kathikāvasthā*); cf. Madhyāntavibhāga, p.190, *21-24*).

6. Finally, the sixth section in the Śgs concerns the tenth *bhūmi*, the Dharmameghā 'Cloud of the Dharma' (see Saṃgraha, pp.202-3), also called Ultimate Abode (*paramavihāra*; cf. Bodh. bhūmi, p.367, *13*), Stage of the Consecration in Omniscience (*sarvajña-jñānābhiṣekabhūmi*: cf. Daśabhūmika, p.82, *8*), or Sphere of Consecration (*abhiṣekāvasthā*; cf. Madhyāntavibhāga, p.190, *24*). In this stage, the predominant virtue is the perfection of knowledge (*jñānapāramitā*). The bs obtains the great *samādhis* (Daśabhūmika, p.82, *9-21*) and has at his command the *dhāraṇīs* and *pratibhāna* (Sūtrālaṃkāra, p.17, *2*). According to the Pañcaviṃśati, p.225, *8*, and the Āloka, p.104, *8-9*: *bodhisattvo daśamyāṃ bhūmau sthitaḥ saṃs tathāgata eveti vaktavyo na tu samyaksaṃbuddhaḥ*: 'the bs who is to be found in the tenth stage should quite simply be called Tathāgata, but not yet Fully and Perfectly Enlightened'.

Thus, § 48 of the Śgs contains an outline of the ten stages proper to the bodhisattvas: an account which is exact in its essentials, but too summary and divergent on several points of what was later to become, in the great Mahāyānist treatises, the traditional teaching.

We will see further on, at § 149, n.299, that the Śgs was not unaware of speculations concerning the stages common to the śrāvakas and bodhisattvas.

113 Phrase, no doubt inadvertently, omitted from the Chinese version. This is the Tibetan version: *byaṅ chub sems dpaḥ dpaḥ bar ḥgro baḥi tiṅ ṅe ḥdzin ḥdi la slob pa na thog ma ñid du bsam pa la slob po // gaṅ gi tshe bsam pa la slobs par gyur pa deḥi tshe sbyor ba la ḥjug go /.*

114 In Tib. *gaṅ gi tshe sbyor ba la bslab par gyur pa deḥi tshe lhag paḥi bsam pa la ḥjug go.* On the difference between *āśaya* and *adhyāśaya*, see Vkn, pp.284-6. In the Saṃbhārabhūmi 'Stage of Accumulation', the *cittotpāda* of the beginner bs (*ādikārmika*) is associated with good wishing (*chanda*), good intentions (*āśaya*) and high resolve (*adhyāśaya*). Associated with *chanda*, the *cittotpāda* is like earth (*pṛthivī*); associated with the *āśayas*, it is like pure gold (*kalyāṇasuvarṇa*); associated with *adhyāśaya*, it is like a new moon in the white fortnight (*śuklapakṣanavacandra*). In the Adhimukticaryābhūmi 'Stage of the Practice of Adherence' preceding the ten stages proper, the *cittotpāda* of the bs, associated with effort (*prayoga*), is like a flame (*jvalana*). See Pañcaviṃśati, pp.19, *4* - 21, *16*; Śatasāh., pp.56-66; Abhisamayālaṃkāra I, v.19*a*; Āloka, p.25, *14-24*; Sūtrālaṃkāra, p.16, *17-21*.

(*karuṇā*), joy (*muditā*) and equanimity[115]. Having learnt the four Noble Brahmā Abodes, he should learn the five superknowledges (*pañcābhijñā*) incurred by fruition (*vipākaja*) and always conform to them[116].

2. Having learnt the superknowledges **[634a]**, he can then complete the six perfections (*ṣaṭpāramitāḥ paripūrayati*)[117].

3. Having completed the six perfections, he understands and penetrates [skilfulness] in means (*upāyakauśalya*)[118]. Having penetrated skilful means, he establishes himself in the second certainty called 'preparatory' (*dvitīyānulomikī kṣānti*)[119]. Being

[115] Cf. the Tibetan version: *gaṅ gi tshe lhag paḥi bsam pa la bslabs par gyur pa deḥi tshe byams pa chen po la ḥjug go / gaṅ gi tshe byams pa chen po la bslabs par gyur pa deḥi tshe sñiṅ rje chen po la ḥjug go / gaṅ gi tshe sñiṅ rje chen po la bslabs par gyur pa deḥi tshe dgaḥ ba chen po la ḥjug go / gaṅ gi tshe dgaḥ ba chen po la bslabs par gyur pa deḥi tshe btaṅ sñoms chen po la ḥjug go / gaṅ gi tshe btaṅ sñoms chen po la bslabs par gyur pa deḥi tshe byaṅ chub sems dpaḥ ḥphags paḥi gnas pa bźi la bslabs pa yin te / bźi gaṅ źe na / byams pa chen po daṅ / sñiṅ rje chen po daṅ / dgaḥ ba chen po daṅ / btaṅ sñoms chen poḥo /.* This clearly concerns the four Brahmavihāras, also called *apramāṇas* or *apramāṇacittas* (cf. Vkn, p.18, n.66). From the outset, Buddhism borrowed these devout practices from ancient Brahmanic Yoga, and the Prajñāpāramitā also recommends them to the bs (see Pañcaviṃśati, pp.181–2).

[116] The Tib. is more precise: *gaṅ gi tshe byaṅ chub sems dpaḥ ḥphags paḥi gnas pa ḥdi bźi la bslabs par gyur ba deḥi tshe rjes su ḥthun paḥi mṅon par śes pa lṅa po mi ñams pa dag la slob po*: 'When the bs has learnt the four noble abodes (*āryavihāra*), he learns the five preparatory (*anulomikī*) Abhijñās which are indestructible (*akṣaya*)'.

In the main, the first five *abhijñās* are supernormal powers common to both worldlings (*pṛthagjana*) and noble ones (*ārya*); only the sixth *abhijñā*, the knowledge of the destruction of the defilements (*āsravakṣayajñāna)*, is reserved for the noble ones (Kośa VII, pp.97 and 100).

This is why the Prajñāpāramitā (Pañcaviṃśati, pp.184-5) does not recommend it to the bs who would be transformed by this *abhijñā* into a *kṣīṇāsrava* arhat, unable to devote himself to the welfare of beings.

[117] The six *pāramitās* are cultivated in the first six *bhūmis*, *dāna* mainly in the first, *śīla* in the second, and so on (Saṃgraha, p.207). They are not perfectly fulfilled (*paripūrṇa*) until the sixth *bhūmi*.

[118] *Upāyakauśalya* is the dominant perfection of the seventh *bhūmi*; see Daśabhūmika, p.60, *6-7*; Saṃgraha, p.207; Siddhi, p.623.

[119] Here and in the following line read *ti êrh* (and not *ti san*) *jou shun jên* 第二柔順忍, according to the Tib. *rjes su ḥthun paḥi bźod pa gñis pa = dvitīyānulomikī kṣānti*.

The problem of *kṣānti*, sometimes 'patience' and sometimes 'certainty', is one of the most complicated ones for scholasticism. J. May (*Candrakīrti*, p.212, n.717) remarks: *Kṣānti* is firstly a *nirvedhabhāgīya*, thus connected to the *prayogamārga* (Kośa VI, p.165; Siddhi, pp.579-82); secondly, eight moments of the *darśanamārga*; thirdly, the third *pāramitā*.

However, we must further distinguish the *kṣāntis* clustered around the *anutpattika-dharmakṣānti* 'certainty of the non-arising of dharmas', a fundamental thesis of the Madhyamaka. In all they number three, ten or five.

I. The three *kṣāntis*.

1. Sometimes they are designated by their numerical order: *prathamā*, *dvitīyā* and *tṛtīyā*:

Sukhāvatīvyūha, ed. U. Wogihara, p.44, *16-17* (T 360, ch.1, p.269*b* 5); Samādhirāja I, p.76, *5-6* (T 639, ch.2, p.556*a* 2).

2. More often they have names: 1. *ghoṣānugā* or *ghoṣānugamī* 'following words' (*yin hsiang* 音響, *sgraḥi rjes su ḥgro ba*); 2. *anulomikī* 'preparatory' or 'conforming' (*jou shun* 柔順, *rjes su ḥthun pa*); 3. *anutpattikadharmakṣānti* 'certainty of the non-arising of dharmas' (*wu shêng fa jên* 無生法忍, *mi skye baḥi chos la bzod pa*); cf. Sukhāvatīvyūha, p.112, *13* (T 360, ch.1, p.271*a* 14-15); Avataṃsaka, T 278, ch.28, p.580*c* 8; T 279, ch.44, p.232*b* 9).

The Avataṃsaka (T 279, ch.44, p.232*b* 12-26) defines them clearly: 'What is the *ghoṣānugā kṣānti* of the bs? Hearing the dharmas expounded by the Buddha, the bs does not fear, does not tremble, does not take fright (*na trasati, na saṃtrasati, na saṃtrāsam āpadyate*); he believes in them deeply, loves them, follows them, remembers them attentively, cultivates (*bhāvayati*) them and dwells (*pratiṣṭhati*) in them.

'What is the *anulomikī kṣānti* of the bs? The bs examines (*vitarkayati*) and appreciates (*vicārayati*) these same dharmas; he assimilates and does not refute (*na virodhayati*) them; he gradually comprehends them so well that his mind is purified; he abides correctly in their cultivation and possesses (*pratipadyate*) them.

'What is the *anutpattikadharmakṣānti* of the bs? The bs does not see that the least dharma arises and does not see that the least dharmas ceases. Why? That which is unarisen (*anutpanna*) is unceasing (*aniruddha*); that which is unceasing is indestructible (*akṣaya*); that which is indestructible is unstained (*viraja*); that which is unstained is undifferentiated (*abhinna*); that which is undifferentiated is abodeless (*anālaya*); that which is abodeless is calm (*śānta*); that which is calm is free from desire (*vītarāga*); that which is free from desire is inactive (*anabhisaṃskṛta*); that which is inactive is wishless (*apraṇihita*); that which is wishless is homeless (*aniketa*); that which is homeless does not leave and does not arrive'.

See a similar definition of the *anutpattikadharmakṣānti* in Daśabhūmika, pp.63, *26* - 64, *6*.

Certain paraphrases clarify the meaning of these three *kṣāntis*: the second is called *śūnyatānulomikī kṣānti* 'certainty conforming to emptiness' (Tathāgataguhyasūtra, T 312, ch.12, p.732*c* 18, quoted in Madh. vṛtti, p.362, *8*). For the third, we find *anutpattikeṣu dharmeṣu kṣāntiḥ* (Lalita, p.36, 9); *nirātmakeṣv anutpattikeṣu dharmeṣu kṣāntiḥ* (Vajracchedikā, p.58, *9*); *anutpattikadharmeṣu kṣāntiḥ* (Sūtrālaṃkāra, p.163, *20*), etc.

3. After having defined the *prathamā, dvitīyā* and *tṛtīyā kṣāntiḥ*, the Samādhirāja I, p.82, *7-10* (see the Chinese tr., T 639, ch.2, p.556*b* 24-25) qualifies them respectively as *ghoṣānugamī kṣāntiḥ, cintāmayī anulomikī kṣāntiḥ* and *bhāvanāmayī anutpattikā kṣāntiḥ*. These details are interesting because they establish a parallel between the three *kṣāntis* of the bs and the three *prajñā*s of the śrāvaka: *śrutamayī* 'based on teaching', *cintāmayī* 'based on reflection' and *bhāvanāmayī* 'based on contemplation' (cf. Dīgha III, p.219; Vibhaṅga, pp.324-5; Visuddhimagga, ed. Warren, p.370; Kośa VI, pp.143-4). However, whereas the three *kṣāntis* of the bs concern emptiness, the three *prajñās* of the śrāvaka concern the general marks of dharmas (*dharmāṇāṃ sāmānyalakṣaṇam*): impermanence, suffering and impersonality.

4. The Dhyānasamādhisūtra (T 614, ch.2, p.285*a* 10 sq.) distinguishes between an *utpādakṣānti*, an *anulomikī dharmakṣānti* and an *anutpādakṣānti*. The first is simply patience in bearing insults and torments (see above, § 28, n.86); the second is the understanding of impermanence and of the *bhūtalakṣaṇa* devoid of any mark; the third marks an advance on the previous one. Here, the 'patience' *kṣānti* and the 'certainty' *kṣānti* are intermixed.

5. A treatise by Vasubandhu (or Maitreya) translated by Kumārajīva, the Bodhicittotpādanaśāstra (T 1659, ch.2, p.516*b-c*), posits three *kṣāntis*: 1. *śraddhākṣānti*, faith in the four *āryasatyas*, the *dvādaśanidānas* of dependent origination, the four *apramāṇacittas* and the six *pāramitās*; 2. *anulomikī kṣānti*, certainty relating to the *pudgala-* and *dharmanairātmya*;

established in the second certainty called 'preparatory', he acquires (*pratilabhate*) the certainty of the non-arising of dharmas (*anutpattikadharmakṣānti*). When he has acquired the *anutpattika-dharmakṣānti*, the Buddhas predict to him (*vyākurvanti*) [that he will reach supreme and perfect enlightenment (*anuttarāṃ samyak-saṃbodhim abhisaṃbhotsyate*)][120].

4. After the Buddhas have given him the prediction (*vyākaraṇa*), he

3. *paramā dharmakṣānti*, which is none other than the *anutpattikadharmakṣānti*. Under slightly different terms, it is always the same theory.

One would like to know at what precise moments in his career the bs acquires these three *kṣāntis*, but the early texts are somewhat reticent. Naturally, it depends on the disposition of each person. In the course of one and the same instruction, certain listeners arouse the *cittotpāda*, others acquire the *ghoṣānugā*, others the *anulomikī*, and yet others the *anutpattikā* (see Vkn, pp.25 and n.84; 58; Samādhirāja II, pp.253, *5*; 280-1).

The texts distinguish between *adhimukti*, adherence, approbation of the non-arising of things, and the definitive acquisition (*pratilābha*, *pratilambha*, *pratilambhatā*) of *kṣānti* (Lalitavistara, pp.36, *9*; 440, *21*; Saddharmapuṇḍ., pp.266, *1*; 437, *1*). See the Aṣṭasāh., p.856, *25*: *bodhisattvāḥ prajñāpāramitāyāṃ carantaḥ sarvadharmā anutpattikā ity adhimuñcanti na ca tāvad anutpattikadharmakṣāntipratilabdhā bhavanti*.

Here, in § 48, the Śgs situates the *anulomikī* and the *anutpattikā* in the seventh *bhūmi*, but this is not the general opinion. The Daśabhūmika places the *anulomikī* in the sixth *bhūmi* (p.47, *19-20*) and the *anutpattikā* in the eighth (p.64, *5*). Equally, nearly all the śāstras situate the *anutpattikā* in the eighth *bhūmi* (Sūtrālaṃkāra, pp.122, *2*; 131, *17*; Madhyāntavibhāga, p.105, *11*; Bodh. bhūmi, pp.350, *27*; 351, *13-14*).

II. The ten *kṣāntis*. Less frequent than the preceding, a list of ten *kṣāntis* is mentioned in the Śatasāhasrikā, p.64, *17* (T 220, ch.3, p.12*b* 16) and itemised in the Avataṃsaka (T 279, ch.44, p.232*b* 9-10): 1. *ghoṣānugā*, 2. *anulomikī*, 3. *anutpattikadharmakṣānti*, 4. *māyopamā*, 5. *marīcyupamā*, 6. *svapnopamā*, 7. *pratiśrabdopamā*, 8. *pratibimbopamā*, 9. *nirmitopamā*, 10. *ākāśopamā*.

III. The five *kṣāntis*. Modern judgement considers the *Jên-Wang hu kuo po-lo-mi ching* 'Perfection of Wisdom of the Good King who protects the State' as an apocryphal Chinese work, of which there exist two editions: that by Kumārajīva (T 245) and that by Amoghavajra (T 246). They mention five *kṣāntis* (T 245, ch.1, p.826*b* 23-24; T 246, ch.1, p.836*b-c*): 1. *damakṣānti* (fu jen), 2. *śraddhākṣānti*, 3. *anulomikī kṣānti*, 4. *anutpādakṣānti*, 5. *nirodhakṣānti*. The first four are subdivided into three categories: strong (*adhimātra*), middling (*madhya*) and weak (*mṛdu*); the fifth and last, into strong and weak categories.

The *damakṣānti* relates to the Adhimukticaryābhūmi, the preparatory stage of the *bhūmis*, the weak category concerning the ten *vihāras*, the middling category the ten *caryās* and the strong category the ten *pariṇāmas*. [Here the Chinese apocryphal text agrees with the Pañcaviṃśati, pp.136, *14* - 141, *24*, and the Bodh. bhūmi, p.324, *14-20*.]

The *śraddhākṣānti* pertains to the first three *bhūmis*: Pramuditā, Vimalā and Prabhākarī.

The *anulomikī kṣānti* pertains to *bhūmis* 4 to 6: Arciṣmatī, Sudurjayā and Abhimukhī.

The *anutpādakṣānti* concerns *bhūmis* 7 to 9: Dūraṃgamā, Acalā and Sādhumatī.

The *nirodhakṣānti* characterises the tenth *bhūmi* (Dharmameghā) and the Buddhabhūmi.

This distribution of the *kṣāntis* among the *bhūmis* became a compulsion among the masters of Chinese Buddhism; cf. Mochizuki's Encyclopaedia, pp.1657-8.

120 The acquisition of the *anutpattikadharmakṣānti* is accompanied by a 'Great Prediction'

penetrates into the eighth bodhisattva stage (*bodhisattvānām aṣṭamakāṃ bhūmiṃ praviśati*). When he has entered the eighth bodhisattva stage, he acquires the Concentration consisting of always being placed facing the Buddhas of the present (*pratyutpannabuddhasaṃmukhāvasthitasamādhi*)[121]. Having obtained the Concentration consisting of always being placed facing the Buddhas of the present, he is never deprived of the sight of the Buddhas (*satatasamitaṃ tathāgatadarśanāvirahito bhavati*). Never being deprived of the sight of the Buddhas, he fulfils the causes and conditions (*hetupratyaya*) necessary for attaining the Buddha attributes

(*mahāvyākaraṇa*) regarding the final triumph of the bs: cf. Lalita, p.35, *21*; Sūtrālaṃkāra, pp.20, *15*; 141, *27*; 166, *12*. This is what stands out clearly in a passage from the Saddharmapuṇḍ., p.266, *1-2*, which attributes to three thousand living beings the joint acquisition of the *anutpattikā* and the *vyākaraṇa: trayāṇāṃ prāṇisahasrāṇām anutpattikadharmakṣāntipratilābho 'bhūt, trayāṇāṃ ca prāṇisahasrāṇām anuttarāyāṃ samyaksaṃbodhau vyākaraṇapratilābho 'bhūt*. This great *vyākaraṇa* will be defined below, in § 108.

[121] This is the last of the nine *bodhisattvasamādhis* listed by the Mahāvyut., No.745; according to the Daśabhūmika, p.82, *14-15*, it concerns the tenth *bhūmi*. A Pratyutpannabuddha-saṃmukhāvasthitasamādhisūtra was translated into Chinese with the title of Pan chou san mei ching (T 418) by Lokakṣema on the eighth day of the tenth moon of the second Kuang-ho year (cf. *Ch'u*, T 2145, ch.2, p.6*b* 12) or 24 November 179. In this sūtra, the Buddha says to the bs Bhadrapāla: 'There is a dharma which should be cultivated ceaselessly, which should be kept ceaselessly, which does not yield to other dharmas and which is the foremost of the virtues (*guṇa*): it is the Pratyutpannabuddhasaṃmukhāvasthitasamādhi' (T 418, ch.1, p.904*b* 19-22). 'It is not with the heavenly eye (*divyacakṣus*) that the bs in *samādhi* sees the Buddha, nor with the heavenly ear (*divyaśrotra*) that he hears him, nor with the *ṛddhipādas* that he goes to his *buddhakṣetra*. Neither does he see the Buddha by dying here and being reborn there in his *buddhakṣetra*: on the contrary, it is here, on the very spot where he is seated in *samādhi*, that the practitioner sees the Buddha and hears the sūtras he expounds' (*ibid*., p.905*a* 23-26).

The *samādhi* in question is independent of the *abhijñās* (superknowledges or powers normally acquired by the yogin) and of infinitely greater import, for it draws its power from the Prajñāpāramitā. Commenting on a passage in the Pañcaviṃśati (ed. Dutt, p.30, *6-12*), the Upadeśa in Nāgārjuna, *Traité* V, p.2272 sq., explains: 'What is seen with the *divyacakṣus* does not go beyond the *trisāhasramahāsāhasralokadhātu*, but here [in this *samādhi*], through the power of the Prajñāpāramitā, the bs sees all the Buddhas to be found, in each of the ten directions, in universes as numerous as the sands of the Ganges. Why? Because from the perspective of the Prajñāpāramitā, nothing is close (*samīpe*) or distant (*dūra*), and there is no obstacle. . .The *divyacakṣus* is undefiled and undefined (*anivṛtāvyākṛta*; cf. Kośa II, p.168). The Pratyutpannasamādhi is obtained as much by a man freed from desire (*vītarāga*) as a man not freed from desire (*avītarāga*); the *divyacakṣus* is obtained only by those who have renounced desire. The Pratyutpannasamādhi is a vision resulting from the constant cultivation and practice of mindfulness (*smṛti*), perception (*saṃjñā*) and subjective imagination (*saṃkalpa*). The *divyacakṣus*, obtained through the practice of the *abhijñās*, is an eye made of clear form derived from the four great elements of the world of form (*rūpadhātoś caturmahābhūtāny upādāya rūpaprasāda*), and that eye enjoys total luminosity. The technique of the *divyacakṣus* is easy: thus, when the sun rises, it is not hard to see colours; conversely, the technique of the *samādhi* is difficult: thus when one lights a lamp at night-time, it is not easy to see colours'.

(*buddhadharma*). Fulfilling the causes and conditions necessary for attaining the Buddha attributes, he achieves (*abhirnirharati*) a Buddha-field of splendid accomplishments (*buddhakṣetravyūhasaṃpad*)[122].

5. Having achieved a Buddha-field of splendid accomplishments, he attains the accomplishments called of birth, family and clan (*janma-kula-gotrasaṃpadaḥ paripūrayati*)[123]. Having attained the accom-

The method of the recollection of the Buddhas (*buddhānusmṛti*) through the Pratyutpannasamādhi or direct visualisation excited great interest in China, particularly among members of the Assocation of the White Lotus (*Po-lien shê*) founded in Lushan by Hui-yuan (334-416 C.E.) who had earlier consulted Kumārajīva. Regarding this particularly interesting phase of Chinese Buddhism, all the details wished for can be found in P. Demieville, 'La Yogācārabhūmi de Saṅgharakṣa', *Bulletin de l'École française d'Extrême-Orient* XLIV, 1954, pp.355-9; see also E. Zürcher, *The Buddhist Conquest of China*, pp.220-1.

[122] According to the Prajñāpāramitā (Pañcaviṃśati, p.217; Śatasāhasrikā, p.1458), it is in the eighth *bhūmi* that the bs practises the vision (*darśanatā*), realisation (*pariniṣpādanatā*) and purification (*pariśodhanatā*) of his *buddhakṣetra*. On this purification, see especially Vkn, pp.14-17.

[123] Read *shêng chia hsing ch'êng chiu* 生家姓成就 with the Tib. *skye ba daṅ rigs daṅ rus phun sum tshogs pa* = *janmakulagotrasaṃpad*.

These three accomplishments are explained in the Prajñāpāramitā (Pañcaviṃśati, p.224; Śata-sāhasrikā, p.1471):

1. *Janmasaṃpad* 'accomplishment of birth': *yad bodhisattvo mahāsattvo jātamātra evāsaṃkhyeyalokadhātūn avabhāsena sphurati tāṃś ca ṣaḍvikāraṃ prakampayati*: 'The bs, at his birth, illuminates with his radiance innumerable universes and shakes them in six ways'.

Cf. Upadeśa in Nāgārjuna, *Traité* V, p.2439: 'When the Bodhisattva is on the point of being born, the devas, nāgas and asuras adorn the *trisāhasramahāsāhasralokadhātu*. Thereupon lotus seats (*padmāsana*) made of the seven jewels (*saptaratnamaya*) emerge spontaneously (*svatas*). From the belly of the mother first come innumerable bss who go and sit on the lotuses; they join their hands, sing praises and wait. Bodhisattvas, and also devas, nāgas, asuras, ṛṣis and noble ladies join their hands and wholeheartedly wish to see the birth of the Bodhisattva. Then the Bodhisattva emerges from the right side of his mother, just like the full moon emerging from clouds. He emits a great radiance (*avabhāsa*) which illuminates immense universes. At that very moment a great voice extends throughout the universes of the ten directions and proclaims that, in such-and-such a place, the Bodhisattva has come to his last existence. Sometimes there are bss who are born in apparitional bodies on lotuses. With regard to the four wombs (*yoni*), the Bodhisattva is born from the chorion (*jarāyuja*) or has an apparitional birth (*upapāduka*). With regard to the four human castes (*jāti*), the Bodhisattva is born into either the kṣatriya caste or that of the brāhmaṇa, since those two castes are respected by men'.

2. *Kulasaṃpad* 'accomplishment of family': *yad bodhisattvo mahāsattvo mahākuleṣu pratyājāyate*: 'The bs goes to be born in great families'.

Cf. Upadesa in Nāgārjuna, *Traité* V, pp.2439-40: 'Brāhmaṇa families possess wisdom (*prajñā*), kṣatriya families possess power (*bala*); the brāhmaṇa favours the future life; the kṣatriya favours the present life, both types of families are useful to the world; that is why the Bodhisattva is born among them. Furthermore, there is the deserving Dharma family, that of irreversible (*avaivartika*) adherents. Taking on birth in those families is the "accomplishment of family"'.

3. *Gotrasaṃpad* 'accomplishment of clan': *yad bodhisattvo mahāsattvo yato gotrāt*

plishments called of birth, family and clan, he attains the accomplishments of the descent into the womb and of the leaving of the world (*garbhāvakrānty-abhiniṣkramaṇasaṃpadaḥ paripūrayati*)[124].

paurvakā bodhisattvā abhūvan tatra gotre pratyājāyate: 'The bs goes to be born in clans from which earlier bss have come'.

Cf. Upadeśa in Nāgārjuna, *Traité* V, p.2440: 'When the Bodhisattva is still found in the Tuṣita heaven, he examines (*vilokayati*) the world, wondering which clan (*gotra*) is the most noble for welcoming a being; it is into that clan that he takes on birth. Thus, of the last seven Buddhas, the first three were born into the Kauṇḍinya clan, the next three into the Kāśyapa clan, and the Buddha Śākyamuni into the Gautama clan. Moreover, the bs who begins with the firmness of high resolve (*adhyāśayadṛḍhatā*) [is born] into the clan of the Buddhas. For others, obtaining the certainty of the non-arising of dharmas (*anutpattikadharmakṣānti*) would be the "clan of the Buddhas", since it is then that the bs acquires a partial influx of the "knowledge of all the aspects" (*sarvākārajñatā*) [proper to the Buddhas]. Compare this level with the *gotrabhūmi* in the śrāvaka system'.

124 Read *ju t'ai ch'u chia ch'êng chiu* 入胎出家成就, with the Tib. *mṅal du ḥjug pa daṅ mṅon par byuṅ ba phun sum tshogs pa* = *garbhāvakrānty-abhiniṣkramaṇasaṃpad*.

These two accomplishments are also explained in the Prajñāpāramitā (Pañcaviṃśati, p.224; Śatasāhasrikā, p.1471):

1. *Garbhāvakrāntisaṃpad* 'accomplishment of the descent into the womb': *yad bodhisattvo mahāsattvaḥ sarvāsu jātiṣūpapāduka upapadyate*: 'In all his births, the bs is born as an apparitional being'.

Cf. Upadeśa in Nāgārjuna, *Traité* V, pp.2438-9: 'According to certain people, the Bodhisattva, mounted on a white elephant, surrounded (*parivṛta*), revered (*satkṛta*), respected (*gurukṛta*), esteemed (*mānita*) and served (*pūjita*) by innumerable Tuṣita gods, enters with them into the womb of his mother. According to others, the mother of the Bodhisattva who possesses the Illusion-like Concentration (*māyopamasamādhi*) acts so that her belly dilates inordinately; all the bss of the *trisāhasramahāsāhasralokadhātu*, the devas, nāgas and asuras can enter and leave there. In that belly is a palace (*bhavana*) and a dais (*kūṭāgāra*). [The deities] arrange a bed (*khaṭvā*) on it, suspend banners (*patākā*) and parasols (*chattra*), scatter flowers and burn perfume; all that results from the meritorious actions (*puṇyakarman*) of the Bodhisattva. Then the Bodhisattva descends and takes his place and, through the power of his *samādhi*, enters that womb even while remaining as before in the heaven of the Tuṣita gods.'

2. *Abhiniṣkramaṇasaṃpad* 'accomplishment of the leaving of the world': *yad bodhisattvo mahāsattvaḥ pravrajito 'nekaiḥ sattvakoṭiniyutaśatasahasraiḥ sārdham abhiniṣkrāmati gṛhāt te ca sattvā niyatā bhavanti triṣu yāneṣu*: 'The bs who is leaving the world takes up the homeless life with innumerable hundreds of thousands of *koṭiniyutas* of beings, and those beings are predestined to the three Vehicles'.

Cf. Upadeśa in Nāgārjuna, *Traité* V, p.2442: 'Thus, one night in his palace, the Bodhisattva Śākyamuni saw that his courtesans resembled corpses. The devas and asuras of the ten directions, bearing banners (*patākā*) and flowers (*puṣpa*), came and offered them to him and, proceeding respectfully to meet him, escorted him outside. Then Chaṇḍaka, despite the order he had received previously from King Śuddhodana, acquiescing to the wishes of the Bodhisattva, arrived leading the horse [Kaṇṭhaka]. The four messenger-kings of the gods supported in their hands the hooves of the horse, which left the town by jumping over the ramparts. It was in order to destroy all the passions (*kleśa*) and Māra in person that the Bodhisattva thus bore witness, before all beings, to his repugnance for the household life, since

6. Having attained the accomplishments of the descent into the womb and of the renunciation of the world, he attains the tenth stage (*daśamāṃ bhūmiṃ paripūrayati*). Having attained the tenth stage, he receives the consecration (*abhiṣeka*) of the Buddhas[125]. Having received the consecration of the Buddhas, he obtains all the bodhisattva concentrations (*sarvabodhisattvasamādhi*). Having obtained all the bodhisattva concentrations, he last of all (*paścāt*) obtains the Śūraṃgamasamādhi. Having obtained the Śūraṃgamasamādhi, he can perform Buddha deeds (*buddhakārya*) for all beings, but he does not abandon the practices (*caryā*) of a bodhisattva.

Dṛḍhamati, if a bodhisattva learns all those dharmas, he obtains the Śūraṃgamasamādhi. A bodhisattva who has obtained the Śūraṃgamasamādhi has no further dharmas to learn. Why? Because he has learnt all dharmas thoroughly. Just as an apprentice-archer who can hit a fraction of a hair has nothing further to learn – and why? Because he has already learnt how to; so, O Dṛḍhamati, a bodhisattva who is in Śūraṃgamasamādhi has no further dharmas to learn, because he has already gained all the concentrations (*samādhi*) and all the merits (*puṇya*).

49. Thereupon the bodhisattva Dṛḍhamati said to the Buddha: Bhagavat, I would like to relate a comparison (*upamā*); may the Bhagavat permit me to do so. The Buddha consented[126].

Bhagavat, just as the devarāja Mahābrahmā, lord of the *trisāhasramahāsāhasralokadhātu*, surveys (*vilokayati*) for himself the

if a person as deserving and noble as himself abandons his home, what should not common worldlings (*pṛthagjana*) do? Episodes (*nidāna*) of that type illustrate the "accomplishment of the leaving of the world"'.

[125] Cf. Madhyāntavibhāga, p.190, *24* sq.: *daśamyāṃ hi bhūmau bodhisattvo mārganiṣṭhāgato daśadiglokadhātuvyavasthitānāṃ buddhabhagavatāṃ raśmibhyo 'bhiṣekeṇābhiṣicyate.*

To consecrate the son of a cakravartin king, water from the four great oceans is poured on his head. To consecrate a bs of the tenth stage, called stage of the Cloud of the Dharma (*dharmameghā*), the Buddhas of the ten regions emit rays which enter the head of the bs and confer on him all the Buddha attributes: he is then said to be *abhiṣikto buddhatve* 'consecrated in Buddhahood' (cf. Daśabhūmika, pp.85-6; Sūtrālaṃkāra, p.178). For the Prajñāpāramitā (Pañcaviṃśati, p.217, *17*; Śatasāhasrikā, p.1458, *19*) the bs in the tenth *bhūmi* should be called Tathāgata: *bodhisattvo mahāsattvo daśamyāṃ bhūmau sthitaḥ saṃs tathāgata eveti vaktavyaḥ.*

[126] The Chinese translation is somewhat free. We have in Tib. *bcom ldan ḥdas bdag spobs so / bde bar gśegs pa bdag spobs so / bcom ldan ḥdas kyis bkaḥ stsal pa / blo gros brtan pa deḥi dus la dbab par śes na khyod spobs par gyis śig*; this gives in Skt *pratibhāti me Bhagavan pratibhāti me Sugata. bhagavān avocat: pratibhātu te Dṛḍhamate yasyedānīṃ kālaṃ manyase*: 'Something comes to my mind, O Bhagavat; something comes to my mind, O Sugata'. The Bhagavat replied: 'Say it, O Dṛḍhamati, if you think the time has come'.

This expression is very common in Pāli and Sanskrit; cf. Majjhima I, pp.230, *10-12*; 234, *6-7*;

trisāhasramahāsāhasralokadhātu without making any effort, so the bodhisattva in Śūraṃgamasamādhi surveys for himself all the dharmas without making any effort, and he also knows the functioning of the mind and mentation (*cittacaittapravṛtti*) of all beings.

The Buddha said to Dṛḍhamati: It is as you say (*evam etad yathā vadasi*): the bodhisattva in Śūraṃgamasamādhi knows all the bodhisattva dharmas and all the Buddha dharmas.

[*Secrets and Mysteries of Meruśikharadhara*]

50. Now, in that assembly, there was a Śakra devendra named Meruśikharadhara[127] 'Holding the Summit of Mount Meru', who lived outside the confines (*prāntadvīpa*) of the *trisāhasramahāsāhasralokadhātu*. He said to the Buddha: Just as [**634b**] a being established on the summit of Sumeru beholds (*vilokayati*) all the continents (*dvīpa*), so a bodhisattva established in Śūraṃgamasamādhi spontaneously (*svatas*) sees the practices (*caryā*) of the Śrāvakas and Pratyekabuddhas as well as the practices of beings.

51. Then the bodhisattva Dṛḍhamati asked the Śakra Meruśikharadhara: From which universe of four continents (*cāturdvīpaka*) do you come? Of which Sumeru do you occupy the summit (*śikhara*)?

The Śakra replied: Kulaputra, a bodhisattva who possesses the Śūraṃgamasamādhi should not be asked the place (*sthāna*) where he dwells. Why? Because such a bodhisattva dwells in all the *buddhakṣetras,* but is not attached to a dwelling place (*sthānaṃ nābhiniviśati*), does not perceive a dwelling place (*sthānaṃ nopalabhate*) and does not

Sanskrit Mahāparinirvāṇa, p.182; Mūlasarv. Vinaya in *Gilgit Manuscripts* III, part 4, p.188, *6*; Divyāvadāna, p.20, *21*; Saddharmapuṇḍ., p.101, *9*.

Commenting upon the passage in Majjhima I, p.230, *10*: *upamā maṃ, bho Gotama, paṭibhātī*, etc., Buddhaghosa (Papañcasūdanī II, p.275) explains: '*Upamā maṃ, bho Gotama, paṭibhātī' ti, bho Gotama, mayhaṃ ekā upamā upaṭṭhāti, āharāmi taṃ upaman ti vadati. 'Paṭibhātu taṃ Aggivessanā' ti upaṭṭhātu te, Aggivessana, āhara taṃ upamaṃ vissattho ti Bhagavā avoca*: 'A comparison comes to my mind means: a comparison comes to me and I would like to say it. The Bhagavat answers *paṭibhātu*, meaning: as the comparison comes to you, say it with confidence'.

Pratibhāti comes from the root *bhā* 'to shine, to gleam', but by giving it as *shuo* 說 and *spobs* respectively, the Chinese and Tibetan translators seem to have confused it with the root *bhaṇ* 'to speak, so say'.

[127] In Tib. *Lhun poḥi rtse ḥdzin* (see Mahāvyut., No.693). This Śakra who holds sway over the great chiliocosm is infinitely superior to the god Śakra who rules over the Trāyastriṃśa gods of our little universe of four continents. On the respective dimensions of these worlds, see Vkn, p.276. [† see Foreword, p.xv, regarding this Śakra's name in Sanskrit].

see a dwelling place (*sthānaṃ na paśyati*).

Dṛḍhamati asked: Friend (*sakhi*), have you obtained the Śūraṃgamasamādhi?

The Śakra replied: Such a *samādhi*, can it be obtained or not?

Dṛḍhamati answered: No!

The Śakra went on: Kulaputra, it must be understood that the bodhisattva who practises this *samādhi* has not obtained any dharma[128].

Dṛḍhamati said further: A man as eloquent (*pratibhānavat*) as yourself must necessarily have obtained the Śūraṃgamasamādhi.

The Śakra said: Kulaputra, I do not see any dharma onto which one can hold; and among all those dharmas onto which one cannot hold must be ranked the Śūraṃgamasamādhi. O Kulaputra, to hold to this *samādhi* is not to hold to anything. If you do not hold to anything, you do not take anything. If you do not take anything, you do not speak of it.

52. Then the Buddha said to the bodhisattva Dṛḍhamati: Do you see this Śakra Meruśikharadhara?

I see him, O Bhagavat.

O Dṛḍhamati, this Śakra, spontaneously (*svatas*) and at will (*yathākāmam*), obtains the Śūraṃgamasamādhi and, dwelling in that *samādhi*, manifests himself (*ātmānaṃ saṃdarśayati*) in all the palaces of the Śakras (*śakrabhavana*) of the *trisāhasramahāsāhasralokadhātu*.

53. Then the Śakra devendra of this universe[129] said to the Buddha: Bhagavat, if the Śakra Meruśikharadhara manifests himself in all the palaces of the Śakras, how is it that I myself have never seen him in any Śakra residence (*śakrasthāna*)?

Then the Śakra Meruśikharadhara said to the Śakra [devendra]: Kauśika, if I were now to show you my true body (*bhūtakāya*), you would feel no joy (*muditā*) in your own palace. I am forever going to the palace where you reside, but you, you do not see me.

54. Then the Śakra devendra said to the Buddha: Bhagavat, I would like to see the perfected body (*pariniṣpannakāya*)[130] of this *satpuruṣa*.

The Buddha said: Kauśika, do you want to see it?

Yes, Bhagavat, I would very much like to see it.

The Buddha said to the Śakra Meruśikharadhara: Kulaputra, then show your true and marvellous body to the Śakra [devendra].

Immediately, the Śakra [Meruśikharadhara] displayed his true and

[128] Compare in the Vkn, p163, § 10, the answer given by the Devī to Śāriputra.

[129] The Śakra of our little universe of four continents (*cāturdvīpaka*) who is often mentioned in the early canonical texts; he is named Kauśika (cf. Vkn, p.101 and n.).

[130] In Tib. *lus yoṅs su grub pa*.

marvellous body. Thereupon, in the assembly, the Śakras, Brahmās, Lokapāla Kings of the gods, śrāvakas and bodhisattvas who had not as yet obtained the Śūraṃgamasamādhi, became invisible [**634c**], like a block of ink (*maṣirāśisadṛśa*)[131]. The body of the Śakra Meruśikharadhara, as lofty (*abhyudgata*) as Meru, king of the mountains, was shining (*bhāsate*), gleaming (*tapati*) and resplendent (*virocate*)[132]. The body of the Buddha was itself doubly luminous.

55. The Śakra devendra said to the Buddha: It is extraordinary (*adbhuta*), O Bhagavat, the body of the *satpuruṣa* present here has colours that are pure, marvellous and unequalled. The bodies of the Śakras, Brahmās and Lokapāla Kings of the gods are all eclipsed (*dhyāmīkṛta*), like blocks of ink (*maṣirāśi*). Bhagavat, when I, in the Sudharmā devasabhā[133] on Mount Sumeru, wear the necklet of jewels (*maṇiratnaniṣka*) called Śakrābhilagna[134] 'Śakra pendant', the bodies of all the devas are eclipsed (*dhyānīkṛta*) by its brilliance. It is I whom am

131 In Tib. *snag tshaḥi phuṅ po bźin*. Compare Mahāvastu II, p.432, *19*: *maṣirāśivarṇa*. *Maṣi*, Tib. *snag tsha*, Ch. *mê* 墨 (cf. Mahāvyut., No.5935) really means ink. The reading *māṣarāśi* and the translation 'heap of beans' proposed by Edgerton, *Dictionary*, p.432, are to be avoided.

132 This is a stock phrase; cf. Vkn, p.6, n.37.

133 Read *shan fa t'ien t'ang* 善法天堂 with the Tib. *chos bzaṅ lhaḥi mdun sa* = Sudharmā devasabhā. Cf. Divyāvadāna, p.220, *6-8*: *eṣā devānāṃ trāyastriṃśānāṃ Sudharmā nāma devasabhā yatra devās trāystriṃśāś catvāraś ca mahārājānaḥ saṃniṣaṇṇāḥ saṃnipatitāḥ*: 'It is the meeting hall of the Trāyastriṃśa gods called Sadharmā, where the Trāyastriṃśa gods and the four Great Kings assemble'.

Sudharmā, one of the four wives of Maghā, was involved in the construction of a rest house for travellers. After her death, she was reborn among the Trāyastriṃśas and, in recompense for her merit, the city of the gods was endowed with a meeting hall which was given the name of Sudharmā (cf. Dhammapada Commentary I, pp.269-74; Jātaka I, p.201). It is in this hall that the gods assembled on the eighth of each month, or else to hear the propounding of the Dharma and to celebrate festivals (cf. Dīgha II, p.268; Majjhima II, p.79; Saṃyutta I, p.221; Jātaka VI, pp.97, 126, etc.).

134 In Tib. *brgya byin thogs pa*. The Śakrābhilagna appears in the list of the forty-seven *maṇiratnas* compiled by the Mahavyutpatti, No.5960. In theory, it is a jewel belonging to Śakra (Gaṇḍavyūha, p.498, *22*), but it is also worn by the bss, notably Mañjuśrī (Mañjuśrīparinirvāṇa, T 463, p.481*a* 1), and used in the way of adornment (Mahāvastu II, p.310, *21*; Sukhāvatīvyūha, p.110, *9*; Lalitavistara, p.297, *16*; Gaṇḍavyūha, p.101, *21*).

Ratnakāraṇḍa, T 462, ch.1, p.468*a* 18-20: 'The Śakrābhilagnamaṇiratna is attached to the neck of Śakra and lights up the Trāyastriṃśa heaven all over. Through the power of this jewel, all that exists is illuminated; nevertheless, this jewel is devoid of reflection'.

Amitāyurbuddhadhyāna, T 365, p.342*b* 10-12: 'In the Sukhāvatī, every young person wears five hundred koṭis of Śakrābhilagnamaṇiratnas by way of a necklet (*niṣka*). The brilliance of those *maṇis* lights up an hundred *yojanas*, as would an hundred koṭis of suns and moons together'.

'Ascent of Maitreya to the Tuṣita heaven', T 452, p.419*c* 22-25: 'He is seated on a lotus, his legs crossed. His body, the colour of the *jaṃbūnadaratna*, is sixteen *yojanas* long now eclipsed by the brilliance of this *satpuruṣa* and the necklet of jewels that I wear no longer shines (*na bhāsate*).

The Buddha said to the Śakra devendra: Kauśika, supposing the *trisāhasramahāsāhasralokadhātu* were filled (*paripūrṇa*) with Śakrābhilagna jewels, there is still another jewel which would eclipse them all: the Sarvadevāloka[135] 'Brilliance of all the gods'. Kauśika, supposing the *trisāhasramahāsāhasralokadhātu* were filled with Sarvadevāloka jewels, there is still another jewel which would eclipse them all: the Vajrāloka[136] 'Diamond Brilliance'. Kauśika, supposing the *trisāhasramahāsāhasralokadhātu* were filled with Vajrāloka jewels, there is still another jewel which would eclipse them all: the Sarvālokasaṃgraha[137] 'Assemblage of all the brilliances'.

Kauśika, do you see the Sarvālokasaṃgraha jewel worn by this Śakra [Meruśikharadhara]?

Yes, I see it, O Bhagavat; but the brilliance of that jewel is so violent that my eyes cannot bear it.

The Buddha said: Kauśika, when bodhisattvas in possession of the Śūraṃgamasamādhi eventually become Śakras, they all wear a necklet of jewels like that.

Then the Śakra devendra said to the Buddha: So, O Bhagavat, those who do not arouse the *anuttarasamyaksaṃbodhicitta* are deprived (*parihīṇa*) of such a perfected body (*pariniṣpannakāya*) and are also deprived of the Śūraṃgamasamādhi.

and is endowed with the thirty-two *lakṣaṇas* and the eighty *anuvyañjanas*. His *uṣṇīṣa* has the violet colour of the *vaiḍurya*. The Śakrābhilagnamaṇi and an hundred thousand myriads of koṭis of *kiṃśukaratnas* adorn his tiara'.

Mahādharmaulkādhāraṇī, T 1340, ch.5, p.681*c* 19-27: 'The Abhilagnaratna is the colour of pure gold and originates from good roots (*kuśalamūla*). It shines by itself; it can even surpass the summit of Sumeru, the heavens of the Trāyastriṃśas, Yamas, Tuṣitas and be found in the palace of Brahmā. When the bs, on leaving Jambudvīpa, is born among the Tuṣitas, it happens that, through the power of its *kuśalamūlas*, this jewel spontaneously springs from its coffers (*karaṇḍa*) and overcomes the Māras. How is this so? If the Māras or their entourage (*parivāra*) arouse a malign thought against the Tuṣita gods, thwart or torment the bs, then even if they try with all their might, they cannot shake him. Why? Because this *maṇiratna* adorns the neck of the bs and, through its power, annihiliates all Māra works. Māra Pāpīmat is deeply troubled by it. Besides, from the moment when the bs leaves the Tuṣita gods to enter his mother's belly, this ornament always accompanies him. Until he leaves home and sits on the *bodhimaṇḍa* and under the *bodhivṛkṣa*, this jewel is constantly there'.

However, here the Śgs reveals to us the existence of jewels infinitely more powerful than the Śakrābhilagna. I have not been able to find any reference to them.

135 In Tib. *lha thams cad snaṅ ba.*

136 In Tib. *rdo rje snaṅ ba.*

137 In Tib. *snaṅ ba thams cad bsdus pa.*

[*Gopaka's Devotion and Change of Sex*]

56. Then the devaputra Gopaka[138] said to the Śakra devendra:

[138] In Tib. *Sbed pa*. This concerns a young woman of the Śākyan clan, named Gopā, Gopī or Gopikā, who knew Śākyamuni while he was still living at home and giving himself over to pleasure. According to certain sources, she was one of Śākyamuni's wives. After her death, she was reborn in the Trāyastriṃśa heaven, where she was known as the devaputra Gopaka.

We have little information on the wife or wives of the Buddha Śākyamuni and their exact names.

1. The Pāli sources only recognise, it seems, that he had but one wife: the one who gave him Rāhula, his only son. She was known by various names: Rāhulamātā (Vin, I. p.82), Bhaddakacā[nā] (Buddhavaṃsa XXVI, v.15; Mahāvaṃsa II, v.24) Yasodharā (Buddhavaṃsa Comm., p.245), Bimbādevī (Jātaka II, p.392, Sumaṅgala II, p.422) and Bimbāsundarī (Jātaka VI, p.478). She was born on the same day as the Buddha (Jātaka I, p.54) and married him at the age of sixteen (Jātaka I, p.58).

The Pāli sources also know of a Gopā or Gopikā, but without stating whether or not she was the wife of the future Buddha. She is mentioned in the Sakkapañha suttanta (Dīgha II, p.271): *Idh' eva Kapilavatthusmiṃ Gopikā nāma Sakyadhītā ahosi Buddhe pasannā dhamme pasannā saṃghe pasannā sīlesu paripūrakārinī. Sā itthicittaṃ virājetvā purisacittaṃ bhāvetvā kāyassa bhedā paraṃ maraṇā sugatiṃ saggaṃ lokaṃ uppannā devānaṃ Tāvatiṃsānaṃ sahavyataṃ, amhākaṃ puttattaṃ ajjhūpagatā*: 'Here, in Kapilavatthu, there was a daughter of the Sakyas, named Gopikā, who believed in the Buddha, the Dhamma and the Community, and kept the precepts. Having given up all female thoughts and having cultivated male thoughts, she had, on the dissolution of her body after her death, a good destiny and was born in the heavenly world, in the company of the Tāvatiṃsa gods, with a filial relationship with us'.

This passage recurs in the corresponding Chinese Āgamas: Dīrgha, T 1, ch.10, p.63*a* 3-4; Madhyama, T 26, ch.33, p.634*b* 5-10. The latter is more prolix: 'Gopī, a daughter of the Śākyas, was a disciple of the Bhagavat. She followed the Bhagavat and practised continence (*brahmacarya*). She abhorred the female body and loved the masculine form: she changed her feminine body and took a masculine form. She renounced desires and abandoned desires. On the dissolution of her body after her death, she was reborn in a good place, among the Trāyastriṃśa gods, where she was our son'.

2. The separate biographies recount how the Buddha came to win the hand of his future wife, during a tournament where he was displaying his skill in the arts (*śilpasaṃdarśana*); in these sources, the wife of the Buddha is sometimes referred to as Yaśodharā (Fang kuang ta chuang yen ching, T 187, ch.4, p.561*c*; Yin kuo ching, T 189, ch.2, p.629*b*; Fo pên hsing chi ching, T 190, ch.13, p.712*c*; Ching hsü mo ho ti ching, T 191, ch.4, p.942*c*; Buddhacarita II, v.26; Mahāvastu II, p.48 sq.), sometimes as Gopā or Gopī (Hsiu hsing pên ch'i ching, T 184, ch.1, p.465*b*; T'ai tzū jui ying pên ch'i ching, T 185, ch.1, p.475*a*; P'u yao ching, T 186, ch.3, p.500*c*; I ch'u p'u sa pên ch'i ching, T 188, p.619*a*; Lalitavistara, p.142 sq.

3. We read in the Mahāyānist Upadeśa (Nāgārjuna, *Traité* II, pp.1002-4): 'It is said in the Rāhulamātṛjātaka that the Bodhisattva Śākyamuni had two wives: the first was called Gopā or Gopiyā, the second Yaśodharā or Yaśodharā Rāhulamātā. Gopā, being sterile (*bandhya*), had no children'.

4. The Mūlasarvāstivādin Vinaya attributes three wives to him, each one surrounded by 20,000 courtesans: Yaśodharā, Gopā and Mṛgajā (Kên pên shuo . . . p'i nai yeh, T 1442, ch.18, p.720*c* 12-13; P'o sêng shih, T 1450, ch.3, p.114*b* 24-26; ch.12, p.160*c* 15). The same Vinaya tells us in what circumstances Śākyamuni married them: 1. He himself chose Yaśodharā from among all the young girls of his clan (T 1450, ch.3, p.111*c*; W.W. Rockhill, *Life of the Buddha,*

Śrāvakas[139] who have already entered the absolute certainty (*avakrāntan-iyāma*)[140], even if they praise and cherish Buddhahood (*buddhatva*), cannot achieve it because they have already set up an obstruction (*āvaraṇa*) to Saṃsāra[141]. Beings who have aroused, are arousing and will arouse the *anuttarasamyaksaṃbodhicitta* should cherish Buddhahood: then they can obtain a physical body (*rūpakāya*) as perfected [as that of Meru-śikharadhara].

57. Just as those born blind (*jātyandha*), even if they praise and cherish the sun (*sūrya*) and moon (*candra*), cannot delight (*anubhāvitum*) in their radiance, so those Śrāvakas entered into the absolute certainty (*avakrāntaniyāma*), even if they praise and cherish the Buddha attributes (*buddhadharma*), cannot personally gain any advantage from those Buddha virtues (*buddhaguṇa*). That is why those who wish to obtain that marvellous body and great wisdom (*mahāprajñā*) should arouse the *anuttarasamyaksaṃbodhicitta* **[635a]**; then they will obtain a perfected physical body.

When the devaputra Gopaka had spoken those words, twelve thousand devaputras aroused the *anuttarasamyaksaṃbodhicitta*.

p.20); 2. He stopped his coach beneath Gopā's terrace; seeing which Śuddhodana took Gopā and gave her to his son (T 1450, ch.3, p.112*c*; Rockhill, *op. cit.*, pp.21-2); 3. Seven days before the Great Departure, when the future Buddha was returning to his palace, Mṛgajā addressed him with the famous stanza, *Nibbutā nūna sā mātā*; Śākyamuni, in thanks, cast his necklet on the young woman; Śuddhodana, learning of the matter, took Mṛgajā and gave her to his son (T 1450, ch.3, p.114*b*; Rockhill, *op. cit.*, pp.23-4). This version of the facts is confirmed by the Chung hsu mo ho ti ching (T 191, ch.4, pp.944*c*-945*a*). Other sources mention the stanza uttered by the young woman whom they call Mṛgī (Fo pên hsing chi ching, T 190, ch.15, p.724*b*; Mahāvastu II, p.157) or Kisāgotamī (Jātaka I, pp.60-1; Dhammapada Comm. I, p.85), but do not say that she married Śākyamuni.

Gopā was a Śākyakanyā and daughter of Daṇḍapāṇi, maternal uncle of the Buddha (Lalitavistara, p.142, *8*; Gaṇḍavyūha, p.420, *19*). Mahāyāna texts consider her the wife or one of the two wives of the Buddha (Lalitavistara, p.157, *3-9*; Suvarṇabhāsa, p.200, *8-9*; Upadeśa in Nāgārjuna, *Traité* II, pp.2002-4; V, p.2236). The Śgs is of the same opinion, as is shown clearly by the Tibetan version (see below, n.143).

139 In the Tibetan translation, Gopā addresses Śakra by saying to him: *kye yab* 'O, my father'. This daughter of the Śākyas had been reborn with the status of devaputra among the Trāyastriṃśa gods; thus it is that Śakra was her father.

140 In Tib. *ṅes par gyur pa la źugs pa*. On the meaning of this expression, cf. Vkn, p.18, n.65. Kumārajīva translates it here by *ju fa wei* 入法位, whereas in his translation of the Vimalakīrti he regularly rendered it by *ju chêng wei* 入正位 (T 475, pp.549*b* 7; 553*c* 8; 554*c* 12), which seems preferable.

141 When he penetrates the *darśanamārga*, the śrāvaka is predestined (*niyata*) to the acquisition of the Absolute Good (*samyaktva*), that is, Nirvāṇa. Turning his back on *saṃsāra*, he will attain the Bodhi of the arhats which will release him from existence, but with the difference from the bodhisattvas that he will never reach the supreme and perfect Bodhi of the Buddhas. Cf. Vkn, pp.179-80.

58. Then the bodhisattva Dṛḍhamati asked the devaputra Gopaka: Through what good-rooted action did you change your female body (*kena kuśalamūlena strīkāyaṃ parāvartiṣṭhāḥ*)[142]?

Gopaka: Kulaputra, those who are pledged to the Great Vehicle (*mahāyānasaṃprasthita*) do not see any difference (*viśeṣa*) between man (*puruṣa*) and woman (*strī*). Why? Because the omniscient thought (*sarvajñacitta*) is not found in the triple world (*traidhātuka*) and because [notions] of man and woman are wrought by discrimination (*vikalpaprabhāvita*). You ask me, O friend (*sakhi*), through what good actions I changed my female body; well, it is because in days gone by I served the Bodhisattva [Śākyamuni][143] with a mind free of hypocrisy (*ahaṃ pūrvakāle bodhisattvasya satkāraṃ cakārācapalena cittena*)[144].

Dṛḍhamati: How did you 'serve' him?

Gopaka: I served the Bodhisattva as the Lord (*bhagavat*).

Dṛḍhamati: How did you serve him 'with a mind free of hypocrisy'?

Gopaka: I conformed my bodily action (*kāyakarman*) to my voice (*vāc*), and I conformed my vocal action (*vākkarman*) to my mind (*manas*): this is, for a woman, a mind free of hypocrisy (*acapalacitta*).

Dṛḍhamati: How did you change your female body?

Gopaka: In conformity with fulfilment (*yathāsādhanam*).

Dṛḍhamati: How did you 'fulfil'?

Gopaka: In conformity with changing (*yathāparāvṛttim*).

Dṛḍhamati: O devaputra, what is the meaning of that word?

Gopaka: Kulaputra, dharmas do not consist of either 'fulfilment' (*sādhana*) or 'changing' (*parāvṛtti*). All dharmas are of a single flavour (*ekarasa*), that is, the flavour of the fundamental element (*dharmadhāturasa*)[145]. It is in conformity with my aspiration (*yathāpraṇidhānam*) that I had a female body (*strīkāya*) and, if now my body is that of a man (*puruṣa*), I have not for all that destroyed or abandoned the signs (*nimitta*) of a female body. That is why, O Kulaputra, it must be understood that [concepts] of man and woman are perverse views (*viparyāsa*), and that all dharmas as well are perverse views: they are

[142] This change took place when Gopā was reborn in the Trāyastriṃśa heaven with the status of a devaputra; see above, n.138 at the beginning.

[143] Instead of saying: 'I served the Bodhisattva', the Tibetan version says: 'I served my husband (*khyim thab*)'; according to the Śgs, Gopā was indeed the wife of Śākyamuni.

[144] According to the canonical sources, if Gopā had changed sex and been reborn in the form of a devaputra, it was because during her life she had 'given up all female thoughts and cultivated male thoughts'. See the references above, n.138 at the beginning.

[145] In Tib. *chos thams cad ni chos kyi dbyiṅs su ro gcig pas na.*

absolutely free of duality (*atyantaṃ dvayavipramukta*)[146].

59. The bodhisattva Dṛḍhamati asked Gopaka: Do you know even the smallest part (*kaṃcid eva pradeśam*) of the Śūraṃgamasamādhi?

Gopaka replied: Kulaputra, what I know of it I learnt from others. I did not acquire it personally (*sākṣātkṛta*). According to my memories, in days gone by (*atīte 'dhvani*), the Buddha Śākyamuni, then an ordinary bodhisattva in the dwelling of King Śuddhodana, was at the palace in the midst of his harem (*antaḥpura*). In the still of the night (*praśāntarātri*), there arrived from the Eastern region (*pūrvā diś*) Brahmarājas as numerous as the sands of the Ganges (*gaṅgānadīvālukopama*); they questioned the Bodhisattva, some of them about the Bodhisattva Vehicle and others about the Śrāvaka Path, and the Bodhisattva replied to all their questions[147].

[146] In the Vkn, pp.169-71, the problem of the equivalence of the sexes is treated in more or less the same terms; the Śgs and the Vkn are manifestly inter-related, but the latter likes to present things in a more theatrical style: it introduces a goddess who changes into a man, whilst her questioner, Śāriputra, is changed into a woman.

[147] An interesting variation on the theme of the Great Departure or, to be more exact, on the reasons that determined it. On this subject like many others, the Buddhist tradition has been the object of more and more complicated anecdotal constructions:

1. The spiritual crisis which determined Śākyamuni to leave home was, in the beginning, confined to three depictions: marriage followed by a life of pleasure in the women's quarters; this led to disgust, and disgust provoked the Great Departure. Such is the most simple and logical version of the facts; it can be found in the Pāli sources (Nidānakathā, in Jātaka I, p.61, *21-31*) and in the Buddhacarita of Aśvaghoṣa, Ch.V, vv.63-8.

2. Most of the separate biographies insert a new event: the intervention of deities who remind the Bodhisattva that the time has come for him to leave home and that his refusal would lead to serious consequences for humanity. This is what is called in Sanskrit the *saṃcodana* 'instigation', not to be confused with the *adhyeṣaṇa* 'invitation' or request which the gods addressed to Śākyamuni, once he had become a Buddha, so that he would consent to expound the Dharma.

The sources are not in agreement over the deities who instigated the Bodhisattva to the Great Departure:

Śuddhāvāsā devāḥ, Īśvara, Maheśvara and Mahābrahmā (Mahāvastu II, pp.158, *4* - 159, *2*).

A group of undefined devas (Hsiu hsing pên ch'i ching, T 184, ch.2, p.467*c* 14; T'ai tzŭ jui ying pên ch'i ching, T 185, ch.1, p.475*b* 19-20).

Devas, nāgas, yakṣas, gandharvas, asuras, garuḍas, kiṃnaras, mahoragas, śakras, brahmās and lokapālas (Lalitavistara, p.159, *20* sq.; T 187, ch.5, p.565*b* 7-8).

The four devarājas (Abhiniṣkramaṇasūtra, T 188, p.619*a* 29).

All the devas, from the four devarājas to the śuddhavāsas (Kuo ch'u hsien tsai yin kuo ching, T 189, ch.2, p.632*b* 24-28).

The Tso-p'ing or ghaṭīkāra gods (Abhiniṣkramaṇasūtra, T 190, ch.16, p.729*b* 11-21).

Śakra devendra and Brahmā devarāja (Chung hsü mo ho ti ching, T 191, ch.5, p.946*a* 16 sq.; Mūlasarv. Vin., T 1450, ch.4, p.115*c* 22 sq.).

The exhortations addressed to Śākyamuni by these deities vary in length depending on the

60. Among those Brahmās, a Brahmarāja who had not grasped the skilful means (*upāya*) being used by the Bodhisattva, put this question to him: Friend, even while being so wise and replying so well to questions, how can you remain attached to royalty (*rājya*) and pleasures (*kāmabhoga*)?

Other Brahmadevas who had understood the wisdom (*prajñā*) and skilful means (*upāya*) of the Bodhisattva said to that Brahmā: The Bodhisattva is not attached to royalty and pleasures; it is in order to ripen and perfect beings that he is here as a layman (*gṛhastha*) and that he appears as a bodhisattva, but at the same time, in other universes, he has already attained complete enlightenment (*abhisaṃbuddha*) and sets turning the Wheel of the Dharma (*dharmacakraṃ pravartayati*)[148].

The Brahmā, having heard this, asked: What *samādhi* has the Bodhisattva acquired in order to perform such transformations (*vikurvaṇa*)[149]?

The other Brahmās replied: He performs them through the might (*sthāma*) of the Śūraṃgamasamādhi.

61. [This narration over, Gopaka said to Dṛḍhamati]: Kulaputra, at

sources but follow the same aim: to remind the Bodhisattva of his duties. No deity seems as yet to suspect that the life of pleasure in the women's quarters is only skill in means. The old school of sculpture in central India has depicted the *adhyeṣaṇa*, the invitation to the Buddha to expound the Dharma (J. Marshall and A. Foucher, *Monuments of Sāñchī* I, p.210; II, pl.49c, and 64a 2), but did not, it seems, devote any sculpture to the *saṃcodana*, the instigation to the Bodhisattva to leave home. This deficiency accords in with the silence held by the earliest literary sources.

In contrast, the Graeco-Buddhist school of Gandhāra depicted both events. In the scenes of the *saṃcodana*, the Bodhisattva wears the hairstyle and jewels of a prince (cf. A. Foucher, *Art gréco-bouddhique* I, p.127, fig.47 in the centre; I, p.321, fig.164*b*; II, p.89, figs 347 and 348), whilst in the scenes of the *adhyeṣaṇa*, he is dressed as a monk (*ibid.*, I, pp.420-7, figs 212, 213, 215).

3. In the present passage, the Śgs gives another version and another interpretation of the facts. From among the deities who instigated the Bodhisattva, it only retains the Brahmarājas, not the single Brahmā reigning over the Rūpadhātu of our universe of four continents, but an infinity of Brahmās as numerous as the sands of the Ganges and come from the Eastern region. This grandiose perspective is in keeping with the taste of the Mahāyāna. It is another Mahāyānist theory that the presence on earth of the Buddhas and bodhisattvas does not relate to an historical truth, but constitutes ordinary skilful means (*upāya*) on their part derived from the prodigious power (*ṛddhi, adhiṣṭhāna, vikurvaṇa*) of the Great Compassionate Ones. In order to bring this theory to light, the Śgs distinguishes between two kinds of Brahmā: on the one hand, Brahmās with a poor understanding, sharing the narrowness of view of the śrāvakas and who believe they can reproach the Bodhisattva for lingering with the pleasures of the women's quarters and the idleness of power; on the other hand, Brahmās who know that the whole conduct of a bodhisattva, whether it seems good or bad, is following no other aim than the winning over of beings.

148 See below, §§ 125-8.

149 *Tzŭ tsai shên pien* 自在神變 corresponds to the Tib. *rnam par ḥphrul ba*.

that moment [**635b**], I had this thought: 'The *samādhi* and supernormal power (*ṛddhibala*) of the Bodhisattva[150] must indeed be extraordinary (*adbhuta*) so that, living in the midst of pleasures (*kāma*) and directing the affairs of the kingdom, he never deviates at all from that *samādhi'*. Having said this to myself, I redoubled my respect and really considered the Bodhisattva as the Lord (*bhagavat*). Resolutely, I aroused the *anuttarasamyaksaṃbodhicitta* and I too wished to fulfil the same virtues (*guṇa*) as he in the future. O Kulaputra, this is what I have seen of the Śūraṃgamasamādhi; it is only a small part of it. I only know that this Śūraṃgamasamādhi possesses virtues (*guṇa*) and might (*sthāma*) which are immense (*apramāṇa*) and inconceivable (*acintya*).

Dṛḍhamati said to the Buddha: Marvellous (*āścarya*), O Bhagavat, are those most deeply inspired words (*adhyāśayanirdeśa*) of the devaputra Gopaka: all that is the work of the Tathāgata. O Bhagavat, ever protected by [the Tathāgata] his spiritual friend (*kalyāṇamitra-parigṛhīta*), the devaputra Gopaka will also be established in the Śūraṃgamasamādhi and will obtain powers of transformation (*vikurvaṇabala*) like those which the Bhagavat at present possesses.

[*Multiple Appearance of a Bodhisattva in the Heroic Progress*]

62. The bodhisattva Dṛḍhamati asked the Buddha: Bhagavat, in this assembly are there persons in possession of the Śūraṃgamasamādhi?

Now, in the assembly, there was a devaputra named *Matyabhimukha[151] 'Close to the intelligence [of a Buddha]' who said to the bodhisattva Dṛḍhamati: It is as if a merchant (*sārthika*) entering the great sea (*samudra*) asked if the great sea contained jewels (*maṇiratna*) to be taken and carried away[152]. Your question is like that. And why is this? At the moment you are sitting in the presence of the Tathāgata, the great sea of knowledge (*mahājñānasamudra*), in an assembly[153] in which there are bodhisattvas endowed with the jewels of the Dharma

[150] Read *p'u sa san mei instead of p'u sa chu san mei.*

[151] To the *Hsien-i* 現意 of the Chinese corresponds the Tib. *Saṅs rgyas blo gros mṅon sum*, which presupposes *Buddhamatyabhimukha* in Sanskrit. I have kept the abridged Chinese reading *Matyabhimukha.*

[152] The great sea possesses eight wonderful and extraordinary qualities; one of the eight is to contain quantities of precious jewels: *Seyyathā pi mahāsamuddo bahuratano anekaratano, tatr' imāni ratanāni seyyathīdaṃ muttā maṇi veḷuriyo saṅkho silā pavāḷaṃ rajataṃ jātarūpaṃ lohitaṅko masāragallaṃ* (Vinaya II, p.239, *35-38*; Aṅguttara IV, p.199, *20-23*; Udāna, p.56, *6-9*; see also Daśabhūmika, p.97, *10*; Vkn, p.179).

[153] The punctuation in the Taishō should be corrected.

(*dharmaratnasamanvāgata*) and displaying great trappings[154]. And you dare to ask if in this assembly there are bodhisattvas who are in possession of the Śūraṃgamasamādhi. O Dṛḍhamati, at present in this assembly there are bodhisattvas in possession of the Śūraṃgamasamādhi who manifest themselves in the body of a Śakra devendra, in the body of a Brahmarāja, or in the bodies of devas, nāgas, yakṣas, gandharvas, asuras, garuḍas, kiṃnaras and mahoragas. There are bodhisattvas in possession of the Śūraṃgamasamādhi who manifest themselves in the bodies of bhikṣus, bhikṣuṇīs, upāsakas and upāsikās. There are bodhisattvas in possession of the Śūraṃgamasamādhi with bodies adorned with the primary and secondary physical marks (*lakṣaṇānuvyañjanasamalaṃkṛta*). There are bodhisattvas who, in order to ripen beings (*sattvaparipācanārtham*), manifest the figure (*saṃsthāna*), colours (*varṇa*) and signs (*nimitta*) of a female body (*strīkāya*); others manifest the figure, colours and signs of a Śrāvaka; yet others, the figure, colours and signs of a Pratyekabuddha.

63. Dṛḍhamati, depending on whether the Tathāgata attends an assembly of Kṣatriyas, Brāhmaṇas, Vaiśyas, Śakras, Brahmās or Lokapālas, the bodhisattvas manifest figures, colours and signs corresponding to those assemblies. It should be known that all these are the special fruits (*phalaviśeṣa*) of the Śūraṃgamasamādhi.

Dṛḍhamati, wherever you see the Tathāgata expounding the Dharma, understand clearly that there there are **[635c]** innumerable great bodhisattvas, masters of great knowledges, displaying great trappings[155], having obtained mastery over all dharmas (*sarvadharmeṣu vaśitāprāpta*); they come in the wake of the Tathāgata to set turning the

154 Kumārajīva usually renders by *fa ta chuang yen* 發大莊嚴 the Sanskrit expression *mahāsaṃnāhasaṃnaddha*, in Tib. *go cha chen po bgos pa* (see further below, notes 155, 216). Literally, the expression means: 'Girded in the great armour'. The Abhisamayālaṃkāra I, v.43, defines it as:

dānādau ṣaḍvidhe teṣāṃ pratyekaṃ saṃgraheṇa yā
saṃnāhapratipattiḥ sā ṣaḍbhiḥ ṣaṭkair yathoditā.

'The action [which consists of girding on] the armour is represented by six sextuples, the six [*pāramitās*], giving, etc., being combined respectively one with the others'.

The *saṃnāhapratipatti* thus includes six sextuples (the combination of giving with the other five *pāramitās*, of morality with the other five *pāramitās*, etc); this adds up in all to thirty-six aspects.

They are detailed in the Pañcaviṃśati, pp.176, *7* - 178, *22*, and the Śatasāhasrikā, pp.1302, *20* - 1309, *12*. See also Aṣṭasāhasrikā, p.84; Āloka, pp.84-5; E. Obermiller, *Analysis of the Abhisamayālaṃkāra* I, p.107-13; E. Conze, *Abhisamayālaṃkāra* translation, pp.19-20.

It must be recognised that the translation *fa ta chuang yen* adopted by Kumārajīva is not a very happy one. That of Hsüan-tsang appearing in T 220, vol.VII, ch.411, p.62*a* 12, is clearer: *pei ta kung tê k'ai* 被大功德鎧 'Dressed in the great armour of the qualities'.

155 See the preceding note.

Wheel of the Dharma.

64. The bodhisattva Dṛḍhamati said to the Buddha: Bhagavat, I now say that this devaputra *Matyabhimukha possesses the Śūraṃgamasamādhi; in fact his wisdom (*prajñā*), eloquence (*pratibhāna*) and unobstructed superknowledges (*apratihatābhijñā*) are so very great!

The Buddha said: Dṛḍhamati, it is exactly as you say (*evam etad yathā vadasi*): that devaputra *Matyabhimukha is already in Śūraṃgamasamādhi; it is because he does penetrate that *samādhi* that he could speak as he did.

[*Various Transformations of the Assembly*]

65. Then the Buddha said to the devaputra *Matyabhimukha: Show, then, be it only a small part (*kaṃcid eva pradeśaṃ darśaya*) of your skill in the Śūraṃgamasamādhi.

The devaputra *Matyabhimukha asked the bodhisattva Dṛḍhamati: Friend, would you like to see a little of the supremacy (*ārṣabha*)[156] of the Śūraṃgamasamādhi?

Dṛḍhamati replied: I would very much like to see it.

1. The devaputra *Matyabhimukha, who had at his disposal the supremacy of the Śūraṃgamasamādhi, performed such a supernormal action (*evaṃrūpam ṛddhyabhisaṃskāram abhisaṃskaroti sma*)[157] that all the members of the assembly (*sarvāvatī parṣad*) were transformed into noble Cakravartin kings, adorned with the thirty-two marks (*dvātriṃśallakṣaṇasamalaṃkṛta*), surrounded by a retinue (*sānucāra*) and accompanied by the seven jewels (*saptaratnasamanvāgata*).

The devaputra asked: What do you see?

Dṛḍhamati replied: I see all the members of the assembly with the colours (*rūpa*) and signs (*nimitta*) of noble Cakravartin kings, surrounded by a retinue and accompanied by the seven jewels.

2. Then the devaputra made all the members of the assembly appear like so many Śakra devendras, dwelling in the palaces (*vimāna*) of the Trāyastriṃśas[158], surrounded by an hundred thousand daughters of the gods (*devakanyā*), playing music (*tūryāṇi pravādayamāna*) and giving themselves over to pleasure in the Grove of Joy (*nandanavane paricārayamāna*)[159].

[156] In Tib., *khyu mchog*.

[157] This is a stock phrase; cf. Vkn, pp.139, 204, 219, 247.

[158] The Vaijayantaprāsāda.

[159] The four parks of the Trāyastriṃśa gods are the Caitraratha, Pāruṣyaka, Miśraka and Nandana.

3. And again, by means of his supernormal power (*ṛddhibala*), he transformed all the members of the assembly into as many Brahmarājas, with their colours (*rūpa*), signs (*nimitta*) and bodily attitudes (*īryāpatha*), dwelling in the palaces (*vimāna*) of the Brahmās[160] and cultivating the four infinite states (*caturapramāṇa*).

Then he asked Dṛḍhamati: What do you see?

The latter replied: Devaputra, I see all the members of the assembly like so many Brahmās.

4. Once again, he displayed such supernormal power that all the members of the assembly were transformed into as many sthavira Mahākāśyapas, with his figure (*saṃsthāna*), colours (*varṇa*) and appearance (*prakāra*), equipped with his robe and alms-bowl (*cīvarapātradhara*), entering the absorptions (*dhyāna*) and attainments (*samāpatti*) and practising the eight liberations (*vimokṣa*): there was not the slightest difference.

5. Yet again, he displayed such supernormal power that all the members of the assembly appeared like so many Śākyamunis with their Buddha-bodies (*buddhakāya*), their primary and secondary marks (*lakṣaṇānuvyañjana*) and their bodily attitudes (*īryāpatha*), each surrounded by a gathering of monks (*bhikṣusaṃghaparivṛta*).

Then he asked: Dṛḍhamati, what do you see?

The latter replied: Devaputra, I see all the members of the assembly like so many Śākyamunis with their Buddha-bodies, their primary and secondary marks and their bodily attitudes, each surrounded by a gathering of monks.

66. The devaputra *Matyabhimukha said to Dṛḍhamati: This is the supremacy (*ārṣabha*) of the Śūraṃgamasamādhi. O Dṛḍhamati, a bodhisattva who possesses the Śūraṃgamasamādhi can insert the *trisāhasramahāsāhasralokadhātu* into a mustard seed (*sarṣapa*) in such a way that the mountains (*parvata*), rivers (*nadī*), suns (*surya*), moons (*candra*) and stars (*tārakā*) all appear as before, without constricting or disturbing beings[161]. Dṛḍhamati, this is the inconceivable supremacy (*acintyārṣabha*) of the Śūraṃgamasamādhi.

[*Necessity of acquiring the Heroic Progress*]

67. Then the Mahāśrāvakas and the devas, nāgas, yakṣas [**636a**], gandharvas, Śakras, Brahmās and Lokapāla Kings of the gods,

160 The spheres of the four *dhyānas*; the first three consist of three stages, and the fourth of eight.

161 See the Vkn, pp.141-50, which describes these abilities, the *acintyavimokṣas* of the bs, in full.

addressing the Buddha with one voice, said to him: Bhagavat, those who have obtained this Śūraṃgamasamādhi have inconceivable virtues (*acintyaguṇa*). Why? Those men are all close to Buddhahood[162] and they are endowed with knowledge (*jñāna*), the superknowledges (*abhijñā*) and the higher knowledges (*vidyā*)[163]. We others, today and in this very place, have seen the various colours (*rūpa*) and various transformations (*vikurvaṇa*) of the assembly, and we think this: Those who have not heard the Śūraṃgamasamādhi are certainly possessed by Māra (*mārādhiṣṭhita*), and those who have heard it are certainly protected by the Buddhas (*buddhaparigṛhīta*). What then can be said (*kaḥ punar vādaḥ*) of those who, having heard it, repeat and practise it?

Bhagavat, the bodhisattva who wishes to penetrate the Buddha attributes (*buddhadharma*) and reach the other shore (*pāra*) should listen attentively (*ekacittaśravaṇa*) to the Śūraṃgamasamādhi, grasp it (*udgrahaṇa*), remember it (*dhāraṇa*), repeat it (*vācana*) and expound it to others (*parebhya uddeśanā*).

Bhagavat, the bodhisattva who wishes to manifest all the figures (*saṃsthāna*), all the colours (*varṇa*) and all the bodily attitudes (*īryāpatha*), the bodhisattva who wishes to understand the functioning of the mind and mentation (*cittacaittapravṛtti*) of all beings, the bodhisattva who wishes to know how to cure all the diseases (*vyādhi*) of beings, that bodhisattva should listen carefully to this jewel of the Dharma (*dharmaratna*) which is the Śūraṃgamasamādhi, grasp it, remember it and repeat it.

Bhagavat, he who has obtained the Śūraṃgamasamādhi has certainly entered the domain of the Buddhas (*buddhaviṣaya*) and into the mastery of knowledge (*jñānavaśita*).

68. The Buddha said: It is so, it is so, it is exactly as you say (*evam etad yathā vadatha*). He who has not obtained the Śūraṃgamasamādhi does not deserve the name of perfectly accomplished (*kṛtacarya*)[164] bodhisattva, and the Tathāgata denies that this man truly possesses giving (*dāna*), morality (*śīla*), patience (*kṣānti*), vigour (*vīrya*), absorptive meditation (*dhyāna*) and wisdom (*prajñā*). That is why, if you wish to tread all the paths [of release (*niryāṇamārga*)[165]], you should seek to obtain the Śūraṃgamasamādhi, but without thinking of any training (*śikṣā*).

[162] *Chiu ching fo tao* 究竟佛道 corresponds here to the Tib. *de bźin gśegs paḥi ḥgros su mchi ba lags*, which gives the Sanskrit *tathāgatagatiṃgata*.

[163] The *traividya* consisting of three of the six *abhijñās*; see Kośa VII, p.108.

[164] *Shên hsing* 深行 corresponds to the Tib. *spyod pa byas pa*.

[165] In Tib. *ṅes par ḥbyuṅ baḥi lam*.

[*Philosophical Discussion*]

1. *The Practice of Heroic Progress*

69. Then the bodhisattva Dṛḍhamati questioned the devaputra *Matyabhimukha: If a bodhisattva wishes to obtain this *samādhi,* what dharmas should he cultivate?

The devaputra: A bodhisattva who wishes to obtain this *samādhi* should cultivate the dharmas of the worldly (*pṛthagjanadharma*). If he sees those *pṛthagjanadharmas* are neither united (*yukta*) with nor separate (*viyukta*) from the *buddhadharmas*, then he is cultivating the Śūraṃgamasamādhi.

Dṛḍhamati: Can there be union (*yoga*) or separation (*viyoga*) in relation to the *buddhadharmas*?

The devaputra: In relation to the *pṛthagjanadharmas*, there is neither union or separation, and even less so in relation to the *buddhadharmas.*

Dṛḍhamati: What is meant by cultivating [dharmas]?

The devaputra: Understanding that the *pṛthagjanadharmas* and the *buddhadharmas* constitute non-duality (*advaya*), that is cultivating dharmas[166]. In reality, between these [two kinds] of dharmas, there is neither union nor separation since, O Kulaputra, all dharmas have a mark of non-arising (*anutpādalakṣaṇa*), all dharmas have a mark of non-cessation (*anirodhalakṣaṇa*), all dharmas have a mark like space (*ākāśasamalakṣaṇa*) and all dharmas have a mark of non-encounter (*asamāgama*)[167].

2. *The End Result of the Heroic Progress*

70. *Dṛḍhamati:* Where does the Śūraṃgamasamādhi go (*kva gacchati*)?

The devaputra: The Śūraṃgamasamādhi goes [**636b**] to the minds (*citta*) and practices (*carita*) of all beings, but does not take for its object (*nālaṃbhate*) those minds and practices.

It goes to all the places of birth (*jātisthāna*), but it is not defiled

166 Regarding the identity of the worldly and the holy ones, see Vkn, pp.44-5, 55-6, 128.

167 The Tib. is clearer: *ḥdi la sbyar baḥam / dgral bar bya baḥi chos ni gaṅ yaṅ med do // de ciḥi phyir że na / rigs kyi bu chos thams cad ni mi skye baḥi de bźin ñid daṅ ldan no // chos thams cad ni mi ḥgog paḥi de bźin ñid daṅ ldan no // chos thams cad ni mi ḥkhrugs paḥi de bźin ñid daṅ ldan no // chos thams cad ni ḥdu ba med paḥi de bźin ñid daṅ ldan no // chos thams cad ni ḥbral ba med paḥi de bźin ñid daṅ ldan no /*: 'Here, there is no united (*yukta*) nor separated (*viyukta*) dharma. Why? O Kulaputra, all dharmas have a suchness (*tathatā*) [comprising] non-arising (*anutpāda*), non-cessation (*anirodha*), non-distraction (*avikṣepa*), non-encounter (*asamāgama*) and non-separation (*aviyoga*)'.

(*kliṣṭa*) by those places of birth.

It goes close to the Buddhas of all the universes, but it does not distinguish (*na vijānāti*) the bodies of those Buddhas with their primary and secondary marks (*lakṣaṇānuvyañjana*).

It goes towards all sounds (*svara*) and all languages (*nirukti*), but it does not distinguish the notion of a syllable (*akṣarasaṃjñā*).

It displays (*saṃdarśayati*) all the *buddhadharmas* but does not go so far as to exhaust them completely.

Kulaputra, you asked me where this *samādhi* goes. Well, everywhere the Buddhas go, this *samādhi* goes as well.

3. The Nirvāṇa of the Buddhas

71. *Dṛḍhamati:* And the Buddhas, where do they go?

The devaputra: The Buddhas, because of the suchness of things (*tathatā*), do not go anywhere.

Dṛḍhamati: Do not the Buddhas go to Nirvāṇa?

The devaputra: All dharmas are [already] in Nirvāṇa (*atyanta-nirvṛta*); that is why the Tathāgatas do not go to Nirvāṇa. Why? Because of the very nature of Nirvāṇa, one does not go to Nirvāṇa.

Dṛḍhamati: In the past did not Buddhas as numerous as the sands of the Ganges (*gaṅgānadīvālukopama*) go to Nirvāṇa?

The devaputra: All those Buddhas as numerous as the sands of the Ganges, do they arise?

Dṛḍhamati: And yet, it has been said by the Tathāgata: 'Buddhas as numerous as the sands of the Ganges, after arising, attain Nirvāṇa'[168].

The devaputra: Kulaputra, has he not also said: 'A single individual arising in the world arises for the benefit and happiness of many beings, [through compassion for the world], for the advantage, benefit and happiness of the great body of beings, [mankind and the gods. Which is that single individual? The Tathāgata, the holy, fully and perfectly enlightened one][169]. What do you think of that (*tat kiṃ manyase*)?

[168] Regarding this idea, see Saddharmapuṇḍ., p.49, *3-4*:
Ye cāpy abhūvan purimās tathāgatāḥ
parinirvṛtā buddhasahasraneke,
atītam adhvānam asaṃkhyakalpe
teṣāṃ pramāṇaṃ na kadāci vidyate.

[169] The Tibetan version quotes the passage in full: *lha daṅ miḥi skye bo maṅ po la phan paḥi phyir / skye bo maṅ po la bde baḥi phyir / ḥjig rten la sñiṅ brtse baḥi phyir / skye bo phal po che daṅ lha daṅ mi rnams kyi don gyi phyir / phan paḥi phyir bde baḥi phyir / gaṅ zag gcig ḥjig rten du ḥbyuṅ ste / ḥdi lta ste / de bźin gśegs pa dgra bcom pa yaṅ dag par rdzogs paḥi saṅs rgyas so /.*

This concerns a well-known passsage in the Aṅguttara I, p.22, *1-4*: *Ekapuggalo bhikkhave*

Would the Tathāgata truly be an individual subject to arising (*utpāda*) and cessation (*nirodha*)[170]?

Dṛḍhamati: O Devaputra, the Tathāgata, in truth, is not possessed of either arising or cessation.

The devaputra: Kulaputra, understand this: Even though the Tathāgata speaks of 'Buddha arising in the world', for the Tathāgata there is no real arising. Even though the Tathāgata speaks of 'Buddha reaching Nirvāṇa', for the Tathāgata there is no real cessation[171].

72. *Dṛḍhamati:* At present, do not innumerable Tathāgatas attain complete enlightenment (*abhisaṃbodhi*)?

The devaputra: It is in accordance with the nature of non-arising (*anutpāda*) and non-cessation (*anirodha*) that the Tathāgatas attain *abhisaṃbodhi.* O Kulaputra, whether the Buddhas appear in the world or enter Nirvāṇa, there is no difference (*viśeṣa*). Why? The Tathāgatas understand completely (*abhisaṃbudhyante*) that all dharmas are essentially appeased (*atyantaparinirvṛta*) and that is why they are called Buddhas.

Dṛḍhamati: If all dharmas are essentially appeased, can Nirvāṇa itself [insofar as it is appeasement] be understood (*abhisaṃbuddha*)?

The devaputra: The fact that all dharmas are essentially appeased (*parinirvṛta*) is identical to Nirvāṇa itself. To understand this is to understand the nature of Nirvāṇa. O Kulaputra, if the Tathāgatas appear in the world, it is not by virtue of an arising (*utpāda*), a duration (*sthiti*) and a destruction (*bhaṅga*)[172]; it is the absence of arising, duration and destruction that is named the appearance of a Buddha (*buddhotpāda*).

4. The Absence of a Base

73. *Dṛḍhamati:* Is it while in Śūraṃgamasamādhi that you say all that?

The devaputra: Kulaputra, what do you think of this (*tat kiṃ manyase*)? On what do the imaginary beings created by the Tathāgata (*tathāgatanirmitanirmāṇa*) base themselves in order to speak?

Dṛḍhamati: They base themselves on the supportive power

loke uppajjamāno uppajjati bahujanahitāya bahujanasukhāya lokānukampāya atthāya hitāya sukhāya devamanussānaṃ. Katamo ekapuggalo? Tathāgato arahaṃ sammā sambuddho. Cf. Ekottara, T 125, ch.3, p.561*a* 9-13; ch.5, p.569*b* 20-23. This text is discussed in Kathāvatthu, p.65, *18-20*; Kośa IX, p.259.

170 The Chinese text is corrupt, though the Tibetan is clear: *ci de bźin gśegs pas gaṅ skye baḥam / ḥgag par ḥgyur baḥi gaṅ zag de sṅed dam /*

171 In other words, Nirvāṇa is possessed in advance and not acquired.

172 Arising, duration and cessation constitute, according to early Buddhism, the three marks of conditioned things (*saṃskṛtalakṣaṇa*).

(*adhiṣṭhāna*)[173] of the Buddha, and then they can speak.

The devaputra: And the Buddha, on what does he base himself in order to create those imaginary beings? [**636c**].

Dṛḍhamati: The Buddha bases himself on the knowledge of non-duality (*advayābhijñā*) in order to create those imaginary beings[174].

The devaputra: Just as the Tathāgata bases himself on the 'absence of a base' (*apratiṣṭhāna*) in order to create those imaginary beings, so those imaginary beings base themselves on the absence of a base in order to speak.

Dṛḍhamati: If they have no base, how can they speak?

The devaputra: In the same way that I speak to you while not basing myself on anything.

5. *The Bodhisattva's Eloquence*

74. *Dṛḍhamati:* Why is a bodhisattva endowed with eloquence (*pratibhānasaṃpanna*)[175]?

The devaputra: A bodhisattva speaks without using the notion of self (*ātmasaṃjñā*), without using the notion of another (*parasaṃjñā*) and without using the notion of dharma[176]; he is therefore 'endowed with eloquence'.

When he expounds the Dharma, syllables (*akṣara*) are inexhaustible (*akṣaya*), and dharmas are also inexhaustible. In so speaking, he does not speak of duality (*dvaya*), he is therefore 'endowed with eloquence'.

Kulaputra, if a bodhisattva does not reject the mark of illusion (*māyālakṣaṇa*) inherent in all dharmas and does not reject the mark of echo (*pratiśrutkālakṣaṇa*) inherent in all sounds (*svara*), he is 'endowed with eloquence'.

Moreover, just as syllables (*akṣara*), sounds (*svara*) and language (*nirukti*) have no sphere (*sthāna*), no place (*deśa*), no inside, no outside,

173 In Tib. *byin gyi rlabs*.

174 The Tib. differs slightly: *de bźin gśegs pa ni gnas med pa la gnas te sprul pa sprul par mdzad do*: 'It is by basing himself on the absence of a base (*apratiṣṭhāna*) that the Tathāgata creates those imaginary beings (*nirmāṇa*)'.

The subject is treated in the same way and in practically the same terms by the Vkn, pp.158-60, 171.

175 The eloquence of the bs is 'philosophical silence': excluding all words and not saying anything, not expressing anything, not uttering anything, not teaching anything, not designating anything, this is to enter into non-duality. See Vkn, pp.202-3, where Mañjuśrī congratulates Vimalakīrti on remaining silent.

176 In the Vkn (p.49), Vimalakīrti explains to Maudgalyāyana that there is no-one to expound, no-one to hear or understand: it is as if an illusory man were to expound the Dharma to other illusory men.

no base (*pratiṣṭhāna*) and originate in dependence (*pratītya-samutpanna*), so also dharmas have no sphere, no place, no inside, no outside and no base; they are neither past (*atīta*), nor future (*anāgata*) nor present (*pratyutpanna*), and they are not expressed by sounds (*svara*) or language (*nirukti*). To speak, in knowing this for oneself, is to be 'endowed with eloquence'. Like an echo (*pratiśrutkā*), for example: it speaks in that all sounds reverberate (*anugacchanti*) in it.

75. *Dṛḍhamati:* What does the word 'reverberation' (*anugama*) mean?

The devaputra: Kulaputra, reverberation means reverberation in space (*ākāśa*). Just as there is no reverberation in space, so all dharmas are devoid of reverberation, all dharmas avoid comparison (*anupama*) and avoid all reconciliation (*asadṛśa*). It is those who hear the echo who speak of reverberation.

Then the Bhagavat congratulated (*sādhukāram adāt*) the devaputra: Excellent, excellent, it is exactly as you say (*sādhu sādhu. evam etad yathā vadasi*). Over this matter a bodhisattva should not fear, tremble or take fright (*nottrasitavyaṃ na saṃtrasitavyaṃ na saṃtrāsam āpattavyam*)[177]. Why? Because if 'reverberation' were to exist, he would not attain *anuttarasamyaksaṃbodhi.*

[*Revelations Concerning the Devaputra *Matyabhimukha*]

76. The bodhisattva Dṛḍhamati asked the Buddha: Bhagavat, from which *buddhakṣetra* did this devaputra *Matyabhimukha come to this [Sahā] universe?

The devaputra said: What is the point of that question?

Dṛḍhamati said: I would like to turn towards that place and pay homage to it, for it is the place travelled through and inhabited by such *satpuruṣas.*

The devaputra said: It is those who hold this Śūraṃgamasamādhi in their hands that the whole world with its gods and mankind (*sadevamanuṣyo loka*) should venerate.

77. Then the Buddha said to the bodhisattva Dṛḍhamati: It is from the Abhirati universe of the Buddha Akṣobhya[178] that this devaputra *Matyabhimukha arrived here [in the Sahāloka]. There, he always expounded the Śūraṃgamasamādhi. O Dṛḍhamati, all the Buddhas without exception expound the Śūraṃgamasamādhi. Dṛḍhamati, this devaputra *Matyabhimukha [**637a**], here in this Sahā universe, will

[177] This is a stock phrase; see Samādhirāja II, p.273, *6-7*; Saddharmapuṇḍ., pp.36, *2*; 37, *1*; 73, *8-9*; 78, *3*; 233, *13-14*.

[178] In the Vkn, pp.243-9, I have assembled some references to the Abhirati universe of the Buddha Akṣobhya. It is from there that Vimalakīrti also came.

reach supreme and perfect enlightenment (*anuttarāṃ samyak-saṃbodhim abhisaṃbhotsyate*). It is in order to destroy the five corruptions (*pañcakaṣāyaprāhāṇa*)[179], to secure a pure Buddha-field (*pariśuddhabuddhakṣetraparigrāhaṇa*), to ripen beings (*sattvaparipācana*), to cultivate (*bhāvanā*) and to enhance (*vardhana*) the Śūraṃgamasamādhi that he has come here.

78. Dṛḍhamati asked the Buddha: After how long (*kiyacciram*) in this universe here will that devaputra reach supreme and perfect enlightenment (*anuttarāṃ samyaksaṃbodhim abhisaṃbhotsyate*)? What will he be called and what will be the name of his universe (*lokadhātu*)?

The Buddha answered: During the sixty-two kalpas that will follow the Nirvāṇa of the thousand Buddhas of the Auspicious Period (*bhadrakalpa*), there will be no more Buddhas; during this lapse of time, there will appear only an hundred thousand *nayutakoṭis* of Pratyekabuddhas, and it is under them that all beings will plant good roots (*kuśalamūlāny avaropsyanti*)[180].

179 See Vkn, pp.84, 264.

180 We are at present in the *mahākalpa* called the Auspicious Period (*bhadrakalpa*), in the course of which a thousand Buddhas appear in the world; four have already come, all the others are yet to come. The *mahākalpa* which will follow will, as always, consist of four *asaṃkhyeyakalpas*: 1. a period of devolution of the world (*saṃvartakalpa*), 2. a period during which the world remains devolved (*saṃvartasthāyikalpa*), 3. a period of evolution (*vivartakalpa*) and, 4. a period during which the world remains evolved (*vivartasthāyikalpa*).

Each of these four periods consists of twenty intermediary kalpas, called *antarakalpas* or 'small kalpas'. It is only during the twenty intermediary kalpas of the period when the world remains evolved (*vivartasthāyikalpa*) that the Buddhas, Pratyekabuddhas and cakravartin kings appear in the world.

During the first *antarakalpa* of this period (the 61st of the *mahākalpa*), the human life-span, infinite in the beginning, continues to diminish until it is no more than ten years.

Antarakalpas Nos 2 to 19 of this period (Nos 62 to 79 of the *mahākalpa*) are each subdivided into two phases: 1. a phase of increase (*utkarṣa*) during which the human life-span, ten years at the beginning, increases until it is 80,000 years, 2. a phase of diminution (*apakarṣa*) during which the human life-span progressively decreases from 80,000 to ten years.

The 20th *antarakalpa* of this period (No.80 and the last of the *mahākalpa*) is only of augmentation: the human life-span increases from ten to 80,0000 years.

The Buddhas appear in the course of the phases of diminution of life, when the life-span is diminishing from 80,000 to 100 years. The Pratyekabuddhas appear during the phases of augmentation and the phases of diminution of life. The cakravartins appear in the era when the human life-span is infinite until the era when life is of 80,000 years.

In the case envisaged here, an hundred thousand *nayutakoṭis* of Pratyekabuddhas will appear during the first two *antarakalpas* of the *vivartasthāyikalpa*, that is, during the 61st and 62nd *antarakalpas* of the *mahākalpa*. During the 63rd *antarakalpa*, the Buddha Vimalaprabhākīrtirāja will appear, and his life-span will last throughout ten *antarakalpas*, that is from the 63rd to the 72nd *antarakalpas* of the *mahākalpa*.

Those [sixty-two] kalpas having elapsed, the devaputra [*Matyabhimukha] will reach supreme and perfect enlightenment. He will be called the Tathāgata Vimalaprabhākīrtirāja[181] 'King Glory of Unstained Brilliance'. His universe [the present Sahālokadhātu] will then have the name of Prasannadarśanā 'Pure vision'[182].

[181] In Tib. *Ḥod dri ma med par grags paḥi rgyal po*. The prediction which concerns him is of great interest. Certain preliminary thoughts are required, which have already been noted by Burnouf: [tr.] 'In extended Sūtras, such as the Saddharmapuṇḍarīka, Samādhirāja, Saddharmalaṅkāvatāra, Lalitavistara and Gaṇḍavyūha, the Buddha does not gather together an assembly unless it consists of an exaggerated number of monks and nuns, devas of all kinds and, above all, bodhisattvas, persons whose merits are no less innumerable than their names are complicated'. These names are the longer the more the bodhisattva is less known. In the case of famous bodhisattvas, their names tend to be abbreviated, but the processes of abbreviation are extremely varied, so much so that it is not always easy to know if one is dealing with the same person. Here are some names of famous Buddhas and bodhisattvas whose names have several variations:

Akṣobhya, Akṣobhyarāja; Amitābha, Amitāyus, Amitaprabha, Amitanātha, Amitāyurjñānaviniścayarājendra; Avalokiteśvara, Avalokita, Avalokitasvara; Dundubhisvara, Dundubhisvaranirghoṣa, Dundubhisvararāja; Bhaiṣajyaguru, Bhaiṣajyaguruvaiḍūryaprabha, Bhaiṣajyaguruvaiḍūryarāja, Bhaiṣajyaguruvaidūryaprabharāja; Mañjuśrī, Mañjughoṣa, Mañjudhvaja, Mañjunātha, Mañjubhāṇin, Mañjusvara, Mañjurava, Mañjuvajra, Mañjuvara, Mañjusvara; Mahāsthāma, Mahāsthāmaprāpta; Maitreya, Maitrīya, Maitraka, Maitranātha, Maitranāman, Ajita, Ajitamaitreya; Vajrapāṇi, Caṇḍavajrapāṇi, Guhyakādhipati, Guhyādhipati, Guhyakendra, Guhyaka Vajrapāṇi Malla (only in Chinese versions?); Vairocana, Vairocanaraśmipratimaṇḍitadhvajarāja; Samantabhadra, Samantatabhadra, Bhadra, Samanta.

The greatest circumspection is required when it is a question of recognising one and the same person among all these diverse variations.

Here, in § 78 of the Śgs, Śākyamuni gives a prediction to the devaputra-bodhisattva Matyabhimukha (or Buddhamatyabhimukha, according to the Tibetan version): In our Sahāloka universe, which will then have the name of Prasannadarśanā, during the 63rd *antarakalpa* of the Mahākalpa which will follow the present Bhadrakalpa, Matyabhimukha will become a Buddha with the name of Vimalaprabhākīrtirāja.

It was said above, at § 77, that before appearing here in the Sahāloka, Matyabhimukha was to be found in the Abhirati universe of the Buddha Akṣobhya. According to the Vkn, p.243, it was from this same Abhirati universe in the Eastern region that Vimalakīrti came, and, as I have pointed out in the notes, the ideas expressed by Matyabhimukha in §§ 62-75 of the Śgs are identical to the theories explained by Vimalakīrti in the Vkn.

So, in the minds of the authors of these two sūtras, Matyabhimukha and Vimalakīrti tend to be confused, and this Buddha Vimalaprabhākīrtirāja whom Matyabhimukha is named to become one day would be none other than the bodhisattva Vimalakīrti in his final existence as a Buddha. In this case, Vimalaprabhākīrtirāja would be to Vimalakīrti what Amitāyurjñāna-viniścayarājendra is to Amitābha, what Bhaiṣajyaguruvaiḍūryaprabharāja is to Bhaiṣajyaguru, etc.: a full name as against a name abbreviated by use.

If this hypothesis is correct, the present passage of the Śgs would be informing us about the final *abhisaṃbodhi* of Vimalakīrti and would thus fill a gap that I regretted in my introduction to the Vkn, p.CIV.

[182] In Tib. *Mthoṅ na daṅ ba*.

79. In that period, the Tathāgata Vimalaprabhākīrtirāja will cause beings to have pure minds (*prasannacitta*), and the beings of that universe will not be beset (*pariveṣṭita*) by craving (*rāga*), hatred (*dveṣa*) or delusion (*moha*); animated by pure faith in the Dharma (*dharmaprasāda*), they will practise the Good Doctrine (*saddharma*).

Dṛḍhamati, the life-span (*āyuṣpramāṇa*) of the Buddha Vimalaprabhākīrtirāja will consist of ten small kalpas *(antarakalpa)*. He will deliver beings by means of the Three Vehicles and, among them, an innumerable (*apramāṇa*) and infinite (*ananta*) number of bodhisattvas will obtain the Śūraṃgamasamādhi and a wondrous power (*vikurvaṇabala*) over all dharmas. In that period, Māra and his kin (*mārajātīya*) will pledge themselves to the Great Vehicle (*mahāyānasaṃprasthita*) and will be compassionate towards beings (*sattvakāruṇika*). That *buddhakṣetra* will be free of the three bad destinies (*durgati*) and the [eight] unfavourable conditions (*akṣaṇa*)[183]; adorned and pure, it will be like the Uttarāvatī[184]. It will be free of the works of Māra (*mārakarman*) and freed from all the false views (*mithyādṛṣṭi*).

After the Nirvāṇa of that Buddha, his Dharma will endure for an hundred thousand *koṭis* of years. Dṛḍhamati, such is the pure universe in which that devaputra will reach supreme and perfect enlightenment.

80. Then the bodhisattva Dṛḍhamati said to the devaputra: It is of great advantage to you (*lābhās te sulabdhāḥ*)[185] that the Tathāgata has predicted your reaching *anuttarasamyaksaṃbodhi.*

The devaputra replied: Kulaputra, the great advantage is not gaining any dharma (*sarvadharmāṇām alābho mahālābha ity utcyate*). To gain any dharma whatsoever is disadvantageous: that is why, O Kulaputra, not gaining any dharmas is a great advantage.

As he was speaking, twenty-five thousand devaputras who had previously planted good roots (*avaropitakuśalamūla*) aroused the

183 Cf. Vkn, pp.20 and n., 57, 79.

184 A continent situated to the north of the *caturdvīpaka* (Kośa III, p.146), the Uttarāvatī or Uttarakuru is the mythical region of the Hyperboreans. Men there are without cupidity (*amamā*) and have no private property (*apariggahā*), they live for a thousand years and are particularly elegant. Without sowing or labouring, they gather rice which is free of blight and husks and cook the grains on oven stones (Dīgha III, p.199; Aṅguttara IV, p.396; other references in Akanuma, *Noms propres*, pp.721-2; Malalasekera, *Proper Names* I, pp.355-6). Their way of life is depicted on the Stūpa at Bhārhut; cf. A. Foucher, 'Sur l'interprétation de quatre bas-reliefs de Bharhut', *Revue des Arts Asiatiques* XIII, pp.1-9.

185 A traditional expression; see Vkn, p.249.

anuttarasamyaksaṃbodhicitta, and ten thousand bodhisattvas acquired the *anutpattikadharmakṣānti.* **[637b]**

[*Māra Tied by the Five Bonds*[186]]

81. Then Śāriputra said to the Buddha: It is extraordinary (*adbhuta*): at present the Śūraṃgamasamādhi is being expounded and yet Māra Pāpīmat[187] 'Māra the Malign' does not come to cause trouble (*vicakṣuḥkaraṇāya*)[188].

The Buddha said to Śāriputra: Do you want to see Māra's troubles?

Yes, I would like to see them.

82. Thereupon the Buddha at that very instant emitted a ray of light from the circle of hair between his two eyebrows, one of the characteristic marks of a great man (*atha khalu buddhas tasyāṃ velāyāṃ mahāpuruṣalakṣaṇād bhrūvivarāntarād ūrṇākośāt prabhāṃ pramumoca*)[189]; the whole of the assembly saw Māra Pāpīmat bound by the five bonds (*pañcabandhanabaddha*) and incapable of freeing himself from them.

The Buddha said to Śāriputra: Do you see Māra Pāpīmat bound by the five bonds?

[Śāriputra replied]: Yes, I have seen him; by what is Māra then bound?

The Buddha replied: He is bound by the supportive power (*adhiṣṭhānabala*) of the Śūraṃgamasamādhi. In *buddhakṣetras* where the Śūraṃgamasamādhi is expounded, ill-willed (*praduṣṭacitta*) Māras oppose it, but through the supportive power (*adhiṣṭhānabala*) of the Śūraṃgamasamādhi and of the Buddhas, all those Māra Pāpīmats find themselves bound by the five bonds. Śāriputra, in the places where the Śūraṃgamasamādhi is expounded, whether I am present in the world or already in Parinirvāṇa, all Māras, kin of Māra (*mārajātīya*) and other ill-willed (*praduṣṭacitta*) beings are bound by the five bonds through

[186] Regarding Māra, see my notes in Vkn, pp.99-101, and the survey by A. Wayman, 'Studies in Yama and Māra', *Indo-Iranian Journal* III, 1959, pp.44-73, 112-31. The conversion of Māra and his daughters is a literary theme frequently exploited by the sūtras of both Vehicles; the present account should be compared with the Mahāsaṃnipāta, *Gilgit Manuscripts* IV, 1959, pp.1-82, the Vkn, pp.99-106, and many other sources.

[187] On the epithet *pāpīmant* or *pāpīyāṃs*, cf. Edgerton, *Dictionary*, p.341.

[188] To the Chinese *jao luan* 嬈亂 corresponds the Tib. *mig gis mi rtsol bar bgyi baḥi slad du*, which gives in Sanskrit *vicakṣuḥkaraṇāya*; cf. Mahāvyut., No.6528. The expression is also found in Mahāvastu III, p.416, *1* and *15*; Lalitavistara, p.378, *15*; Aṣṭasāhasrikā, p.243, *2*; Śikṣāmuccaya, p.96, *10* (cf. Edgerton, *Dictionary,* p.483).

[189] A stock phrase; see Saddharmapuṇḍ, p.423, *1-2*, and, with slight variations, *ibid.*, pp.20, *8-9*; 243, *3*; Lalitavistara, pp.300, *6-8*; 393, *17-18*; Laṅkāvatāra, p.13, *4*.

the supportive power of the Śūraṃgamasamādhi[190].

[*The Twelve Bonds of False Views*]

83. Then, in the assembly, the devas, nāgas, yakṣas, gandharvas, etc., said to the Buddha: Bhagavat, with regard to this *samādhi,* we do not feel any doubt (*saṃśaya*) and we have no opposition (*antarāya*) to it. We do not want to be bound by the five bonds (*pañcabandhana*). O Bhagavat, we respect this *samādhi,* and that is why we have all come to protect (*parigrāhaṇa*) its instructors (*dharmabhāṇaka).* We consider this *samādhi* like the Bhagavat himself.

84. The Buddha said to the devas, nāgas and other divine beings: It is for this reason that you must free (*parimoktum*) yourselves from the twelve bonds of false views (*dṛṣṭigatabandhana*). What are those twelve?

Those twelve bonds are:

1. the view of a self (*ātmadṛṣṭi*),
2. the view of a being (*sattvadṛṣṭi*),
3. the view of a living being (*jīvadṛṣṭi*),
4. the view of an individual (*pudgaladṛṣṭi*),
5. the view of nihilism (*ucchedadṛṣṭi*),
6. the view of eternalism (*śāśvatadṛṣṭi*),
7. the view of the belief in a self (*ātmagrāhadṛṣṭi*),
8. the view of the belief in what pertains to the self (*ātmīyagrāha-dṛṣṭi*),
9. the view of existence (*bhavadṛṣṭi*),
10. the view of non-existence (*vibhavadṛṣṭi*),
11. the view of a personality (*satkāyadṛṣṭi*),
12. the view of all dharmas (*sarvadharmadṛṣṭi*)[191].

Such are the twelve bonds. Know that if beings have any feelings of hatred (*dveṣa*) for the Buddhadharma and seek to destroy (*nivartitum*) it, they are entangled in those twelve bonds of false views. Those who believe (*adhimucyante*) in the Buddhadharma, follow (*anuvartante*) it and do not oppose it will be freed from those twelve bonds.

190 As we shall see at the end of § 87, these bonds are fixed to both hands, both feet and the neck of Māra. In the Legend of Aśoka and related sources (cf. Divyāvadāna, p.357), three corpses, those of a serpent, a dog and a man, are bound to the nape of Māra's neck.

191 We have in Tib. *chos thams cad la mṅon par źen par lta ba*, which gives in Sanskrit *sarvadharmābhiniveśadṛṣṭi.*

[*The Virtue of the Name*]

85. Then Śāriputra said to the Buddha: Bhagavat, at the moment, does Māra Pāpīmat [**637c**] hear the name of this Śūraṃgamasamādhi?

The Buddha replied: He too hears it but, since he is bound, he cannot come here.

Śāriputra said: Why does the Tathāgata not make use of his supportive power (*adhiṣṭhānabala*) so that Māra cannot hear the name of that Śūraṃgamasamādhi?

The Buddha said: Stop (*tiṣṭha*), do not say such words! Supposing that universes as numerous as the sands of the Ganges (*gaṅgā-nadīvālukopama lokadhātu*) were filled with a great fire (*mahāgni*) [and that they would have to be crossed] in order to hear the Śūraṃgamasamādhi being expounded, they would have to be crossed all the same. Why? If someone hears the Śūraṃgamasamādhi being expounded, I claim that he would gain from it great advantages (*lābha*) far superior to the obtaining of the four absorptions (*dhyāna*) or the four Brahmā Abodes (*brahmavihāra*).

86. Śāriputra, if Māra Pāpīmat now hears the name of the Śūraṃgamasamādhi being uttered, he will succeed in transcending (*samatikrāntum*) the works of Māra (*mārakarman*). And, even if they are bound, those who hear this *samādhi* will free themselves from the twelve bonds of false views (*dvādaśa dṛṣṭigatabandhana*). That is why, O Śāriputra, perverse and malign men, caught in the net of Māra (*mārajālapraviṣṭa*), should hear this Śūraṃgamasamādhi. How much more so (*kaḥ punar vādaḥ*) should beings with pure thoughts (*prasannacitta*) delight in hearing it.

[*Bondage and Deliverance*]

87. Now there was in the assembly a bodhisattva named Māragocarānupalipta[192] 'Undefiled by the Domain of Māra'; he said to the Buddha: In truth, Bhagavat, I would like to go now to the world of Māra and, by means of my wondrous power (*vikurvaṇabala*), compel Māra to establish himself in the Śūraṃgamasamādhi.

The Buddha said: Yes, if you consider now to be the right time (*yasyedānīṃ kālaṃ manyase*).

Then the bodhisattva Māragocarānupalipta suddenly disappeared from the assembly and appeared in Māra's palace (*mārabhavana*). He said to Māra Pāpīmat: Do you not hear the Buddha expounding the

[192] In Tib. *Bdud kyi spyod paḥi yul gyis mi gos pa.*

Śūraṃgamasamādhi? Innumerable beings arouse the *anuttarasamyaksaṃbodhicitta* and escape from your domain (*gocara*), and [that instruction] will deliver many more persons by enabling them all to leave your domain[193].

Māra replied: I hear the Buddha expounding the name of the Śūraṃgamasamādhi but, being bound by the five bonds (*pañcabandhanabaddha*), I am not able to go there. They are the bonds I have at my two hands, two feet and neck.

88. [Māragocarānupalipta] asked Māra Pāpīmat: Who bound you?

Māra replied: At the precise moment that I made the resolve to go there in order to disturb those who are listening attentively to the Śūraṃgamasamādhi, I was immediately bound by the five bonds. At that precise moment I said to myself: 'The Buddhas and bodhisattvas have great might (*anubhāva*) and are not easily disturbed; if I go there, I shall be overcome, so it is better to stay here in this palace'. I had scarcely finished that thought when I was [† momentarily] delivered (*mukta*) from the five bonds.

The bodhisattva responded: [† Similarly], those foolish worldlings (*bālapṛthagjana*) are bound (*baddha*) by their own notions (*saṃjñā*), imaginations (*vikalpa*), perverse views (*viparyāsa*) and apprehensions (*nimittograhaṇa*); they are bound by their movements (*iñjita*), reflections (*manyanā*) and idle talk (*prapañca*); they are bound by what they have seen, heard, thought and known (*dṛṣṭaśrutamatavijñāta*)[194]. But in reality, there is nothing which is 'bound' (*baddha*) or 'delivered' (*mukta*). Why? Dharmas are not 'bound' because they are originally delivered (*svabhāvena mukta*); dharmas are not 'delivered' because originally they were not bound[195]. Regarding this mark of eternal deliverance (*nityavimuktilakṣaṇa*), there is no possible error: it is by means of this exposition of the Dharma (*dharmamukha*) that the Tathāgata expounds the Dharma; [**638a**] beings who understand its meaning and seek deliverance attentively and vigorously are delivered from the bonds.

[*Conversion of the Daughters of the Gods*]

89. Then, in Māra's entourage, seven hundred devakanyās 'daughters

193 In Tib. *gźan yaṅ sems can śin tu dpag tu med pa dag khyod kyi yul las ḥdaḥ bar ḥgyur ro*: 'Besides, innumerable beings will still leave your domain'.

194 See Vkn, p.138, n.5.

195 The identity of *bandhana* and *mokṣa* is also one of the theses of the Pañcaviṃśati, p.192, *12-13*, and the Vkn, pp.192, 201.

of the gods' strewed the bodhisattva Māragocarānupalipta with celestial perfumes (*divyagandha*), flowers (*puṣpa*), powders (*cūrṇa*), unguents (*vilepana*) and necklets (*niṣka*). They said to him: When shall we be delivered (*mukta*) from the domain of Māra?

The bodhisattva replied: If you do not destroy the bonds of Māra (*mārabandhana*), you will be delivered.

They asked: What are the bonds of Māra?

He said: They are the sixty-two kinds of false views (*dṛṣṭigata).* If you do not destroy those false views, you will be delivered from the bonds of Māra[196].

90. The devakanyās said further: How can deliverance be obtained by not destroying false views?

He replied: False views do not originally come from anywhere and do not go anywhere. To know the mark of the non-coming and non-going (*anāgamanirgama*) of the false views is to be delivered from the bonds of Māra.

False views are neither existent nor non-existent. Not to distinguish between either existence (*bhāva*) or non-existence is to be delivered from the bonds of Māra.

Not to see anything is the right view (*samyagdṛṣṭi*) and this right view is neither right (*samyak*) nor wrong (*mithyā*). Dharmas are neither right nor wrong, neither actors (*kāraka*) nor reactors (*vedaka*), and this is to be delivered from the bonds of Māra.

Those false views are not found inwardly (*adhyātmam*) or outwardly (*bahirdhā*) or beyond the two (*nobhayam antareṇa*). Not to muse (*amanyanā*) on those false views is to be delivered from the bonds of Māra.

The seven hundred devakanyās, having heard that discourse, obtained the preparatory certainty (*anulomikī kṣānti*) and said: When we are no longer defiled by the domain of Māra (*māragocarānupalipta*), we shall set free (*parimocayiṣyāmaḥ*) all those who are bound by Māra (*mārabaddha*).

[*Self-interested Conversion of Māra*]

91. Then the bodhisattva Māragocarānupalipta said to Māra Pāpīmat: Your handmaids (*bhṛtyā*) have aroused the *anuttarasamyaksaṃbodhicitta;* what are you going to do?

Māra replied: Being bound by the five bonds (*pañcabandhana-*

[196] According to the Vkn as well, the sixty-two kinds of false views are identical to deliverance and constitute the Tathāgatagotra; cf. Vkn, pp.44, 57, 119, 127, 129 and n., 177, 183.

baddha), I do not know what to do.

The bodhisattva went on: Arouse the *anuttarasamyaksaṃbodhicitta*, and you will be delivered from those bonds.

Then the devakanyās, through pity (*anukampā*) for Māra, said to him: You can arouse the *anuttarasamyaksaṃbodhicitta.* Do not take for the fearful (*bhaya*) what is security (*kṣema*); do not take for suffering (*duḥkha*) what is happiness (*sukha*); do not take for bondage (*bandhana*) what is deliverance (*mukti*).

92. Then Māra framed a thought of deceit (*māyācitta*) and said: If you renounce (*visarjatha*) the *bodhicitta,* I consent to arouse it.

Then the devakanyās, resorting to skilful means (*upāya*), said to Māra: We have already renounced the *bodhicitta,* therefore you can arouse the *anuttarasamyaksaṃbodhicitta.* If a single bodhisattva arouses the *bodhicitta,* all bodhisattvas arouse it as well. Why? The *citta* is undifferentiated (*nirviśiṣṭa*); among all beings the *citta* is the same (*sama*).

Thereupon Māra Pāpīmat said to the bodhisattva Māragocarānupalipta [**638b**]: I arouse the *anuttarasamyaksaṃbodhicitta;* may I through that good root (*kuśalamūla*) be delivered from the bonds!

Scarcely had he said those words than he found himself delivered from the bonds.

[*Conversion of the Lustful Devakanyās*]

93. Then the bodhisattva Māragocarānupalipta, by means of his supernormal power (*ṛddhibala*), emitted a great light (*mahāprabhā*) and showed his marvellous body (*pariniṣpannakāya*): he illuminated all the palaces of Māra (*mārabhavana*), and Māra found himself eclipsed (*dhyāmīkṛta*) like a block of ink (*maṣirāśisadṛśa*).

Now there were in Māra's entourage two hundred devakanyās deeply attached to the pleasures of the senses (*kāmarāgātisakta*). Seeing the perfect beauty (*rūpasaṃpad*) of that bodhisattva, they became enamoured (*saṃrakta*) of him. Each one declared separately: If that man makes love to us[197], we will all comply with his orders (*sarvās tasya śāsanam anuvartsyāmaḥ*).

94. Then the bodhisattva, knowing that they fulfilled the requisite conditions (*pūrvapratyaya*) for being delivered, created through transformation (*abhinirmimīte sma*) two hundred devaputras of perfect

[197] With *ts'ung chih* 從事, Kumārajīva summarises the long traditional Sanskrit periphrase *krīḍati ramate paricārayati* (cf. Divyāvadāna, pp.1, *6*; 98, *19*; Saddharmapuṇḍ., pp.72, *13*; 78, *2*, etc.).

beauty, identical to his own. He also created two hundred magnificent belvederes (*kūṭāgāra*) for intimacy, superior to all the palaces of Māra. The devakanyās, finding themselves in those magnificent belvederes, each thought apart: 'It is I who am disporting myself with the bodhisattva'. When their desires (*āśaya*) were fully gratified (*paripūrṇa*), their craving (*kāmarāga*) disappeared. They aroused the high resolve (*adhyāśaya*) and honoured the bodhisattva. Then the latter expounded the Dharma as was suitable (*yathāpratyarham*) to them, and they all aroused the *anuttarasamyaksaṃbodhicitta.*

[*Further Guile of Māra*]

95. Then the bodhisattva Māragocarānupalipta said to Māra Pāpīmat: You can go to the Buddha.

Māra had this thought: Now that I am delivered from the bonds, I shall go to the Buddha and disturb the instruction of the Dharma.

Thereupon Māra Pāpīmat, surrounded by his retinue, went to the Buddha and said to him: Bhagavat, do not expound the Śūraṃgamasamādhi any more. Why? When you expound that *samādhi,* I am bound by the five bonds. I would like the Tathāgata to expound something else.

Then the bodhisattva Dṛḍhamati said to Māra Pāpīmat: Who unbound your bonds?

Māra replied: The bodhisattva Māragocarānupalipta unbound my bonds.

[Dṛḍhamati went on]: What did you promise, in return for being unbound?

Māra said: I promised to arouse the *anuttarasamyaksaṃbodhicitta.*

96. Then the Buddha said to the bodhisattva Dṛḍhamati: Today Māra Pāpīmat aroused the *bodhicitta* in order to be unbound, and not with a pure intention (*adhyāśaya*). Equally, O Dṛḍhamati, after my Nirvāṇa [at the end of time, in the final period], in the last five hundred years (*mama parinirvṛtasya, paścime kāle, paścime samaye, paścimāyāṃ pañcaśatyāṃ vartamānāyām*)[198], numerous bhikṣus will arouse the bodhicitta for material gains (*lābha*) and not with a pure intention (*adhyāśaya*).

97. O Dṛḍhamati, consider the might (*sthāma*) of the Śūraṃgamasamādhi and the supportive action (*adhiṣṭhāna*) of the Buddhadharma: bhikṣus, bhikṣuṇīs, upāsakas and upāsikās who, through derision

[198] The Tibetan version reproduces in full this well-known stock phrase; cf. Vkn, p.264, in the notes.

(*viḍambanā*), through love of gain (*lābhakāma*) or to imitate others (*parānuparivartana*), will listen to this *samādhi* and arouse the *bodhicitta,* I know that for them that *cittotpāda* will be the cause and condition (*hetupratyaya*) of arrival at *anuttarasamyaksaṃbodhi.* How much more so can it be said (*kaḥ punar vādaḥ*) of those who will listen to this Śūraṃgamasamādhi with a pure intention (*adhyāśaya*) and will arouse the *anuttarasamyaksaṃbodhicitta.*? **[638c]**. It must be known that the latter are predestined to the Buddha attributes (*buddhadharmaniyata*).

[*Prediction to Māra*]

98. The bodhisattva Dṛḍhamati said to the Buddha: Bhagavat, today Māra Pāpīmat, after having heard the Śūraṃgamasamādhi expounded, aroused the *bodhicitta* in order to be delivered from his bonds. Will that *cittotpāda* enable him one day to obtain the perfected Buddha attributes (*paripūrṇabuddhadharma*)?

The Buddha replied: It is indeed as you say (*evam etad yathā vadasi*). Because Māra Pāpīmat has the merit (= good roots, (*kuśalamūla*) of having heard[199] this *samādhi* and because he aroused the *bodhicitta,* he will in the future (*anāgate 'dhvani*) come to eliminate (*vyantīkartum*) the works of Māra (*mārakarman*), the practices of Māra (*māracaryā*), the hypocrisy of Māra (*māraśāṭhya*) and the guiles of Māra (*māramāyā*). As from today (*adyāgreṇa*) he will gradually (*krameṇa*) gain the power of the Śūraṃgamasamādhi and will finally reach supreme and perfect enlightenment (*anuttarāyāṃ samyaksaṃbodhim abhisaṃbhotsyate*).

99. The bodhisattva Dṛḍhamati said to Māra Pāpīmat: The Tathāgata has just given you the prediction (*vyākaraṇa*).

Māra said: Kulaputra, it was not with a pure intention (*adhyāśaya*) that today I aroused the *anuttarasamyaksaṃbodhicitta.* How then could the Tathāgata give me the prediction? The Buddha has said: 'From thought (*citta*) arises action (*karman*) and from action arises fruition (*vipāka*)'. Since I have never had the thought [that is, the intention] of seeking Bodhi, how could the Tathāgata give me the prediction?

[*The Four Kinds of Prediction*[200]]

100. Then the Buddha, in order to destroy the doubts of the assembly

199 Adopt the variant *i wên* 以聞.

200 1.The Avataṃsaka (T 278, ch.37, 633*c* 8-19; T 279, ch.53, p.281*a* 16-25; Tib. Trip., vol.26, p.62, fol.150*b* 4 - 151*a* 3) is familiar with the ten *vyākaraṇas* by virtue of which the bs knows himself to be *vyākṛta.* Further on (T 278, ch.39, p.646*c* 7-15; T 279, ch.55, p.292*c* 16-23;

Tib. Trip., vol.26, p.80, fol.194*b* 1-5), the same text draws up a list of the ten *vyākaraṇas* of which at least three can be compared with the present passage of the Śgs: 4. *saṃmukha-vyākaraṇa*, prediction made in the presence of the one concerned; 5. *asaṃmukhavyākaraṇa*, prediction made in the absence of the one concerned; 7. *kṣāntilābhavyākaraṇa*, prediction conferred after the acquisition of the *anutpattikadharmakṣānti*.

2. The four *vyākaraṇas* of which the Śgs speaks here are mentioned in the Bodhisaṃbhāraśāstra, a work translated into Chinese at Lo-yang between 590 and 616 by Dharmagupta of the Sui, with the title of P'u ti tzŭ liang lun (T 1660). It is a work in verse and prose; according to the K'ai (T 2154, ch.7, p.551*c* 1), the kārikās are by Nāgārjuna and the commentary by the bhikṣu Īśvara. Here is a translation of the passage referring to the *vyākaraṇas* (T 1660, ch.3, p.528*b* 16-25):

'In the Mahāyāna, four *vyākaraṇas* are spoken of: 1. *Anutpāditabodhicittavyākaraṇa*: A man is *tīkṣṇendriya* and *udārādhimuktika*, and the Bhagavat Buddhas having considered him with their *apratihatabuddhacakṣus* give him the *vyākaraṇa*. 2. *Utpāditabodhicittavyākaraṇa*: A man has ripened the *kuśalamūlas*, planted and cultivated the seed of Bodhi; his faculties are very sharp, he has obtained the superior practices and he wants only to liberate beings. This is why, as soon as he has aroused the *bodhicitta*, he has entered the state of *avaivartika*; he is *avinipātadharman* and freed from the eight *akṣaṇas*. 3. It can happen that a man, hearing his own *vyākaraṇa*, loses his zeal (*vīrya*) for the six *pāramitās*, but he proves to be ever more vigorous if he does not hear it: this is why the Buddha does not let him hear it. However, desiring other men to hear the *vyākaraṇa* so that they may cut off their doubts (*saṃśayacchedanāya*), the Buddha, through *adhiṣṭhāna*, confers the *vyākaraṇa* unbeknown to the one concerned. 4. If the bs has ripened the five *lokottarendriyas*, he acquires the *anutpattikadharmakṣānti* and dwells in [the eighth stage] of the bs, namely the *acalābhūmi*. It is to him that the *saṃmukhavyākaraṇa* applies'.

3. The Upadeśa, also attributed to Nāgārjuna, refers twice to the four *vyākaraṇas* of the Śgs (T 1509, ch.4, p.92*b* 3-6; ch.40, p.349*c* 19). I should here correct the translation of the first passage which I gave earlier in Nāgārjuna, *Traité* I, p.293. It should read: 'In the Śūraṃgamasamādhi, there are four kinds of bs and four kinds of *vyākaraṇa*: 1. The *anutpāditabodhicittavyākaraṇa*; 2. the *utpāditabodhicittavyākaraṇa*; 3. the *saṃmukhavyākaraṇa* [given in such a way] that [only] all other men know it, but the one concerned does not know it; 4. the *saṃmukhavyākaraṇa* given in such a way that all men and the one concerned know it'.

[In this passage, the term used for the third *vyākaraṇa* is wrong; it should read *asaṃmukha-vyākaraṇa* instead of *saṃmukhavyākaraṇa*].

Further on (ch.76, p.597*a* 23 - *b* 2), the Upadeśa goes into more detailed explanations:

'According to some people, there are two kinds of irreversible (*avaivartika*) bs: 1. he who has already obtained the *vyākaraṇa*; 2. he who has not yet obtained the *vyākaraṇa*.

'He who has already obtained the *vyākaraṇa* is of two kinds: 1. he who obtained the *vyākaraṇa* while he was present (*saṃmukha*); 2. he who obtained the *vyākaraṇa* while he was not present (*asaṃmukha*).

'He who has obtained the *vyākaraṇa* while he was not present is of two kinds: 1. he who has obtained the *vyākaraṇa* while he was already perfected (*saṃpanna*); 2. he who has obtained the *vyākaraṇa* while he was not perfected (*asaṃpanna*).

'He who has obtained the *vyākaraṇa* while he was already perfected is he who knows the true nature (*bhūtalakṣaṇa* or *bhūtanaya*) of all dharmas and who fulfills to perfection (*paripūrayati*) the six *pāramitās*.

'He who has obtained the *vyākaraṇa* while he was not perfected is he who knows only the true nature of all dharmas but who has obtained only a part of the *prajñāpāramitā* and does not perfectly fulfil the other *pāramitās*.

4. The quotations that preceded demonstrate the importance that the Mādhyamikas attached to the predictions. However, the theory of the *vyākaraṇa* which disregards the *pudgalanairātmya* and runs counter to the absolute sameness among beings, is only valid for Saṃvṛti and does not apply absolutely speaking. Thus the Vkn does not pay much attention to it: Vimalakīrti explains to the future Buddha Maitreya that supreme Bodhi being possessed by everybody, from the beginning and by right, any prediction concerning it is null and void and no bs can pride himself on having received it (see Vkn, pp.86-90). Nevertheless, scholars continued to discuss the *vyākaraṇa* and the Yogācārins developed the system still further.

5. Mahāyānasūtrālaṃkāra, p.166, *9-17*: *Tatra pudgalabhedena vyākaraṇaṃ gotrasthotpāditacittasaṃmukhāsamakṣapudgalavyākaraṇāt. kālabhedena parimitāparimita-kālavyākaraṇāt. punar bodhau vyākaraṇaṃ bhavati vyākaraṇe vā evaṃnāmā tathāgata evam amuṣmin kāle vyākariṣyatīti. anyat punar mahāvyākaraṇaṃ yad aṣṭamyāṃ bhūmāv anutpattikadharmakṣāntilābhataḥ, ahaṃ buddho bhaviṣyāmīti mānaprahāṇataḥ, sarvanimittābhogaprahāṇataḥ, sarvabuddhabodhisattvaiś ca sārdham ekībhāvopagamanataḥ, tadātma-saṃtānabhedādarśanāt, punaḥ kṣetrādibhir vyākaraṇam īdṛśe buddhakṣetre evaṃnāmā iyatā kālena buddho bhaviṣyati, evaṃnāmake kalpe, īdṛśaś cāsya parivāro bhaviṣyati, etāvad antaraṃ kālam asya saddharmānuvṛttir bhaviṣyatīti.*

Free translation: 1. Depending on the various individuals to whom it is addressed, the prediction is conferred: *a.* on an individual belonging to the lineage of the Tathāgata; *b.* on a bs who has already aroused the thought of Bodhi; *c.* on a bs who is present; *d.* or finally, on a bs who is absent. 2. According to the various methods of predicting the time, we can distinguish: *a.* the prediction which fixes the time required for attaining supreme and perfect enlightenment; *b.* the prediction which does not fix it. 3. Again there are: *a.* the prediction having a bearing on Bodhi, that is, prophesying the attainment of Bodhi; *b.* the prediction having a bearing on the prediction, announcing that a Tathāgata with such-and-such a name, at such-and-such a time, will make such-and-such a prophecy. 4. Yet another is the Great Prediction: it is addressed to a bs in the eighth stage who has acquired the certainty of the non-arising of dharmas, who has destroyed any feeling of pride making him say: 'I shall become a Buddha!', who has eliminated every object and every effort of thought, who has understood the fundamental sameness uniting him with all the Buddhas and bodhisattvas and who no longer sees any distinction between their mental series and his own mental series. 5. The prediction which specifies the field and the rest, saying: 'In such-and-such a Buddha-field, the so-named, after so long, will become a Buddha, in the cosmic period of such-and-such a name; he will have such-and-such an entourage, and his Saddharma will last for such-and-such a length of time'.

6. The Madhyāntavibhāga, p.190, *18-21*, defines the Great Prediction (No.4 of the preceding text) in the following way: *Vyākaraṇāvasthāṣṭamyāṃ bhūmāv iti. sarvathā sarvanimittābhogasaṃjñāvigamād aṣṭamyāṃ bhūmau niyatipatito bhavati buddhatva iti buddhair bhagavadbhiḥ saṃmukhavyākaraṇena vyākriyate*: The state of prediction is related to the eighth stage: in the eighth stage, through the complete elimination of every object of thought, every mental effort and every notion, the bs is predestined to Buddhahood; this is why the Blessed Lord Buddhas confer the prediction on him in his presence'.

7. Bodh. bhūmi, p.290, *4-10*: *Ṣaḍbhir ākāraiḥ samāsatas tathāgatā bodhisattvam anuttarāyāṃ samyaksaṃbodhau vyākurvanti. katamaiḥ ṣaḍbhiḥ. gotrastham anutpāditacittaṃ, tathotpāditacittaṃ, saṃmukhāvasthitaṃ, viparokṣāvasthitaṃ, parimitakālam iyatā kālenānuttarāṃ samyaksaṃbodhim abhisaṃbhotsyata iti, aparimitakālaṃ vyākaroti na tu kālaniyamaṃ karoti*: 'In short, the Tathāgatas predict to a bodhisattva his arrival at supreme and perfect enlightenment in six different ways. What are those six? They confer the prediction:

(*tasyāḥ parṣadaḥ saṃśayacchedanāya*), said to Dṛḍhamati: The prediction conferred on a bodhisattva is of four kinds. What are those four?

1. The prediction concerning him who has not yet aroused the thought of Bodhi (*anutpāditabodhicittavyākaraṇa*).

2. The prediction conferred on him who has just aroused the thought of Bodhi (*utpāditabodhicittavyākaraṇa*).

3. The prediction made unbeknown to the one concerned (*rahovyākaraṇa*)[201].

4. The prediction made in the presence of him who has acquired the certainty of the non-arising of dharmas (*anutpattikadharmakṣānti-labdhasaṃmukhavyākaraṇa*)[202].

These four predictions can only be known by the Tathāgatas; Śrāvakas and Pratyekabuddhas do not know them.

1. *Anutpāditabodhicittavyākaraṇa*

101. *Tatra Dṛḍhamate katamad anutpāditabodhicittavyākaraṇam. iha Dṛḍhamate sa pudgalaḥ pāñcagatike saṃsāre upapanno bhavati, yadi vā nirayeṣu yadi vā tiryagyonau yadi vā yamaloke yadi vā deveṣu yadi vā manuṣyeṣu; sa ca pudgalas tīkṣṇendriyo bhavati, udārādhimuktikaḥ; tam enaṃ tathāgataḥ prajānāti: ayaṃ puruṣa-pudgalo yāvadiyadbhiḥ kalpakoṭīniyutaśatasahasrair anuttarāyāṃ samyaksaṃbodhau cittam utpādayiṣyati, iyadbhir asaṃkhyeya-kalpakoṭīniyutaśatasahasrair bodhisattvacaryāś cariṣyati, iyanti buddhakoṭīniyutaśatasahasrāṇi satkariṣyati, iyanty apramāṇāni sattvakoṭīniyutaśatasahasrāṇi paripācayiṣyati bodhipratiṣṭhāpanāya, iyadbhiś cāsaṃkhyeyakalpaśatasahasrair bodhim abhisaṃbhotsyate, evaṃnāmā bhaviṣyati, īdṛśaṃ cāsya buddhakṣetraṃ bhaviṣyati, īdṛśaś*

1. on a bs who belongs to the lineage of the Tathāgatas, but who has not yet aroused the thought of Bodhi; 2. on a bs who has just aroused that thought; 3. on a bs who is present; 4. on a bs who is absent; 5. they predict a specific time by saying that at the end of a certain length of time the bs will reach supreme and perfect enlightenment; 6. they predict an indeterminate time and give no set date'.

8. At the Council of Lhasa, the Indian party referred to the present passage of the Śgs in support of their gradualist thesis. The Chinese Sudden Way supporters responded by opposing them with a passage from the Viśeṣacintibrahmaparipṛcchā (T 586, ch.2, pp.45*c* - 46*a*) where it is said that the Buddha confers the prediction on the bss who practise neither the dharmas of arising nor the dharmas of cessation… (cf. P. Demiéville, *Le Concile de Lhasa*, pp.141-6). They could also have quoted the Vkn which, as we have just seen, considers the prophecy as null and void, even if given to Maitreya.

201 In Tib. *gsaṅ luṅ bstan pa*. It is also called *asaṃmukha-* or *viparokṣavyākaraṇa*.

202 The Tib. simply says: *bźod pa thob nas mṅon sum du luṅ bstan pa = kṣāntilabdhasaṃmukhavyākaraṇa*.

cāsya śrāvakaparivāro bhaviṣyati, īdṛśaṃ cāsyāyuṣpramāṇaṃ bhaviṣyati, etāvad antaraṃ kālam asya parinirvṛttasya saddharmaḥ sthāsyati. idaṃ Dṛḍhamate tathāgataḥ prajānāti taduttaraṃ ca. idaṃ Dṛḍhamate ucyate bodhisattvasyānutpāditabodhicittavyākaraṇam[203].

Dṛḍhamati, what is the prediction concerning him who has not yet aroused the thought of Bodhi? Here, Dṛḍhamati, a man has taken on birth in the round of rebirth with five destinies, among the hell-born, animals, the world of Death, gods and mankind: this man has sharp faculties and aspires to the noble teaching. The Tathāgata knows this man well and says: This individual, after so many hundreds of thousands of koṭīniyutas of cosmic periods, will arouse the thought of supreme and perfect enlightenment; for so many hundreds of thousands of koṭīniyutas of incalculable cosmic periods, he will perform the practices of the bodhisattvas; he will revere so many hundreds of thousands of koṭīniyutas of Buddhas; he will ripen so many innumerable hundreds of thousands of koṭīniyutas of beings so as to establish them in Bodhi; after so many hundreds of thousands of incalculable cosmic periods, he will attain perfect Bodhi; he will have such-and-such a name, his Buddha-field will have such-and-such characteristics; his entourage of disciples will number so many; his life-span will last for so long and after his Nirvāṇa his Good Dharma will endure for so many years. This, Dṛḍhamati, the Tathāgata knows well, and other things also. Such is, O Dṛḍhamati, the prediction concerning the bodhisattva who has not yet aroused the thought of Bodhi.

102. *Atha khalv āyuṣmān Mahākāśyapo bhagavantam etad avocat. adyagreṇāsmābhir bhagavan sarvasatvānām antike śāstṛsaṃjñotpādayitavyā. tat kasya hetoḥ. na hy asmākam etaj jñānaṃ pravartate: katamasya bodhisatvasya bodhiparipācakānīndriyāṇi saṃvidyante, katamasya na saṃvidyante. tato vayaṃ bhagavann ajānānās tathārūpeṣu, hīnasaṃjñām utpādayema. tena vayaṃ kṣaṇyema*[204].

Then the Venerable Mahākāśyapa said to the Bhagavat: As from today, O Bhagavat, we **[639a]** should consider all beings as being the Master in person. Why? It is because we do not possess your knowledge and we do not know in which bodhisattva spiritual faculties ripening in

203 The underlined text represents an original passage of the Śgs quoted in Śikṣāsamuccaya, p.91, *8-14*.

204 This is a fragment of the original text quoted in Śikṣāsamuccaya, pp.91, *14* - 92, *1*. The form *kṣaṇyema*, from the verb *kṣan* (*kṣaṇoti, kṣaṇute*) is a passive optative with an active flexional ending (*kṣaṇyema* for *kṣaṇyemahi*); cf. L. Renou, *Grammaire sanscrite* II, p.465; F. Edgerton, *Buddhist Hybrid Sanskrit Grammar*, p.182.

Bodhi are to be found and in which bodhisattva they are not to be found. So therefore, O Bhagavat, not knowing this, it comes about that we conceive scorn for such men and, through this, we can harm ourselves.

103. *Bhagavān āha. sādhu sādhu Kāśyapa subhāṣitā te iyaṃ vāk. idaṃ ca mayā Kāśyapārthavaśaṃ saṃpaśyamānena yuṣmākam evaṃ dharmo deśito: 'Mā bhikṣavaḥ pudgalena pudgalaṃ pravicetavyaṃ. yac chīghraṃ kṣaṇyati*[205] *hi bhikṣavaḥ pudgalaḥ pudgalaṃ pravicinvan. ahaṃ vā pudgalaṃ pramiṇuyāṃ yo vā syān mādṛśaḥ'. etena Kāśyapa nirdeśena bodhisatvena vā śrāvakena vā sarvasatvānām antike śāstṛsaṃjotpādayitavyā. mātra kaścid bodhisatvayānikaḥ pudgalo bhavet tena tatrātmā rakṣitavya iti*[206].

The Bhagavat said: Excellent, excellent, Kāśyapa, what you have just said was well spoken. It is in considering the importance of the subject, O Kāśyapa, that I taught you the following rule: 'Monks, a man should not judge a man, for he harms himself very quickly, O monks, that man who judges a man. I myself or someone like me can assess a man'[207]. In accordance with this teaching, O Kāśyapa, a bodhisattva and a śrāvaka should consider all beings as being the Master himself, and ask themselves cautiously if some individual adhering to the Bodhisattva Vehicle is not before them.

2. *Utpāditabodhicittavyākaraṇa*

104. 'The prediction conferred on him who has just aroused the thought of Bodhi'. There are also beings having long since planted good roots (*avaropitakuśalamūla*), having accomplished the good practices (*kṛtacarya*)[208], given over to vigour (*ārabdhavīrya*), with sharp faculties (*tīkṣṇendriya*), aspiring to the noble teaching (*udārādhimuktika*),

[205] *Kṣaṇyati* is a passive present indicative with an active ending. To this form, attested in Śikṣāsamuccaya, p.92, *3*, corresponds the Pāli *khaññati* attested in Aṅguttara III, p.350, *6*; V, p.140, *19*, etc. The verb is therefore connected with the Sanskrit root *kṣan* 'to harm' and not with the root *khan* 'to dig' as the Rhys Davids and W. Stede *Pali-English Dictionary* II, p.60, and Woodward and Hare, *Pali Concordance* II, p.74, would have us believe.

[206] A fragment of the original text quoted in Śikṣāsamuccaya, p.92, *1-6*.

[207] A canonical saying taken from the Saṃyuktāgama, T 99, ch.35, p.258*a* 23-25; *c* 7-8. The Pāli phrasing attested in Aṅguttara III, pp.350, *4-8*; 351, *13-16*; V, pp.140, *18-22*; 143, *17-21*, differs slightly: *Tasmā ti h'Ānanda mā puggalesu pamāṇikā ahuvattha, mā puggalesu pamāṇaṃ gaṇhittha. Khaññati h'Ānanda puggalesu pamāṇaṃ gaṇhanto. Ahaṃ vā Ānanda puggalesu pamāṇaṃ gaṇheyyaṃ, yo vā pan' assa mādiso*: 'This is why, Ānanda, do not be among those who take the measure of men; do not take the measure of men, for he harms himself, O Ānanda, he who takes the measure of men. It is I, Ānanda, who can take the measure of men, or someone who may be like me'.

[208] In Tib. *spyad ba byas pa*.

greatly compassionate (*mahākaruṇāsamanvāgata*) and seeking to deliver beings (*sattvavimoktukāma*). Immediately after their *cittotpāda*, those men are:

irreversible (*avaivartika*)[209],

entered into the absolute certainty of the bodhisattvas

[209] We saw earlier, § 5, n.5, that the bs is truly *avaivartika* when he is in possession of the *anutpattikadharmakṣānti*, a virtue of the eighth *bhūmi*, the Acalā, also called *avivartyabhūmi* or *avaivartikabhūmi*. However, the problem of the *avaivartika* is one of the most obscure of the Mahāyāna, and the long chapter devoted to it by the Prajñāpāramitā (Aṣṭasāhasrikā, pp.665-92; Pañcaviṃśati, T 223, ch.16, pp.339*a* - 341*b*) is not enough to clarify it.

In fact, the eighth *bhūmi* is not the only one to be qualified as *avivartanya-* or *avaivartikabhūmi*: the epithet can also be applied to the first *bhūmi,* the Pramuditā, classified in the Path of Vision *(darśanamārga)* of the bs, a path in the course of which the bs is *avakrāntabodhisattvaniyāma* 'entered into the certainty of the Bodhisattva', predestined as to his future accession to Saṃbodhi (see above, § 7, n.13).

Here are some texts where it appears quite clearly that the bs is *avaivartika* from the start of his career, from the first bhūmi:

a. Pañcaviṃśati, p.66, *15-16*; Śatasāhasrikā, p.272, *7-9*: *santi bodhisattvā mahāsattvā ye prathamacittotpādenaiva bodhisattvaniyāmam avakrāmanty avinivartanīyabhūmau vāvatiṣṭhante*: 'There are bss who simply by means of the first *cittotpāda* enter the certainty of the bs or establish themselves in the irreversible stage'.

b. Pañcaviṃśati, p.107, *10-11* (cf. Śatasāhasrikā, p.381, *20*): *evaṃ hi bodhisattvo mahāsattvaḥ prajñāpāramitāyāṃ carann avinivartanīyāṃ bhūmim avakrāmati: iti nirodhe dharmajñānakṣāntiḥ*: 'And so the bs moving in the perfection of wisdom enters the irreversible stage: this is the *nirodhe dharmajñānakṣāntiḥ*', or ninth moment of the Darśanamārga having as its object the cessation (*nirodha*) of suffering connected with the Kāmadhātu (Kośa VII, p.5).

c. The Upadeśa (T 1509, ch.75, p.586*a* 10-11) defines the Darśanabhūmi, a stage common to both śrāvakas and bodhisattvas: 'The Darśanabhūmi [for the śrāvaka], is the Prathamaphalapratipannaka, that is, the candidate to the srotaāpanna fruit [grade covering the first fifteen moments of the Darśanamārga; see Kośa VI, p.194; Āloka, p.35, *16-17*; Abhidharmasamuccaya, p.88, *19-20*]; for the bodhisattva, it is the *avaivartikabhūmi*'.

d. The Upadeśa (T 1509, ch.74, pp.579*c* 21- 580*a* 11; passage noted and translated by L. de La Vallée Poussin in Siddhi, pp.738-9):

'What should a bs obtain in order to receive the name of *avaivartika*?

'According to the Abhidharmavibhāṣā, when the bs, having passed through three *asaṃkhyeyakalpas*, plants the causes which will produce the thirty-two marks: from that moment, he is called *avaivartika* (see Kośa IV, pp.222-3).

'According to the Vinaya-Avadāna, from the time he saw the Buddha, Dīpaṃkara scattered the five flowers, spread his hair out on the ground, received the 'prediction of *avaivartika*' from the Buddha, rose in the air and praised the Buddha: from that moment, he is named *avaivartika*.

'However, in the Prajñāpāramitā, when the bs is possessed of the practice of the six *pāramitās*, obtains *jñāna* and *upāya*, is no longer attached to the *pāramitās* which are absolutely empty, sees that all dharmas are free of arising-cessation-increase-diminution-defilement-purity-coming-going-unity-multiplicity-permanence-impermanence-existence-non-existence, free of any dualities whatsoever; when, by reason of this *jñāna*, he sees and severs every note of impermanence after having severed every note of permanence; abandons the view of non-arising-cessation, the view of impermanence, is not attached to non-arising-cessation . . . he is *(avakrāntabodhisattvaniyāma)*[210],

graded in absolute certainty *(niyatipatita)*[211],

called "bs who has acquired the *anutpattikadharmakṣānti*", he enters the bs predestination *(bodhisattvaniyāma)*, he is named *avaivartika*.

'Doubtless, from the first arousal of the thought of Bodhi, the bs is *avaivartika*, but he is not endowed with the characteristics of *avaivartika*'.

It follows from this passage that the Upadeśa, faithful interpreter of the Prajñāpāramitā, distinguishes two kinds of *avaivartika*: 1. an *avaivartika* incorrectly so called, from the time of entering the *bhūmis*; 2. an *avaivartika* correctly so called, starting with the eighth *bhūmi*. Hence, the term leads to confusion and only the context allows us to decide which kind of *avaivartika* we are dealing with. Here in § 104 of the Śgs, it obviously concerns an *avaivartika incorrectly so called*, while in § 108, it will be a question of an *avaivartika correctly so called*.

e. To complicate matters still further, the Āloka, p.665, *5-8*, posits three kinds of *avaivartika* bs: 1. he who is on the Preparatory Path [where he cultivates the practices] favourable to the penetration of the Truths *(nivedhabhāgīyaprayogamārgastha)*; 2. he who is on the Path of Vision consisting of [eight] *kṣāntis* and [eight] *jñānas* *(kṣāntijñānasaṃgṛhīta-darśanamārgastha)*; 3. he who is on the Path of Meditation which follows *(prābandhika-bhāvanāmārgastha)*.

210 Regarding the *bodhisattvaniyāma*, parallel to the *samyaktvaniyāma* of the śrāvaka, see above, § 7, n.13.

211 This concerns the second of the three *niyatipātas* enumerated in Bodh. bhūmi, p.290, *11-23* (or T 1579, ch.46, p.547*a* 5-17): *traya ime bodhisattvasya niyatipātāḥ. katame trayaḥ. gotrastha eva bodhisattvo niyatipatita ity ucyate. tat kasya hetoḥ. bhavyo 'sau pratyayān āsādya niyatam anuttarāṃ samyaksaṃbodhim abhisaṃboddhum. punar ekatyo bodhisattvo niyataṃ cittam utpādayati anuttarāyāṃ samyaksaṃbodhau na punas tasmāt pratyudāvartayati yāvad anuttarāṃ samyaksaṃbodhim abhisaṃbudhyate. punar bodhisattvo vaśitāprāptaḥ sarvāṃ sattvārthacaryāṃ yathecchati yathārabhate tathaivābandhyāṃ karoti. ta ete trayo niyatipatitā bhavanti. gotrasthaniyatipātaś cittotpādaniyatipāto 'bandhyacaryāniyatipātaś ca. tatra paścimaṃ niyatipātam ārabhya tathāgatā niyatipatitaṃ bodhisattvaṃ vyākurvāṇā vyākurvanti*: 'There are three certainties [= predestinations] for the bs: 1. The bs who is to be found in the spiritual lineage is said to be predestined, in fact if he meets with favourable conditions, he is capable of certainly reaching supreme and perfect enlightenment. 2. Furthermore, a certain bs arouses a thought of 'predestination' regarding supreme and perfect enlightenment and does not swerve from it until he reaches the latter. 3. Finally, the bs, in possession of the sovereign powers, infallibly achieves whatever he wishes and whatever he undertakes in the service of all beings. These three kinds of bs have 'fallen into predestination': predestination consisting respectively of the fact of belonging to the lineage, of the *cittotpāda* and of the infallible practice. With regard to the third and last predestination, the Tathāgatas give the prediction to the *niyatipatita* bs'. Compare the six *niyatipātas* of Sūtrālaṃkāra, pp.166, *21* - 167, *1*.

However, in the paragraph which concerns us, the epithet *niyatipatita* appears only in the Chinese version by Kumārajīva who renders it by *to-pi-ting-shu* 墮畢定數. The Tibetan version replaces it with another expression: *log par ltuṅ baḥi chos can ma yin pa*, corresponding to the Sanskrit *avinipātadharman* and meaning 'free from falling into the bad destinies'. It is a standard epithet which the Hīnayāna texts apply to the srotaāpanna: *avinipātadharman, niyata, saṃbodhiparāyaṇa*; see Dīgha I, p.156, *9*; II, p.200, *17*; Divyāvadāna, p.534, *4*. The Mahāyāna texts also apply it, altering details as appropriate, to certain bss; the Sukhāvatīvyūha, p.114, *16*, talks of *avinipātadharmāṇo yāvadbodhiparyantam* bss 'free of falling or reversal until their attainment of Bodhi'.

and have transcended the eight unfavourable conditions of existence (*aṣṭākṣaṇasamatikrānta*)[212].

As soon as such men have aroused the *cittotpāda*, the Buddhas predict to them that they will one day reach *anuttarasamyaksaṃbodhi*, that they will have such-and-such a name, such-and-such a field (*kṣetra*) and such-and-such a life-span (*āyuṣpramāṇa*).

When the Tathāgatas, knowing the tendencies (*āśaya*) of men like that, give them the prediction, it is a 'prediction conferred on him who has just aroused the thought of Bodhi'.

3. *Rahovyākaraṇa*[213]

105. 'The prediction made unbeknown to the one concerned'. There are bodhisattvas[214] who, as long as they have not received the prediction, always vigorously seek *anuttarasamyaksaṃbodhi*.

1. Delighting in all kinds of giving (*nānāvidhadānādhimukta*), they love to bestow all gifts[215].

2. Undertaking strict commitments (*dṛḍhasamādānastha*), they do not trangress against morality (*śīlaskandhaṃ na tyajanti*).

3. Displaying great trappings[216], possessing the power of great patience (*mahākṣāntibalopeta*), they are evenminded (*samacitta*) towards all beings.

4. Giving themselves over to vigour (*ārabdhavīrya*), they seek all the good dharmas (*sarvakuśaladharmān paryeṣante*). Their bodies (*kāya*) and minds (*citta*) are not idle (*akusīda*); they seem like men trying to save their hair which is ablaze[217].

5. Skilled in mindfulness and attention (*smṛtisaṃprajanyakuśala*)[218], they can acquire the four absorptions (*dhyāna*).

6. Seeking wisdom (*prajñāparyeṣin*), they exercise the Bodhi of the Buddhas.

Having long practised those six perfections (*ṣaṭpāramitā*), they

212 See Vkn, p.20 and n.

213 Also called *asaṃmukha, asamakṣa* or *viparokṣa*; cf. above, n.200.

214 The Tib. says: lazy (*kusīda*) bss.

215 In Tib.: *bdog pa thams cad yoṅs su gtoṅ ba* 'abandon all their riches (*sarvasvaṃ parityajanti*)'.

216 In Skt. *mahāsaṃnāhasaṃnaddha*; cf. n.154.

217 The Tib. is more literal: *mgo daṅ gos la me ḥbar ba ltar* = *ādīptaśiraścailopama* 'Like someone whose head and clothes were on fire'. This is a well-known expression; see Gaṇḍavyūha, p.493, *2*; Śikṣāsamuccaya, p.54, *3-4*; Mahāvyutpatti, No.1802; and for the Pāli, Saṃyutta V, p.440, *7*; Aṅguttara II, p.93, *18*; III, p.307, *12*; IV, p.320, *27*; V, p.98, *3*.

218 In Tib. *dran pa daṅ śes bźin la mkhas pa*.

realise the Buddha marks (*buddhalakṣaṇa*)[219].

106. Then other bodhisattvas, the devas, nāgas, yakṣas, gandharvas, etc., reflect thus: 'So vigorous (*evaṃvidhārabdhavīrya*) a bodhisattva is truly extraordinary (*adbhuta*). After how long will he attain *anuttarasamyaksaṃbodhi*? What will his name be? Which will be his field (*kṣetra*)? What will be the number of his śrāvakas?

107. The Buddha, in order to cut off the doubts (*saṃśayacchedana*) of those beings, then gives the prediction: the whole of the assembly (*sarvāvatī parṣad*) hears and understands the prediction; only, and because of the supportive power (*adhiṣṭhānabala*) of the Buddha, the bodhisattva concerned is not able to hear it. The whole of the assembly knows that this bodhisattva will become a Buddha, what his name will be, which will be his field and the number of his srāvakas. Those who doubted will then be sure and will consider this bodhisattva as being the Bhagavat himself (*tasya bodhisattvasyāntike bhagavatsaṃjñām utpādayiṣyanti*). However, the bodhisattva himself [**639b**] will not know whether or not he has obtained the prediction. Such is the 'prediction made unbeknown to the one concerned'.

4. *Anutpattikadharmakṣāntilabdhasaṃmukhavyākaraṇa*

108. 'The prediction conferred in the presence [of him who has acquired the certainty of the non-arising of dharmas]'. A certain bodhisattva has accumulated good roots (*saṃcitakuśalamūla*) for a long time; there is nothing he does not see; he has always practised continence (*brahmacarya*)[220]; he contemplates the not-self (*anātman*) and the empty (*śūnya*)[221] and, concerning all dharmas, he has acquired the certainty that they do not arise (*anutpādakṣānti*).

The Buddha knows that the merits (*puṇya*) and wisdom (*prajñā*) of that man are perfected (*saṃpanna*)[222]; and so, in the midst of a great assembly

[219] They accomplish acts productive of the marks, and it is from this moment that they are predestined; see Kośa IV, p.220 sq.

[220] It is doubtful whether Kumārajīva caught the meaning. The Tib. is more coherent: *ḥdi la byaṅ chub sems dpaḥ dge baḥi rtsa ba bsdus pa yin, yun riṅ po nas tshaṅs par spyod pa mi dmigs par spyad pa . . . yin te*: 'Now, however, the bs has accumulated good roots (*saṃcitakuśalamūla*) and, long since, imperceptibly (*anupalambhena*) observed continence'.

[221] The *pudgala-* and *dharmanairātmyas*.

[222] This concerns a bs of the eighth stage, free of all grasping of an object (*nimittodgrahaṇa*) and effort of thought (*ābhoga*), possessing the 'absolute patience' (*paramārthakṣānti*), namely, the *anutpattikadharmakṣānti*, understanding the true principle (*bhūtanaya*) of things and its fundamental identity (*advaya*) with the Buddhas, definitively (*atyantam*) entered into the predestination of the bss (*avakrāntabodhisattvaniyāma*) and possessing the third certainty (*niyatipāta*): that of the infallible practice (*abandhyacaryā*) which supremely ensures the welfare of

of devas, manuṣyas, Māras, Brahmās, śramaṇas and brāhmaṇas, he confers the prediction on him openly (*saṃmukha*) and says to him: 'Kulaputra, in so many hundreds of thousands of koṭīniyutas of kalpas, you will become a Buddha having such-and-such a name, such-and-such a field, such-and-such a number of śrāvakas and such-and-such a life-span'.

Then innumerable persons, in imitation of that bodhisattva, will arouse the *anuttarasamyaksaṃbodhicitta*. As for him, having received the prediction face to face with the Buddha, he will rise into the air to the height of seven palm trees (*saptatālamātraṃ vaihāyasam abhyudgamiṣyati*)[223]. Such is, O Dṛḍhamati, the fourth prediction, conferred 'in the presence'.

[*Bodhisattvas Having Received the Prediction*]

109. Then the bodhisattva Dṛḍhamati said to the Buddha: Here, in this assembly, are there bodhisattvas who have been the object of the four predictions?

The Buddha replied: Yes, there are some.

Dṛḍhamati asked: Who are they?

The Buddha said:

1. The bodhisattva Siṃhanādanādin[224] 'Roaring the Lion's Roar' and the gṛhapatiputra 'Pleasure-loving'[225] have received the prediction before arousing the thought of Bodhi (*anutpāditacittavyākaraṇa*). Equally, in universes in other regions, innumerable bodhisattvas have also received the prediction before arousing the thought of Bodhi.

2. Moreover, the bodhisattva Śāntimat[226] 'Appeased', the bodhisattva kumārabhūta 'Great Virtue'[227], the bodhisattva Mañjuśrī kumārabhūta[228]

beings. It is on this bs that the Buddhas confer the Great Prediction (*mahāvyākaraṇa*) which always takes place, it seems, in the presence (*saṃmukha*) of the one concerned.

[223] This is a traditional expression, frequently used in Buddhist Sanskrit: Lalitavistara, pp.18, *16*; 350, *20-21*; Divyāvadāna, p.252, *16*; Samādhirāja I, p.88, *12*; Saddharmapuṇḍ., pp.459, *11*; 465, *7*; Laṅkāvatāra, p.16, *6*. It is rarer in Pāli which usually says *vehāsaṃ abbhuggantvā* without defining the height (however, see Dhammapada Comm. II, pp.62, *14*; 100, *5*). The translations in Chinese and Tibetan (*śiṅ ta la bdun tsam du*) show that it does indeed concern the height of the palm tree, and not the span as is sometimes translated.

[224] In Tib. *Seṅ geḥi sgra sgrags*; see Mahāvyut. No.685; Vkn, p.5.

[225] To the Chinese Lo-yu 樂欲 (Chanda?) here corresponds the Tib. Dgaḥi ḥdod (Nandakāma?).

[226] In Tib. Źi ba ldan pa.

[227] *Ta tê* 大德 (Bhadanta?) is not mentioned in the Tibetan version.

[228] In time gone by, in the Anutpādā universe in the Eastern region, when he was the cakravartin king Ākāśa, Mañjuśrī aroused the *cittotpāda* and at the same moment received the prediction from the Buddha Meghasvara; see the Mañjuśrībuddhakṣetraguṇavyūha in T 310, ch.59, p.345*c* 26, and for details, my article on 'Mañjuśrī', *T'oung Pao* XLVIII, pp.17-23.

and innumerable other bodhisattvas have received the prediction after having aroused the thought of Bodhi (*utpāditacittavyākaraṇa*). They are all at the irreversible stage (*avaivartikabhūmi*)[229].

3. Moreover, the bodhisattva Jñānaśūra[230] 'Hero of Knowledge', the bodhisattva Viśeṣamati[231] 'Special Intelligence' and innumerable other bodhisattvas have received the prediction unbeknown to themselves (*rahovyākaraṇa*).

4. Finally, O Dṛḍhamati, I myself[232], Maitreya[233] and the thousand bodhisattvas of the Auspicious Period (*bhadrakalpa*)[234] have all received the prediction conferred in the presence of those who have acquired the certainty of the non-arising of dharmas (*anutpattikadharmakṣāntilabdhasaṃmukhavyākaraṇa*).

The Bodhisattva Dṛḍhamati said to the Buddha: Extraordinary (*adbhuta*), O Bhagavat, are the inconceivable practices of the bodhisattvas (*acintyabodhisattvacaryā*) and the inconceivable predictions

229 This remark, missing in the Tibetan version, is perhaps a note added to the text. It should only be accepted with the reservations formulated in n.209 above.

230 In Tib. *Ye śes dpaḥ bo.*

231 In Tib. *Ḥkhyad par blo gros*. The bs Viśeṣamati is a member of a group of sixteen Satpuruṣas, starting with Bhadrapāla, enumerated with some variants in several Mahāyāna sūtras (cf. Vkn, p.6, n.38). In the Saddharmapuṇḍ., p.19, *4*, Viśeṣamati is one of the eight sons of the Buddha Candrasūryapradīpa.

232 The career of a bs is usually divided into three incalculable periods (*asaṃkhyeyakalpa*). Śākyamuni revered 75,000 Buddhas during the course of the first Asaṃkhyeya, 76,000 during the course of the second, and 77,000 during the course of the third.

For Śākyamuni, the first Asaṃkhyeya ended under the Buddha Ratnaśikhin, at the same time as the *adhimukticaryābhūmi*. The second comprised *bhūmis* 1-7 and ended with Dīpaṃkara. The third comprised *bhūmis* 8-10 and ended with Vipaśyin. See Vibhāṣā, T 1545, ch.178, p.892*c*; Kośa IV, p.227; Nyāyānusāra, T 1562, ch.44, p.591*b*; Upadeśa, T 1509, ch.4, p.87*a* (tr. and notes in Nāgārjuna, *Traité* I, p.248); Sūtrālaṃkāra, p.172; Saṃgraha, pp.209-10.

233 We possess in Sanskrit, Tibetan, Chinese, Tocharian, Old Turkish and Khotanese several accounts or adaptations of the 'Prediction to Maitreya'; see the references in Lamotte, *History*, pp.701-2. The Maitreyavyākaraṇa of Gilgit has been edited by N. Dutt in *Gilgit Manuscripts* IV, pp.187-214.

234 The thousand sons of a cakravartin king – including Śākyamuni and Maitreya – who are or will be the thousand Buddhas of the present Bhadrakalpa received the prediction on several occasions, as it appears in two long jātakas:

1. According to the Tathāgataguhyasūtra (T 310, ch.9, pp.49*a* - 53*a*; T 312, ch.4, pp.712*c* - 716*c*; Tib. Trip. vol.22, pp.56-9, fols 135*a* - 143*a*), the thousand sons of the cakravartin Dhṛtarāṣṭra received the prediction from the Buddha Anantaguṇanānāratnavyūharāja who appeared, during the Vibhūṣaṇakalpa, in the Sudarśanā universe.

2. According to the Vimalakīrtinirdeśa (Vkn, pp.255-7), the thousand sons of the cakravartin Ratnacchattra received the prediction from the Buddha Bhaiṣajyarāja who appeared, during the Vicaraṇakalpa, in the Mahāvyūha universe.

In both cases, the thousand princes were in possession of the *anutpattikadharmakṣānti*.

(*acintyavyākaraṇa*) that they receive! The Śrāvakas and Pratyekabuddhas cannot understand them and, even less so, other beings.

The Buddha said: Dṛḍhamati, the practices (*caryā*) of the bodhisattvas and the vigour (*vīrya*) that they develop as well as their supportive power (*adhiṣṭhānabala*) are inconceivable (*acintya*).

[*Prediction Conferred on the Daughters of the Gods*]

110. Then the devakanyās who had been won over (*vinīta*) by the bodhisattva Māragocarānupalipta and who had aroused the *anuttarasamyaksaṃbodhicitta* scattered celestial flowers (*divyapuṣpa*) over the Buddha and said to him: Bhagavat, we do not like the prediction conferred unbeknown to the one concerned (*rahovyākaraṇa*); we would like to obtain the prediction conferred in the presence of whoever has acquired the certainty of the non-arising of dharmas (*anutpattikadharmakṣāntilabdhasaṃmukhavyākaraṇa*). We would like the Bhagavat to give us now [**639c**] that prediction with regard to *anuttarasamyaksaṃbodhi*.

111. Thereupon the Buddha smiled (*smitam akarot*): from his lips flashed forth rays (*arcis*) of various colours (*nānāvidhavarṇa*) which illuminated all the universes, returned to the Bhagavat and disappeared into his cranial protuberance (*uṣṇīṣe 'ntarhita*)[235].

Ānanda asked: Bhagavat, for what reason are you smiling?

The Buddha said to Ānanda: Do you see these two hundred devakanyās who, with joined hands, are bowing down before the Tathāgata?

Yes, I see them, O Bhagavat.

112. [The Buddha went on]: Ānanda, those devakanyās, in days gone by, in the presence of five hundred Buddhas, deeply planted good roots (*avaropitakuśalamūla*). Henceforth, they will pay homage (*pūjayiṣyanti*) to innumerable Buddhas and, at the end of seven hundred incalculable cosmic periods (*asaṃkhyeyakalpa*), they will become a Buddha with the name of *Vyūharāja[236]. Ānanda, those devakanyās, after their death (*maraṇakālakriyākāle*), will change their female bodies (*strīkāya*) and will all be reborn in the dwelling of the Tuṣita gods where they will pay homage to (*pūjayiṣyanti*) and serve (*upasthāpayiṣyanti*) the bodhisattva Maitreya.

[235] Depending on whether the Buddha intends this or that prediction, the rays that he emits return to him in a fixed part of the body. If he predicts supreme and perfect enlightenment, the rays disappear into his *uṣṇīṣa*. See Divyāvadāna, p.69, *6-7*; Avadānaśataka I, p.6, *1-2*: *yadi Bhagavān anuttarāṃ samyaksaṃbodhiṃ vyākartukāmo bhavaty, uṣṇīṣe 'ntardhīyante.*

[236] In Tib. *Chos bkod pa* = Dharmavyūha.

[*Fallacious Departure of Māra*]

113. Then Māra Pāpīmat, learning that the devakanyās had received the prediction, said to the Buddha: Bhagavat, I have lost all command (*vaśitā*) over my entourage (*parijana*) since it heard the Śūraṃgamasamādhi expounded. What then can be said (*kaḥ punar vādaḥ*) of my other subjects (*anubaddha*)? If they hear the Śūraṃgamasamādhi, they will also become certain of the Buddha attributes (*buddhadharmeṣu niyatā bhaviṣyanti*).

114. Then the devakanyās bold-mindedly (*alīnacittena*) said to Māra Pāpīmat: Do not be distressed, we are not leaving your world (*dhātu*). Why?

The suchness of the world of Māra (*māradhātutathatā*)[237] is the suchness of the world of the Buddha (*buddhadhātutathatā*). Between the *māradhātutathatā* and the *buddhadhātutathatā* there is neither duality (*dvaya*) nor difference (*viśeṣa*). And we do not swerve from that suchness.

The true nature of the world of Māra (*māradhatudharmatā*)[238] is the true nature of the world of the Buddha (*buddhadhātudharmatā*). Between the *māradhātudharmatā* and the *buddhadhātudharmatā* there is neither duality (*dvaya*) nor difference (*viśeṣa*). And we do not leave, do not exceed that true nature.

The world of Māra (*māradhātu*) is nothing precise or definable, and the world of the Buddha (*buddhadhātu*) is also nothing precise or definable. Between the *māradhātu* and the *buddhadhātu* there is neither duality (*dvaya*) nor difference (*viśeṣa*). And we do not leave, nor do we exceed that true nature of things (*dharmatā*)[239].

That is why it should be known that all dharmas are imprecise (*aniyata*) and, since they are imprecise, [for you] there is neither presence of retinue (*parivāra*) nor absence of retinue (*aparivāra*).

115. The Māra Pāpīmat, saddened and aggrieved, wanted to return to his paradise.

The bodhisattva Māragocarānupalipta said to Māra Pāpīmat: Where are you going?

Māra replied: I want to return to the palace where I live.

The bodhisattva went on: Do not leave this assembly, this is your palace.

[237] To *ju* in the Chinese corresponds the Tibetan *de bźin ñid.*

[238] To *hsiang* in the Chinese corresponds the *chos ñid* of the Tibetan.

[239] Cf. the Vkn, p.105, where, even while staying in the Garden of the Dharma (*dharmārāma*), the devakanyās are returned to Māra.

At that very moment Māra Pāpīmat found himself in his own palace.

The bodhisattva asked him: What do you see?

Māra Pāpīmat answered: I find myself back in my own palace: these lovely groves (*ramaṇīyārāma*) and these rivers (*nadī*) belong to me.

The bodhisattva said to him: Well then, now offer them (*niryātaya*) to the Tathāgata.

Māra replied: Agreed!

At the precise moment that he uttered that word, he saw the Tathāgata, the śrāvakas and bodhisattvas: the whole assembly was in his residence and the Buddha was expounding the Śūraṃgamasamādhi [**640a**].

[*Respective Value of Offerings to the Buddha*]

116. Then Ānanda said to the Buddha: Bhagavat, the Buddha was offered the place where he expounds the Śūraṃgamasamādhi, and he was offered the meal (*bhojana*) which he ate before attaining complete enlightenment (*abhisaṃbodhi*). How great are the merits (*puṇya*) gained by the two masters of giving (*dānapati*) who made those offerings to him[240]?

[240] In other words, what are the merits of the two generous *dānapatis* who respectively made an offering to the Buddha of the vihāra where he expounded the Śgs and the meal which he took before reaching enlightenment? The Tibetan version differs and asks which were the respective merits of the two *dānapatis* who offered Śākyamuni the vihāra where he expounded the Śgs and the meal he took before expounding this same sūtra.

According to the text itself (§ 1), the Śgs was expounded at Rājagṛha on the Gṛdhrakūṭaparvata. This is a piece of pious fiction, the principle works of the Great Vehicle having been published around five centuries after Śākyamuni's Nirvāṇa. However, Mahāyāna scholars and Chinese pilgrims accepted to the letter the anachronisms put forward by the Mahāyāna sūtras, and commentators such as Nāgārjuna, Paramārtha, Hsüan-tsang, Hsüan-ts'ê, etc., elaborated a whole theory on the places and dates that the three phases, or more exactly, three 'turnings of the wheel' of the Buddha's teaching took place (cf. É. Lamotte, 'Sur la formation du Mahāyāna', *Festschrift F. Weller*, *Asiatica*, Leipzig 1954, pp.381-2).

Several Mahāyāna sūtras, including the Prajñāpāramitā, Saddharmapuṇḍ., Śgs, etc., were propounded on the Gṛdhrakūṭaparvata. This was one of five mountains surrounding Rājagṛha, present-day Rajgir. Archaeologists still argue over its exact position and hesitate between Śailagiri (Cunningham), Chhathagiri (Sir John Marshall, M.H. Kuraishi and A. Ghosh, D.N. Sen), Udayagiri (B.C. Law) and Ratnagiri (L. Petech). See the bibliography on this question in A. Ghosh, 'Rajgir 1950', *Ancient India* VII, 1951, p.68; L. Petech, *Northern India*..., Rome 1950, pp.44-8; D.N. Sen, 'Sites in Rajgir', *Journal of the Bihar Research Society*, Patna, Buddha Jayanti Issue, 1956, pp.136-58.

At the time of Śākyamuni, the Gṛdhrakūṭa already contained a certain number of residences such as the Paṭibhānakūṭa, the Sītavana, the bank of the river Sappinī, the Paribbājakārāma, the Moranivāpa, the Maddakucchi, the Sūkarakhatalena, etc. When it comes to establishing the site where the great teaching of the Mahāyāna sūtras took place, the choice is superabundant. Fa-hsien and Hsüan-tsang, who respectively visited the Gṛdhrakūṭa in about 404 and 637 C.E., brought back information which they collected on the spot (see T 2085, pp.862*c*-863*a*, tr. Legge, pp.82-4; T 2087, ch.9, p.921*a*-*b*, tr. Watters II, pp.151-2). They are relatively in agreement, but manifestly apocryphal. On the summit of the Gṛdhrakūṭa, Fa-hsien saw the 'temple' (*t'ang*) where the Buddha expounded the Dharma: it was in ruins and only the brick foundations of the walls remained. The pilgrim stayed for a whole night on the spot and, in memory of the earlier divulgation, chanted the Śūraṃgamasamādhi himself. When, two centuries later, Hsüan-tsang went to the same site, the temple had been restored: 'where the Tathāgata had in the past stayed for a long time and expounded the Dharma' there now stood a tall brick vihāra (*chüan ching-shê*) enclosing a life-sized statue of the Buddha. Not far from there, a stūpa marked the spot where the Buddha had uttered the Saddharmapuṇḍarīka.

Fa-hsien and Hsüan-tsang are both agreed in situating the temple of the teaching in the immediate neighbourhood of the places where Devadatta had thrown the rock which injured Śākyamuni on the foot and where Māra, in the shape of a vulture, had terrified Ānanda. The first event is well known to the canonical sources while the second is completely unknown to them. At the time of the two Chinese masters, the Guide to the Pilgrimage to the Gṛdhrakūṭa had already been compiled; mixing the old with the new, it betrays its apocryphal nature.

In such conditions, it is pointless to wonder, with the Śgs, who might have offered the Buddha the vihāra where he expounded the Śgs. In the mind of Hsüan-tsang or the Indian who gave him the information, it was doubtless Bimbisāra, the king of Magadha who, so he could go and hear the Buddha, had built, from the foot of the mountain to its summit, a stone stairway more than ten paces wide and five or six *li* long (T 2087, ch.9, p.921*a* 24-26). All this is mere hypothesis.

Conversely, the Indians were fully informed on the person who offered the Buddha the meal before his Bodhi. According to the Pāli sources, this was Sujātā, daughter of Senāni 'General', from the village of Senani in Uruvelā. She presented the Bodhisattva with a cake prepared with cream collected from the milk of a thousand cows and a handful of new rice (see Nidānakathā in Jātaka I, p.68; Dhammapada Comm. I, p.85; Manorathapūraṇī I, pp.402-3).

However, the Sanskrito-Chinese sources differ slightly from this tradition and sometimes split the generous donatrix into two: according to them, there would have been:

1. A single donatrix: Sujātā (Mahāvastu II, pp.131, *10*; 200, *17*; 205, *3*; 263, *15*; Lalitavistara, pp.265-7, which makes Sujātā one of the ten daughters of the grāmika Nandika; P'u yao ching, T 186, ch.5, p.511*c* 23, which presents the young lady as the daughter of a śreṣṭhin (merchant) from Sujātaka; Tang kuang ta chuang yen ching, T 187, ch.7, p.583*a* 29; Shen mao hsi shu ching, T 757, ch.2, p.599*b* 6).

2. A single donatrix: Nandabalā (Buddhacarita of Aśvaghoṣa XII, v.109, which makes Nandabalā the daughter of a gopādhipa). In the corresponding Chinese version, she is sometimes called Nandā and sometimes Nandabalā (T 192, ch.3, p.24*c* 9 and 11).

3. Two donatrices: the daughters of Sena (Hsiu hsing pên ch'i ching, T 184, ch.2, p.469*c* 13).

4. Two donatrices: the two daughers of the grāmika Sujāta (Fo pên hsing chi ching, T 190, ch.25, p.771*b* 23).

5. Two donatrices: Nandā and Nandabalā, daughters of a gopādhipa (Mūlasarv. Vin, T 1443, ch.1, p.911*a* 8; T 1444, ch.2, p.1026*c* 24; T 1450, ch.5, p.121*c* 9; Chung hsü mo ho ti ching, T 191, ch.6, p.949*b* 24; Fo pên hsing ching, T 193, ch.3, p.75*b* 3).

In the weeks that followed his enlightenment, the Buddha went alms-seeking in Uruvilvā. Sujātā filled his bowl and took 'the two refuges' in the Buddha and the Dharma. The fact is reported in the Mahīśāsaka Vin. (T 1421, ch.15, p.103*b*) and the Dharmaguptaka Vin., where Sujātā is called Sucarā (T 1428, ch.31, p.786*a* 22). On this subject, see the translation and

117. The Buddha replied: Ānanda, the Buddha was offered the meal which he ate before his reaching *anuttarasamyaksaṃbodhi,* he was offered the meal which he ate before setting turning the Wheel of the Dharma (*dharmacakrapravartana*)[241], and he was offered the meal which he ate before expounding the Śūraṃgamasamādhi. Well, the respective merits resulting from those three gifts of food are undifferentiated (*nirviśeṣa*).

118. Ānanda, the place where I attained *anuttarasamyaksaṃbodhi* is the Diamond [Seat] (*vajrāsana*) where all the Buddhas, past (*atīta*), future (*anāgata*) and present (*pratyutpanna*), reach complete enlightenment (*abhisaṃbodhi*). Well, all the places where the Śūraṃgamasamādhi is expounded are absolutely the same (*sama, nirviśeṣa*) as that Diamond Seat[242]. It is also the same for all the places

commentaries by A. Bareau, *Recherches sur la biographie du Buddha*, Paris 1963, pp.127-34.

On that occasion the Buddha proclaimed Sujātā, daughter of Senāni, the foremost of the upāsikā-disciples having been the first to take refuge (Aṅguttara I, p.26, *16-17*). However, in the corresponding passage in the Ekottara (T 125, ch.3, p.560*b* 1), the upāsikā Sujātā is replaced by the upāsikā Nandānandabalā, as if both names designated one and the same person.

However it may be, Buddhists have always considered Sujātā's offering as supremely meritorious because of the excellence of the beneficiary, on this occasion the Buddha who is the best field of merit. Its value is only equalled by the meal, indigestible though it may have been, which the blacksmith Cunda offered to the Master immediately before his Nirvāṇa. This resulted in a formal declaration by the Buddha (Dīgha II, pp.135-6; Sanskrit Mahāparinirvāṇa, pp.282-4): *Dve 'me piṇḍapātā samasamaphalā samasamavipākā ativiya aññehi piṇḍapātehi mahapphalatarā ca mahānisaṃsatarā ca. katame dve. yañ ca piṇḍapātaṃ bhuñjitvā tathāgato anuttaraṃ sammāsambodhiṃ abhisambujjhati yañ ca piṇḍapātaṃ bhuñjitvā tathāgato anupādisesāya nibbānadhātuyā parinibbāyati.*

The thesis upheld here by the Śgs is that all gifts, of vihāra or piṇḍapāta, made to the Buddha or to Dharma instructors are equal and without difference.

241 As far as I know, no Buddhist text mentions a meal taken by the Buddha before the Discourse at Vārāṇaṣī.

242 In the proper meaning of the word, the *bodhimaṇḍa* is the site of the enlightenment at Bodh-Gayā, the Diamond Seat (*vajrāsana*) where the thousand Buddhas of the Bhadrakalpa have attained or will attain enlightenment. In the figurative sense, the *bodhimaṇḍa* indicates the wholly spiritual presence of the Dharma or of the *dharmakāya* of the Buddhas, and this independently of any material location (for details, see Vkn, pp.94-9, n.105). Conceived originally as the place sanctified by the presence of the material body of the Buddhas, the *bodhimaṇḍa* is considered by several Mahāyāna sūtras to be the symbol or quintessence of the Dharma or Buddhist Path. Thus for the Saddharmapuṇḍ., p.391, *6-13*, anywhere that the Sūtra has just been recited, monastery, convent, house, etc., should be considered as the *bodhimaṇḍa*. For the Vimalakīrtinirdeśa (Vkn, pp.94-9), the *bodhimaṇḍa* is quite simply the great Bodhi of the Buddhas and bodhisattvas: wherever they may come from or go to, the bodhisattvas come from the *bodhimaṇḍa*. The Śgs expresses an identical idea by saying that all the places where the Sūtra is expounded are absolutely identical to the Diamond Seat. This is an outline of the theory regarding the bodies of the Buddhas which contrasts the *dharmakāya*, or body of

where the Śūraṃgamasamādhi is taught (*deśita*), recited (*vācita*) or written down (*likhita*).

119. Ānanda, the Buddha was offered the meal which he ate before setting turning the Wheel of the Dharma for the first time. Well, if a Dharma-master (*dharmācārya*) who is about to recite or expound the Śūraṃgamasamādhi is offered a meal, the respective merits resulting from those two offerings are the same (*sama*) and undifferentiated (*nirviśeṣa*).

120. Furthermore, O Ānanda, the Buddha was offered the monastery (*vihāra*) where he won over beings by means of the eighteen supernormal wonders (*ṛddhiprātihārya*)[243]; he was also offered the monastery where he recites and expounds the Śūraṃgamasamādhi. Well, the merits resulting from those two gifts do not differ between themselves.

Then Ānanda said to Māra Pāpīmat: It is of great advantage for you (*mahālābhās te sulabdhāḥ*) to have been able to give your palace to the Buddha so that he may dwell in it.

Māra said: That is the result of the supportive action (*adhiṣṭhāna*)[244] of the bodhisattva Māragocarānupalipta.

[*Exploits of Māragocarānupalipta in the Heroic Progress*]

121. The bodhisattva Dṛḍhamati said to the Buddha: Bhagavat, to perform such great wonders (*vikurvaṇa*), is not the bodhisattva Māragocarānupalipta in Śūraṃgamasamādhi?

The Buddha replied: Dṛḍhamati, it is indeed as you say (*evam etad yathā vadasi*). This bodhisattva is in Śūraṃgamasamādhi and can thus, by means of his supernormal power, proceed at will:

He manifests himself in all the domains of Māra (*māragocara*), but he is not defiled (*upalipta*) by the domains of Māra.

He disports himself (*ramati*) with the daughters of the gods (*devakanyā*), but he does not experience any illicit sexual pleasures (*maithunarati*)[245].

immutable truth, with the *nirmāṇakāyas*, fictitional and provisional bodies which the Buddhas assume out of compassion so as to win over beings.

243 The author doubtless has in mind the Pavilion of Wonders (*prātihāryamaṇḍapa*) which Prasenajit, king of Kosala, built for the Buddha between the town of Śrāvastī and the Jetavana Grove (cf. Mūlasarv. Vin., T 1451, ch.26, p.331*a* 3-5; Divyāvadāna, p.155, *17-19*). It was there that the Buddha performed the *yamakaprātihārya*, multiplied images of himself up to the Akaniṣṭha heaven and where a violent storm raised by the yakṣas completed the routing of the six sectarian masters.

244 Correct *ên li* 恩力 to *shên li* 神力. The Tibetan has *byin gyi rlabs.*

245 In Tib. *ḥkhrig paḥi dgaḥ ba.*

This kulaputra is to be found in Śūraṃgamasamādhi: he enters the palaces of Māra, and yet he never leaves the assembly (*parṣad*) gathered around the Buddha.

He seems to travel through the world of Māra (*māradhātu*), to stroll and amuse himself there, but he makes use of the *buddhadharmas* to win over beings.

[*Exploits of the Buddha in the Heroic Progress*]

122. The bodhisattva Dṛḍhamati said to the Buddha: Bhagavat, when the Tathāgata is in Śūraṃgamasamādhi, how many wondrous feats (*vikurvaṇavyūha*) does he manifest? It would be good, O Bhagavat, if you would reveal to me be it only a small part of it (*kaṃcid eva pradeśam*).

The Buddha said: Dṛḍhamati, I am at present in Śūraṃgamasamādhi.

In this *trisāhasramahāsāhasralokadhātu,* there are a thousand million (*koṭiśata*) Caturdvīpakas, Candrasuryas, Cāturmahārāja devas, Trāyastriṃśa devas, Yāma devas, Tuṣita devas, Nirmāṇarati devas, Paranirmitavaśavartin devas, etc., up to Akaniṣṭha devas [**640b**], Sumeru parvatarājas and Mahāsamudras: this is called a *trisāhasramahāsāhasralokadhātu*[246].

Dṛḍhamati, even while dwelling in Śūraṃgamasamādhi, I am in the *trisāhasramahāsāhasralokadhātu* and, eventually, in Jambudvīpa, I practice, as the case may be, the perfections (*pāramitā*) of giving (*dāna*), morality (*śīla*), patience (*kṣānti*), vigour (*vīrya*), absorptive meditation (*dhyāna*) or wisdom (*prajñā*). In Jambudvīpa I am, as the case may be, a recluse with the five superknowledges (*pañcābhijñarṣi*), or again, a layman householder (*gṛhastha*) or a monk (*pravrajita*).

In Caturdvīpaka, I am, should the occasion arise, a Tuṣita deva separated from Buddhahood by only one existence (*ekajātipratibaddha*), or again a noble Cakravartin king, a Śakra devendra, Brahmarāja, Caturmahādevarāja, Yāma devarāja, Tuṣita devarāja, Nirmāṇarati devarāja, Para-nirmitavaśavartin devarāja, or again a merchant (*śreṣṭhin*), householder (*gṛhapati*), minor king (*koṭṭarāja*), great king (*mahārāja*), kṣatriya, brāhmaṇa or śūdra.

123. In Caturdvīpaka, should the occasion arise, I leave the Tuṣita heaven and descend to be born in the world, or again, I enter the womb, I dwell in the womb, I am born, after my birth I take the seven steps (*saptapada*) and, raising my hand, I proclaim: 'I am the eldest (*jyeṣṭha*) of

246 For details, see Vkn, pp.275-6.

heaven and earth'[247], I dwell in the palace in the midst of the harem (*antaḥpura*), I renounce the world, I practise the austerities (*duṣkaracaryā*), I receive the grass[248], I sit on the *bodhimaṇḍa,* I vanquish Māra, I become Buddha, I meditate [under] the king of trees, Śakra and Brahmā invite me to set turning the Wheel of the Dharma, I set turning the Wheel of the Dharma, I reject the life forces (*āyuḥsaṃskārān utsṛjāmi*)[249], I enter Nirvāṇa, my body is burnt, all my bodily relics (*śarīra*) are preserved, my relics are distributed, my Dharma is on the point of disappearing, my Dharma has disappeared, my life-span (*āyuḥpramāṇa*) is immense, my life-span is short, my field (*kṣetra*) does not contain any bad destinies (*apāya*), my field does contain bad destinies.

Now Jambudvīpa is pure and adorned like a royal palace, now it seems wretched[250], now again, it seems superior (*adhimātra*), middling (*madhya*) or inferior (*avara*).

124. Such is, O Dṛḍhamati, the wondrous power (*vikurvaṇabala*) of the Śūraṃgamasamādhi. The bodhisattva seems to enter Nirvāṇa, but he does not entirely disappear: in the *trisāhasramahāsāhasralokadhātu*, he continues to manifest this wondrous power (*vikurvaṇabala*) and display such marvels (*vyūha*).

Dṛḍhamati, consider the Buddha: for the moment (*etarhi*), in this *caturdvīpaka* here he sets turning the Wheel of the Dharma, but in other Jambudvīpas he has not yet reached Buddhahood and, in yet other Jambudvīpas [**640c**], he is already in Nirvāṇa. This is called the Exposition of the Dharma leading to the Concentration of Heroic Progress (*śūraṃgamasamādhipraveśadharmamukha*).

[*Extension of the Heroic Progress to Other World Systems*]

125. Then, in the assembly, the devas, nāgas, yakṣas, gandharvas, etc., the bodhisattvas and mahāśrāvakas reflected thus: Is it only in this present *trisāhasramahāsāhasralokadhātu* that the Buddha Sākyamuni possesses this supernormal power (*ṛddhibala*), or does he exercise it equally in other universes?

247 Cf. Majjhima III, p.123: *Sampatijāto bodhisatto samehi pādehi patiṭṭhahitvā uttarābhimukho sattapadavītihāre gacchati, setamhi chatte anubhīramāne sabbā ca disā viloketi, āsabhiñ ca vācaṃ bhāsati : Aggo 'ham asmi lokassa, seṭṭho 'ham asmi lokassa, jeṭṭho 'ham asmi lokassa, ayam antimā jāti, na 'tthi dāni punabbhavo ti.*

On the seven steps of the Bs, see Nāgārjuna, *Traité* I, p.6, in the notes.

248 *Kuśa* grass, to be laid on the seat of enlightenment. Śākyamuni received his from Svastika.

249 A traditional expression; cf. Sanskrit Mahāparinirvāṇa, p.212.

250 See in the Vkn, p.22 sq., the transformation of the Sahāloka on the supernormal intervention of the Buddha: Śāriputra, who saw it as impure, suddenly sees all its splendours.

Thereupon Mañjuśrī, knowing the thoughts of the assembly and desiring to cut off the doubts (*saṃśayacchedana*) of the latter, said to the Buddha: Bhagavat, I travel through all the Buddha-fields (*buddha-kṣetra*). Now, in the zenith region (*upariṣṭhād diśi*), if, leaving this universe here, one traverses universes as numerous as the sands of the sixty Ganges (*ito buddhakṣetrāt ṣaṣṭigaṅgānadīvālukopamāni buddha-kṣetrāṇy atikramya*), there is a Buddha universe (*buddhalokadhātu*) called Ekapradīpa 'Single Lamp'; there a Buddha expounds the Dharma to mankind. I went to him and, after saluting his feet by touching them with my head (*tasya pādau śirasābhivandya*), I asked him: 'Bhagavat, what is your name and how should I address you (*ko nāma tvaṃ, kathaṃ dhārayāmi*)?' That Buddha answered me: 'Go and find the Buddha Śākyamuni and he himself will answer you'.

O Bhagavat, the virtues and marvels (*guṇavyūha*) of that Buddha-field are such that, were one to spend a kalpa or more at it, one could not enumerate them all. In that field, the name of Śrāvaka or of Pratyekabuddha is not even mentioned; there is only an assembly of bodhisattvas ceaselessly expounding the irreversible Wheel of the Dharma (*avaivartikadharmacakra*).

Bhagavat, do tell me the name of that Buddha who expounds the Dharma in the Ekapradīpa universe.

126. Then the Buddha [Śākyamuni] said to Mañjuśrī kumārabhūta: Now listen carefully and engrave it well in your mind (*tena hi śṛṇu sādhu ca suṣṭhu ca manasikuru*)[251], but you must not fear or tremble or take fright, or hesitate or doubt (*nottrasitavyaṃ na saṃtrasitavyaṃ na saṃtrāsam āpattavyaṃ na vimativicikitsā utpādayitavyāḥ*)[252]. Why? The supernormal power (*ṛddhibala*) of the Buddhas is inconceivable (*acintya*) and the supremacy (*ārṣabha*) of the Śūraṃgamasamādhi is also inconceivable. Mañjuśrī, he who expounds the Dharma in the Ekapradīpa universe is the Buddha named Sarvaguṇadharmasaṃdarśaka-vikurvaṇaprabhārāja[253] 'King of Wondrous Brilliance manifesting all the Virtues'. O Mañjuśrī, that Buddha Sarvaguṇadharmasaṃdarśaka-vikurvaṇaprabhārāja of the Ekapradīpa universe is myself. In that universe I manifest (*saṃdarśayāmi*) the supportive power of the Buddhas; in that universe I expound the irreversible Wheel of the

[251] Kumārajīva abbreviates this formula which the Tibetan reproduces in full.

[252] This is a stock phrase; cf. Samādhirāja II, p.273, *5-6*; Saddharmapuṇḍ., pp.73, *8-9*; 78, *3*.

[253] In Tib. *Yon tan gyi chos thams cad ston par snaṅ ba rnam par ḥphrul baḥi rgyal po*. He is a Buddha of the zenith region. Further on, in § 170, Śākyamuni will also identify himself with a Buddha from the eastern region.

Dharma (*avaivartikadharmacakra*): it is a 'pure land'[254] cultivated (*prabhāvita*) by me in days gone by.

127. Mañjuśrī, you should know that I exercise this supernormal power everywhere in innumerable (*apramāṇa*) and infinite (*ananta*) koṭinayutaśatasahasrāṇis of *buddhakṣetras,* but the Śrāvakas and Pratyekabuddhas do not know this. Such is, O Mañjuśrī, the supremacy (*ārṣabha*) of the Śūraṃgamasamādhi: bodhisattvas, even while always manifesting such wondrous feats (*vikurvaṇa*) in innumerable universes, never swerve from this *samādhi.*

128. Mañjuśrī, just as the sun (*sūrya*) and moon (*candra*), without ever leaving their palaces (*vimāna*), illuminate villages (*grāma*), towns (*nagara*) and districts (*nigama*)[255], so the bodhisattvas, without ever swerving from the Śūraṃgamasamādhi, manifest themselves everywhere in innumerable universes and expound the Dharma according to the aspirations (*adhimukti*) of beings [**641a**].

[*Faith in the Heroic Progress*]

129. Then the whole assembly was filled with astonishment (*adbhutaprāpta*): well-pleased (*tuṣṭa*), delighted (*udagra*), transported (*āttamanās*), filled with joy and gladness (*prītisaumanasyajāta*)[256]. The innumerable onlookers made salutations, their hands joined (*pragṛhītāñjali*). The devas, nāgas, yakṣas, gandharvas, asuras, garuḍas, kiṃnaras, mahoragas, etc., showered the Buddha with pearl necklaces (*ardhahāra*), marvellous flowers of various colours, powders (*cūrṇa*) and unguents (*vilepana*); they caused every musical instrument (*tūrya*) at the disposal of the gods to sound and praised the Tathāgata. The śrāvakas[257] removed their outer garments (*uttarāsaṅga*) and offered them to the Buddha. The bodhisattvas showered the Buddha with wonderfully coloured flowers, as big as Sumeru, as well as various perfumes (*gandha*), powders (*cūrṇa*), unguents (*vilepana*), necklets of pearls and jewels (*maṇiratnaniska*).

They all exclaimed: Yes, Bhavagat, all the places (*pradeśa*) where the Śūraṃgamasamādhi is expounded are diamond-like (*vajrasama*).

254 *Ching t'u* 淨土 'pure land' belonging to the vocabulary of Chinese Buddhism. Going by the Tibetan version which has *saṅs rgyas kyi źiṅ*, the Sanskrit original translated here was simply *buddhakṣetra*.

255 Kumārajīva abbreviates the traditional enumeration *grāma-nagara-nigama-janapada-rāṣṭra-rājadhānyāḥ*; cf. Vkn, pp.8, 140, 141, 150, 246, 253, 272.

256 Here again, Kumārajīva abbreviates a well-known stock phrase; cf. Vkn, pp.8-9, 160, 234, 264, 270.

257 The punctuation of the Taishō should be corrected.

Those who, having heard this *samādhi,* will believe (*adhimokṣyanti*), grasp (*udgrahīṣyanti*), repeat (*vācayiṣyanti*) and expound it widely to others (*parebhyaś ca vistareṇa saṃprakāśayiṣyanti*), will not fear (*nottrasiṣyanti*) and will not tremble (*na saṃtrasiṣyanti*), those most surely are also diamond-like (*vajrasama*), prompted by an indestructible certainty (*abhedyakṣāntipratilabdha*), firmly established in faith (*prasādaniśrita*), protected by the Buddhas (*tathāgata-parigṛhīta*), endowed with strong good roots (*sthūlakuśalamūla*), having great advantages at their disposal (*sulabdhalābha*), vanquishers of Māra and adversaries (*nihatamārapratyarthika*), freed from the bad destinies (*kṣīṇāpāya*) and protected by spiritual friends (*kalyāṇa-mitraparigṛhīta*).

Bhagavat, as we understand the meaning of the Bhagavat's words (*yāthā vayaṃ, bhagavan, bhagavato bhāṣitasyārtham ājānīmaḥ*)[258], beings who, having heard this Śūraṃgamasamādhi, will believe (*adhimokṣyanti*), grasp it (*udgrahīṣyanti*), repeat it (*vācayiṣyanti*), penetrate it in depth (*paryavāpsyanti*), expound it widely to others (*parebhyo vistareṇa saṃprakāśayiṣyanti*) and apply their effort to it (*bhāvanākāreṇa prayokṣyante*), those beings will definitively and irreversibly be predestined regarding the Buddha attributes (*buddha-dharmaniyata*).

130. The Buddha said: Excellent, excellent, it is indeed as you say (*sādhu sādhu, evam etad yathā vadatha*). Those, however, who have not firmly planted good roots (*anavaropitakuśalamūla*), when they hear this Śūraṃgamasamādhi, do not believe it (*na pattīyanti*)[259]. Few are the beings who, hearing this Śūraṃgamasamādhi, believe it; many are those who, hearing the Śūraṃgamasamādhi, do not believe it.

Kulaputras, if he is endowed with four qualities (*caturbhir dharmaiḥ samanvāgataḥ*), a man can believe (*pattīyati*) this *samādhi* when he hears it. What are those four?

1. In times gone by, under the Buddhas of the past (*atītabuddha*), he heard this *samādhi.*

2. Protected by spiritual friends (*kalyāṇamitraparigṛhīta*), he aspires profoundly (*adhyāśayati*) to Buddhahood.

3. Having accumulated good roots (*kuśalamūla*), he is an aspirant to the good teaching (*udārādhimuktika*).

258 A stock phrase; cf. Vkn, p.252.

259 Cf. Śikṣāsamuccaya, p.174, *15*. On the verb *pattīyati*, *pratīyati*, see Edgerton, *Dictionary*, pp.317, 374.

4. He is a bodily witness to the profound dharmas of the Great Vehicle (*mahāyānagambhīradharmakāyasākṣin*)[260].

If he is endowed with these four qualities, a man can believe the Śūraṃgamasamādhi.

131. Kulaputras, there are also the arhats whose aims are fulfilled (*paripūrṇasaṃkalpa*), those who possess the right view (*dṛṣṭi-saṃpanna*)[261], those who pursue [the truth] under the impulse of faith (*śraddhānusārin*) and those who pursue the truth by means of the Dharma (*dharmānusārin*)[262]. Those men who adhere through faith (*śraddhādhimukta*) to the word of the Buddha (*tathāgatapravacana*) believe the Śūraṃgamasamādhi, but do not witness it bodily (*na tu kāyena sākṣātkurvanti*)[263]. Why? Because this *samādhi* cannot be

260 Regarding *kāyasākṣin*, see below, n.263.

261 The Tib. has *lta ba phun sum tshogs paḥam / rgyun du źugs pa:* 'the *dṛṣṭisaṃpanna* or *srotaāpanna*'. One becomes *srotaāpanna* on the sixteenth and last thought-moment of the *darśanamārga*. The *srotaāpanna* has definitively abandoned the passions which are wrong views (*dṛṣṭi*) of their nature: *satkāyadṛṣṭi*, etc., those which the Kośa (VI, p.257) calls the *avastuka kleśas*. Thus put in possession of right view (*dṛṣṭisaṃpanna*), the *srotaāpanna* is assured of a swift deliverance: he will attain Nirvāṇa after seven rebirths at the most. See also Puggalapaññatti, p.26.

262 Correct *chien-hsing* 見行 to *fa-hsing* 法行.

During the first fifteen thought-moments of the *darśanamārga*, the ascetic, qualified as an ārya and who has entered the predestination (*avakrāntaniyāma*), is a candidate to the first fruit (*prathamaphalapratipannaka*), namely, the fruit of *srotaāpanna*. If his spiritual faculties – *śraddhā*, *vīrya*, *smṛti*, *samādhi* and *prajñā* – are weak (*mṛdvindriya*), the ascetic is a *śraddhānusārin* 'faith-devotee': he pursues the truth (*arthānusevin*) and becomes acquainted with the truths relating to suffering etc. (*duḥkhādisatya*) under the impulse of others, through confidence in others (*parapratyayena*). Conversely, if his spiritual faculties are sharp (*tīkṣṇendriya*), he is a *dharmānusārin* 'Dharma-devotee': he pursues the truth by means of the twelve-limbed texts, sūtras, etc. (see Kośa VI, p.194).

The distinction between *śraddhā-* and *dharmānusārin*, qualifying respectively the ascetic with weak faculties and the ascetic with sharp faculties, persists into the *bhāvanāmārga*, but the wording differs.

The candidate to the fruit of *sakṛdāgāmin*, called candidate to the second fruit (*dvitīyaphalapratipannaka*), who has destroyed the five categories of the passions relating to the Kāmadhātu, and the candidate to the fruit of *anāgāmin*, or candidate to the third fruit (*tṛtīyaphalapratipannaka*), who has destroyed seven or eight categories of the passions relating to the Kāmadhātu, are, according to the degree of their faculties, either *śraddhāprāpta* or *dṛṣṭiprāpta* in that they are informed (*prabhāvita*), the former by faith and the latter by speculative views.

Regarding all this, see Visuddhimagga, ed. Warren, p.566; Kośa VI, p.196; Āloka, p.35 and many other sources as well.

263 The *kāyasākṣin* 'bodily witness' is a type of *anāgāmin*. The clearest explanation, in my opinion, is found in the Āloka, p.36, *3-4*: *Bhavāgraparamaś ca rūparāgavītarāgo dṛṣṭa-dharmaśamaḥ kāyasākṣīti dvividhaḥ*: [The anāgāmin] who has reached [by a rebirth or an

penetrated (*gatimgata*) by the Śrāvakas and Pratyekabuddhas and even less so by other beings.

132. Then the sthavira Mahākāśyapa[264] said to the Buddha: Bhagavat, it is like a man blind from birth (*jātyandha*) who, in a dream (*svapna*), regains his sight (*cakṣus*): he sees all kinds of colours (*rūpa*) and feels great joy; still in a dream [**641b**], he mixes and converses (*pralapati*) with those who enjoy normal sight. However, this blind man, once awakened (*pratibuddha*), no longer sees the colours. Thus we, having heard this Śūraṃgamasamādhi, were well-pleased (*tuṣṭa*), delighted (*udagra*) and transported (*āttamanas*); we thought we had obtained the heavenly eye (*divyacakṣus*)[265], we mixed, we conversed and we debated

attainment] the summit of existence [or fourth and last level of the Ārūpyadhātu] and who is freed from all attachment regarding form [because he has eliminated all the categories of the passions relating to the Kāmadhātu and Rūpadhātu], this anāgāmin is of two kinds: 1. he who has attained Calmness [or Nirvāṇa] during the course of his present existence [in the summit of existence where he was reborn]; 2. he who bodily witnesses Nirvāṇa [in the attainment called *saṃjñāvedayitanirodha* 'cessation of perception and feeling' constituting Nirvāṇa-on-Earth].

Indeed, as defined by the Kośa VI, pp.223-4, the anāgāmin who has acquired *nirodha* is considered as a *kāyasākṣin* (*nirodhalābhy anāgāmī kāyasākṣī punar mataḥ*). The anāgāmin, whichever he may be, who has acquired the attainment of the cessation of perception and feeling, experiences, through his body only – since he has no more mind – a dharma similar to Nirvāṇa (*nirvāṇasādṛśa dharma*), namely, the *nirodhasamāpatti*. How can he immediately experience it through his body only? Because, in the absence of mind, that immediate discernment arises by relying on the body (*cittābhāvāt kāyāśrayotpatteḥ . . . sākṣātkriyā*).

On the *kāyasākṣin* in the writings of the Hīnayāna, see Dīgha III, pp.105, *28*; 254, *1*; Majjhima I, pp.439, *30*; 478, *4-8*; Madhyama, T 26, ch.30, p.616*a* 13 (in the list of the eighteen *śaikṣas*); Aṅguttara I, pp.74, *1*; 118-19; IV, pp.10, *25*; 77, *18*; 215, *10*; Paṭisambhidā II, p.52, *26-33*; Puggalapaññatti, p.14, *29*; Visuddhimagga, ed. Warren, p.566, *5-6 (yo dukkhato manasikaronto passaddhibahulo samādhindriyaṃ paṭilabhati so sabbattha kāyasakkhī nāma hoti*); Vibhāṣā, T 1545, ch.152, p.776*b* 5-7; Kośa VI, pp.223, 273; Kośavyākhyā, p.566; Abhidharmadīpa, p.348; Satyasiddhiśāstra, T 1646, ch.1, p.246*b* 25; Mahāvyutpatti, No.1020 (in the list of the twenty śrāvakapudgalas).

Among the sūtras and śāstras of the Mahāyāna where the *kāyasākṣin* is mentioned, we can consult the Pañcaviṃśati, pp.70, *14* - 71, *7*; Śatasāhasrikā, pp.272, *18* - 273, *18*; Abhisamayālaṃkāra I, vv.23-4 (on the twenty types of holy ones) and its Āloka, pp.35, *14* - 36, *7* (cf. the excellent analysis by E. Obermiller, *Analysis of the Abhisamayālaṃkāra*, London 1933, pp.51-6); Yogācārabhūmi, T 1579, ch.26, p.424*c* 24-26 (in the list of the twenty-eight pudgalas; cf. A. Wayman, *Analysis of the Śrāvakabhūmi*, p.84).

Here the Śgs posits the thesis that the śrāvaka, whatever may be his level on the ladder of the satpuruṣas, is incapable of witnessing bodily the profound realities (*gambhīradharma*) of the Mahāyāna, and in particular the Heroic Progress reserved for the Buddhas and bodhisattvas of the tenth *bhūmi*.

264 In Mahāyāna sūtras, the śrāvakas, particularly Mahākāśyapa, often confess their own inferiority; see Vkn, pp.53, 60-1, 149, 166, 178-80, 228; Saddharmapuṇḍ., pp.60, 210, 211.

265 Regarding the *divyacakṣus*, see Vkn, pp.66-8 and note, 247.

with the bodhisattvas. But now that, from the lips of the Buddha, we have heard this *samādhi*, we know nothing at all of the matter and, like those blind from birth, we know nothing of the dharmas practised by the Buddhas and bodhisattvas. As from today (*adyāgreṇa*), we consider ourselves like those blind from birth, not knowing the profound dharmas (*gambhīradharma*) of the Buddhas, not knowing and not seeing the domain (*gocara*) of the Bhagavat. As from today, we know that the bodhisattvas really possess the heavenly eye and have the profound knowledges (*gambhīrajñāna*). Bhagavat, if a man does not possess the thought of omniscience (*sarvajñacitta*), how could he assert he is knowledgeable (*jñānin*) and that he is a field of merit (*puṇya-kṣetra*)?

The Buddha said: Excellent, excellent, Kāśyapa, it is indeed as you say (*sādhu sādhu, Kāśyapa, evam etad yathā vadasi*). These profound knowledges obtained by the bodhisattvas cannot be attained by either the Śrāvakas or Pratyekabuddhas.

While Mahākāśyapa had been speaking, eight thousand beings aroused the *anuttarasamyaksaṃbodhicitta*.

[*The Field of Merit*]

133. Then the bodhisattva Dṛḍhamati questioned Mañjuśrī kumārabhūta: Mañjuśrī, one speaks of a field of merit (*puṇyakṣetra*)[266]. What is a *puṇyakṣetra*?

[266] On the whole, the merit (*puṇya*) resulting from a gift varies according to the excellence of the giver (*dāyaka*), the thing given (*deya*) and the beneficiary (*pratigrāhaka*). The last, who brings about the fruition of alms bestowed on him, is called a field of merit (*puṇyakṣetra*).

In the scale of values, four kinds of *puṇyakṣetra* can be discerned: the field of merit is distinguished by destiny (*gati*), suffering (*duḥkha*), benefaction (*upakaraṇa*) or virtues (*guṇa*); see Kośa IV, p.236 sq.

1. Field distinguished by destiny. A fruition an hundred times greater is to be expected from a gift made to an animal; a fruition a thousand times greater is to be expected from a gift made to an immoral man, etc.; see Majjhima III, p.255, *14* sq.; Kośavyākhyā, p.320, *31* sq.

2. Field distinguished by suffering. The poor and wretched who are 'a sorry field of merit' and provoke compassion (*karuṇā*); see Abhidharmāmṛtasāra, T 1553, ch.1, p.966*a*; Upadeśa, T 1509, ch.12, p.147*a* (Nāgārjuna, *Traité* II, pp.722-3).

3. Field distinguished by benefaction. The father, mother, master, the benefactors who constitute a 'field of indebtedness' and provoke gratitude. Nevertheless, this still concerns a worldly (*laukika*) and conditioned (*saṃskṛta*) field; see Saddharmasmṛtyupasthāna, T 721, ch.61, p.359*b*; Ta fang pien pao ên ching, T 156, ch.3, p.141*b* 28; ch.5, p.148*c* 12; Upāsakaśīla, T 1488, ch.3, p.1051*c*.

On the subject of filial piety, in no way unknown in India, a particularly noteworthy canonical topic should be pointed out: Aṅguttara I, pp.61-2; Ekottara, T 125, ch.11, p.601*a*; Avadānaśataka I, p.205; Mūlasarv. Vin., T 1448, ch.4, p.16*a* 19-27; Divyāvadāna, pp.51, *19* -

---

52, 3: *Dvinnāhaṃ bhikkhave na suppatikāraṃ vadāmi. Katamesaṃ dvinnaṃ? Mātucca pitucca. Ekena bhikkhave aṃsena mātaraṃ hareyya ekena aṃsena pitaraṃ parihareyya vassasatāyuko vassasatajīvī. So ca tesaṃ ucchādanaparimaddananahāpanasambāhanena te pi tatth' eva muttakarīsaṃ cajeyyuṃ na tveva bhikkhave mātāpitunnaṃ kataṃ vā hoti patikataṃ vā. Imissā ca bhikkhave mahāpaṭhaviyā pahūtasattaratanāya mātāpitaro issarādhipacce rajje patiṭṭhāpeyya na tveva bhikkhave mātāpitunnaṃ kataṃ vā hoti patikataṃ vā. Taṃ kissa hetu? Bahukārā bhikkhave mātāpitaro puttānaṃ āpādakā posakā imassa lokassa dassetāro.*

4. Field distinguished by virtues. These are the members of the Community of disciples (*śrāvakasaṃgha)* which is, by definition (see Woodward, *Pāli Concordance*, p.353*a*), *āhuneyyo pāhuṇeyyo dakkhiṇeyyo añjalikaraṇīyo anuttaraṃ puññakkhettaṃ lokassa* 'Worthy of sacrifices, worthy of offerings, worthy of alms, worthy of being saluted with joined hands, the best field of merit in the world'.

This Community is subdivided into two large classes: the śaikṣas 'those who still train' and the aśaikṣas 'those who have no more to train in' (see the Dakkhiṇeyasutta in Aṅguttara I, p.63; Saṃyukta, T 99, ch.35, p.258*c*). The Madhyamāgama, in a more developed version of the same sutta (T 26, ch.30, p.616*a*) distinguishes eighteen kinds of śaikṣa and nine kinds of aśaikṣa.

The eighteen kinds of śaikṣas are: 1. *śraddhānusārin*, 2. *dharmānusārin*, 3. *śraddhādhimukta*, 4. *dṛṣṭiprāpta*, 5. *kāyasākṣin*, 6. *kulaṃkula*, 7. *ekavīcika*, 8. *srotaāpattiphalapratipannaka*, 9. *srotaāpanna*, 10. *sakṛdāgāmiphalapratipannaka*, 11. *sakṛdāgāmin*, 12. *anāgāmiphalapratipannaka*, 13. *anāgāmin*, 14. *antarāparinirvāyin*, 15. *upapadyaparinirvāyin*, 16. *sābhisaṃskāraparinirvāyin*, 17. *anabhisaṃskāraparinirvāyin*, 18. *ūrdhvasrotas-rūpopaga*.

The nine kinds of aśaikṣa are: 1. *cetanādharman*, 2. *prativedhanādharman*, 3. *akopyadharman*, 4. *parihāṇadharman*, 5. *aparihāṇadharman*, 6. *anurakṣaṇādharman*, 7. *sthitākampya*, 8. *prajñāvimukta*. 9. *ubhayatobhāgavimukta*.

These technical terms are defined in the Abhidharmas, particularly the Kośa, Ch.VI; Āloka, pp.35-6; Abhidharmasamuccaya, pp.88-91.

According to the Ta fang pien fo pao ên ching, T 156, ch.3, p.141*b*; ch.5, p.148*c*, the field of merit constituted by the Saṃgha is transcendental (*lokottara*) and unconditioned (*asaṃskṛta*). According to the Upāsakaśīla, T 1488, ch.3, p.1051*c*, this field of virtues (*guṇakṣetra*) encompasses all the holy ones, from possession of the *uṣmagata* (the first of the *nirvedhabhāgīyas*) up to arrival at *anuttarā samyaksaṃbodhi*. Thus, the Buddha is included in this, and he is considered as the best of all *puṇyakṣetras*; see Avataṃsaka, T 279, ch.13, p.67*b-c*; Mahāmāyāsūtra, T 383. ch.2, p.1013*a* 13; Upadeśa in Nāgārjuna, *Traité* I, p.524.

Regarding the virtues (*guṇa*) which make the Saṃgha a superior field of merit, the texts do not agree: the lists compiled in the early writings differ from those drawn up by the Mahāyānists.

According to Majjhima I, pp.446, *29* - 447, *6*, ten virtues, called of the aśaikṣa, are required of a bhikṣu for him to be a *puṇyakṣetra*: the Eightfold Path, *samyagdṛṣṭi*, etc., plus right knowledge (*samyagjñāna*) and right deliverance (*samyagvimukti*). Harivarman, a Hīnayāna master and native of Kāśmīr who lived in the third century, counts twelve of them: having destroyed the *kleśas* of *rāga-dveṣa-moha*, etc. (Satyasiddhiśāstra, T 1646, ch.1, p.246*c* - 247*a*.

The Mahāyāna claims a special place for the bodhisattvas in the honours list of the holy ones. If the sūtras, in their introductions (*nidāna*), usually mention the arhats before the bodhisattvas, this is bowing to tradition. The Upadeśa in Nāgārjuna, *Traité* I, p.235, remarks on this subject: 'Even though the bss come after the Buddha, they have not destroyed all their passions; this is why the arhats are spoken of first [in the *nidānas*]. Among arhats, wisdom is paltry, but they are already ripened (*paripakva*); among bss, wisdom is rich, but they have not destroyed their passions. That is why the arhats are spoken of first. But there are two kinds of

Mañjuśrī replied: If one is endowed with ten qualities (*daśabhir dharmaiḥ samanvāgataḥ*), one is a *puṇyakṣetra*. What are those ten?

1. Dwelling in the three doors to deliverance (*vimokṣamukha*): emptiness (*śūnyatā*), signlessness (*ānimitta*) and wishlessness (*apraṇihita*)[267], but not entering into absolute certainty (*dharmaniyāma*)[268].

2. Seeing and knowing the four Noble Truths (*catuḥsatyajñāna-darśana*), but not reaping the fruit of the Path (*na tu mārgaphala-sākṣātkāraḥ*)[269].

3. Arousing the eight liberations (*aṣṭavimokṣa*)[270], but not abandoning

Buddhadharmas: the esoteric (*abhisaṃdhidharma*) and the exoteric (*prakāśitadharma*). In the exoteric, the Buddhas, Pratyekabuddhas and arhats are all fields of merit, because their passions are destroyed without any remainder. In the esoteric it is said that the bss have acquired the *anutpattikadharmakṣānti*, that their passions are destroyed, that they are possessed of the six *abhijñās* and work for the benefit of beings. It is by putting itself in the exoteric point of view that the sūtra places the arhats before the bss'.

From this new concept comes the tendency henceforth of defining the *puṇyakṣetra*, no longer as a function of the śaikṣas and aśaikṣas, but as a function of the bss. The present passage of the Śgs (§§ 133-4) is quite categorical in this respect. It admits that the Buddha declared the great arhat Subhūti to be 'foremost of the *dakṣiṇeyas*', that is, of the *puṇyakṣetras*, but only in relation to the other śrāvakas and not in relation to the bss. Subhūti admits here to not himself possessing any of the ten virtues required for being a true *puṇyakṣetra* as conceived by Mañjuśrī. The ten virtues listed in § 133 pertain exclusively to the bss, coupling with wisdom (*prajñā*) that skill in means (*upāyakauśalya*) which makes their conduct seem apparently contradictory because it has no other aim than to win over beings (see the references in Vkn, pp.LVII-LVIII).

The same point of view is represented by the Guṇapuṇyakṣetra, T 683, p.777*a* 17-22: 'In the Saṃgha, there are five pure virtues constituting a *puṇyakṣetra*; to venerate it is to gain merit and progress towards Buddhahood. What are those five? 1. to arouse the thought (*cittotpāda*) and leave the world so as to embrace the Path; 2. to destroy one's own ornaments (*anuvyañjana*) so as to dress as a monk; 3. to reject definitively affections so as not to be for or against anyone; 4. to sacrifice one's life so as to follow the Good; 5. to seek resolutely the Mahāyāna so as to deliver mankind'.

All the above discussions arise from the perfection of giving (*dānapāramitā*) known as worldly (*laukikī*), which practises alms-giving while remaining attached to the provisional notions of a giving subject, recipient and thing given (see Pañcaviṃśati, pp.263, *22* - 264, *13*). However, there exists a transcendental (*lokottarā*), triply pure (*trimaṇḍalapariśuddhā*) *dānapāramitā*: the bs, when he makes a gift, no longer perceives either a giver, beneficiary or object given, or fruition (*bodhisattvo dānaṃ dadan nātmānam upalabhate pratigrāhakaṃ nopalabhate dānaṃ ca nopalabhate tadvipākaṃ ca nopalabhate*); he applies this giving to supreme Bodhi, but does not perceive Bodhi; see Pañcaviṃśati, pp.18, *7-9*; 183, *20-22*; 264, *16-22*; Upadeśa in Nāgārjuna, *Traité* II, p.724.

[267] Cf. Vkn, p.48, n.16.

[268] See above, § 104, n.210.

[269] The fruit of the Path, namely, Nirvāṇa which normally results from the knowledge and practice of the four Noble Truths.

[270] Cf. Vkn, p.53, n.25.

the bodhisattva practices (*bodhisattvacaryā*).

4. Arousing the triple knowledge (*traividyā*)[271], and still travelling through the triple world (*traidhātuka*).

5. Manifesting the figure (*saṃsthāna*), colours (*varṇa*) and bodily attitudes (*īryāpatha*) of a śrāvaka, but not being a mere repeater (*ghoṣānuga*)[272] seeking to learn the Dharma from the lips of another (*parato dharmaparyeṣin*).

6. Manifesting the figure, colours and bodily attitudes of a Pratyekabuddha[273], but expounding the Dharma with unfailing eloquence (*anācchedyapratibhāna*).

7. Dwelling always in absorption (*dhyāna*) and attainment (*samāpatti*), but at the same time exercising the bodhisattva practices (*bodhisattvacaryā*).

8. Never swerving from the right Path (*mārga*), but pretending to enter the wrong paths (*kumārga*)[274].

9. Seeming to be strongly attached to pleasures (*saṃrakta*), but being detached (*virakta*) from all the passions (*kleśa*).

10. Entering Nirvāṇa, but not destroying or abandoning Saṃsāra[275].

It should be known that a man endowed with these ten qualities is a true *puṇyakṣetra*.

134. Then the bodhisattva Dṛḍhamati said to Subhūti: Āyuṣmat Subhūti, the Bhagavat has called you the foremost among the *puṇyakṣetras*[276]. Do you possess those ten qualities?

Subhūti replied: I do not possess even one of them, let alone all ten.

Dṛḍhamati went on: Then why are you called the foremost among the *puṇyakṣetras*?

Subhūti replied: Compared with the Buddhas and bodhisattvas, I am not the foremost among *puṇyakṣetras*; it is only in relation to śrāvakas

[271] Cf. Vkn, p.40, n.38.

[272] In Tib. *sgraḥi rjes su soṅ*.

[273] In theory, if the Pratyekabuddhas do not teach the Dharma, this is through timidity and lack of courage (Kośa III, p.196). According to the Mahāyāna, their Nirvāṇa is not definitive: at the end of their career, they are in a sort of catalepsy called 'Nirvāṇa resembling an extinguished light' (*pradīpanirvāṇaprākhyanirvāṇa*), but they are awakened from it by the exhortations of a Buddha and they then enter the Mahāyāna Path, the one and only way leading to deliverance (Āloka, pp.133-4).

[274] See above, § 31, n.91.

[275] Regarding this *apratiṣṭhitanirvāṇa*, see Vkn, p.45, n.8.

[276] Subhūti was proclaimed by the Buddha to be the foremost of those who are worthy of offerings (*dakkhiṇeyyānaṃ aggo*), *dakkhiṇeyya* being synonymous with *puṇyakṣetra*; see Aṅguttara I, p.24, *9*; Manorathapūraṇī I, p.221, *12-13*. He was also the foremost of the *araṇavihārins* and of those who practise the *śūnyatāsamādhi*. See the references in Vkn, pp.54-5, in the notes.

and Pratyekabuddhas that the Buddha proclaimed me the foremost among *puṇyakṣetras* [**641c**].

O Dṛḍhamati*, it is like a minor border king (*pratyantajanapadānāṃ koṭṭarājaḥ*): he also is called king, but if a noble Cakravartin king goes to the border, all the minor kings lose the title of king, for then there is only a noble Cakravartin king whose royal majesty is infinitely superior (*bahvantaraviśiṣṭa*) to theirs. Equally, O Dṛḍhamati, in the kingdoms, villages (*grāma*), towns (*nagara*) and districts (*nigama*)[277] where there are no bodhisattvas, I have the title of *puṇyakṣetra*, but wherever there are Buddhas or great bodhisattvas, I lose the title of *puṇyakṣetra*. Indeed, bodhisattvas possess omniscience (*sarvajñacitta*): that is why they are superior to me.

Thereupon, the Buddha congratulated (*sādhukāram adāt*) Subhūti: Excellent, excellent, it is indeed as you say (*evam etad yathā vadasi*): that is the word of a great śrāvaka devoid of pride (*anabhimānika*).

[*The Truly Learned*]

135. Again, the bodhisattva Dṛḍhamati asked Mañjuśrī kumārabhūta: Mañjuśrī, one speaks of the learned (*bahuśruta*)[278] What is a *bahuśruta*?

*† the original French version had Subhūti's name twice in this paragraph – corrected to Dṛḍhamati with the agreement of É. Lamotte.

277 See above, § 128, n.255.

278 Already in the early texts, the *bahuśruta* 'he who has heard much' holds an important place. *Bahuśruta* is the term given to him who has heard and retained the Word of the Buddha, specifically the nine or twelvefold Dharma. Here are a few canonical texts where this notion is defined:

1. Vinaya II, p.95, *32-36*; Majjhima III, p.11, *19-24*; Aṅguttara II, pp.22, *23* - 23, *5*; III, p.114, *21-26* (the Cullaniddesa II, p.212, gives a typical definition): *Bahussuto hoti sutadharo sutasannicayo; ye te dhammā ādikalyāṇā majjhimakalyāṇā pariyosānakalyāṇā sātthaṃ sabyañjanaṃ kevalaparipuṇṇaṃ parisuddhaṃ brahmacariyaṃ abhivadanti tathārūpā 'ssa dhammā bahussutā honti dhātā vacasā paricitā manasānupekkhitā diṭṭhiyā suppaṭividdhā*: 'He has heard much, he memorises what he has heard and stores up what he has heard; the teachings, good in the beginning, good in the middle and good at the end, whose meaning is good and whose letter is good (cf. the corresponding Sanskrit phrasing: *svartha, suvyañjana*), which propounds the entirely fulfilled and perfectly purified brahman conduct, these teachings are much heard by him, recalled, familiar in their enunciation, examined by the mind and well penetrated by right view'.

2. The dharmas in question are indeed the authentic teachings: it is the Word of the Buddha as it appears in the writings.

Aṅguttara II, pp.147, *28-29*; 170, *1-2*: *Bhikkhu bahussuto āgatāgamo dhammadharo vinayadharo mātikādharo*: 'The *bahussuta,* monks, knows the texts and has memorised the Dharma, the Discipline and the moral teachings.'

Aṅguttara II, p.178, *12-16*: *Bahu kho bhikkhu mayā dhammā desitā – suttaṃ geyyaṃ*

Mañjuśrī replied: If someone, hearing a religious discourse of a single phrase (*ekapādika dharmamukha*), can analyse the hundred thousand koṭīnayutas of meanings (*artha*) in it, develop and explain it for an hundred, a thousand or ten thousand kalpas without exhausting

veyyakaraṇaṃ gāthā udānaṃ itivuttakaṃ jātakaṃ abbhutadhammaṃ vedallaṃ. Catuppādāya ce pi bhikkhu gāthāya atthaṃ aññāya dhammaṃ aññāya dhammānudhammapaṭipanno hoti bahussuto dhammadharo ti alaṃ vacanāyā ti: 'Monks, I have widely imparted the teachings: suttas, etc. Now, if a monk knows the meaning and knows the teaching, be it only a verse of four feet, and behaves in conformity with the teaching, that is sufficient for him to be called a *bahussuta* who has memorised the teaching'.

The present wording refers only to the ninefold writings, suttas, etc., while the corresponding passage in the Madhyamāgama (T 26, ch.45, p.709*b* 7-8) mentions the twelvefold writings. Regarding the distribution of these two classifications throughout the canonical texts, see Lamotte, *History*, pp.143-7.

3. The *bahussuta* appears in a canonical list of seven good dhammas, faith, etc. (Dīgha III, pp.252, *11*; 282, *26*; Majjhima III, p.23, *15*).

4. Erudition also has a place in the series of predictions which relate to the duration of the Saddharma, predictions which diverge considerably from each other (see Lamotte, *History*, 191-202). According to the Vinayamātṛkā of the Haimavatas (T 1463, ch.3, p.818*c* 8), the Saddharma lasts for five centuries, and the fourth is characterised by the predominance of the *bahuśruta*. According to the Mahāsaṃnipāta (T 397, ch.55, p.363b 3), the Saddharma continues for five periods of five centuries and, during the third, the bhikṣus are *bahuśruta*.

5. In Aṅguttara I, pp.24, *32* - 25, *3*, the Buddha proclaimed the five pre-eminences of Ānanda: *aggo bahussutānaṃ, satimantānaṃ, gatimantānaṃ dhitimantānaṃ upaṭṭhākānaṃ*. During the twentieth year of his public ministry he attached Ānanda to his person as an *upasthāyaka* or attendant (see Vkn, p.79 in the notes). The reason which dictated this choice to him was less the unflinching devotion of the disciple as his prodigious erudition, which enabled him to memorise the words of the Teacher and to expound the Dharma correctly.

In the Hīnayānist Mahāparinirvāṇasūtra (Dīgha II, pp.144-6; Sanskrit Mahāparinirvāṇa, pp.298-302; Aṅguttara II, p.132), the Buddha declares that Ānanda is the best of all the attendants that the Tathāgatas have had or will ever have. The great disciple is learned (*paṇḍita*) and knows when to introduce into the Teacher's presence those who come to visit him. Besides, he possesses four wonderful qualities (*āścarya-adbhūta-dharma*): all the assemblies that come to him rejoice at the sight of him and delight in his teachings.

These considerations are taken up and amplified in the Mahāyānist Mahāparinirvāṇasūtra (T 374, ch.40, p.601*c* 18 sq; T 375, ch.36, p.850*a* 17): 'Endowed with eight qualities, the bhikṣu Ānanda is capable of memorising perfectly the twelvefold writings: 1. his faculty of faith (*śraddhendriya*) is firm; 2. his thought is correct; 3. his body is free of disease; 4. he constantly exerts vigour (*vīrya*); 5. he is gifted with mindfulness (*smṛti*); 6. his mind is free of pride (*abhimāna*); 7. he has perfected *samādhi* and *prajñā*; 8. he is gifted with wisdom born of listening (*śrutamayī prajñā*)'. These eight qualities characterised the *upasthāyakas* who succeeded each other in the service of the last seven Buddhas; these *upasthāyakas* were named Aśoka, Kṣemakara, Upaśānta, Bhadrika, Svastika, Sarvamitra and, finally, Ānanda.

However, the thesis upheld here by the Śgs, which once again is in unison with the Vkn, p.228, is that the pre-eminences in which the great disciples rejoice apply only to śrāvakas and are worthless with regard to bodhisattvas. The least bodhisattva is infinitely superior to the greatest of the śrāvakas.

either his knowledge (*jñāna*) or his eloquence (*pratibhāna*), then he is a *bahuśruta*.

Moreover, O Dṛḍhamati, the bodhisattva[279] who, as soon as he hears them, can remember (*dhāraṇa*) all the words of the innumerable Buddhas of the ten regions, the bodhisattva for whom there does not exist a single phrase (*pada*) not already heard before (*apūrvaśruta*), the bodhisattva for whom what is commonly heard is the already-heard, the bodhisattva who remembers (*dhārayati*) things just as he hears them (*yathāśrutam*) and without forgetting them (*asaṃpramoṣam*), the bodhisattva who expounds to beings while there are no beings, the bodhisattva who does not make any distinction (*viśeṣa*) between his own self (*ātman*), the beings (*sattva*) and the thing expounded[280] that bodhisattva, say I, is *bahuśruta*.

136. Now there was in the assembly a bodhisattva devaputra named Vimalacandragarbha[281] 'Spotless Moon Essence', who had this thought: The Buddha proclaimed Ānanda the foremost of the *bahuśrutas*; is Ānanda truly a *bahuśruta* such as Mañjuśrī has just defined it? Having had that thought, he questioned Ānanda: The Tathāgata, he said to him, has proclaimed you the foremost of the *bahuśrutas*. Is your learning (*bahuśrutya*) like that which Mañjuśrī has just defined?

Ānanda replied: I do not in any way possess the learning that Mañjuśrī has just defined.

Vimalacandragarbha asked: Why then has the Tathāgata always proclaimed you the foremost of the *bahuśrutas*?

Ānanda replied: The disciples (*śrāvaka*) of the Buddha obtain deliverance (*vimukti*) in so far as they repeat the words of the Master (*ghoṣānuga*): it is among them that the Buddha proclaimed me the foremost. But he never said that I was the foremost of the *bahuśrutas* among the bodhisattvas, immense seas of knowledge (*apramāṇajñāna-samudra*), endowed with unequalled wisdom (*asamaprajñā*) and unobstructed eloquence (*apratihatapratibhāna*).

O devaputra, it is because the sun (*sūrya*) and moon (*candra*) illuminate them that the men of Jambudvīpa see figures (*saṃsthāna*) and colours (*varṇa*) and carry out their activities (*karmakāraka*). Equally, it is only because of the brilliance of the wisdom (*prajñāprabhā*) of the Tathāgata that I have managed to remember his Dharma. In this respect I

279 The punctuation of the Taishō should be corrected.

280 The same idea is expressed in the Vkn, p.48, § 7.

281 In Tib. *Zla ba dri ma med paḥi sñiṅ po* [† on the correct name of this devaputra in Sanskrit, see Foreword, p.xv].

have no personal power at my disposal; the matter should be attributed to the supernormal power (*ṛddhibala*) of the Tathāgata.

Then the Bhagavat congratulated (*sādhukāram adāt*) Ānanda: Excellent, excellent, it is indeed as you say (*sādhu sādhu, evam etad yathā vadasi*) [**642a**]. If you remember and if you have memorised the teachings, that is due to the supernormal power of the Tathāgata.

137. Then the Buddha said to Vimalacandragarbha: The dharmas remembered by Ānanda are very few; those that he has not understood are innumerable and infinite.

O devaputra, of all the dharmas that I acquired on the seat of enlightenment (*bodhimaṇḍa*), I have not expounded the hundred-thousand-hundred-millionth part of them, and of the little that I have expounded Ānanda has not remembered an hundred-thousand-hundred-millionth part of them[282].

Let us consider, O devaputra, what the Tathāgata, in a single day and a single night, expounds to the Śakras, Brahmarājas, Lokapāla devarājas, devas, nāgas, yakṣas, gandharvas, devaputras and bodhisattvas who inhabit all the universes of the ten regions. By means of the power of his knowledge (*jñānabala*) he composes *gāthās*, he expounds *sūtras*, *nidānas*, *avadānas*[283] *sattvacaritas* and *pāramitās*, he expounds the Śrāvaka- and Pratyekabuddhayānas, and the Anuttarayāna of the Buddhas containing the Mahāyāna Teaching, he belittles Saṃsāra and upholds Nirvāṇa. Let us suppose that all the beings of Jambudvīpa were as learned as Ānanda. Well now, were they to devote an hundred thousand kalpas to it, they would not be able to memorise [the teachings which have just been mentioned]. That is why, O devaputra, it should be known that the dharmas expounded by the Tathāgata are innumerable and infinite and that what Ānanda has remembered of them is very little.

[*Prediction to Vimalacandragarbha*]

138. Then the devaputra Vimalacandragarbha offered the Tathāgata

282 A minor matter in relation to all that the Buddha taught, but objectively considerable if we refer to the old stanza uttered by Ānanda (Theragāthā, v.1024; Mahāsāṃghika Vin., T 1425, ch.32, p.491*c* 23; Vibhāṣā, T 1545, ch.74, p.385*c* 11; Avadānaśataka II, p.155, *8*:

Dvāsītiṃ buddhato gaṇhi, dve sahassāni bhikkhuto
caturāsīti sahassāni ye 'me dhammā pavattino.

'I have learnt 82,000 articles of the Dharma from the lips of the Buddha and 2,000 from the lips of the bhikṣu (Śāriputra); therefore 84,000 dharmas exist within me'.

283 Kumārajīva abbreviates as usual, mentioning only the four *aṅgas* of the writings, whereas the Tibetan version quotes all twelve of them (see Lamotte, *History*, pp.145-6).

an hundred thousand parasols (*chattra*) adorned with the seven jewels (*saptaratnamaya*). At the same instant those parasols covered (*ācchādayanti sma*) the firmament (*antarikṣa*), and the beings who were covered by them took on the colour of gold (*suvarṇavarṇa*)[284].

After having offered those parasols, the devaputra said: O Bhagavat, I wish that, owing to my merit (*puṇya*), all beings may expound the Dharma with the same eloquence (*pratibhāna*) as yours and that they may remember the Dharma as well as does Mañjuśrī kumārabhūta.

Thereupon the Buddha, knowing the high resolve (*adhyāśaya*) concerning Buddhahood which motivated the bodhisattva devaputra, predicted (*vyākaroti sma*) *anuttarasamyaksaṃbodhi* to him, saying: This devaputra, in four hundred and four hundreds of thousands of kalpas, will become a Buddha under the name of Ekaratnacchattra[285] 'Single Precious Parasol', and his *kṣetra* will be called Sarvaratnacitā[286] 'Set with all the Jewels'.

[*Provisional Nature of Pratyekabodhi*]

139. When the Buddha had ended those words, two hundred bodhisattvas experienced discouragement (*līnacitta*) and thought: The teachings (*dharma*) of the Bhagavat Buddhas are too profound (*atigambhīra*) and *anuttarasamyaksaṃbodhi* is too difficult to attain (*sudurlabha*); we are not capable of achieving these things; it would be better to enter Nirvāṇa by means of the Vehicle of the Pratyekabuddhas[287].

284 See in Vkn, pp.6-9, an identical offering and wonder.

285 In Tib. *Rin po cheḥi gdugs gcig pa.*

286 In Tib. *Rin po che thams cad kyis spras pa* [† see Foreword, p.xv, for a more accurate name in Sanskrit].

287 The text mentions several falterings (*vyāvartana*) of this type. The Vkn, p.60, presents us with some monks who 'formerly were pledged to the Great Vehicle', but had just lost the *bodhicitta*. Vimalakīrti expounded the Dharma so eloquently to them that they became incapable of turning back (*avaivartika*) from supreme and perfect enlightenment.

However, the strangest case is that of Śāriputra, the greatest of the śrāvakas. The Upadeśa, T 1509, ch.12, p.145*a* (cf. Nāgārjuna, *Traité* II, p.701), reproduced by the Ching lü i hsiang, T 2121, ch.14, p.69*b*, relates an unusual story about him. Śāriputra had, for sixty kalpas, practised the 'way of the bss' (the Great Vehicle). One day, a beggar asked him for his eye. Śāriputra, who wanted to 'cross the stream of giving', hesitated but gave it to him and the beggar threw it to the ground and trod on it. Upset by this attitude, Śāriputra renounced 'the way of the bss' and returned to the Small Vehicle.

Nonetheless, if we are to believe the Saddharmapuṇḍ., p.65, this faltering was only temporary: according to the Buddha's prediction, Śāriputra will be a bs in the future and, after an incalculable number of kalpas, will become the Tathāgata Padmaprabha.

A special property of the bss known as *avaivartika* 'irreversible' is to be sheltered from

Why? Because the Buddha has said: 'Bodhisattvas who falter become either Pratyekabuddhas or Śrāvakas'.

140. Thereupon Mañjuśrī kumārabhūta, comprehending the discouragement (*līnacitta*) of those two hundred bodhisattvas, wished to dissuade them from their resolve so as to cause them to acquire *anuttarasamyaksaṃbodhi*. He also wished to ripen (*paripācana*) the assembly with its devas, nāgas, yakṣas, gandharvas, asuras, garuḍas, kiṃnaras and mahoragas. That is why he said to the Buddha: Bhagavat, I remember [**642b**] that in days gone by (*atīte 'dhvani*), during the kalpa called Virocana[288] 'Shining', in the course of three hundred and sixty hundreds of thousands of existences, I entered Nirvāṇa[289] by means of the Vehicle of the Pratyekabuddhas.

Then the whole assembly (*sarvāvatī parṣad*), utterly disconcerted (*saṃśayajāta*), thought: If he has entered Nirvāṇa, he would not have returned to new births (*pratisaṃdhibandha*)[290]. So why does Mañjuśrī say: 'Bhagavat, I remember that in days gone by, during the kalpa called Virocana, in the course of three hundred and sixty hundreds of thousands of existences, I entered Nirvāṇa by means of the Vehicle of the Pratyekabuddhas'? What does this mean?

141. Then Śāriputra, empowered by the Buddha (*buddhānubhāvena*), asked the latter: Bhagavat, if someone has already entered Nirvāṇa, he

such vicissitudes and, as we have seen earlier, the bs is not absolutely *avaivartika* until the eighth *bhūmi*, when he is in possession of the *anutpattikadharmakṣānti*.

The career of the bs functions from his first *cittotpāda*, as is shown in a passage of the Bodh. bhūmi, p.13, *13-20*: *sa ca bodhisattvasya prathamaś cittotpādaḥ samāsena dvividhaḥ: nairyāṇikaś cānairyāṇikaś ca. tatra nairyāṇiko ya utpanno 'tyantam anuvartate na punar vyāvartate. anairyāṇikaḥ punar ya utpanno nātyantam anuvartate punar era vyāvartate. tasya ca cittotpādasya vyāvṛttir api dvividhā: ātyantikī cānātayantikī ca. tatrātyantikī yat sakṛdvyāvṛttaṃ cittaṃ na punar utpadyate bodhāya. anātyantikī punaḥ yad vyāvṛttaṃ cittaṃ punaḥ punar utpadyate bodhāya*: 'Briefly, the first arousal of the thought by the bs is twofold: conducive to deliverance or not conducive to deliverance. Conducive to deliverance is that which, once aroused, continues to the end and does not waver. Not conducive to deliverance is that which, once aroused, does not continue to the end but wavers. The wavering of this arousal of the thought is also twofold: definitive or non-definitive. It is definitive when the thought, once wavering, never more aims at Bodhi. It is non-definitive when the thought, after wavering, once again always aims at Bodhi'.

All this deserves to be compared with the theories relating to the Gotras (cf. Vkn, pp.303-7), but there is some lack of clarity.

288 In Tib. *Rnam par snaṅ ba*.

289 Parinirvāṇa, according to the Tib.

290 To *shêng ssŭ hsiang hsü* 生死相續, in Chinese, corresponds *ñid mtshams sbyor ba* in the Tibetan version, which gives the Skt *pratisaṃdhi* (cf. Mahāvyut., No.2164). This is 'rebirth'; see Kośa III, pp.50-3.

cannot return to new births. So how could Mañjuśrī, after having entered Nirvāṇa, have been reborn again?

The Buddha replied: You can ask Mañjuśrī yourself and he will answer you.

[*Mañjuśrī's Fictitious Nirvāṇa*]

142. Then Śāriputra questioned Mañjuśrī and said to him: If someone has already entered Nirvāṇa, he cannot return to new births. So how can you say: 'Bhagavat, I remember that in days gone by, during the kalpa called Virocana, in the course of three hundred and sixty hundreds of thousands of existences, I entered Nirvāṇa by means of the Vehicle of the Pratyekabuddhas'? What does this mean?

Mañjuśrī replied: The Tathāgata now present is all-knowing (*sarvajña*) and all-seeing (*sarvadarśin*)[291]; he tells the truth (*satyavādin*), he tells of reality (*tattvavādin*) and he does not lie (*na vañcayati*); never does he deceive the world with its gods and mankind (*sadevamanuṣya loka*). Now this Buddha in person bears witness (*sākṣin*) to my words and, if I were to speak otherwise (*anyathā*), I would deceive the Buddha.

143. O Śāriputra, at that time, during the Virocana kalpa, there appeared in the world a Buddha named Puṣya[292]. After having been of benefit to the world with its gods and mankind, he entered Nirvāṇa. After his Nirvāṇa, his Good Dharma lasted for one hundred thousand years. After the disappearance of that Good Dharma (*saddharma-vipralopa*), beings could not find the conditions for deliverance except with the Pratyekabuddhas. Even if hundreds of thousands of koṭis of Buddhas had expounded the Dharma to them, they would not have believed and would not have accepted it. It was only through the bodies (*kāya*), bodily attitudes (*īryāpatha*) or teachings (*dharma*) of the Pratyekabuddhas[293] that they could be won over. And all those beings aspired to the Bodhi of the Pratyekabuddhas. At that time, no Pratyekabuddha was present, and those beings had no opportunity whatsoever to plant good roots (*kuśalamūla*).

144. So it was then that, in order to ripen them (*paripācanārtham*), I

[291] Cf. Saddharmapuṇḍ., p.123, *4*.

[292] In Tib. *Rgyal*, the name of an asterism (Mahāvyut., No.3192) borne by a Buddha, the eighteenth of the twenty-four Tathāgatas of the past, according to the Buddhavaṃsa, pp.50-1. He also appears in Mahāvastu, III, p.240, *6* and sq.; Avadānaśataka II, p.175, *14*; Lalitavistara, pp.5, *10*, 172, *7*; Gaṇḍavyūha, p.206, *12*. The reading Puṣpa given in certain manuscripts is doubtless wrong (cf. Edgerton, *Dictionary*, p.350).

[293] The punctuation of the Taishō should be corrected.

pretended to be a Pratyekabuddha. In all the kingdoms (*rāṣṭra*), villages (*grāma*), towns (*nagara*) and districts (*nigama*)[294], I was believed to be a Pratyekabuddha. Furthermore, I manifested (*saṃdarśayāmi sma*) the figure (*saṃsthāna*), colours (*varṇa*) and bodily attitudes (*īryāpatha*) of a Pratyekabuddha. All those beings revered me (*pūjayanti sma*) deeply and offered me alms-food (*piṇḍapāta*). After having received and eaten it, I considered their previous conditions (*pūrvapratyaya*) and the teachings which it suited them to hear; I expounded to them, then I rose into the air (*antarikṣam abhyudgamam*), like the swan king (*rāja-haṃsa*)[295]. Then the beings felt great joy and, filled with respect, they saluted me with their heads, saying: 'We would like, in future times (*anāgate 'dhvani*), **[642c]** to obtain virtues and advantages like those of this man'. O Śāriputra, it is with this method (*tena paryayeṇa*) that I led an innumerable and incalculable number of beings to plant good roots (*kuśalamūla*).

145. Then, considering and knowing that those men who offered me my food were having feelings of discouragement (*līnacitta*), I declared to them: 'The time of my Nirvāṇa has arrived'. The hundred thousand beings, having heard those words, took up flowers (*puṣpa*), perfumes (*gandha*), various essences and oil (*taila*), and came to me. Then I entered the attainment of cessation (*nirodhasamāpatti*) but, in accordance with my previous aspirations (*pūrvapraṇidhāna*)[296], I did not enter Parinirvāṇa entirely (*atyantam*). The beings said that I was dead; in order to honour me, they burnt my body with perfumed fuel (*gandhendhana*) and asserted that I was truly in Parinirvāṇa.

146. Afterwards, I once more went to other capitals (*rājadhānī*); I represented myself as a Pratyekabuddha; there again, the beings came to offer me alms-food (*piṇḍapāta*). At that time, I pretended to enter Nirvāṇa and, once again, I was said to be in Parinirvāṇa. The people came to revere me and burnt my body.

[294] See above, § 128, n.255.

[295] This is a traditional expression.

[296] Earlier aspirations formulated before the Buddha Meghasvaraghoṣa by Mañjuśrī who was, at that time, the good king Ākāśa of the Anutpāda universe. See my article, 'Mañjuśrī', *T'oung Pao* XLVIII, 1960, pp.17-23, and, for the aspiration in question, the Mañjuśrībuddhakṣetra-guṇavyūha (T 318, ch.2, pp.896*c* - 899*b*; T 310, ch.59, pp.345*b* - 347c; T 319, ch.2-3, pp.912*b* - 915*b*; Tib. Trip., Vol.23, pp.128-32, fols 315*a* - 325*b*). The most characteristic is reproduced in its original text by the Śikṣāsamuccaya, p.13:

Nāhaṃ tvaritarūpeṇa bodhiṃ prāptum ihotsahe/ parāntakoṭiṃ sthāsyāmi satvasyaikasya kāraṇāt//

'I am in no hurry to attain enlightenment and I will remain here below until the end, as long as there is a being to be delivered'.

147. So it is, Śāriputra, that at that time, for a whole small kalpa (*antarakalpa*), in the course of three hundred and sixty hundreds of thousands of existences, I was a Pratyekabuddha and pretended to enter Nirvāṇa. In all the capitals (*rājadhānī*), one after the other, I delivered thirty-six hundreds of thousands of beings through the Vehicle of the Pratyekabuddhas. So it is, Śāriputra, that a bodhisattva who enters Nirvāṇa through the Vehicle of the Pratyekabuddhas is not in Parinirvāṇa for ever[297].

148. When Mañjuśrī had spoken those words, the *trisāhasmahāsāhasralokadhātu* trembled in six ways (*ṣaḍvikāram akampata*)[298] and was filled with a great radiance (*mahatā prabhayā pariṣphuto 'bhūt*). In order to pay homage to Mañjuśrī kumārabhūta, a thousand hundreds of thousands of devas caused celestial flowers (*divyapuṣpa*) to shower down and said: It is truly extraordinary (*adbhuta*): today we have obtained great advantages (*lābhā naḥ sulabdhāḥ*), we have seen the Bhagavat Buddha, we have seen Mañjuśrī kumārabhūta and we have heard the Śūraṃgamasamādhi. O Bhagavat, Mañjuśrī kumārabhūta possesses truly extraordinary qualities (*adbhutadharma*). In which *samādhi* is he to be found to manifest such extraordinary qualities?

[*Exploits of the Bodhisattvas in the Heroic Progress*]

149. The Buddha said to the devas: Mañjuśrī kumārabhūta is to be found in the Śūraṃgamasamādhi; that is why he can do such extraordinary (*adbhuta*) and difficult (*duṣkara*) things.

1. The bodhisattva in Śūramgamasamādhi affects to be following the truth under the impulse of faith (*śraddhānusārin*)[299], but he does not rely

[297] See the Upadeśa, T 1509, ch.75, p.586*a* 28 sq.: 'The bss know perfectly well the beings who can be delivered [only] by the Pratyekabuddhas; that is why, knowing this, they carry out the feats of a Pratyekabuddha. Thus, according to the Śūraṃgamasamādhisūtra, Mañjuśrī made himself a Pratyekabuddha seventy-two hundreds of thousands of times. And it is the same with the other bss'.

[298] See Mahāvyut., Nos 3019-30: 1. *Pūrvā dig unnamati paścimā dig avanamati*; 2. *paścimā dig unnamati pūrvā dig avanamati*; 3. *dakṣiṇā dig unnamaty uttarā dig avanamati*; 4. *uttarā dig unnamati dakṣiṇā dig avanamati*; 5. *antād unnamati madhyād avanamati*; 6. *madhyād unnamaty antād avanamati*.

The phrasing differs; see Lalitavisatra, pp.51-2, 410-11; Pañcaviṃśati, p.8; Śatasāhasrikā, p.13.

According to the Upadeśa in Nāgārjuna, *Traité* I, pp.473-4, this is the 'superior' earthquake, with six movements. The middling and inferior ones have four and two respectively.

[299] The canonical sources (Saṃyutta V, p.202; Saṃyukta, T 99, ch.26, p.183*a*) distinguish eight classes of 'noble individuals' (*āryapudgala*) pledged to the Buddhist Path; four are already in possession of the fruit of the religious life (*śrāmaṇyaphala*), four are merely candidates to those fruit (*phalapratipannaka*). These eight *āryapudgalas* are:

---

1. The arhat.
2. The candidate to the fruit of arhat (*arhatphalapratipannaka*).
3. The anāgāmin.
4. The candidate to the fruit of anāgāmin.
5. The sakṛdāgāmin.
6. The candidate to the fruit of sakṛdāgāmin.
7. The srotaāpanna.
8. The candidate to the fruit of srotaāpanna, also called the candidate to the first fruit (*prathamaphalapratipannaka*).

This classification is in descending order, the first step to be taken chronologically being that of the *prathamaphalapratipannaka*. That is why this last is also known as an eighth-level holy one: *aṣṭamaka* in Sanskrit, *aṭṭhamaka* in Pāli (see Patisambhidāmagga II, p.193, *34*; Kathāvatthu I, pp.243-51; Nettipakaraṇa, pp.49, *33*; 50, *1*; Mahāvastu I, pp.120, *9*; 159, *8*; Kośa VI, p.201).

While the other seven holy ones are pledged to the path of meditation (*bhāvanāmārga*), the *prathamaphalapratipannaka* or *aṣṭamaka* is still on the path of the vision of the Truths (*satyadarśanamārga*). The latter, as we know, consists of sixteen thought-moments (*cittakṣaṇa*) the details of which can be found in my *History*, pp.614-16.

Scholars of the Small and Great Vehicles are in agreement in placing the *prathamaphalapratipannaka* in the first fifteen moments of the path of vision. Here are three definitions taken respectively from Vasubandhu, Haribhadra and Asaṅga:

a. Kośa VI, pp.191-4: *Dṛṅmārgas tatra pañcadaśa kṣaṇāḥ, mṛdutīkṣṇendriyau teṣu śraddhādharmānusāriṇau, ahīnabhāvanāheyau phalādyapratipannakau*: 'In the path of vision, during the [first] fifteen [thought-] moments, the ascetic with dull faculties and the ascetic with sharp faculties who are [respectively] *śraddhānusārin* and *dharmānusārin* and who have not yet destroyed [the passions of the Kāmadhātu] to be abandoned on the path of meditation, are both "candidates to the first fruit"'.

b. Āloka, p.35, *15-17*: *Ṣoḍaśakṣaṇadarśanamārgam āśritya pañcadaśasu darśanamārgacittakṣaṇeṣu śraddhādharmānusāribhedena prathamaphalapratipannako dvividhaḥ*: 'The holy one who, moving through the path of vision consisting of sixteen moments, finds himself in the [first] fifteen thought-moments of the path of vision is a candidate to the first fruit, and he is of two kinds depending on whether he is a *śraddhānusārin* or a *dharmānusārin*'.

c. Abhidharmasamuccaya, ed. Pradhan (original part), p.88, *19*: *Srotaāpattiphalapratipannakaḥ katamaḥ. Nirvedhabhāgīyeṣu pañcadaśasu darśanamārgacittakṣaṇeṣu yaḥ pudgalaḥ*: 'What is the candidate to the fruit of srotaāpanna [or first fruit]? It is the man who is to be found in the [first] fifteen thought-moments of the path of vision, moments referring to the penetration [of the four Noble Truths]'.

Between these identical formulas, however, hide different realities, since śrāvakas and bss pursue different aims:

a. In the perspective of the former, we can say that the *prathamaphalapratipannaka* is a *saṃyaktvaniyāmāvakrānta* Ārya 'entered into the certainty of acquiring the Absolute Good or Nirvāṇa'. In fact, this is a quality which is obtained from the very first thought-moment of the Darśanamārga (cf. Kośa VI, p.180 sq.). Besides, this candidate to the first fruit is assuredly inferior to the holder of the first fruit, namely, the srotaāpanna. The prerogatives of the latter are well known: he occupies the sixteenth thought-moment of the Darśanamārga, which coincides with the first moment of the Bhāvanāmārga; his deliverance is certain and rapid: he will attain Nirvāṇa after seven rebirths at the most among the men or gods of the Kāmadhātu (*saptakṛdbhāvaparama*) and he is incapable of falling into a bad destiny (*avinipātadharman*).

---

b. However, from the point of view of the Mahāyāna, the ideal is not to attain Nirvāṇa, definitive *nirodha*, but to reach supreme and perfect enlightenment by devoting onself to the welfare and happiness of all beings. Also, the career of a bs, parallel to that of a śrāvaka, differs from it in respect of its fruit and results. The Prajñāpāramitās have applied themselves to drawing up its stages and, borrowing from the vocabulary of the śrāvakayāna, distinguish twenty categories of holy ones, but – and this is essential – the final outcome of this career is not entry into Nirvāṇa but arrival at Buddhahood through the winning of *anuttarasamyaksaṃbodhi*.

Detailed explanations of this career can be found in the Pañcaviṃśati, pp.60-72 (tr. E. Conze, *The Large Sūtra on Perfect Wisdom*, London 1961, pp.33-41) and the Śatasāhasrikā, pp.266-81; a concise explanation in the Abhisamayālaṃkāra I, vv.23-4 (tr. E. Conze, *Abhisamayālaṃkāra*, Rome 1954, pp.11-13) and its commentary, the Āloka of Haribhadra, pp.35-6 (tr. E. Obermiller, *Analysis of the Abhisamayālaṃkāra* I, London 1933, pp.51-6).

To return to the *prathamaphalapratipannaka* or *aṣṭamaka*, a holy one of lesser degree, we find in the Pañcaviṃśati, p.60, *7-10*, the following definition: *yo bodhisattvo mahāsattvo 'nena prajñāpāramitāvihāreṇa viharati sa itaś cyuta ihaiva buddhakṣetre upapadyate anyebhyo vā buddhakṣetrebhyaś cyutas tuṣitebhyo vā devebhyaś cyuta ihopapadyate, iti bodhisattvāṣṭamakaḥ*: 'The bs residing in this residence of perfect wisdom dies in this world here and is reborn in this buddhakṣetra here, or else he dies in other buddhakṣetras or among the Tuṣita gods and is reborn here: such is an *aṣṭamaka* bs'.

If I properly understand the elliptical thought of this passage, the *aṣṭamaka* bs is he who, after a career of greater or lesser length, will attain *samyaksaṃbodhi* in the present buddhakṣetra, and this no matter where he comes from. Concurrently, the *aṣṭamaka* śrāvaka, after a certain number of rebirths among the gods or humans of the Kāmadhātu, reaches his end in the Kāmadhātu, but the end for him is Nirvāṇa and not *samyaksaṃbodhi*.

The mere mention of the *aṣṭamaka* in § 149 of the Śgs proves that its author knew of the speculations relating to the career of the holy ones. He was also fully informed on the ten stages of the bss which he mentioned in § 21. This is because, independently of the speculations on the twenty types of holy ones, the larger Prajñāpāramitās (Pañcaviṃśati, pp.214-25; Śatasāhasrikā, pp.1454-73; Aṣṭādaśāḥ., T 220, ch.490-1. pp.490*b* - 497*b*) have devoted a whole section to the ten bs stages. These do not yet have the characteristic names of Pramuditā, etc., which were to designate them later on, starting with the Daśabhūmikasūtra. Nonetheless, they are the object of a very detailed and completely original analysis, without any reference to the levels of the traditional Buddhist Path. Nevertheless, since nothing is wasted in the Buddhist tradition, very early on there was an attempt to establish a more general format encompassing within a single framework the śrāvaka stages and the bs stages, while still maintaining the necessary differences. This is what the Upadeśa in Nāgārjuna, *Traité* V, p.2383, calls the *Kung-ti* 共地, the stages common (*sādhāraṇabhūmi*) to both Vehicles.

These common stages are listed in the following sources:

a. Pañcaviṃśati, pp.225, *16-18*; 235, *18-19*; T 221, ch.4, p.29*b* 25-26; T 222, ch.7, p.199*a* 1-2; T 223, ch.6, p.259*c*, 12-14; ch.17, p.346*b* 5-6; T 220, Vol.VII, ch.416, p.88*c* 20-21.

b. Śatasāhasrikā, pp.1473, *11-16*; 1520, *20-22*; T 220, Vol.V, ch.55, p.309*b* 21-23.

c. Aṣṭādaśasāhasrikā, pp.183, *24-26*; 197, *4-8*; T 220, Vol.VII, ch.491, p.497*b* 14-15.

d. Āloka, p.104, *3-11*.

e. Mahāvyutpatti, Nos 1141-7 (listing the first nine only).

These common stages (s.) are eleven in number:

1. *Śuklavipaśyanā*- or *Suklavidarśanabhūmi*, s. of insight (but the old Chinese translations and notably Kumārajīva read *Śuṣkavidarśanabhūmi* and in consequence translated as *Kan-hui-ti* 乾慧地, s. of dry wisdom).

2. *Gotrabhūmi*, s. of spiritual lineage.
3. *Aṣṭamakabhūmi*, s. of the eighth-level holy one.
4. *Darśanabhūmi*, s. of vision.
5. *Tanubhūmi*, refined s.
6. *Vītarāgabhūmi*, s. of renunciation.
7. *Kṛtāvibhūmi*, s. of the one who has ended his career.
8. *Śrāvakabhūmi*, s. of the śrāvakas.
9. *Pratyekabuddhabhūmi*, s. of the Pratyekabuddhas.
10. *Bodhisattvabhūmi*, s. of the bodhisattvas.
11. *Buddhabhūmi*, s. of the Buddhas.

Haribhadra, in his Āloka, p.104, *3-9*, supplies the following details: 1. The *gotrabhūmi* pertains to those who possess the lineage of the śrāvakas, etc.; 2. the *aṣṭamakabhūmi* pertains to the prathamaphalapratipannaka (see above); 3. the *darśanabhūmi* pertains to the srotaāpanna; 4. the *tanubhūmi* pertains to the sakṛdāgāmin; 5. the *vītarāgabhūmi* pertains to the anāgāmin; 6. the *kṛtāvibhūmi* pertains to the arhat; 7. in the absence of a special word to designate it (*viśeṣavacanābhāvena*), the *śrāvakabhūmi* pertains to the pratipannakatraya [i.e. śrāvakas who are respectively candidates to the second, third and fourth fruits]; 8. the *pratyekabuddhabhūmi* pertains to the Pratyekabuddhas; 9. the *bodhisattvabhūmi* pertains to the bss of whom we have spoken and is of nine kinds [Pramuditā, Vimalā, Prabhākarī, Arciṣmatī, Sudurjayā, Abhimukhī, Dūraṃgamā, Acalā and Sādhumatī]; 10. having gone beyond these nine *bhūmis* and being found in the tenth *bhūmi* [the Dharmameghā], the bs should quite simply be called Buddha but not yet Samyaksaṃbuddha, according to the assertion of the Pañcaviṃśatisāhasrikā'.

Haribhadra's interpretation has become essential to modern exegesis. E. Obermiller, who was the first to study it in detail, seems to have made it his own (cf. *Analysis of the Abhisamayālaṃkāra*, London 1933-43, pp.176-9; 'The Doctrine of the Prajñā-pāramitā', *Acta Orientalia* XI, 1932, pp.48-51). And in his turn, E. Conze was inspired by him in the useful tables he devoted to the Path of the śrāvakas pratyekabuddhas on the one hand, and the bss on the other (cf. 'Maitreya's Abhisamayālaṃkāra', *East and West* V, 1954, pp.6-7; 'Marginal Notes to the Abhisamayālaṃkāra', *Sino-Indian Studies* V, Nos 3-4, 1957, pp.6-11; *The Large Sūtra on Perfect Wisdom*, London 1961, p.200).

Haribhadra's interpretation establishes a definite division between the śravaka stages (the first eight on the list, Śuklavipaśyanā, etc.) and those of the bs (No.10 on the list). However, in so doing, it runs directly counter to the spirit and intentions of the Prajñāpāramitā and the Mahāyāna. Undoubtedly bodhisattvas have their own stages (Pramuditā, etc.), but they can *also* occupy the stages of the career of the śrāvakas and Pratyekabuddhas.

Indeed, we read in the Pañcaviṃśati, p.225, *16-18*, and the Śatasāhasrikā, p.1473, *11-16*, that the bs, after having gone beyond (*atikramya*) nine *bhūmis*: Gotrabhūmi, Aṣṭamaka, Darśana, Tanu, Vītarāga, Kṛtāvin, Śrāvaka, Pratyekabuddha and Bodhisattvabhūmi, is established in the Buddhabhūmi, the tenth bs stage. It therefore follows that the first eight are not reserved *exclusively* for the śrāvakas and Pratyekabuddhas, but pertain *also* to the bss.

The Vimalakīrtinirdeśa (Vkn, pp.128-33), expatiates at length on the immensity of the domain (*gocara*) traversed by the bss, the domain, it says, where, among others, the attitudes of the śrāvakas and Pratyekabuddhas are manifested (*ibid.*, p.132).

§ 149 of the Śgs which occupies us here is also just as categoric: its bs affects to be at will a *śraddhānusārin* or *dharmānusārin* (the two types of *prathamaphalapratipannaka*), *aṣṭamaka*, *srotaāpanna*, *sakṛdāgāmin*, *anāgāmin*, *arhat*, *śrāvaka*, *pratyekabuddha*. In §§ 140-7, it showed us Mañjuśrī entering Nirvāṇa via the Pratyekabuddha Vehicle throughout 360 hundreds of thousands of existences. In § 156, it will show us Maitreya simultaneously occupying, in various places in the cosmos, the most varied of states and stages. In § 157, it will be said that the bs penetrates the practices of all the paths (*sarvamārgacaryā*): śrāvakayāna, Pratyekabuddhayāna and Mahābuddhayāna.

None should object too much that such a mastery of practice is only valid for the bss in the tenth stage, in Śūraṃgamasamādhi, for the answer has already been given by Dṛḍhamati in § 51: to be in Śgs is not to be anywhere.

It is pointless to pursue any further the demonstration of a thesis harped on eternally by all the Mahāyāna sūtras. We simply note the narrowness of view of a Haribhadra who attributes certain stages to the śrāvakas and Pratyekabuddhas and reserves others for the bss.

However, other exegetes have been able to see more clearly, particularly the author or authors of the Upadeśa (Nāgārjuna, *Traité* V, p.2382 sq.): 'There are two kinds of stages: 1. the stages pertaining only to the bss; 2. the stages in common (*sādhāraṇabhūmi*). The common stages go from the Śuṣkavidarśanabhūmi to the Buddhabhūmi. The stages particular to the bss are Pramuditā, Vimalā, Prabhākarī, Arciṣmatī, Sudurjayā, Abhimukhī, Dūraṃgamā, Acalā, Sādhumatī and Dharmameghā: their characteristics are described at length in the Daśabhūmikasūtra'.

It goes without saying that the stages common to the Small and Great Vehicles are not practised in the same way or in the same spirit, as it depends on whether a śrāvaka or a bs is concerned. On this subject once again the Upadeśa (T 1509, ch.75, pp.585*c* 26 - 586*a* 25) supplies useful though somewhat summary details:

'Here the Buddha explains again how peerless Bodhi can be attained. From the first arousal of the thought (*prathamacittotpāda*), bss exercise Prajñāpāramitā and accomplish (*paripūrayanti*) the *bhūmis* from the first to the tenth. These *bhūmis* are the aids which achieve peerless Bodhi. These ten bhūmis are the Śuṣkavidarśanabhūmi, etc.

'1. The *Śuṣkavidarśanabhūmi* is of two kinds: of a śrāvaka or of a bs. For a śrāvaka, it is only for Nirvāṇa that he exerts his vigour (*vīrya*), morality (*śīla*), purification of the mind (*cittaviśodhana*) and things profitable for deliverance (*mokṣabhāgīya*). Sometimes he practises-contemplates the *samādhis* of the Buddhas or the meditation on the repulsive (*aśubhabhāvanā*); sometimes he practises good-will (*maitrī*), compassion (*karuṇā*) or the contemplation of impermanence etc. (*anityādivipaśyanā*). He particularly assembles all the good dharmas and rejects bad dharmas. But even though he possesses *jñāna* and *prajñā,* he does not acquire the waters of the *dhyānas* and *samāpattis* and, since he cannot attain Bodhi, this stage is called stage of dry wisdom. For a bs, this stage begins with the first arousal of the thought (*prathamacittotpāda*) and continues for as long as he has not obtained the preparatory certainty (*anulomikī kṣānti*).

'2. The *Gotrabhūmi*. For a śrāvaka, this is [the four aids to penetration (*nirvedha-bhāgīya*)] from heat (*uṣmagata*) to supreme worldly dharmas (*laukikāgradharma*). For the bs, it is the obtaining of the preparatory certainty (*anulomikī kṣānti*); he is attached to the true nature of things (*dharmāṇāṃ bhūtanaya*), no longer holds false views (*mithyādṛṣṭi*) and obtains the waters of the *dhyānas* and *samāpattis*.

'3. The *Aṣṭamakabhūmi*. [For a śrāvaka], this goes from the *duḥkhe dharmajñānakṣānti* to the *mārge 'nvayajñānakṣānti*: namely the [first] fifteen thought-moments (*cittakṣaṇa*) [of the Darśanamārga]. For a bs, it is the *anutpattikadharmakṣānti* and entry into the bs pre-destination (*bodhisattvaniyāma*).

'4. The *Darśanabhūmi*. [For a śrāvaka], it is the candidate to the first fruit (*prathamaphala-pratipannaka*), that is, the srotaāpanna fruit. For a bs, it is the irreversible stage (*avaivartikabhūmi*).

'5. The *Tanubhūmi*. [For a śrāvaka], it is either the srotaāpanna or sakṛdāgāmin, for then six [read *liu* 六 instead of *chiu* 九] categories of the passions relating to the Kāmadhātu are on others in order to believe.

2. He affects to be following the truth by means of the Dharma (*dharmānusārin*) but, concerning the nature of things (*dharmatā*) and the turning of the Wheel of the Dharma (*dharmacakrapravartana*), he is without irreversibility or shortcoming.

3. He affects to be an eighth-level holy one (*aṣṭamaka*)[300], but for innumerable incalculable cosmic periods (*asaṃkhyeyakalpa*), he travels the Path (*mārgaṃ carati*) for those who have fallen into the eight corruptions (*aṣṭamithyātvapatita*)[301].

4. He affects to have entered the stream of Nirvāṇa (*srotaāpanna*) but, for beings drawn into the stream of Saṃsāra (*saṃsārasrotovāhita*), he does not enter the certainty (*niyāma*) [concerning the acquisition of the absolute good][302].

5. He affects to return only once [among mankind] (*sakṛdāgāmin*),

destroyed (*kāmāvacaraṣaṭprakāraklesaprahāṇāt*). For a bs, it is the stage that goes beyond the irreversible stage and continues as long as he has not become a Buddha: he destroys the passions (*kleśa*), and the pervasions of the passions (*kleśavāsanā*) which still remain are slight (*tanu*).

'6. The *Vītarāgabhūmi*. [The śrāvaka] who has destoyed all attachments and passions relating to the Kāmadhātu is named anāgāmin. The bs, by reason of the abandoning of the passions (*vairāgya*), obtains the five Abhijñās.

'7. The *Kṛtāvibhūmi*. The śrāvaka obtains the knowledge of the destruction of defilements (*āsravakṣayajñāna*) and the knowledge of their non re-arising (*anutpādajñāna*): he becomes an arhat. As for the bs, he reaches the Buddhabhūmi.

'8. The *Pratyekabuddhabhūmi*. In former existences, [the Pratyekabuddha] had planted the causes and conditions of the Bodhi of the Pratyekabuddhas. In the present existence, obtaining a partial [view] of causality, he leaves the world (*pravrajati*) and, contemplating the profound causality (*gambhīredaṃpratyayatābhāvanayā*), he achieves Bodhi and is called a Pratyekabuddha. Pratyeka in the language of the Ch'in means 'causality' and [he who knows it] is also called Buddha.

'9. The *Bodhisattvabhūmi*. It goes from the *Śuṣkavidarśanabhūmi* to the *Vītarāgabhūmi* of which we have just spoken. Besides, [the stages] from the *Pramuditābhūmi* to the *Dharmameghābhūmi* are called Bodhisattvabhūmis. Some say that [the stages] which go from the first arousal of the thought (*prathamacittotpāda*) to the diamond-like concentration (*vajropamasamādhi*) [consisting of the destruction of the ninth and last category of the passions of the Bhavāgra] are called bs stages.

'10. The *Buddhabhūmi*. This consists of the Buddha attributes: knowledge of things in all their aspects (*sarvākārajñāna*), etc. The bs, in the stages that are his own (*svabhūmi*) is perfected with regard to the practice (*ācārasaṃpanna*) of the stages of others (*parabhūmi*), he is perfected with regard to deliberation (*vicārasaṃpanna*). [Here], he is perfected with regard to two things: that is why he is called Perfect'.

Obviously, the author of the Śgs knows of all these speculations, but he has not yet systematised them.

300 *Aṣṭamaka* or *prathamaphalapratipannaka*; see preceding note.

301 See Vkn, p.53, n.25, and p.177.

302 Cf. above, § 7, n.13.

but he shows himself everywhere in all the worlds (*lokadhātu*).

6. He affects not to be reborn again [in the Kāmadhātu] (*anāgāmin*), but he returns once again in order to ripen beings (*sattvaparipācanārtham*).

7. He affects to be a holy one (*arhat*), but he continues to exert his vigour (*vīryam ārabhate*) in search of the Buddha attributes (*buddhadharmaparyeṣanārtham*).

8. He affects to be an ordinary listener (*śrāvaka*), but he teaches the Dharma (*dharma deśayati*) to mankind with unobstructed eloquence (*anācchedyapratibhāna*).

9. He affects to be a Pratyekabuddha but, in order to ripen beings endowed with the power of the conditions (*pratyayabalopeta*)[303], he seems to enter Nirvāṇa, then [**643a**] through the power of this *samādhi* he returns to new births.

10. O devaputras, the bodhisattva who dwells in Śūraṃgamasamādhi can make use of various noble modes of speech (*āryavyavahāra*)[304] but, in all the stages (*bhūmi*) where he expounds the Dharma, he does not truly dwell (*na viharati*).

[*Superiority of the Offender over the Holy One*]

150. The devas, on hearing the Buddha explaining those things, dissolved into tears and said: Bhagavat, beings who have already entered

303 To the Chinese *yin yüan chung shêng* 因緣眾生 corresponds the Tib. *sems can rkyen gyi stobs can* 'beings gifted with the power of the conditions', that is to say, particularly versed in the system of the dependent origination of phenomena (*pratītyasamutpāda*) and, as such, easily won over to the Pratyekabuddha Vehicle. The Āloka, p.155, *25-27*, quotes another sūtra where it is said: *eta eva daśa kuśalāḥ karmapathāḥ svayamabhisaṃbodhatayā gambhīredaṃpratyayatānubodhena ca pratyekabuddhajñānaṃ nirvartayanti*: 'These beings, knowing for themselves the ten paths of good action and understanding the profound causality of phenomena, achieve the Bodhi of the Pratyekabuddhas'. For more details see A. Wayman 'The Sācittikā and Acittikābhūmi and the Pratyekabuddhabhūmi (Sanskrit Texts)', *Journal of Indian and Buddhist Studies* VIII, No.1, 1960, pp.375-6.

304 To the *shêng hsing* 賢行 of the Chinese corresponds the *ḥphags paḥi tha sñad* of the Tibetan version. This concerns the *āryavyavahāras* (*ariyavohāra* in Pāli) or noble manners of speaking. Three groups of four are mentioned (Dīgha III, p.232; Majjhima III, p.29; Aṅguttara II, p.246; IV, p.307; Kośa IV, pp.159-60; Bodh. Bhūmi, p.220):

a. To abstain from false speech (*mṛṣāvāda*), slander (*paiśunya*), harmful (*pāruṣya*) and idle words (*saṃbhinnapralāpa*); in other words, to observe *śīlas* 4-7.

b. When one has seen something, to say one has seen it; when one has heard something… etc. (*dṛṣṭe dṛṣṭavāditā, śrute mate vijñāte vijñātavāditā*).

c. When one has not seen something, to say one has not seen it…, etc. (*adṛṣṭe adṛṣṭavāditā, aśrute amate avijñāte avijñātavāditā).*

the certainty (*niyāma*) of the śrāvakas and Prateykabuddhas[305] are definitively deprived (*vipanna*) of this Śūraṃgamasamādhi. O Bhagavat, a man guilty of the five offences of immediate fruition (*pañcānantarya*) who hears the Śūraṃgamasamādhi expounded is superior to the [holy one who has] entered into the certainty (*avakrāntaniyāma*) and to the arhat who has destroyed all the defilements (*kṣīṇāsrava)*[306]. Why? The man who is guilty of the *pañcānantaryas*, on hearing the Śūraṃgamasamādhi expounded, arouses the *anuttarasamyaksaṃbodhicitta* and even if, because of his previous misdeeds (*pūrvapāpakarman*), he falls into the hells (*naraka*), the merit (*kuśalamūla*) of having heard the Śūraṃgamasamādhi enables him to become a Buddha. Conversely, the arhat who has destroyed the defilements (*kṣīṇāsrava*) is like a broken receptacle (*chinnabhājana*): never could he make use of the Śūraṃgamasamādhi.

151. Thus, Bhagavat, one day when a distribution of ghee (*ghṛta*), oil (*taila*) and honey (*madhu*) was taking place, a crowd of people presented themselves with all kinds of receptacles (*bhājana*). Among those people a man, through inadvertence (*smṛtihāni*), broke the receptacle he was holding. He went to the distribution but gained no profit from the ghee, oil and honey. He refreshed himself only on the spot, but could not take anything home to give to others. In contrast, another man who had an intact receptacle at his disposal not only refreshed himself on the spot, but could take away a well-filled bowl (*paripūrṇabhājana*) to offer to other people.

The ghee, oil and honey denote the Good Dharma (*saddharma*) of the Buddhas. The man with the broken bowl who gained only personal satisfaction from the distribution but could not take home anything to give to others denotes the śrāvakas and Pratyekabuddhas. The man with the intact bowl denotes the bodhisattva who, while ensuring his own welfare (*svahita*), can still give to all beings[307].

[*Two Hundred Discouraged Bodhisattvas Obtain the Ten Powers*]

152. When the two hundred bodhisattvas[308] who had wanted to with-

305 Regarding the *niyāma* of the śrāvakas and Pratyekabuddhas, see above, § 7, n.13; § 56, n.140; § 104, nn.210 and 211.

306 A man guilty of the five *ānantaryas* is privileged in relation to the arhat since he can still reach Saṃbodhi, while an arhat whose passions are destroyed (*kṣīṇāsrava*) will immediately pass into Nirvāṇa. Regarding this commonplace widespread in Mahāyāna sūtras, see Vkn, p.55, n.33.

307 Unlike the śrāvaka only interested in his own personal deliverance, the bs assures both his own welfare and that of others (*svaparārtha*) at the same time.

308 Read *p'u-sa* (bodhisattva) instead of *tien-tz'ŭ* (devaputra); as can be seen from the Tib. version, *byaṅ chub sems dpaḥ sems zum pa*, this concerns the two hundred 'discouraged bss

draw from *anuttarasamyaksaṃbodhi* heard the words of those devaputras and learnt of the inconceivable virtues and potency (*acintyaguṇaprabhāva*) of Mañjuśrī kumārabhūta, they renewed their high resolve (*adhyāśaya*) and aroused the *anuttarasamyaksaṃbodhicitta*. Fully decided on not withdrawing from it again, they said to the Buddha: Even if we should have to face dangers and lose our lives, never again will we renounce the *bodhicitta* and never will we abandon beings. O Bhagavat, by virtue of the merit (*kuśalamūla*) resulting from hearing this Śūraṃgamasamādhi, may we obtain the ten bodhisattva powers (*daśabodhisattvabala*)[309]. What are those ten powers?

1. Steadfastness in the thought of Bodhi (*bodhicittasāratābala*),
2. faith in the inconceivable Buddha attributes (*acintyabuddhadharmaśraddhābala*),
3. retention of learning (*bahuśrutyāsaṃpramoṣabala*),
4. tirelessness in the journey through the rounds of rebirth (*saṃsāraṇāparikhedabala*),
5. steadfastness in great compassion towards beings (*sattveṣu mahākaruṇāsāratābala*),
6. firm generosity in giving (*dānadṛḍhatyāgabala)*,
7. not renouncing commitment as regards morality (*śīlasamādānāparihāṇibala*),
8. settling firmly into patience and kindness (*kṣāntisauratyaniveśanabala*),
9. wisdom that Māra cannot destroy[310], **[643b]**
10. belief in the profound teachings (*gambhīradharmādhimuktibala*).

Then the Buddha said to the bodhisattva Dṛḍhamati: If someone, now

who were mentioned at the beginning of § 139.

309 The canonical list of the ten Tathāgatabalas (Majjhima I, pp.69-70; Aṅguttara V, pp.32-6) has remained unchanged throughout the entire Buddhist tradition; conversely, the ten bodhisattvabalas have been subjected to differing lists:

a. The list in the Avataṃsaka (T 278, ch.39, p.649*c* 4-13; T 279, ch.56, p.295*c* 1-10), reproduced in Mahāvyut. Nos 760-9: 1. *āśaya*, 2. *adhyāśaya*, 3. *prayoga*, 4. *prajñā*, 5. *praṇidhāna*, 6. *yāna*, 7. *caryā*, 8. *vikurvaṇa*, 9. *bodhi*, 10. *dharmacakrapravartana-bala*.

b. The list in the Dharmasaṃgraha, § 75: 1. *adhimukti*, 2. *pratisaṃkhyāna*, 3. *bhāva*, 4. *kṣānti*, 5. *jñāna*, 6. *prahāṇa*, 7. *samādhi*, 8. *pratibhāna*, 9. *puṇya*, 10. *pratipatti-bala*.

c. The list in the Vikurvaṇarājaparipṛcchā (T 420, ch.2, p.632*c* 13-26) and the Upadeśa (Nāgārjuna, *Traité* III, pp.1611-12) which has factors in common with the present list in the Śgs: 1. *sāratā*, 2. *sarvasattvāparityāga*, 3. *mahākaruṇā*, 4. *mahāvīrya*, 5. *dhyānasamāpatti*, 6. *prajñā*, 7. *saṃsārāparikheda*, 8. *anutpattikadharmakṣānti*, 9. *vimukti*, 10. *pratisaṃvid-bala*.

310 We have in Tib. *bdud ḥdul baḥi śes rab kyi stobs* 'The wisdom that triumphs over Māra' (*māradharṣaṇaprajñābala*).

or after my Parinirvāṇa, hears this Śūraṃgamasamādhi and believes it, he will certainly obtain those ten *bodhisattvabalas*.

[*Why and How to Practise the Heroic Progress*[311]]

153. Now, in the assembly there was a bodhisattva named *Nāmamati[312] who said to the Buddha: Bhagavat,

1. He who seeks merit should pay homage to the Buddha (*puṇyaparyeṣiṇā buddhapūjanaṃ kartavyam*).

2. He who seeks wisdom (*prajñā*) should devote himself to learning (*śrutābhiyoga*).

3. He who seeks heaven (*svarga*) should observe morality (*śīlarakṣaṇa*).

4. He who seeks riches (*upabhoga*) should multiply gifts (*dānavardhana*).

5. He who seeks beauty (*rūpa*) should cultivate patience (*kṣāntibhāvanā*).

6. He who seeks eloquence (*pratibhāna*) should be devoted to his teacher (*gurubhakti*).

7. He who seeks memory (*dhāraṇī*) should avoid pride (*abhimānaparivarjana*).

8. He who seeks knowledge (*jñāna*) should cultivate right attention (*yoniśo manasikāra*).

9. He who seeks happiness (*sukha*) should avoid all wrong actions (*sarvapāpākaraṇa*).

10. He who seeks to be of benefit to beings (*sattvārthakriyā*) should arouse the thought of enlightenment (*bodhicittotpāda*).

11. He who seeks a sweet voice (*madhurasvara*) should cultivate the truthful word (*satyavāgbhāvanā*).

12. He who seeks virtues (*guṇa*) should delight in solitude (*pravivekaprīti*).

13. He who seeks the Teaching (*dharma*) should frequent spiritual friends (*kalyāṇamitrasevana*).

14. He who seeks tranquillity (*śamatha*) should avoid crowds (*saṃsargavipravāsa*).

15. He who seeks insight (*vipaśyanā*)[313] should cultivate attention

[311] This paragraph seems to be inspired by a sūtra on the fruition of actions; cf. the two Kammavibhaṅgas of Majjhima III, pp.202-15, and the Mahākarmavibhaṅga edited by S. Lévi, Paris 1932.

[312] *Ming i* 名意 which I have retained, but in the Tibetan we have *Rgyal baḥi blo gros* (Rājamati), which seems preferable.

[313] On *śamatha* and *vipaśyanā*, cf. P. Demiéville, *Le Concile de Lhasa*, Paris 1952, pp.79, 336-48.

(*manasikārabhāvanā*).

16. He who wishes to be reborn in the world of Brahmā (*brahmaloka*) should practise the four infinite states (*caturapramāṇacittabhāvanā*).

17. He who wishes to be reborn among the divine and human [blisses] (*devamanuṣyasaṃpad*) should follow the ten paths of good action (*daśakuśalakarmapatha*).

[18. He who seeks Nirvāṇa should adhere to the emptiness of dharmas (*dharmaśūnyatādhimukti*)[314].]

O Bhagavat, he who seeks at the same time merit, wisdom, heaven, riches, beauty, eloquence, memory, knowledge, happiness, the benefit of beings, a sweet voice, virtues, the Dharma, tranquillity, insight, the world of Brahmā, the divine and human blisses and Nirvāṇa, that man, say I, should hear the Śūraṃgamasamādhi, grasp, remember, expound it to others and put it into practice. Bhagavat, how then should a bodhisattva practise this *samādhi*?

154. The Buddha replied: *Nāmamati,

1. The bodhisattva who regards dharmas as empty (*śūnya*), unresisting (*apratigha*) and perishing from instant to instant (*kṣaṇika*), without aversion or affection (*ananunayapratigha*), that bodhisattva practises this *samādhi*.

2. Moroever, O *Nāmamati, there is not just a single method of pursuance (*ekapratipatti*) in practising this *samādhi*. How is that so? As many as there are functionings (*pravṛtti*) in the minds and mentations (*cittacaitta*) of beings, are there functionings in this *samādhi*. As many as there are entrances (*praveśa*) into the minds and mentations (*cittacaitta*) of beings, are there entrances into this *samādhi*. As many as there are entrance doors (*praveśamukha*) into the faculties (*indriya*) of beings, are there entrance doors into this *samādhi*. As many as there are names and forms (*nāmarūpa*) among beings, are there names and forms in this *samādhi*. Knowing this to be so is practising this *samādhi*.

3. As many as there are names (*nāman*), forms (*rūpa*) and marks (*lakṣaṇa*) in the Buddhas, are there names, forms and marks in this *samādhi*. [**643c**] Knowing this to be so is practising this *samādhi*.

4. The bodhisattva himself acquires as many fields (*kṣetra*) as he sees of them among the Buddhas: that is practising this *samādhi*.

The bodhisattva *Nāmamati said to the Buddha: Bhagavat, the method of pursuance (*pratipatti*) in this *samādhi* is very difficult (*atiduṣkara*).

[314] Sentence omitted, doubtless inadvertently, in the Chinese translation. In Tib. we have *mya ṅan las ḥdaḥ par ḥtshal bas chos la stoṅ par mos par bgyiḥo.*

The Buddha said to *Nāmamati: That is why few are the bodhisattvas who dwell in this *samādhi*, and many are the bodhisattvas who practise other *samādhis*.

[*Maitreya in the Heroic Progress*]

155. Then the bodhisattva *Nāmamati said to the Buddha: Bhagavat, the bodhisattva Maitreya here is separated from Buddhahood by only one existence (*ekajātipratibaddha*) and according to you, Bhagavat, he should attain *anuttarasamyaksaṃbodhi*. Does Maitreya possess the Śūraṃgamasamādhi?

The Buddha replied: *Nāmamati, the bodhisattvas who are in the tenth stage (*daśabhūmistha*), who are *ekajātipratibaddha* and who have received the consecration (*abhiṣeka*)[315] from the Buddhas all possess the Śūraṃgamasamādhi.

156. Then the bodhisattva Maitreya performed such a supernormal action (*evaṃrūpam ṛddhyabhisaṃskāram abhisaṃskaroti sma*)[316] that the bodhisattva *Nāmamati and the whole assembly (*sarvāvatī parṣad*) saw the bodhisattva Maitreya in all the Jambudvīpas of the *trisāhasramahāsāhasralokadhātu*.

Here he was among the gods (*devaloka*), there among mankind (*manuṣyaloka*). Here he was a religious mendicant (*pravrajita*), there he was a layman (*gṛhastha*).

Here he was an attendant (*upasthāyaka*) of the Buddha like Ānanda, there he was the foremost of the great sages (*mahāprajñāvatām agryaḥ*) like Śāriputra, there he was the foremost of those who possess supernormal powers (*ṛddhimatām agryaḥ*) like Maudgalyāyana, there he was the foremost of those who observe ascetic practices (*dhūtaguṇavādinām agryaḥ*) like Mahākāśyapa, there he was the foremost of those who expound the Dharma (*dharmakathikānām agryaḥ*) like Pūrṇa, there he was the foremost of those who like to train themselves (*śikṣākāmānām agryaḥ*) like Rāhula, there he was the foremost of the guardians of the Vinaya (*vinayadharāṇām agryaḥ*) like Upāli, there he was the foremost of those who possess the heavenly eye (*divyacakṣukānām agryaḥ*) like Aniruddha, there he was the foremost of the absorbed (*dhyāyinām agryaḥ*) like Revata, [there he was the

315 Kumārajīva usually renders *niyāma* by *chêng wei* 正位 (cf. above, § 56, n.140), but the *niyāma* is not received from the Buddhas. Here *chêng wei* translates *abhiṣeka* as it appears in the Tibetan version *dbaṅ bskur ba thob pa* = *abhiṣekaprāpta*. Regarding this consecration, see above, § 48, n.125.

316 This is a stock phrase; see Vkn, pp.139, 204, 219, 247.

foremost of those who dwell in the absence of discord (*araṇavihāriṇām agryaḥ*) like Subhuti[317]]. So it was that they saw Maitreya to be the foremost among all.

Here they saw him entering the villages (*grāma*), towns (*nagara*) and provinces (*nigama*) to beg for his food, there they saw him expounding the Dharma, or again, seated in solitary meditation (*pratisaṃlīna*).

157. The bodhisattva *Nāmamati and the great assembly saw the bodhisattva Maitreya thus manifesting the supportive power of the Śūraṃgamasamādhi and, having seen him, they rejoiced greatly and said to the Buddha: Bhagavat, just as gold (*kāñcana*), even if it has gone through the forge, never loses its self-nature (*svabhāva*), so these great Satpuruṣas, wherever they may go, manifest everywhere their natures of inconceivable qualities (*acintyadharma*).

Then the bodhisattva *Nāmamati said to the Buddha: Bhagavat, I claim that the bodhisattvas who can penetrate the Śūraṃgamasamādhi also penetrate the practices of all the paths (*sarvamārgacaryā*) and penetrate the śrāvakayāna, the Pratyekabuddhayāna and the Mahābuddhayāṇa.

[317] Here again, doubtless through inadvertence, Kumārajīva has omitted Subhūti. We have in Tib. *la la na ni rab ḥbyor bźin du ñon moṅs pa med par gnas paḥi mchog tu gyur to*.

With the exception of Revata, the great śrāvakas given here as examples all appear in the third chapter of the Vkn, where I have devoted short notes to them. The pre-eminences that characterise them are recorded in Aṅguttara I, p.23 sq.

The early texts mention no less than ten Revatas, but the one concerned here is certainly Kaṅkhā-Revata 'Revata the Scrupulous', proclaimed by the Buddha to be *aggo jhāyīnaṃ* (Aṅguttara I, p.24, *11*). The Udāna, p.60, tells us in what circumstances: 'Near the Jetavana of Śrāvastī, Revata, seated with his legs crossed and his body straight, was contemplating that purity which was his and which consisted in having overcome scruples (*attano kaṅkhāvitaraṇavisuddhiṃ paccavekkhamāno*). The Buddha perceived him and uttered this stanza:

yā kāci kaṅkhā idha vā huraṃ vā
sakavediyā vā paravediyā vā
jhāyino tā pajahanti sabbā
ātāpino brahmacariyaṃ carantā.

'The scruples which, in the present existence or in future existences, are experienced personally or felt by others, the meditative reject them all and, filled with zeal, practise pure conduct'.

Before he reached arhatship, Revata was tortured by scruples. We know from the Vinayas that these were of an alimentary kind: he refused to eat, outside the time prescribed for meals (*vikāle*), treacle (*guḍa*) mixed with flour (*kaṇena badhyamāna*) under the pretext that such a mixture constituted true food (*āmiṣa*); in the same way, he disapproved of beans (*mudga*) which had been grown on manure (*vaccas*) because, he said, they were already cooked; see Pāli Vinaya I, p.210; Mahīśāsaka Vin., T 1421, ch.22, p.147*c* (where Revata is replaced by Aniruddha); Sarvāstivādin Vin., T 1435, ch.26, p.185*b* 11-21; Mūlasarv. Vin. in *Gilgit Manuscripts* III, part 1, pp.XI, *6* - XII, *19*, and T 1448, ch.1, p.3*a* 13 - *b* 9.

The Buddha replied: Yes, it is indeed as you say: the bodhisattvas who can penetrate the Śūraṃgamasamādhi also penetrate the practices of all the paths.

[*Mañjuśrī Identical to the Buddha Nāgavaṃśāgra*]

158. Then the sthavira [**644a**] Mahākāśyapa said to the Buddha: Bhagavat, I claim that Mañjuśrī kumārabhūta, in days gone by (*bhūtapūrvam*), in times long past (*atīte 'dhvani*), performed Buddha deeds (*buddhakārya*), that he sat on the seat of enlightenment (*bodhimaṇḍa*), that he set turning the Wheel of the Dharma, that he taught beings and that he entered great Nirvāṇa.

159. The Buddha replied: It is indeed so, it is indeed as you say (*evam etad evam etad yathā vadasi*). In times long past, well before immense (*aprameya*), infinite (*ananta*) and inconceivable (*acintya*) *asaṃkhyeyakalpas*, there was a Buddha named Nāgavaṃśāgra[318] 'Acme of the Dragons' Race', the Tathāgata, holy one (*arhat*), fully and perfectly enlightened one (*samyaksaṃbuddha*), gifted with knowledge and conduct (*vidyācaraṇasaṃpanna*), the Sugata, knower of the world (*lokavid*), incomparable leader of men, those beings to be tamed (*anuttara puruṣadamyasārathi*), instructor of gods and mankind (*śāstā devānāṃ ca manuṣyānāṃ ca*), the Buddha, the Blessed One (*bhagavat*)[319].

In the southern region (*dakṣiṇasyāṃ diśi*), if leaving this universe here one traverses a thousand Buddha-fields (*ito buddhakṣetrād buddhakṣetrasahasrāṇy atikramya*), there is a field called Samā[320] 'Even', devoid of mountains and rivers (*apagataparvatanada*) devoid of sand, gravel and stones, without hill or hillock, even like the palm of a hand (*sama pāṇitalajāta*), yielding a tender grass (*mṛdutṛṇa*) like the Kācilindika[321].

160. It was in that universe (*lokadhātu*) that the Buddha Nāgavaṃśāgra attained *anuttarasamyaksaṃbodhi*, set turning the

[318] In Tib. *Kluḥi rigs mchog*. Indian and Chinese texts, referring to the present passage of the Śgs, mention him frequently: Hsin ti kuang ching, T 159, ch.3, p.304*b* 10; Upadeśa in Nāgārjuna, *Traité* I, p.602; IV, p.1097; Ku ch'ing liang chuan, T 2098, ch.1, p.1093*a* 21.

[319] A traditional formula to recall the appearance of a Buddha of the past. See below, § 170, and the references in Vkn, p.257, n.12.

[320] In Tib. *Mñam pa.*

[321] The Tibetan version renders these traditional epithets more literally: ḥjig rten gyi khams mñam pa źes bya ba ri daṅ rdo med pa / boṅ ba daṅ gyo mo daṅ gseg ma med pa / lag mthil ltar mñam par gyur pa / ka tsa lin ḥdi ka ltar reg na bde baḥi rtsa ḥjam po skyes par gyur te; in Skt. Samā lokadhātur apagataparvatapāṣāṇo 'pagataloṣṭakathallaśarkaraḥ samaḥ pāṇitalajātaḥ kācilindikasukhasaṃsparśamṛdutṛṇotpannaḥ. See identical and similar epithets in Saddharmapuṇḍ., pp.144, 9 - 145, 1; 202, 2.

Wheel of the Dharma, ripened and won over seventy koṭis of bodhisattvas. Eighty koṭis of men became arhats and ninety-six thousand men were established in the doctrine of causality of the Pratyekabuddhas[322]. The Buddha Nāgavaṃśāgra had an immense assembly of śrāvakas in his following. O Kāśyapa, his lifespan (*ayuṣpramāṇa*) was of four hundred and forty myriad years. When he

Regarding *kācilindika* (*var. kācalindika*), F. Edgerton has collated many references in Sanskrit (*Dictionary*, p.175*b*) as has Lin Li-kouang in Chinese (*L'Aide-mémoire de la Vraie Loi*, Paris 1949, pp.253-4 in the notes). The grass and wonderful flowers which grow in the paradises are often compared to the *kācilindika*:

Lalitavistara, p.82, *20-21*: *karatalanibhe bhūmibhāge suvibhaktavistīrṇanīlatṛṇe mayūragrīvasaṃnibhe kācilindikasukhasaṃsparśe dharaṇītale saṃsthitaḥ.*

Sukhāvatīvyūha, ed. U. Wogihara, p.88, *10-12*: *tāni ca puṣpajātāni mṛdūni kācilindikasukhasaṃsparśāny aupamyamātreṇa yāni nikṣipte pāde caturaṅgulam avanamanti, utkṣipte pāde caturaṅgulam evonnamanti.*

Two glosses incorporated into the Saddharmasmṛtyupasthāna (T 721, ch.2, p.8*c* 5-7; ch.30, p.176*b* 6) define the *kācilindika* as a bird of maritime islands. For Li Lin-kouang (*loc. cit.*) these glosses are due to a purely Chinese confusion with *kalaviṅka*, the name of a fabulous bird, the lovely voices of whose young are supposedly audible while they are still in the shell.

That the similarity of the Chinese transcriptions serving to render *kācilindika* and *kalavinka* may have led to confusion is possible, even probable. However, we can bring into the discussion texts of Indian origin – and not only Chinese glosses – where *kācilindika* does indeed indicate an aquatic bird.

I will limit myself here to quoting the Mahāyānist Mahāparinirvāṇasūtra (T 374, ch.8, p.414*b* 19-21; T 375, ch.8, p.655*b* 13-16; T 376, ch.5, p.889*a* 16-17): 'There are two kinds of bird, the *Chia-lin-t'i* (*kācilindika*) and the *Yüan-yang* (*cakravāka*; cf. Mahāvyut., No.4885) which, moving or standing still, stay in groups and never separate; equally, the dharmas *duḥkha*, *anitya* and *anātman* never separate'. A little further on (T 374, ch.8, p.415*b* 21-23) we read: 'These kācilindikas and cakravākas, at the height of summer, when the waters are in spate, choose high streams and place their young in them to bring them up there; then, as before, they move about peacefully'.

The kācilindika has a particularly soft down; that is why when a lawn, flowers, horses or even thoughts are soft they are called *kācilindikasādṛśa* (Mahāvastu II, p.307, *2*), *kācilindikamṛdūpama* (*ibid.*, pp.261, *2*; 262, *4*) or *kācilindikasukhasaṃsparśa* 'having the pleasant touch of the k.' (Lalita, p.17, *12*, etc.).

It is also possible that the down or plumage of the bird served to make clothes; hence the expression *mṛdukācilindikapraveṇī* (Mahāvastu I, pp.152, *16*; 226, *10*; II, p.29, *13*) and the Tibetan translations like *ka-tsa-lin-daḥi gos* (Mahāvyut., No.5879) where the adjunction of *gos* shows that clothing is definitely indicated.

I think that we can accept the explanations supplied by the Kashgarian Hui-lin (737-820) in his I ch'ieh ching yin i (T 2128, ch.19, p.423*c* 21-22): The wadding *Chia-chih-li-na* is also the name of the lovely bird, *Chia-chên-lin-ti-chia* (Kācilindika). Its body has a fine and soft down and it is unusually light and beautiful, like wadding. This down is woven so as to make clothing or padding from it. The noble cakravartin kings alone use it as clothing. This type of bird exists at present, but it is not the one that concerns us; its plumage, coarse and unpleasant, is unfit for weaving'.

[322] See above, § 149, n.303.

had delivered gods and mankind, he entered Nirvāṇa. His bodily relics (*śarīra*) were distributed throughout the land; thirty-six koṭis of stūpas were erected over them which beings came to venerate. After the Parinirvāṇa of that Buddha, his Good Dharma (*saddharma*) lasted a further ten myriad years.

161. The Buddha Nāgavaṃśagra, being on the point of entering Nirvāṇa, had given the prediction (*vyākaraṇa*) to the bodhisattva Jñānaprabha[323] 'Brilliance of Knowledge' and declared: 'This bodhisattva Jñānaprabha, after myself, will attain *anuttarasamyaksaṃbodhi* and will bear the name of Jñānaprabha'.

162. O Kāśyapa, do not start wondering if, at that time, the Buddha Nāgavaṃśagra of the Samā Universe was none other [than Mañjuśrī]. Why? Because the present Mañjuśrī kumārabhūta was then [the Buddha Nāgavaṃśāgra][324].

163. Kāśyapa, now consider the might of the Śūraṃgamasamādhi. It is through its power that the great bodhisattvas manifest:

1. the descent into the womb (*garbhāvakrānti*),
2. the birth (*janman*),
3. the renunciation of the world (*abhiniṣkramaṇa*),
[4. the practice of the austerities (*duṣkaracaryā*)[325]],
5. the going to the tree of enlightenment (*bodhivṛkṣagamana*),
6. the installation on the seat of enlightenment (*bodhimaṇḍa-niṣīdana*),
[7. the victory over Māra (*māradharṣaṇa*)[326]],
[8. the attaining of enlightenment (*abhisaṃbodhana*[327]],
9. the turning of the Wheel of the Dharma (*dharmacakrapravartana*),
10. the Mahāparinirvāṇa,
11. the disposal of the relics (*śarīranikṣepa*)[328].

Nevertheless, those great bodhisattvas never abandon their bodhi-

323 In Tib. *Ye śes ḥod*; a bs mentioned in Mahāvyut., No.691.

324 As is his custom, Kumārajīva summarises a standard stock phrase used to identify persons from the past who come into the jātakas; see the references in Vkn, p.265, n.28. The Tibetan version makes it easy to reconstruct the original Sanskrit: *syāt khalu punas te Kāśyapaivaṃ kāṅkṣā vā vimatir vā vicikitsā vānyaḥ sa tena kālena tena samayena tasminn eva Samalokadhātau Nāgavaṃśāgro nāmābhūt tathāgataḥ. na khalu punas tvayā Kāśyapaivaṃ draṣṭavyam. tat kasya hetoḥ. sa eva Mañjuśrīḥ kumārabhūtas tena kālena tena samayena Nāgavaṃśāgro nāmābhūt tathāgato 'rhan samyaksaṃbuddhaḥ.*

325 According to the Tibetan version: *dkaḥ ba spyod pa.*

326 According to the Tibetan version: *bdud ḥdul ba.*

327 According to the Tibetan version: *byaṅ chub mṅon par rdzogs par ḥtshaṅ rgya ba.*

328 This is a further summary of the requisite exploits of a Buddha; see above, § 7 at the end; § 21, Nos.96-100; § 123.

sattva nature (*bodhisattvadharmatāṃ notsṛjanti*) and, [even] in Mahāparinirvāṇa, they are not absolutely in Parinirvāṇa (*atyantaparinirvṛtta*).

164. Then the āyuṣmant Mahākāśyapa said to Mañjuśrī: Friend, you have accomplished a most difficult thing (*atiduṣkara*) by thus manifesting yourself to beings.

Mañjuśrī replied: Kāśyapa, what do you think of this (*tat kiṃ manyase*): who produced this Gṛdhrakūṭaparvata and where does this universe (*lokadhātu*) come from?

Kāśyapa answered: Mañjuśrī, all universes are produced like foam and they come from the inconceivable fruition of actions (*acintyakarmavipāka*) accomplished by beings[329]. [**644b**]

Mañjuśrī said: All dharmas also come from the inconceivable fruition of actions. In this sphere, I do not have to make any effort (*abhisaṃskāra*). Why? All dharmas depend on causes and conditions (*hetu-pratyayādhīna*); not being independent (*asvāmika*) they are forged at will (*yathākāmaviṭhapita*). Nothing is difficult (*duṣkara*) for him who has understood this. O Kāśyapa, for a man who has not seen the four Noble Truths (*na dṛṣṭasatya*) to hear these things and believe them, that is what is difficult. But for a man who has seen the four Truths (*dṛṣṭasatya*) and obtained the superknowledges (*abhijñāprāpta*) to hear this and believe it, that is not difficult.

[*Appearance of the Buddhas of the Ten Regions*]

165. Thereupon the Bhagavat, rising into the air to the height of seven palm trees (*saptatālamātraṃ vaihāyasam abhyudgamya*), sat down cross-legged (*paryaṅkam ābhujya nyaṣīdat*) and emitted a radiance (*avabhāsa*) which illuminated the innumerable universes of the ten regions. The whole assembly saw the innumerable Buddhas of the ten regions who were all expounding the Śūraṃgamasamādhi, adding nothing and omitting nothing (*anūnānadhikam*)[330], and from afar the assembly heard them.

In their own turn the Buddhas of the ten regions, rising into the air to the height of seven palm trees, sat down crossed-legged and emitted a radiance which illuminated the innumerable universes of the ten regions. The beings of those universes also saw the Buddha Śākyamuni

[329] According to traditional acceptance, the receptacle-world (*bhājanaloka*) is produced by the good and bad actions of all living beings; see Kośa II, p.288, n.1.

[330] In Tib. *lhag chad med ciṅ lhag pa med par*, giving the Skt. *anūnānadhikam*; cf. Laṅkāvatāra, p.142,*4*.

sitting in the air, his legs crossed[331]. Those assemblies took up flowers (*puṣpa*) and, from afar, scattered them over the Buddha Śākyamuni. They saw those flowers join together in the air in the shape of a flowery parasol (*puṣpacchattra*).

The bodhisattvas of this universe[332], as well as the devas, nāgas, yakṣas, gandharvas, etc., also took up flowers and scattered them over those Buddhas [of the ten regions]. And, above the Buddhas, those flowers were transformed into a flowery parasol.

166. Then the Buddha withdrew the bases of his supernormal power (*ṛddhipādān pratisaṃharati sma*) and resumed his original seat. He said to Dṛḍhamati: That is the wondrous power (*prātihāryabala*) of the Tathāgata. It is so that the virtues (*guṇa*) of beings may increase that the Tathāgata manifests these things.

167. At the moment that the Buddha manifested his wondrous powers (*prātihāryabala*), eight thousand devas and manuṣyas aroused the *anuttarasamyaksaṃbodhicitta*. And, as the instruction of the Śūraṃgamasamādhi came to an end, the bodhisattva Dṛḍhamati and five hundred bodhisattvas obtained the Śūraṃgamasamādhi. They saw the prodigious power (*vikurvaṇabala*) of the Buddhas of the ten regions; they obtained the light of knowledge (*jñānāloka*) regarding the profound teachings (*gambhīradharma*) of the Buddha; they established themselves in the tenth stage (*daśamā bhūmi*) and received the consecration of the Buddhas (*buddhābhiṣeka*). The *trisāhasramahāsāhasralokadhātu* shook in six ways (*ṣaḍvikāram akampata*); a great radiance (*mahāvabhāsa*) filled the universe; a thousand myriad musical instruments (*tūrya*) played simultaneously and, from the sky (*upary antarikṣāt*), the devas showered down all kinds of flowers.

[*Protection Assured to the Heroic Progress*]

168. Then the Buddha said to Ānanda: Grasp, Ānanda, this Śūraṃgamasamādhi, remember, recite and expound it widely to others (*udgṛhṇīṣva tvam Ānandemaṃ Śūraṃgamasamādhiṃ dhāraya vācaya parebhyaś ca vistareṇa saṃprakāśaya*)[333].

Thereupon the Śakra Meruśikharadhara said to the Buddha:

[331] Through the supernormal power of the Buddha, the inhabitants of the Sahāloka see the beings populating the innumerable universes of the ten regions, and vice versa. This concerns a common wonder in the Prajñā literature; cf. Pañcaviṃśati, p.12, *5-16*, and its commentary in Nāgārjuna, *Traité* I, pp.526-8.

[332] The Sahālokadhātu.

[333] This is a stock phrase; see Vkn, p.272.

Bhagavat, the knowledge (*jñāna*) and mindfulness (*smṛti*) of Ānanda are limited (*prādeśika*)[334], and the śrāvakas restrict themselves to repeating the words of others (*parato ghoṣānuga*); how can you entrust (*parindātum*) to Ānanda this jewel of the Dharma (*dharmaratna*) which is the Śūraṃgamasamādhi?

The Śakra Meruśikharadhara [**644c**] then made this declaration of truth (*satyavacanam akarot*)[335]: If it is indeed true that, at the present time (*pratyutpanne 'dhvani*) and in future times (*anāgate 'dhvani*) I shall propagate (*upabṛṃhayiṣyāmi*) this Śūraṃgamasamādhi, may the trees (*vṛkṣa*) covering the Gṛdhrakūṭaparvata all change into *bodhivṛkṣas* of the Buddha and, under each of them, may there be a bodhisattva.

Scarcely had the Śakra Meruśikharadhara said those words than he saw all the trees as *bodhivṛkṣas* and, under each one of them, a bodhisattva. All those *bodhivṛkṣas*[336] uttered the following words: What is said by the Śakra Meruśikharadhara is the truth (*satya*): that man will widely expound and propagate the Śūraṃgamasamādhi.

169. Then the devas, nāgas, yakṣas, gandharvas, etc., with one voice said to the Buddha: Bhagavat, let us suppose that the Tathāgata were to remain alive for a whole kalpa, doing nothing but expounding the śrāvakayāna to mankind; let us further suppose that at each one of his instructions he were to win over as many beings as he won over during the first turning of the Wheel of the Dharma (*prathamadharma-cakrapravartana*)[337]. Well now, the beings won over (*vinītasattva*) by the instructing of the Śūraṃgamasamādhi would outnumber them still more. Why? Because the beings won over by the śrāvakayāna do not attain an hundredth part (*śatatamīm api kālaṃ nopayanti*) of that of the beings won over by the bodhisattvayāna, nor a thousandth (*sahasratamīm api*), nor a ten-thousandth (*daśasahasratamīm api*), nor an hundredth-thousandth (*śatasahasratamīm api*), and so on as far as (*yāvat*) do not bear numbering, or calculation, or comparison, or resemblance (*saṃkhyām api gaṇanām apy upamām apy upaniṣām api*

334 See above, § 137.

335 Cf. Saddharmapuṇḍ., p.413, *8*: *satyādhiṣṭhānaṃ karomi yena satyena satyavacanena...* Burnouf translated: 'Je prononce une bénédiction de vérité et, au nom de cette vérité et par la déclaration de cette véritée... [I utter a benediction of truth and, in the name of that truth and by the declaration of that truth...]'. Also see Samādhirāja, p.464, *1-4*.

336 Equally, in the Sukhāvatīvyūha, the *bodhivṛkṣa* of Amitābha utters words (p.110 sq.). In the *buddhakṣetras*, Buddha deeds (*buddhakārya*) are carried out by countless means; see Vkn, pp.223-5.

337 Viz. the discourse at Vārāṇasī.

na kṣamante)[338]. This Śuraṃgamasamādhi possesses immense power; it can perfect beings and cause them to obtain the Buddha attributes.

[*Identity of the Buddhas Śākyamuni and Vairocana*[339]]

170. Then the bodhisattva Dṛḍhamati asked the Buddha: Bhagavat,

338 Here again Kumārajīva translates in abridged form a stock phrase found widespread in the comparisons; see Aṣṭasāhasrikā, pp.231, 364, 370, 863; Pañcaviṃśati, p.39; Śatasāh., p.122; Vajracchedikā, p.46; Saddharmapuṇḍ., pp.333, 349: *śatatamīm api kalāṃ nopaiti sahasratamīm api śatasahasratamīm api koṭītamīm api koṭīśatatamīm api koṭīsahasratamīm api koṭīśatasahasratamīm api koṭīniyutaśatasahasratamīm api kalāṃ nopaiti saṃkhyām api kalām api gaṇanām apy upamām api aupamyam apy upaniśām apy upaniṣadam api na kṣamate.*

339 After having created 84,000 koṭinayutas of imaginary Buddhas, Śākyamuni, in § 18, declared them all to be as real and as unreal as himself, for all dharmas, Buddhas included, are only magical illusions and mirages. Further on, in § 126, he identified himself with the Buddha Sarvaguṇadharmasaṃdarśakavikurvaṇaprabhārāja reigning over the Ekapradīpa universe in the zenith region. Here, he identifies himself with the Buddha Vairocanaraśmipratimaṇḍita-vikurvaṇarāja reigning over the Pratimaṇḍitā universe in the Eastern region.

The subject of the Pratimaṇḍitā universe is dealt with at length in the Saddharmapuṇḍ., pp.423, *4-5*; 427, *3-4*; 457, *6*, which designates it by its long title of Vairocanaraśmipratimaṇḍitā 'Universe adorned with the Rays of the Sun'.

In Ch.25, the Saddharmapuṇḍ. brings this universe into a jātaka which I will summarise briefly. In the most distant past, during the Priyadarśana kalpa, the Buddha Jaladharagarjitaghoṣa-susvaranakṣatrarājasaṃkusumitābhijña appeared in the Pratimaṇḍitā universe. At the same time and in the same place reigned King Śubhavyūha whose wife Vimaladattā had given him two sons: the bss Vimalagarbha and Vimalanetra. After having won over their parents, the two princes invited them to go with them to the Buddha Jaladhara... abhijña. No sooner said than done: the Buddha instructed the court and the king, queen and two princes left home to take up the religious life. The Buddha Jaladhara... abhijña predicted to King Śubhavyūha that he himself would become a Buddha with the name of Śālendrarāja, in the Vistīrṇavatī universe, during the Abhyudgatarāja kalpa.

The *samavadhāna* which ends the jātaka established the connection between the hero of the past and the persons of the present. The king Śubhavyūha of that period is the present bs Padmaśrī; the queen Vimaladattā is now the bs Vairocanaraśmipratimaṇḍitadhvajarāja. As for the two princes Vimalagarbha and Vimalanetra, they are at present represented by the bss Bhaiṣajyarāja and Bhaiṣajyasamudgata.

In Ch.23 of the Saddharmapuṇḍ., the Vairocanaraśmipratimaṇḍitā universe in the Eastern region is again mentioned. At the time when Śākyamuni is expounding the *Lotus*, this universe is ruled over by the Buddha Kamaladalavimalanakṣatrarājasaṃkusumitābhijña. The bs Gadgadasvara, who is a member of his entourage, asks for and receives permission to go to the Sahāloka of Śākyamuni. The latter, questioned by the bs Padmaśrī, expatiates at length on the past and present of Gadgadasvara. Formerly, in the Priyadarśana kalpa, Gadgadasvara had made an offering of 84,000 precious vases to the Buddha Meghadundubhisvararāja reigning over the Sarvabuddhasaṃdarśana universe. At present Gadgadasvara, in possession of the Sarvarūpasaṃdarśana *samādhi*, assumes various forms in order to teach the *Lotus* in innumerable universes. He is particularly 'the protector of creatures who are born in the Sahā universe and the Vairocanaraśmipratimaṇḍitā universe' (Saddharmapuṇḍ., p.434, *5-7*, with the variant in n.10).

There is no doubt that the Eastern universe, Pratimaṇḍitā 'Adorned', or Vairocana-how long will your life-span be (*kiyat tavāyuṣpramāṇam*) and after how long (*kiyacciram*) will you enter definitive Parinirvāṇa?

The Buddha replied: Dṛḍhamati, in the Eastern region (*pūrvasyāṃ diśi*) if, leaving this universe, one traverses thirty-two thousand Buddha-fields (*ito buddhakṣetrād dvātriṃśadbuddhakṣetrāṇy atikramya*), there is a universe (*lokadhātu*) called Pratimaṇḍitā[340] 'Adorned': there there can be found Vairocanaraśmipratimaṇḍitavikurvaṇarāja[341] 'Prodigious King adorned with Solar Rays', the Tathāgata, holy one (*arhat*), perfectly and fully enlightened one (*samyaksaṃbuddha*), gifted with knowledge and conduct (*vidyācaraṇasaṃpanna*), the Sugata, knower of the world (*lokavid*), incomparable leader of men, those beings to be tamed (*anuttara puruṣadamyasārathi*), instructor of gods and mankind (*śāstā devānāṃ ca manuṣyānāṃ ca*), the Buddha, the Blessed One (*bhagavat*)[342]. At the moment, he is expounding the Dharma[343].

O Dṛḍhamati, my life-span (*āyuṣpramāṇa*) is exactly the same as the life-span of that Buddha Vairocanaraśmipratimaṇḍitavikurvaṇarāja.

[Dṛḍhamati asked]: Bhagavat, how long is the life-span of that Buddha Vairocanaraśmipratimaṇḍitavikurvaṇarāja?

The Buddha answered Dṛḍhamati: Go and ask him yourself and he himself will answer you.

171. Then Dṛḍhamati, through the supernormal power (*ṛddhibala*) of the Buddha, through the supernormal power of the Śūraṃgamasamādhi and also through the supernormal power of his own good roots

raśmipratimaṇḍitā 'Adorned with the Rays of the Sun', to which the Śgs and the *Lotus* refer, is none other than the universe or paradise of the Buddha Vairocana. In his work on *Barabuḍur* II, Hanoi 1935, p.584, P. Mus attempts to show 'that the aspect, name, emblem and activity of Vairocana denote an episode in Śākyamuni's career'. A reading of the Śgs would have spared him the effort since, in § 172, Śākyamuni declares that the 'Prodigious king inhabiting the universe adorned with the rays of Vairocana' is himself. Besides, the Mahāvairocanasūtra clearly defined the relationship between Śākyamuni and Vairocana: Vairocana is the historical Buddha Śākyamuni, but idealised as the *dharmakāya* 'which is neither born nor dies' (cf. R. Tajima, *Étude sur le Mahāvairocanasūtra*, Paris 1936, pp.47-8).

However, it would be to disregard completely the scope of the Mahāyāna to identify Śākyamuni with such and such a particular Buddha. Śākyamuni is not only identical to the Sarvaguṇa... prabhārāja of the zenith region (Śgs, § 126) and to the Vairocana... vikurvaṇarāja of the Eastern region (Śgs, § 172), he is identical to all the Buddhas, whose true suchness (*tathatā*) is an inconceivable 'non-existence' (see Śgs, § 18; Vkn, pp.238-42).

340 In Tib. *Rnam par spuṅ ba.*

341 In Tib. *Rnam par snaṅ mdzad ḥod zer gyis brgyan pa rnam par ḥphrul baḥi rgyal po.*

342 This is a stock phrase, see above, § 159, n.319.

343 Kumārajīva abbreviates. In Tib. we have *de ltar bźugs śiṅ ḥtshol gźes śiṅ chos kyaṅ ston to*, which gives the Skt. *tatra tiṣṭhati dhriyate yāpayati dharmaṃ ca deśayati.* Regarding this stock phrase, see Vkn, p.139, n.8.

(*kuśalamūla*), went in an instant (*ekasminn eva kṣaṇalavamuhūrte*) to the Pratimaṇḍitā universe and, having saluted the feet of that Buddha with his head (*tasya bhagavataḥ pādau śirasābhivandya*) and having circumambulated him three times (*triṣpradakṣiṇīkṛtya*), he stood to one side (*ekānte 'sthāt*). Then he said to the Buddha: Bhagavat, how long will your life-span be and after how long will you enter Parinirvāṇa?

That Buddha replied: My life-span is exactly the same as the life-span of the Buddha Śākyamuni. O Dṛḍhamati, if you want to know, my life-span will last for seven hundred incalculable cosmic periods (*asaṃkhyeyakalpa*) [**645a**], and it is exactly the same for that of the Buddha Śākyamuni.

Thereupon the bodhisattva Dṛḍhamati experienced great joy and, having returned to the Sahā Lokadhātu, he said to the Buddha [Śākyamuni]: Bhagavat, the life-span of that Buddha Vairocanaraśmipratimaṇḍitavikurvaṇarāja will last for seven hundred *asaṃkhyeyakalpas* and he told me: 'My life-span is exactly the same as the life-span of the Buddha Śākyamuni'.

172. Then Ānanda, having risen from his seat, having arranged his upper garment on one shoulder, having placed his right knee on the ground and having extended his joined hands in the direction of the Bhagavat, said to the latter (*athānanda utthāyāsanād ekāṃsam uttarāsaṅgaṃ kṛtvā dakṣiṇaṃ jānumaṇḍalaṃ pṛthivyāṃ pratiṣṭhāpya yena bhagavāṃs tenāñjaliṃ praṇamya bhagavantam idam avocat*): Bhagavat, as I understand the meaning of the Bhagavat's words (*yathāhaṃ, bhagavan, bhagavato bhāṣitasyārtham ājānāmi*)[344], I say that it is you, O Bhagavat, who are in the Pratimaṇḍitā Lokadhātu where, under a different name (*anyena nāmnā*), you bring about the welfare and happiness (*hitasukha*) of all beings.

Then the Buddha congratulated (*sādhukāram adāt*) Ānanda: Excellent, excellent (*sādhu sādhu*), it is through the power of the Buddha that you know that; that Buddha [Vairocanaraśmipratimaṇḍitavikurvaṇarāja] is myself who, under a different name, expounds the Dharma in that [Pratimaṇḍitā] universe and delivers beings. Ānanda, this supernormal and prodigious power (*ṛddhivikurvaṇabala*) is the might itself of the Śūraṃgamasamādhi.

Then the Buddha, addressing the bodhisattva Dṛḍhamati, said to him: Hence it should be known that my life-span (*āyuṣpramāṇa*) will last for seven hundred *asaṃkhyeyakalpas* and that after that I shall definitively enter Parinirvāṇa.

[344] See above, § 129, n.258.

[*The Wonderful Effects of the Heroic Progress*]

1. *Longevity and Security*

173. Then the whole assembly (*sarvāvatī parṣad*), on learning that the life-span of the Buddha was so inconceivable (*acintya*), experienced great joy and, filled with astonishment (*adbhutaprāpta*), said to the Buddha: Bhagavat, the supernormal power (*ṛddhibala*) of the Buddhas is astonishing (*adbhuta*) and all their practices (*caryā*) are inconceivable (*acintya*). Even while, in this universe [the Sahā Lokadhātu], you manifest a very short (*atihrasva*) life-span[345], in that universe [the Pratimaṇḍitā Lokadhātu], your life-span lasts for seven hundred *asaṃkhyeyakalpas*! O Bhagavat, we would like all beings to have such an inconceivable life-span.

Then the Buddha said to Dṛḍhamati: In all the kingdoms (*rāṣṭra*), villages (*grāma*), towns (*nagara*), provinces (*nigama*), dwellings (*vihāra*) and deserted places (*araṇya*) where this Śūraṃgamasamādhi will penetrate, neither Māra nor the kin of Māra (*mārajātīya*) will have a hold over it (*avatāraṃ na lapsyante*)[346].

He further said to Dṛḍhamati: If a master of the Dharma (*dharmācārya*) writes down (*likhayati*), studies (*svādhyāyati*) or teaches (*uddeśayati*) the Śūraṃgamasamādhi, he will experience neither fear nor trembling in the presence of human or non-human beings (*manuṣyāmanuṣyānām antike nottrasiṣyati na saṃtrasiṣyati na saṃtrāsam āpatsyate*). Furthermore, he will obtain twenty kinds of inconceivable virtues (*acintyaguṇaviśeṣa*).

345 The majority of sources assign to Śākyamuni a life-span of about eighty years. In an early stanza affirmed in both Sanskrit and Pāli, Śākyamuni, at the moment of his Nirvāṇa, confides to Subhadra:

Ekonatriṃśo vayasā Subhadra
yat prāvrajaṃ kiṃ kuśalaṃ gavesī
pañcaśad varṣāṇi samādhikāni
yataś cāhaṃ pravrajitaḥ Subhadra.

'I was twenty-nine years old, O Subhadra, when I left home in search of the Good; fifty years and more have gone by since I left home'.

This stanza is reproduced frequently; cf. Sanskrit Mahāparinirvāṇa, p.376; Avadānaśataka I, p.231; Dīgha II, p.151; Dīrghāgama, T 1, ch.4, p.25*b*; T 5, ch.2, p.172*a* 16; Saṃyuktāgama, T 99, ch.35, p.254*b*; Mūlasarv. Vin., T 1451, ch.38, p.396*c*.

To my knowledge the 'Sūtra of the Descent of the Bodhisattva' (T 384, ch.2, p.1024*a* 17) is the only one to attribute eighty-four years of life to Śākyamuni.

For A. Foucher, *La Vie du Bouddha*, Paris 1949, pp.322-3, the Buddha in fact died at the age of sixty-five and not eighty.

346 This is a traditional expression; see Vkn, p.272, n.39.

2. *Twenty Inconceivable Virtues*

174. What are those twenty inconceivable (*acintya*) virtues?

1. Inconceivable merit (*puṇya*).
2. Inconceivable knowledge (*jñāna*).
3. Inconceivable wisdom (*prajñā*).
4. Inconceivable skilful means (*upāya*).
5. Inconceivable eloquence (*pratibhāna*).
6. Inconceivable light of knowledge (*jñānāloka*).
7. Inconceivable *dhāraṇīs*.
8. Inconceivable expositions of the Dharma (*dharmamukha*).
9. Inconceivable mindfulness (*smṛti*) and intelligence (*mati*), in conformity with the truth.
10. Inconceivable power of the superknowledges (*abhijñābala*).
11. Inconceivable penetration of the language of all beings (*sarvasattvaniruktipraveśa*).
12. Inconceivable penetration of the practices and aspirations of all beings (*sarvasattvacaryāśayapraveśa*).
13. Inconceivable vision of all the Buddhas (*sarvabuddhadarśana*).
14. Inconceivable learning (*śruta*).
15. Inconceivable ripening of beings (*sattvaparipācana*). **[645b]**
16. Inconceivable power over the concentrations (*samādhivikurvaṇa*).
17. Inconceivable achievement of pure lands (*kṣetrābhinirhāra*).
18. Inconceivable beauty of shapes and colouring (*saṃsthānavarṇaprasāda*).
19. Inconceivable virtues (*guṇa*) and sovereign powers (*vaśitā*).
20. Inconceivable practice of the perfections (*pāramitābhāvanā*).
21. Inconceivable irreversible Wheel of the Dharma (*avaivartikadharmacakra*).

Such are the twenty virtues. Dṛḍhamati, whoever writes down (*likhati*) and studies (*svādhyāyati*) this Śūraṃgamasamādhi obtains those twenty kinds of inconceivable virtues (*acintyaguṇaviśeṣa*). That is why, O Dṛḍhamati, whoever wants to obtain those advantages (*artha*) in this and future existences (*ihāparajanmani*) should write down, study, penetrate and practise this Śūraṃgamasamādhi.

3. *Reaching Enlightenment*[347]

175. Dṛḍhamati, the kulaputra or kuladuhitā who seeks

[347] The sands of Central Asia have delivered up to us the last folio of the Śgs, covering

enlightenment practises the six perfections for an hundred thousand kalpas. But whoever, hearing this Śūraṃgamasamādhi, would believe it, not be discouraged, not fear, not tremble [and not take fright], would surpass the former in merit and would even more quickly be established in supreme and perfect enlightenment. What can then be said of those who, after having heard it, would grasp, retain, repeat and expound it while applying every effort to it? (*Dṛḍhamate, bodhyarthikaḥ kulaputro vā kuladuhitā vā kalpaśatasahasreṣu ṣaṭpāramitāś carati. yaś ca khalu punaḥ śūraṃgamasya samādheḥ saha śravaṇenādhimucyeta nāvalīyen nottrasen na saṃtrasen na saṃtrāsam āpadyet*[348] *sa eva bahutaraṃ puṇyaskandhaṃ prasavati*[349], *kṣiprataraṃ niryāty anuttarāyāṃ samyaksaṃbodhau. kaḥ punar vādo yaḥ śrutvodgṛhṇīyād dhārayed vācayet parebhya uddiśed*[350] *bhāvanāyogam anuyuktaḥ*).

4. *Confident Faith*

176. The bodhisattva who, having heard of the inconceivability of the Buddhas, does not want to fear and does not want to tremble, the bodhisattva who wants to know though personal experience all the Buddha attributes, without relying on the teaching of others, that bodhisattva, say I, should cultivate the Śūraṃgamasamādhi. The bodhisattva who, on hearing teachings not heard before, wants to believe them and does not want to reject them, that bodhisattva should listen to the Śūraṃgamasamādhi (*bodhisattvena tathāgatācintikatāṃ śrutvānuttrasitukāmenāsaṃtrasitukāmena, bodhisattvena parato ghoṣam aniśritya sarvabuddhadharmāṇāṃ pratyātmajñānam anugantukāmena śūraṃgamasamādhir bhāvayitavyaḥ. bodhisattvenāśrutapūrvān dharmān śrutvādhimoktukāmena na nikṣiptukāmena śūraṃgamasamādhiḥ śrotavyaḥ*).

§§175-178 of the present translation. It is a mutilated folio abounding in Prakritisms (*duhitrā* for *duhitā*, *olīyet* for *avalīyet*, *imasmin* for *asmin*), even mistakes (*sattvāni* for *sattvāḥ*; *abhūṣit* for *abhūṣīt* or *abhūt*). This fragment, from which the Chinese and Tibetan versions differ considerably, has been published by A.F.R. Hoernle, *Manuscript Remains* I, Oxford 1916, pp.125-32. The edition is followed by a Sanskrit conjectural rendering and a translation into English based on the Tibetan version: a highly approximative translation, the inaccuracies of which result in part from a lack of familiarity with the traditional stock phrases. [† see Foreword, p.xiv sq., and R.E. Emmerick, *The Khotanese Śūraṅgamasamādhisūtra.*]

I have tried here to reconstruct a Sanskrit text as close as possible to Kumārajīva's Chinese version.

348 Cf. Saddharmapuṇḍ., p.233, *13-14*.

349 Cf. Vajracchedikā, pp.33, *20*; 37, *9-10*.

350 Cf. *ibid.*, p.43, *17-19*.

[*Final Conversions*]

177. While the Śūraṃgamasamādhi was thus being taught, innumerable beings aroused the thought of supreme and perfect enlightenment; more numerous were those who were established in the irreversible stage; yet more numerous were those who obtained the certainty of the non-arising of dharmas. Eighteen thousand bodhisattvas acquired the Śūraṃgamasamādhi; the minds of eighteen thousand monks and nuns were, through detachment, delivered from their defilements[351]; twenty-six thousand upāsakas and upāsikās obtained the pure Dharma eye without dust or stain regarding dharmas; thirty nayutas of deities entered into the noble certainty (*asmiñ śūraṃgamasamādhau nirdiśyamāne 'prameyāṇāṃ sattvānām anuttarāyāṃ samyaksaṃbodhau cittāny utpannāni*[352], *apramāṇatarā ye 'vaivartikabhūmau pratiṣṭhitāḥ. apramāṇatarāś ca yeṣām anutpattikadharmakṣāntiḥ pratilabdhā*[353]. *aṣṭādaśānāṃ bodhisattvasahasrāṇāṃ śūraṃgamasamādhiḥ pratilabdhah. aṣṭādaśānāṃ bhikṣubhikṣuṇīsahasrāṇām anupādāyāsravebhyaś cittāni vimuktāni*[354]. *ṣaḍviṃśatīnāṃ copāsakopāsikāsahasrāṇāṃ virajo vigatamalaṃ dharmeṣu dharmacakṣur viśuddham*[355]. *triṃśatīnāṃ ca devanayutānāṃ niyāmāvakrantir abhūṣīt*).

178. Thus spoke the Bhagavat[356]. Transported with joy, Mañjuśrī kumārabhūta, the bodhisattva Dṛḍhamati, the other great-being bodhisattvas, the great disciples and the world with its gods, humans, demons and gandharvas praised the words spoken by the Bhagavat (*idam avocad bhagavān. āttamanā Mañjuśrīḥ kumārabhūtaḥ sa ca Dṛḍhamatir bodhisattvas te cānye bodhisattvā mahāsattvās te ca mahāśrāvakāḥ sadevamanuṣyāsuragandharvaś ca loko bhagavato bhāṣitam abhyanandann iti*)[357].

[351] The Chinese translation adds: 'and became arhats', a gloss which does not belong to the traditional formula.

[352] Cf. Sukhāvatīvyūha, ed. Wogihara, p.154, *5-6*; Saddharmapuṇḍ., p.456, *8*.

[353] Cf. Sukhāvatīvyūha, p.154, *4*.

[354] Cf. *ibid.*, p.154, *2-3*; Saddharmapuṇḍ., p.179, *17*.

[355] Cf. Sukhāvatīvyūha, p.154, *1*; Saddharmapuṇḍ., p.471, *4*. Other references in Vkn, p.26 in the notes.

[356] Before this conclusion, the Tibetan version introduces a long partly versified passage (Tib. Trip., Vol.32, pp.96-8, fols 338*b* 8 - 344*a* 1). Without a doubt, it did not belong to the original edition; see above, § 21, n.43.

[357] This is the customary conclusion at the end of Mahāyāna sūtras; see Vkn, p.273, n.43.

SYNOPSIS OF FORMULAS AND STOCK PHRASES

Not all these formulas and stock phrases have always been translated literally and in full by Kumārajīva

INDEX

Abbreviations: B.(s) = Buddha(s); bs(s) = bodhisattva(s); emp. = emperor; w. = worked.